THE POLITICAL
ELITE OF
Iran

PRINCETON

STUDIES ON THE

NEAR EAST

THE POLITICAL
ELITE OF

Iran

MARVIN ZONIS

PRINCETON
UNIVERSITY PRESS

This book was composed in Times Roman

Printed in the United States of America

by Princeton University Press,

Princeton, New Jersey

First PRINCETON PAPERBACK Printing, 1976

To My Mother,

Clara Zonis

and

the Memory of My Father,

Leonard Zonis

PREFACE

$\mathcal{R}$ecent years have witnessed a remarkable convergence in formerly disparate disciplines and distant geographical areas. Concern for the fate of that two-thirds of the world's population living in dire poverty was occasioned by the emergence of those nations from colonialism to independence and the growth of the United States and then the Soviet Union to superpowers whose interests, always extending beyond their boundaries, now became truly international. Into these new and little understood waters ventured social scientists whose intellectual concerns could be useful for both facilitating the modernization of these new nations and formulating the foreign diplomatic and aid policies of their own nations.

Where the anthropologist had long studied went the economists, followed by political scientists, sociologists, and psychologists. The early works on development were quick to indicate that no one of these disciplines could offer a satisfactory answer to what proved the devilishly complicated problems of "underdevelopment," or "development," as it is now more fashionably conceived. Interdisciplinary studies were called for and then undertaken, not only intraculturally, but, in increasing number, interculturally as well.

It is in this latter stream that this work most neatly fits. Concerned with the course of political development in one of the oldest of the new nations, it is predicated on the assumption that the "political" concerns the interrelationships of people. And to understand and analyze those interrelationships, we must consider not only the form of government, the political institutions, and the ideologies, but also the attitudes and values of the political actors, the norms of the culture, and the structure of the social system. For all affect, in varying degree, the very inter-relations that constitute politics, the political process, and political development.

In this work, no attempt will be made to attribute responsibility for either the political successes or the failures of the system under investigation. Nor are sides taken in a political system whose partisan battle lines have long since been drawn. Rather, we seek to understand and generalize, to analyze and explicate the lessons for students of political development that can be drawn from an interdisciplinary approach to but one political system. At the same time, however, it is also hoped that the lessons of this political system will be noted. For the contribution that this study was designed to offer was for those social scientists who seek to formulate and refine theories that will enhance, initially, our under-standing of the processes of development and assist, ultimately, in facili-tating such development. But to use this work to leap from the first of these purposes to the second, to seek its relevance in the virulent politics that occasionally characterize its subject, is both premature and unwise. If this study but fulfills the former of these dual aims, it will be counted as a success by its author.

But no work of this kind ever has but a single author. The contribu-tions of others, both material, intellectual, and emotional, are never slight and collectively may exceed those of the writer himself. For the material assistance without which neither the research nor the analysis on which this study is based could have been accomplished, I acknowl-edge with gratitude a Research Training Fellowship of the Social Science Research Council, held from 1963 to 1965, and supplemental grants from the Carnegie Corporation, and the College Faculty Research Fund and the Social Sciences Faculty Research Fund, both of the University of Chicago.

The intellectual contributors to this work are varied and numerous. Professors Daniel Lerner, Ithiel de Sola Pool, Lucian W. Pye, and espe-cially Frederick W. Frey of the Department of Political Science of the Massachusetts Institute of Technology, all served as my mentors. But more importantly, they transmitted a sense of the excitement of intel-lectual inquiry at the frontiers of the social sciences and provided me with tools that I would require to conduct my own explorations. Profes-sor Robert A. LeVine of the Committee on Human Development of the University of Chicago was particularly helpful in the later stages of the work, when the data were voluminous and order had to be established in that informational chaos that only the computer can generate. For that chaos and the hours of tedious and laborious work that generated the data processing on which this study is based, Howard Rotblat, Department of Sociology, the University of Chicago, is responsible. The counsel of Frank Bamberger and Allan Herzog of that university's Computation Center is also gratefully acknowledged.

For incisive comments on the final manuscript, I wish to thank Professors Sidney Verba, Nikki Keddie, Phyllis Levenstein, and Sidney Levenstein.

For all these, there would have been no project without the research opportunities so graciously offered me in Iran and the cooperation of the many hundreds of Iranians who participated in the project. The most important of these were the 170 respondents who subjected themselves to an aggressive and often brash foreign researcher. To spare them the embarrassment that might result from their being singled out, suffice it to acknowledge here my appreciation. But none of these interviews would have been carried out in the absence of official cooperation and royal assent. His Imperial Majesty, Mohammad Reza Pahlavi, Shahanshah, made that available with speed and kingly grace. His willingness to welcome foreign scholars is both courageous and laudable. To identify but one other Iranian whose intellectual integrity and training were perpetually at my service, I wish to thank Dr. Iraj Ayman, former director, Institute for Educational Research and Studies of the National Teachers' College in Tehran. If Iran is to take its place in the ranks of developed nations it will be through the national devotion and toil of men like him.

Finally, I thank my wife, Ella Zonis. Without her aid, this project would still be just that, a project.

CONTENTS

xi

TABLES

FIGURES

THE POLITICAL
ELITE OF
Iran

:1:

INTRODUCTION

*I*ran has been called the oldest of the new nations, a distinction accurately reflecting not only its lengthy history and venerable culture, but also its impressive successes in avoiding the status of a European colony. In recent years, Iran has augmented this reputation as her remarkable political continuity has set the stage for rapid economic growth and social development.

Iran's ruling monarch, Shah Mohammad Reza Pahlavi, acceded to the throne in 1941 amidst foreign occupation, economic disintegration, and savage attacks on the twenty-year rule of his father, Reza Shah. Since those chaotic days, the present shah has made a series of attempts to establish solid bases of political support. During the years following his accession, his relatively insecure throne depended primarily on the graces of the British and Russians who had deposed his father. Supported by these foreign powers and many of the elite who had served the ex-monarch, the shah reconstructed his defeated army. With his civil and military elites, the shah continued to maintain a tenuous grip on the throne after the withdrawal of the British and American troops, who had joined the occupiers in 1942, and the ultimate withdrawal of the Soviets and the collapse of their ill-fated "autonomous" People's Republics of Azarbaijan and Kurdistan.

An abortive assassination attempt in 1949 and the near overthrow of the shah by Prime Minister Mohammad Mossadegh (1951–1953) gave testimony to the ethereal nature of this coalition of civil and military elites. But following Mossadegh's overthrow and the shah's return to the throne after a hasty exile to Italy in 1953, kingly power was regained by an almost solitary reliance on the Imperial Iranian Armed Forces. For despite the efforts of Mossadegh and the Iranian Communist party, the Tudeh, the shah had never totally lost control over the military, a control that was then augmented by a burgeoning program of United States technical and military assistance.

Using the power of the military, the king extirpated Tudeh supporters within the ranks of the officer corps of his army. He then turned to eliminating the Tudeh throughout Iran and subduing the most ardent partisans of Mossadegh. After the most threatening of his opponents had been neutralized, the shah began to experiment with new forms of control. From 1957 to 1960, a royally chartered and directed two-party system was created. But its "tweedledum-tweedledee" character failed to provide a meaningful channel for political expression. The debacle of the two elections for the twentieth session of the Parliament in 1960–1961—a debacle that resulted in the dissolution of the Majles until new elections were held in the fall of 1963—testified to the bankruptcy of the two political parties.

The monarch's response to the political turmoil following the closing of the Parliament, while unexpected, was not atypical. He answered his increasingly vocal opposition by liberalizing political life. A new prime minister known to be suspicious of the royal prerogatives, independent ministers, and an easing of censorship all followed. By 1963, the shah launched a new experiment. He appealed for support directly to the masses through his Six-Point Reform Program and a national referendum. With the almost universal popular support that these moves generated, the shah once again turned to narrowing the limits of acceptable political behavior. In 1964, he gave official support to a single political party encompassing all of the elite he classed as progressive.

Building on his increased control over the political life of his nation, the shah then began to lessen and, finally, virtually to eliminate his reliance on the United States. What had initially been an absolutely necessary basis for maintaining control, had by mid-1960 become a burden with its implications of neoimperialism and foreign subservience. New commercial and aid treaties with Communist states were contracted, and these new diplomatic and economic relations were capped by a military aid pact with the Soviet Union in 1967.

Now, at last, the throne appears secure. Organized internal opposition has been decimated, while even the expression of antiregime sentiment is absent. International support for the shah's rule has been broadened to include not only the United States and its Western allies, but also the USSR and other Communist nations as well. With a firm grasp over the political process, the shah has devoted himself and Iran's continually increasing oil income to internal development. A mounting gross national product, social reforms, educational development, land distribution, and even a massive program of heavy industries have been the rewards.

But in the face of these widely admired triumphs, it is generally agreed that Mohammad Reza Shah has not located the majoritarian political base he has so ardently sought. The general support of the masses exists, but such support is an intangible base for royal strength. The single party remains an artificially nourished collectivity of office seekers. Thus, the shah maintains and continues to operate the Iranian political system only by incurring substantial political costs—costs that are largely determined by the relationship of the shahanshah to his political elite.

The basic assumption on which this study is based is that the attitudes and behavior of powerful individuals in societies whose political processes are less institutionalized within the formal structures of government are valid guides to political change.[1] Operating on such an assumption, we have examined the course of recent political development in Iran by analyzing its political elite.

The concept of the political elite, as used in this study, is an empirical, behavioral one. No attempt was made on a priori grounds to equate the political elite with holders of official positions in Iran's government or social structure.[2] Rather, the political elite were defined as those members of Iranian society, i.e., Iranian nationals,[3] who exercised and pos-

---

[1] "When a society is organized in such a way that the will of one man, or a small group, is the most powerful of the political and social forces, such explanation must give way, at least to a very considerable degree, to a more psychological style" (Robert Conquest, *The Great Terror: Stalin's Purge of the Thirties* [New York: Macmillan Co., 1968], as quoted in "On Dictatorship," by Alexander Gerschenkron, *New York Review of Books*, 12, no. 12 [June 19, 1969]: 3). Gerschenkron criticizes Conquest's psychological emphasis and replies that "riveting our attention to the personality of the dictator tends to blind us to the *force des choses*, to the fact that is, that recurring conditions produce analogous recurring responses" (*ibid.*, p. 4). I would argue that there is no *necessary* incompatibility here but rather that structural and psychological explanations are complementary. Similar structural conditions will tend to call forth similar political practices. But this is only a tendency not a certainty. Moreover, it is through individuals that structural factors are manifested. The intervening variables cannot be ignored.

[2] A matter for empirical investigation is the "fit" between the holders of official political positions and participants in the making of important political decisions or persons to whom political power is attributed. See, for example, Fatma Mansur, *Process of Independence* (London: Routledge & Kegan Paul, 1962), pp. 2–3. It was an assumption of this study that no significant correlation between official position holders and actual political power (as measured by the attribution of power) could be expected on a priori grounds in the Iranian context. The assumption is based on the hypothesis that the less representative (accountable, democratic) a political system is estimated to be, the less the correlation between formal positions and actual power is likely to be.

[3] It has been assumed that non-Iranian nationals who exercised significant political power in Iranian society were not independent actors but "base values" for Iranian national political actors. See Harold D. Lasswell, "Introduction: The Study

sessed political power to a greater degree than other members of Iranian society. By power we mean an interpersonal relationship such that the behavior of one (or more) actor(s) alters the behavior of another (other) actor(s). By behavior is meant any change in the state of an individual from a given time to a later time.[4] As Frey indicates, several subordinate concepts relating to "power" must be introduced. Two such concepts that are vital in this study may be mentioned. The scope of a power relationship may be considered "the set of behaviors of the influencee altered by the influencer."[5] The domain refers to "the set of persons whose behavior [the influencer] alters within a given scope."[6] The powerful, then, are those individuals whose behavior alters the widest scope of the largest domain, that is, the widest range of behavior of the largest set of persons within that society.

This definition of power does not yet sufficiently narrow our interests, for with it the investigator would find himself studying thespians, athletes, and others, who by being thespians and athletes do manage to alter the behavior of significant numbers of people. Rather we are interested in political power, that is, power exercised within the political system.

The meaning and nature of *the* political system continues to be a matter of debate even for political scientists whose legitimate concern it is considered to be.[7] For purposes of research in Iran, the political system was defined as that pattern of interactions among actors seeking to exercise power over the allocation of values at the most comprehensive level —the national, social system level.

Another problem that confronts the wary investigator seeking to identify the politically powerful in Iran relates to the persistence or longevity of patterns of power interactions.[8] An individual may be con-

---

of Political Elites," in *World Revolutionary Elites: Studies in Coercive Ideological Movements*, by Harold D. Lasswell and Daniel Lerner (Cambridge: M.I.T. Press, 1966), pp. 16–17.

[4] Frederick W. Frey, "Power Analysis," mimeo, n.d., p. 1.

[5] Frederick W. Frey, "Political Development: Power and Communications in Turkey," in *Communications and Political Development*, ed. Lucian W. Pye (Princeton: Princeton University Press, 1963), p. 302.

[6] *Ibid.*

[7] For various formulations of the concept, see Gabriel A. Almond and James S. Coleman, eds., *The Politics of the Developing Areas* (Princeton: Princeton University Press, 1960), especially the introduction by Almond; David Easton, *A Framework for Political Analysis* (Englewood Cliffs: Prentice-Hall, 1965), especially chap. 2; and Robert A. Dahl, *Modern Political Analysis* (Englewood Cliffs: Prentice-Hall, 1963), especially chap. 1. For a critical look at these formulations of the political system and a further elaboration of the concept, see Frederick W. Frey, "Political Science, Education, and National Development" (Paper delivered at the Conference on Comparative Education, University of California at Berkeley, March 25–27, 1966), especially pp. 1–10.

[8] Dahl mentions the "persistent" nature of power relations as a feature of political systems (*Modern Political Analysis*, p. 6).

sidered to exercise substantial power in the society-wide political system. But the power which that individual exercises may be a highly transitory phenomenon. A second individual may exercise power to a lesser extent, i.e., his power may be of a narrower scope or smaller domain or he may exercise that power over less-valued resources. But the lesser power of the latter individual may have existed over a longer time period than the greater power of the former actor. Or the lesser power of the latter may be widely perceived as likely to be efficacious for a longer period in the future than that of the former. In such a case, the less immediately powerful but politically longer lived individual may be considered more powerful for our purposes.[9] The phenomenon of lasting political power tends to be especially relevant for the behind-the-scenes political manipulator or the archetypal civil servant. Never attaining to high or visible position, he nonetheless manages to exercise power continually.[10]

The political elite of Iran, then, consists of those Iranians who more or less persistently exercise power over significant behaviors of large numbers of people with regard to the allocation of highly prized values in the national political system.

But how to locate these men? Initially, an attempt was made to identify the politically powerful by seeking out decision makers, those Iranians who had participated in the making of crucial political decisions in recent times. Information was sought about the land reform, oil negotiations, military pacts and aid, and the like. But such inquiry in the secretive Iranian system, which strives to disperse and mask responsibility, proved fruitless. A new approach was initiated, an approach that sought to identify the powerful by locating those with reputations for exercising such power.

First, the holders of formal position within the government were identified. Then the occupants of key social roles—doctors, tribal leaders, members of the royal family, opposition leaders—were identified and a list of three thousand "general elite" was constructed.[11] A panel of ten persons knowledgeable about Iranian politics then attributed

[9] Evaluations of members of the political elite based on this criterion may help to account for the lack of "fit" between reputational analyses and decision makers' issue-orientation in community power structures.

[10] Cf. Thomas Balogh, "The Apotheosis of the Dilettante" in *The Establishment*, ed. Hugh Thomas (New York: Clarkson N. Potter, 1959), pp. 83–126, passim.

[11] "The Search for a political elite may begin with what is conventionally known as the Government. *Conventionally* speaking, government is the institution which is so named by the members of the community in question. *Functionally*, however, only the institution which makes the severely sanctioned choices can qualify. Since the true decision makers are not necessarily known at the beginning of research, the investigator can select government in the conventional sense as a convenient starting point" (Harold D. Lasswell, "The Comparative Study of Elites," in *World Revolutionary Elites*, ed. by Lasswell and Lerner, p. 8).

various levels of political power to the three thousand, and a rank ordering of these general elite was made. The 10 per cent of those who boasted the greatest reputations for political power were specified as the political elite. (See Appendix I for a detailed account of this procedure.)

But why 10 per cent, why three hundred men? There is no especially telling answer for this question. All three thousand could have been referred to as the political elite. Equally arbitrarily we could have limited the political elite to four persons: His Imperial Majesty, the Shahanshah, Mohammad Reza Pahlavi; his twin sister, Her Royal Highness, the Princess Ashraf; the boyhood companion of the shah and virtually his only trusted Iranian confidant, an ex-prime minister and now minister of the Imperial Court, Assadollah Alam; and the then chief of the State Security and Intelligence Organization, General Hassan Pakravan. Of all three thousand members of the general elite, only these four were reputed to be politically very powerful by all ten of the rankers.[12]

Three hundred were specified, not so much because a convenient cutting point fell there, but because we wished a universe large enough to allow for statements about the elite that could be considered statistically valid. Just as Tocqueville noted that the "moral authority of the majority [in America] is partly based upon the notion that there is more intelligence and wisdom in a number of men united than in a single individual," so we sought to be able to make relevant statements about the Iranian political process on the basis of a majority of the political elite.[13]

Coincidentally, this same figure of three hundred has been recognized before. Prior to the rule of Reza Shah, a perceptive foreign observer noted that "Persia is ruled by Tehran and Tehran is ruled by perhaps three hundred men, including the ins and outs."[14]

In the process of identifying the most politically powerful individuals in Iran, it became clear that to speak of a single political elite is, in fact, a misreading of the realities of Iranian politics. For the power attributed to one member of the general elite was sufficient to merit assigning that individual to a category distinct from and above his fellow members of

---

[12] The crudity of this means for identifying the political elite became evident not long after the completion of the interviews. General Pakravan was relieved of his post and assigned as ambassador to Pakistan, where he is currently serving. But within our categorization system, there would be no means of predicting that the shah had sufficient political power to dismiss Pakravan, for both received exactly equal scores of reputed power. Thus not only did this reputation scheme not result in a cardinal scale of power, but even its ordinality must be considered suspect.

[13] Alexis de Tocqueville, *Democracy in America*, 2 vols. (New York: Vintage Books, 1945), 1: 265.

[14] J. M. Balfour, *Recent Happenings in Persia* (Edinburgh: W. Blackwood and Sons, 1922), p. 90.

the political elite.[15] We refer, of course, to His Imperial Majesty, Mohammad Reza Pahlavi. The extraordinary power that the shah is able to wield vis-à-vis any other member of the elite suggests that Iranian politics can most fruitfully be analyzed through separate but complementary investigations of the shah on the one hand and the remainder of the elite on the other.

The Iranian political process, then, constitutes a system in which the two principal actors may be considered as the shah and his political elite. The decisions of the king, the dominant political actor, directly affect the political elite. But, although unanticipated and frequently undesired by the shah, the behavior of the political elite operates as an important influence on him. There is a feedback system at work in which the shah and the elite, whose makeup he has largely determined, interact and together elaborate Iranian politics.

Once this universe of the elite was identified, the goal became to study that universe in the most productive fashion, defined as an analysis fruitful for explaining the present course of politics and for predicting the likely immediate future of politics in Iran, i.e., to analyze and explain the interactions of the shah and the elite. Plutarch long ago gave one clue as to how this might best be done:

. . . the most glorious exploits do not always furnish us with the clearest discoveries of virtue or vice in men; sometimes a matter of less moment, an expression or a jest, informs us better of their characters and inclinations than the most famous sieges, the greatest armaments, or the bloodiest battles whatsoever. Therefore, as portrait painters are most exact in the lines and features of the face, in which the character is seen, than in the other parts of the body, so I must be allowed to give more attention to the marks and indications of the souls of men, and while I endeavor by these to portray their lives, may be free to leave more weighty matters and great battles to be treated of by others.[16]

Just as great and momentous events may be less useful indications of the souls of men, so may they be less useful than those "souls" for the kind of analysis contemplated for the elite in Iran. In a political system

[15] Thus while empirical investigations of a society may reveal a marked break between the "elite" and the "nonelite," it is also the case that the elite category does not consist of an undifferentiated aggregation of individuals. For us the concept of the elite is in the nature of a continuous rather than a discrete variable. Within the elite category itself, some people are "more elite" than others. Thus the identification of an elite must reveal at least two things if it is to prove useful for empirical systemic analysis: first, who are the individuals who are in the "elite," and second, within the elite itself, what is the hierarchy of "eliteness"?

[16] *The Lives of Noble Grecians and Romans*, trans. John Dryden (New York: Random House, Modern Library, n.d.), p. 801 (a discussion of the life of Alexander the Great).

where institutions are not paramount but where individuals in their interactions constitute the essence of the political process, the souls of men,
or their personalities, to use a more contemporary formulation, are of
primary importance. So it was that in Iran insights to the personalities
of the most powerful political actors and the interactions of these
actors with each other were sought. As Talcott Parsons has cogently
argued:

On the one hand, Freud and his followers, by concentrating on the single
personality, have failed to consider adequately the implications of the individual's interactions with other personalities to form a system. On the
other hand, Durkheim and the other sociologists have failed in their concentration on the social system as a system to consider systematically the
implications of the fact that it is the interactions of personalities which
constitutes the social system. . . . Therefore, adequate analysis of motiva-
tional process in such a system must reckon with the problem of personality.[17]

As description and explanation were the ultimate ends, an analysis that
would consider both aspects of the actors' personalities as well as their
interactions was contemplated. In short, we sought the "code" of the
Iranian political elite.[18]

To do so, it was clear that ideally some form of projective tests,
administered to the elite themselves, would be essential. Because of their
ease of administration, it was decided to employ a series of projective
questions that would allow the elite respondents maximal opportunities
for externalizing subjective feelings. A search of already developed psychological testing instruments was conducted and a number of items,
valid in the American context, were included in the questionnaire. Additionally, standard items pertaining to social background data, communications patterns, and political and social attitudes were included. After
extensive pretesting, translation into Persian, more pretests, and revisions
throughout these stages, a final instrument with some 250 questions
whose data were to fill eleven IBM cards was ready for administration.

Our analysis was based primarily on the responses of 167 members

[17] *Social Structure and Personality* (New York: Free Press, 1964), p. 20.
[18] "By proper methods, it is possible to ascertain the 'code' of an elite, and to
describe the values and objectives sought; the base values typically relied upon;
and the detailed patterns of expectation, identification, and operation which are
present. A scientific observer will take into consideration the principles and maxims
made articulate among the decision-makers. In addition, the analyst will examine
the mode of conduct displayed in typical circumstances, estimating the degree of
elaboration and the intensity of all manifestations. Hence the 'code' of an elite
summarizes both conscious perspectives and unconscious demands, identifications,
and expectations. The measure of intensity is the degree to which the total personality is involved" (Lasswell, "Comparative Study of Elites," p. 12). See also
Nathan Leites, *The Operational Code of the Politburo* (New York: McGraw-Hill,
1951).

of the Iranian political elite to that Persian-language questionnaire through interviews conducted by the author. While access to active duty military officers was denied the author by the shah, those of the elite who were interviewed constitute, impressionistically, a fair cross section of the civilian political elite. Interviews were obtained with present and past officeholders (including a large number of retired military officers as well as those serving in the Senate and the cabinet), supporters and opponents of the monarch, political "comers" and those whose political star has clearly descended, members of the royal family, and commoners.

In many cases, these interviews were simple to arrange. A telephone call to an official's secretary brought a welcome response or even a direct call to the home of the individual was frequently sufficient. Some potential respondents required several telephone calls or even a letter. Others agreed only upon the intervention of a third party. In some cases a document presented to me by the shah supporting the whole undertaking was used to provide legitimacy. But that was used sparingly for fear of placing the whole project too squarely under the aegis of the royal court. (See Appendix II for a comparison of those of the elite who were interviewed and the nonrespondents.)

Impressionistically, as well as on the basis of an analysis of the data generated through the interviews, the respondents seem to have been unusually candid. Obviously, the style of politics in Iran as well as the general character orientations here described argue for caution and discrimination in interpreting the results. It remains for the reader to determine whether this has been done.

It is a major contention of this study that a remarkably small set of significant variables characterize the interpersonal relations that constitute the essence of politics in Iran. By means of a factor analysis applied to data derived from the elite interviews, four principal attitudinal dimensions were uncovered. They have been labeled political cynicism, personal mistrust, manifest insecurity, and interpersonal exploitation. They are assumed to represent the general characterological orientations that underlie elite political behavior.

These general attitudes are not unknown to other students of Iranian politics. Similar attitudes have been ascribed to the Persians by Iranian and foreign observers alike. Leonard Binder has described the means available to those "who engaged in negative system challenging."[19] "Silent resistance" and "the refusal to believe" are two such techniques. Professor Binder adds that the national complement of such disbelief is "cynicism."[20] It is our contention that a cynical response to one's envi-

[19] *Iran: Political Development in a Changing Society* (Berkeley: University of California Press, 1962), p. 288.
[20] *Ibid.*, p. 289.

ronment is by no means restricted to the opponents of the regime. Rather, the attitude permeates the elite itself. An Iranian satirist captured some of the essentials of this cynicism in an "interview" with a mythical deputy to the lower house of the Parliament. The interviewer is questioning Deputy Qurbanali (Ali, the Sacrifice):

Q: What is the population of your constituency?
A: Ten thousand.
Q: How many votes did you get?
A: One hundred and fifty thousand.
Q: Don't you think there is some discrepancy here?
A: I do, but I was told to shut up.
Q: How many rival candidates were there? Did anyone really get more votes than you did?
A: There were many. All of them got more votes.
Q: Then how did you manage to get elected?
A: That was a miracle of the ballot box.
Q: Have you been a member of Parliament before?
A: No.
Q: Why?
A: Because they did not choose me.
Q: What parties have you belonged to in the past, and now?
A: As far as I recall I have been a member of all sorts of parties. At the moment I am a member of the Old Iran party, but I shall soon join the Future Iran party.
Q: Why?
A: Because my experience has shown me that it would be the right thing to do.
Q: What's wrong with the present party?
A: There is nothing wrong with it, but the Future party has better prospects.
Q: How many times did you speak in the present term; and what is the total length of your speeches?
A: I spoke as many times, and for as long, as the speeches they gave me lasted.
Q: Who is "they"?
A: Don't you know?
Q: How many bills did you vote against and which ones are they?
A: Well, . . . about none!
Q: Why?
A: Because the bills were presented by the Government.
Q: Are you saying that one should vote for any bill presented by the Government?
A: Would you give a vote against them?
Q: What are the three most important events during your term?
A: The first important event occurred when I was sitting one day in my home, minding my own business and wondering what kind of

a job I should try for. The radio suddenly announced in the news bulletin that I had been elected a member of Parliament! The second event was the day when the Parliament voted an increase in our salaries to 70,000 rials [$1,000] a month. The third, when they gave us a big housing grant.[21]

As cynicism is a typical response of the Iranian elite to the political process, so is its counterpart, mistrust, typical of interpersonal relations. In discussing the place of mistrust in Persian society, one foreigner noted: "Iranians claim that it is not that they basically are distrustful or that they prefer the interpersonal relations to be the way they are, but that since no basis for altruistic trust exists in Iranian society, they can but respond accordingly to protect themselves; or, as more than one Iranian has expressed himself on the matter, 'If I am trustful, I will only be taken advantage of by others.' "[22] But Iranians themselves put it more strongly. Two Tehran magazines, *Khandaniha* and *Khushe*, printed a series of vitriolic articles castigating Tehranis for their seeming indifference to the reforms of the shah and the implementation of those reforms by the civil service. A third journal responded:

The people are not indifferent, they are distrustful. If you want the truth, the people have lost confidence in everybody and everything. . . .

This distrust begins with the people themselves. People are no longer sure of their own ideas, beliefs, attitudes, or even their decisions.

This distrust in oneself, gained through actual experience, extends, naturally, to others too. They no longer trust anyone. They have heard so many lies, have seen so much creeping and crawling. . . . Whom can they trust? The people do not even trust "the people."[23]

Exploitation or manipulation of others is a third orientation of the elite. A perception of others as self-interested and hostile coupled with a predilection for opportunism in dealing with other persons is a stance that has been noted in Iran for centuries. Adroitness and cleverness have been particularly valued as weapons in what is perceived as an unending interpersonal struggle. Anne Sinclair Mehdevi, an American woman who lived in Iran with her Persian husband, relates not only the extent to which interpersonal relations are governed by Machiavellianism but also how its successful application is lauded: "I was constantly regaled with stories of rascality and guile, stories told with pretenses of censure but which really gave all kudos to the trespasser . . . almost every

[21] K. Shahani, "Interviewing a Majles Deputy," *Khandaniha* (Tehran), Jan. 17, 1967.

[22] Norman Jacobs, *The Sociology of Development, Iran as an Asian Case Study*, Praeger Special Studies in International Economics and Development (New York: Praeger, 1966), p. 260.

[23] "Not Indifferent but Distrustful," *Sahar* (Tehran), July 30, 1966 (Editorial).

13

day some member of our family came home with a tale of how he had been shamelessly but cleverly fleeced."[24] An Iranian writer has put it differently: "All this modernity in Iran is a facade, a pretense. The man's appearance has changed but his mentality is the same. The clean appearance has not stamped out the dirt of dishonesty; the calculating machines have not made us any less calculating."[25]

Finally, the Persian elite are beset with feelings of insecurity. Joseph M. Upton, one of the most perceptive interpreters of Iranian history, states on the first page of his study, "This lively and persistent feeling of both national and individual insecurity is perhaps the dominant characteristic of modern Persian history."[26] An Iranian, trained in the ways of social science, has written a monograph to examine what he senses as "the manic drive of the socially active Iranian for money."[27] He concludes that most of his countrymen view money or wealth as the only meaningful source of security in the face of sweeping social changes.

Clearly, then, others have sensed the presence of these attitudes among certain sectors of the population. Our data, which do not permit generalizations about any sector of the society save the political elite, support the existence of these variables. But these data not only establish and verify the presence of such attitudes among the politically most powerful individuals in the society, they also allow for an analysis that deepens our understanding of the Iranian political process. Who, for example, manifests higher levels of cynicism, of insecurity, of mistrust? What types of social background characteristics are likely to be associated with such personal attitudes? Indeed, from among the millions of eligible and would-be elite, who is recruited into elite membership? Finally, of what relevance to the political process are these variables? Is there any policy significance to the presence of these characteristics among the elite? Does it make any difference to the political system that its most powerful members have a particular set of attitudes? Or is it more important to consider the extrapersonal factors—the Iranian constitution, the influence of foreign powers, the economic and social conditions of the country, etc.?

In the course of this study, we shall examine a number of similar issues. Suffice it to say here that the data suggest unexpected results. Where we had expected that the older Iranians would have become cynical from their participation in the political system, we find the opposite. The younger elites manifest higher levels of cynicism than their

[24] *Persian Adventure* (New York: Alfred A. Knopf, 1953).

[25] Esma'il Pourvali, "What Is Civilization," *Bamshad* (Tehran), Sept. 29, 1964.

[26] *The History of Modern Iran: An Interpretation*, Harvard Middle Eastern Monographs (Cambridge: Harvard University Press, 1960), p. 3.

[27] Khodadad Farmanfarmaian, "Social Change and Economic Behavior in Iran," *Explorations in Entrepreneurial History*, 9, no. 3 (1957): 178-83.

older counterparts. Where we looked for higher levels of manifest insecurity among those of the elite who had fewer institutional ties and thus fewer bases of support, we found the opposite. The more active the elite—the more occupations they have and the more organizations they have joined—the higher their levels of insecurity. Where we had expected the more politically powerful to be more involved and thus more committed to the political system and its objectives, we were again surprised. The more powerful manifested the highest levels of cynicism. The younger elite, then, are more cynical; the active are more insecure; and the powerful, the least committed.

An additional unexpected finding of our research is that these variables do not increase concurrently. For the type of career patterns that the elite have experienced alter their general character orientations. Those members of the elite who have enjoyed lengthy tenure in formal positions within the hierarchies manifest a greater tendency towards interpersonal exploitation, but less cynicism, mistrust, and insecurity. That set of variables that has been labeled exploitation appears to be the attitudinal counterpart to interpersonal manipulation and political conflict. The elite whose attitudes are the most exploitative, and, thus, appear able to manipulate others, also demonstrate higher levels of trust, security, and commitment than do their nonexploitative counterparts. But the latter are by far the more numerous. The majority of the elite, buffeted by frequent alterations of position, seem unable to establish the attitudinal bases for such behavior. Consequently, manipulation is not their forte.

In short, the data indicate that the longer and more thoroughly a member of the elite participates in the Iranian political system, the more he manifests personal attributes of insecurity, cynicism, and mistrust. The incidence of these orientations among the more powerful, more active, and older members of the political elite is above the mode for the entire panel of elite respondents. Moreover, the data suggest that individuals more recently co-opted into elite status are socialized into these patterns and manifest higher levels of these attributes as they mount the elite hierarchy.

The significance of such variables is not principally in their presence nor solely in the assumption that the mode for their distribution is higher among the elite of Iran than it would be for the elites of other political systems. Their importance also lies in two other areas. First, the variables to which single-word labels have been attached are, in fact, composites of a number of subconceptualizations whose nature and meaning reveal the theoretical bases of the general character orientations. Second, the orientations of insecurity, cynicism, mistrust, and tendency towards exploitation are highly correlated with attitudes of the

elite that are more specifically political. A number of political attitudes
were similarly derived from another factor analysis of interview data and
labeled xenophobia, social disdain, populist-nonelite orientation, government disdain, and orientation to the shah. Higher levels of cynicism,
mistrust, and insecurity go together with higher levels of xenophobia,
social disdain, elitism, and a lesser orientation to the shah.

What is being suggested is that there exist modal distributions of these
attitudes that resemble, in actuality, the descriptions of Iranian society
made by so many observers; that these qualities of cynicism, mistrust,
insecurity, and interpersonal exploitation are then the central character
variables that explicate that which is peculiar to Iranian politics; and,
moreover, that these very variables are related in essential ways to the
outputs of the political process in Iran.

To put it another way, the more thoroughly acculturated members of
the political elite, on the one hand, display political attitudes that reflect
their own general character orientations. And on the other hand, the
political attitudes of the elite tend to form the foundation of the political
policies of the Iranian government as those policies are influenced by the
political elite. The basic relationships of influence are illustrated in
figure 1.1.

FIGURE 1.1

Relationships of Influence between the Shah and the Political Elite

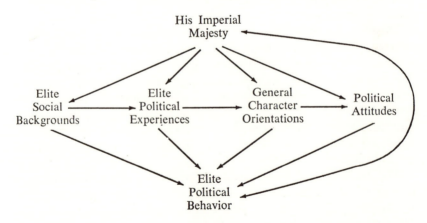

The decisions of the monarch affect the social backgrounds from
which the elite are recruited as well as the political experiences that the
members of the political elite undergo. These in turn affect the general
character orientations that these individuals develop. The more specifically political attitudes that the elite hold are shaped by their back-

grounds, the lives they have led, and the diffuse orientations they have adopted. All in turn influence the political behavior of the elite and the direction of the political system. But these patterns of influence are not unidimensional. All feed back to limit the freedom with which the shah can direct his country's domestic and foreign policies.

Nonetheless, there is no allusion here to either of the exaggerated notions advanced to explain the relationship between the king and his elite. Apologists for the monarch have rationalized his failures in terms of an allegedly refractory and powerfully entrenched clique of elite courtiers. While these courtiers allegedly filter from the royal ears all that would cause the shah discomfort, they simultaneously impede the implementation of his democratic reforms.[28] At the opposite pole sit bitter and outcast antiroyalists who charge the shah and his elite with fraud. They allege that the shah has purposely surrounded himself with venal, sycophantic, and obsequious rogues enlisted to satisfy every royal impulse. Together this coterie is said to milk the nation of its resources while driving its most talented and upright citizens to exile.

Neither extremity represents the entire truth, but both contain some measure of realism. An accurate assessment of the relationship between the shah and his elite must take account of the time period and the momentum of the political system. For while this relationship has been grounded in the shah's demand for unfailing loyalty, its precise nature is a product of the political situation of the moment and the political vision then motivating His Majesty. To detail this relationship between the shah and his elite, and in the process the nature of politics in the Iranian system, we shall examine the principal actors in that system. It is to the most elite of elites to whom we first turn.

[28] Tocqueville commented that "the French under the old monarchy held it for a maxim that the king could do no wrong; and if he did do wrong, the blame was imputed to his advisers. This motion made obedience very easy; it enabled the subject to complain of the law without ceasing to love and honor the law giver. The Americans entertain the same opinion with respect to the majority" (*Democracy in America*, 1: 266).

:2:

THE SHAHANSHAH OF IRAN

AND THE COMPOSITION OF THE POLITICAL ELITE

*The Shah wouldn't know he were Shah
if it weren't written down.*
Brecht, *The Caucasian Chalk Circle*

*H*is Imperial Majesty, Mohammad Reza Pahlavi, Shah of Shahs, Light of the Aryans, is, as his titles might indicate, the central figure in Iranian politics. Since coming to the throne in 1941, the shah has demonstrated a capacity for preserving his position all but unheard of among the nations of the developing world. Through foreign occupations and foreign-sponsored separatist states, internal uprisings, tribal challenges, assassination efforts, and thwarted military *coups d'état*, the shah has managed to husband his support, to experiment with new forms of control, and, ultimately, to expand his political power.

Indeed, the entire reign of the shah, with temporary setbacks, can be characterized as a quarter century in which the civil and military bureaucracies have continually expanded their control over the activities of the population at large while the shah has even more relentlessly expanded his power over the bureaucracies. In both relative and absolute terms, this monarch is more powerful than his father and than any previous Iranian ruler. This king of kings can, in no political sense, be considered merely the "first among equals." He, personally, without the aid of advisory councils, alter egos, or close confidants, makes the thousands of decisions that allow the government to function. From the appointment or promotion of officers in the army to the decisions as to whether or not to pave the main street of Tabas, His Imperial Majesty is the arbiter.

Mohammad Reza was the first son and third-born child of Reza Khan, an illiterate or semiliterate officer in the Russian-commanded Persian Cossack Brigade. Two years after the birth of his son, Reza Khan was to command the Cossack Brigade, and with it provide military support for a coup led by a journalist, Seyyed Zia ed-Din Tabatabaie, against the ailing Qajar regime. Six years after the boy's birth, Reza Khan, having long since replaced the Seyyed as prime minister, exiled him along with a number of his more vocal opponents, silenced most of his remaining internal critics, ousted the last Qajar, and established himself as Reza Shah, the first ruler of the new Pahlavi dynasty.[1] With his coronation in 1925 came the designation of Mohammad Reza as crown prince.

The crown prince's childhood appears to be a near parody of a future monarch's upbringing. Surrounded by servants and sycophants, protected by older military officers, and supplied with playmates from the children of the elite, he always managed to be the first in his class at school. Numerous photographs show the youth dressed in military uniform taking the salute of honor: from the graduates of the Officer Academy to the Boy Scouts of Iran, he early was the subject of immense deference. Besides the servility of the court, the crown prince had other significant childhood experiences. As a young child, he was considered rather weak and sickly. Shortly after he became crown prince, he was struck by typhoid fever and wavered near death for weeks. His frail nature and childhood illnesses heightened the protective and almost isolated atmosphere in which he was raised.

One final experience contributed to heightening the effects of these others. Until the age of six, the boy lived with his mother and brothers and sisters. When he was invested as crown prince, however, his father decided that the future monarch needed a more "manly education." Thereafter, he was separated from his mother and sisters, raised by a French governess, and educated in a specially organized school with a group of "carefully selected" elite boys.[2]

Perhaps to isolate his son from the debilitating atmosphere surrounding the court, Reza Shah sent the boy to study at Le Rosey secondary school in Switzerland. The king was later to look back at this period and recall: "I was to stay in Switzerland about four years, a tremendously important period in my life. The democratic Western environment moulded my character to an extent that was second only to my father's influence."[3] Other evidence suggests that the crown prince was not, in

[1] It is interesting that perhaps the most articulate critic of Reza Khan's decision to assume the throne was Dr. Mohammad Mossadegh, then a member of Parliament. As the prime minister in 1953, Mossadegh nearly brought about the downfall of the Pahlavi dynasty.

[2] Mohammad Reza Shah Pahlavi, *Mission for My Country* (New York: McGraw-Hill, 1961), p. 52.

[3] *Ibid.*, p. 60.

fact, subject to quite the "democratic Western environment" reported. Reza Shah, concerned with his son's "original frailty," dispatched a personal physician to supervise the crown prince's health.[4] A Persian tutor, his brother, and two boyhood friends comprised the remainder of the retinue.[5] It would seem likely that this Iranian clique and ready-made peer group isolated the aspiring monarch from some of the ruder consequences of the democratic environment of Le Rosey.

Whatever the influence on the crown prince of his experience abroad, his return to Iran in 1936 found him once again immersed in the atmosphere of the court. He entered the Military Academy, graduating two years later as a second lieutenant at the head of his class. Shortly afterwards, he was appointed by his father to be inspector of the Imperial Iranian Armed Forces.

In 1939, in what was apparently his first great service to the monarchy, his country, and the legitimacy of his father's rule, he was married to Princess Fawzia, the sister of King Farouk of Egypt. Although a daughter was born a year later, the marriage apparently was a personal failure—the Egyptian ruling family proving no more compatible to an Iranian than it did to the Egyptians.

And so the boy lived until the age of twenty-one, when in 1941 Great Britain and Russia invaded his country. Wary of growing German influence on Reza Shah and fearing an Iraqi-type pro-Axis coup, the two powers demanded Reza Shah's abdication, sent him into exile, and established his son on the throne. It seems clear that the young king was ill-prepared for his new role. A deadening court atmosphere of servility and sycophancy had isolated the new king from many of the pervasive problems of Iran and their possible solutions, and limited his own capability for dealing with them. His father had been a strict disciplinarian at home and an authoritarian at court. His Imperial Majesty remembered that as crown prince he used to discuss details of Iran's domestic and foreign policy with his father. But he hastily added, "I, and all the officials of my father's Government, had such respect for him and were so much in awe of him that 'discussion' with him had none of the give-and-take the word implies. I advanced my views and made hints and suggestions, but discussion in any usual sense was out of the question."[6]

The king also had countless examples of his father's forceful methods for dealing with his officials. To this day, Iranians look back with wonder at Reza Shah's lightning and unannounced inspection tours of public projects. In the earlier years of his rule, he would almost invariably find

---

[4] *Ibid.*

[5] One of the four boys was the son of the ill-fated minister of court, Teimourtash, who, falling afoul of Reza Shah's temper, was relieved of his post. At that point, his son was forced to leave Mohammad Reza and return home.

[6] Mohammad Reza Shah Pahlavi, *Mission for My Country*, p. 64.

the project in near collapse and decay, despite the glowing reports of progress sent to Tehran. Charging the responsible official with completion by a given date, Reza Shah would return on that very day, weeks or months later, and find the project completed, or else. That it was frequently the "or else" alternative was clear to the crown prince: "Proverbially, to get things done in Persia, one must both reward and punish. My father relied more on punishment than he did on reward or even encouragement. In his view there was no reason to wax sentimental about a man doing something well, because that was his duty. On the other hand if my father learned of a man who was doing something poorly or dishonestly, he would live to regret it."[7]

All these elements—personal sickliness; enforced separation from his mother and sisters; a stern, powerful, and dominating father; and a milieu replete with sycophants—seem to have resulted in the young king's being filled with self-doubt and fears of his own weakness.[8] In his autobiography, the shah relates a conversation revealing these perceived inadequacies:

My father said that he wanted to improve the government machinery to such a degree that, if he should die, the day-to-day process of administration would operate almost automatically without the need of continuous supervision from the top.

I was still rather young and perhaps not very mature; and I took his remark as an insult. "What does he mean?" I thought. "Does he think that if he were gone I couldn't take over and continue his work?"[9]

With the Allied invasion and the abdication of his father, then, this young and self-doubting man took the throne. His country was occupied and effectively controlled by powerful foreign nations that had recently destroyed, in a matter of hours, the Imperial Iranian Armed Forces. These were the same armed forces that his father had devoted his life to modernizing and to which he had directed the major share of his country's resources during his rule. Among his own people, the new shah was surrounded by courtiers, politicians, and generals, more experienced and older, who had served his father for years. They quickly moved to consolidate their own power bases, independent of the throne. Finally, a torrent of domestic opposition, silenced, exiled, or incarcerated by Reza

[7] *Ibid.*, p. 49. Widely held charges against Reza Shah suggest that this recollection is faulty, i.e., not all disgraced officials "lived to regret it." Minister Teimourtash, some claim, lost his post and his life as a result of Reza Shah's ill will.

[8] It is not unlikely that His Majesty's avid commitment to vigorous, physical activities, such as skiing, is in the form of compensation for perceived self-weaknesses.

[9] Mohammed Reza Shah Pahlavi, *Mission for My Country*, p. 65. Note that His Imperial Majesty refers to his thoughts rather than to an expression of those thoughts to his obviously stern and overbearing father.

Shah, was released. Enveloped in flowing praise and panegyric a few months before, Reza Shah was suddenly vilified and damned by his enemies, not surprisingly, but also by many of his apparently warmest supporters.

None of this was lost on the young king. His self-doubts and fears of weakness were reinforced by an actual inability to do as his father had done or as Iranian kings before Reza Shah had always done: to rule. All that which the crown prince had been taught to revere had crumbled. His father was debased and maligned for his alleged corruption, ignorance, and tyranny. The much-heralded Iranian army—in whose uniform he had been invested as crown prince—now resembled the rabble of Qajar times. The modern bureaucracy that Reza Shah had hoped to build more nearly resembled an inefficient and virtually autonomous collection of corrupt and nepotistic cliques. And the ultimate trust of the monarchy—the very independence of Iran—had been lost.

To the amazement of many foreign observers and at least grudging admiration from domestic opponents, the shah faced and overcame these early obstacles. Working within the weaknesses of self and system, the shah strengthened his hold on the throne and the hold of the throne over the political elite. With interruptions and setbacks, he has continued the process to the present day. As Farouk, Feisal, Ben Bella, Sukarno, Menderes, Nkrumah, Batista, and Trujillo have fallen by the wayside of political leadership, the shah has preserved his throne, enhanced his power, and maintained the integrity of Iran.

Many answers have been advanced to account for the shah's political longevity, but they all share the common failings of oversimplicity and a lack of exclusivity. That the shah has the support of foreign governments, well-equipped and efficient armed forces for internal control, a pervasive secret police, a subservient and cowed political elite, and rigid control over the civil liberties and personal freedom of the population may or may not be true. If these are true of Iran or, at least, partly true of Iran, they were also true or partly true of other nations whose rulers did not enhance and ultimately preserve their positions. And more importantly, if these phenomena are true of the Iranian political system, they constitute second-order explanations. That is, they do not account for the successes of His Imperial Majesty in strengthening his position. Rather, these phenomena are characteristics of that success. A more adequate explanation must be sought in the interplay of his style of rule with the attitudes and expectations of the political elite, those whose relations to the political process allow them to execute, thwart, or alter his wishes.

The style of rule that His Imperial Majesty has unfolded and elaborated since coming to power centers about (1) controlling the size and compositions of the politically influential segments of the Iranian population; (2) manipulating the behavior of the politically active and influential segments of the Iranian population, including the political elite;[10] (3) limiting the nature of the demands made by the political process as articulated by the general population; and (4) satisfying, to the maximum extent, those demands that are articulated.

CONTROLLING ACCESS TO ELITE STATUS

The basis of the shah's policy of controlling the size and composition of the politically influential is one of recruitment by co-optation. That is, all elites and those who because of unusual popularity, charisma, wealth, skills, or knowledge are considered potential elites or counterelites are co-opted into elite membership by being offered prestigious office or other rewards. High-status positions in the civil bureaucracy, Imperial Court, Parliament, universities, or any number of royal commissions are used as counters in the shah's attempts to incorporate all potentially relevant individuals.

Specific representatives of the Ministry of Imperial Court have been commissioned by the ruler to designate and seek out politically relevant individuals. Working through personal contacts, reports of the intelligence services, and the ambassadors of Iran (for students abroad), these representatives are then charged with offering the kinds of rewards or positions that would recruit the designee into the system.

This co-optative method of recruitment to the ranks of the elite fills two principal functions: uncovering talent and hindering the formation of counterelites. In the former sense, personal representatives of the shah are able to identify individuals with valuable skills or training, but individuals who are currently outside the monarch's immediate scrutiny. There may be an individual of unusual capability filling a relatively menial post. A young student in Iran, Europe, or America may demonstrate unusual capacity in his university work. An Iranian with valuable skills may have finished his foreign studies and, attracted by the higher salaries, remained abroad. All these individuals can be located and induced, with suitable material or other blandishments, to use their skills and training for the regime and Iran.

The second function that this recruitment–by–co-optation serves is to restrain the formation of counterelites. In the words of Fred W. Riggs, "the rise of counter-elites [is] part of a much broader phenomenon . . .

[10] By "politically influential" we refer to a far larger number of Iranians than the political elite whom we have ambitiously specified as the most politically powerful 10 per cent of a general elite. The politically influential would include the remaining general elite and a substantial number of others.

namely the 'differentiation' of a population as it becomes mobilized but not assimilated."[11] In Iran, individuals with the qualities to lead or, indeed, form, a mobilized counterelite rarely do so. They lack the incentive, for they are rapidly assimilated. And precisely that which they value, they receive as elites: be it status, power, money, or foreign travel, the rewards of recruitment by seduction are usually satisfying.

Like so many other political practices in Iran, this one—buying off the potential opposition—has a long history. In the early twentieth century, W. Morgan Shuster, an American brought to reorganize Persia's finances, commented on one aspect of this:

One of the most remarkable examples of Persia's peculiar financial chaos was a system of "pensions." According to the loosely kept records of the different Ministries, the Government was expected to pay out each year to nearly 100,000 different people throughout the Empire the sum of about 3,000,000 tumans, in money and grain.

The greater part of this strange burden had been inherited by the Constitutional Government from the regime of the former Shahs. . . .

. . . Fully nine-tenths of the pensions allotted were pure graft. All the grandees enjoyed large pensions.[12]

Presently, the co-optative system takes several forms. Outright pensions are still granted to elites or counterelites, the monarch's Pahlavi Foundation frequently serving as a conduit.[13] In addition, facilities and conveniences are provided the elites and potential elites. Thus a building originally designed to serve as a headquarters for the secret police was completed at a cost of some $1 1/2 million and designated a Palace of Youth. Entrance to the building is restricted, however, to "those, from 19 to 30, who have higher than secondary school educations."[14] But the most frequent reward for co-optation remains a high-status position within the bureaucracy.

One major effect of this method for the recruitment of new elements into the elite may be found in the nature of the political process that ensues. Politics becomes intraelite, rather than interelite. Political issues are not formulated to serve as rallying points for elite cliques. The role

[11] *The Ecology of Public Administration* (New Delhi: Indian Institute of Public Administration, 1961), p. 125.

[12] *The Strangling of Persia: A Record of European Diplomacy and Oriental Intrigue* (London: T. Fisher Unwin, 1912), pp. 267–68. In addition, Professor Nikki R. Keddie informs me (personal communication, Feb. 2, 1969) of the widespread co-optative use of pensions to the ulema (religious preachers, scholars, and jurists) to lessen their protests in the late nineteenth and early twentieth centuries.

[13] See, for example, the reports that Majles Deputy Habibi (an ex-Olympic wrestling champion) had his Pahlavi Foundation "allowances" cut for refusing to follow directions in the Parliament (*Farman Magazine* [Tehran], July 14, 1966).

[14] *Kayhan International* (Tehran), Nov. 17, 1966.

of ideology is minimized and politics, as enacted at the elite level in Iran, consists of the adjustment of personal differences within an elite perspective. While individuals may gain or lose status within the elite hierarchy, whole groups do not. Moreover, neither groups nor individuals are likely to pass out of the limits of the elite. Thus, the incentives for adopting radical methods of holding or taking political elite status are lessened.

Another effect to which the co-optation policy contributes is a surprisingly democratic character in elite politics. The goal of the regime vis-à-vis the elite is inclusivity rather than exclusivity. When combined with a cynical perspective on political activities, there are relatively few political acts that may not be forgiven or that the shah perceives as sufficiently ominous to result in the exclusion of an elite from his elite status or, once excluded, that prohibit eventual return.

One example is found in a well-educated Iranian who became active in the Tudeh party, Iran's organized Communists, in the 1940s. At one stage, he was a member of the central committee and actively working towards Soviet suzerainty. After quitting the party and retiring from active political life, however, the man returned in the early 1960s as minister of justice. Being a member of the Tudeh in the 1940s is now perceived as a tolerable and, for that time, a personally useful form of political expression. In addition, this was a man of demonstrated qualities of leadership and administration: better within the elite than without.

Another example may be found in a youthful activist in the National Front, the pro-Mossadegh political grouping now, in effect, illegal. One of His Imperial Majesty's representatives stressed the valuable services that he could perform for Iran were he in the government's service rather than out of it. And he was offered a position as deputy minister. This particular aspiring counterelite agreed that he could serve best within the government, but only in a National Front government. He refused the offer, and is now living abroad.

The shah attends to matters other than the immediate co-optation of potential elites or counterelites. He also influences the distribution of resources that serve as bases for the acquisition of political power. By regulating the apportionment of these resources, His Majesty attempts to circumscribe entry into the political elite to those who will probably sustain his rule. Presently, membership into the political elite of Iran is most facilitated by control over two resources—wealth and education. The monarch has labored long to control these power bases.

WEALTH AS A POWER BASE

The principal criterion for membership in the Iranian political elite of Qajar times was wealth—wealth to buy offices and political power. The most feasible method of accumulating wealth was the ownership of land. What national wealth there was in Iran stemmed almost entirely from agricultural production and herding. Land gave one a share in that wealth—a portion of the crop or the wool, rents from tenants. But while landownership was the most prevalent base for the accumulation of wealth, it was by no means the sole source of wealth. Profits from internal commerce or production and exporting and importing financed the elite status of some.

In contemporary Iran, wealth remains an important but no longer, in a direct sense, the most important criterion for membership in the elite or the generally influential. Wealth as a power base in Iran has been supplemented and occasionally supplanted by what Frederick W. Frey has called the "hallmark" of the Turkish elite—education.[15] The progressive expansion in the power of the political center means that the center now has more control than ever before over these bases for elite membership. Not only do the government, and in turn, the shah, control the sources of wealth in Iran, but they also control access to institutions of formal education. The government's hold over the economy, and thus over the possibilities for accumulating and retaining wealth, is most strikingly seen in the recent Land Reform Program. As of 1971, land reform had progressed through two phases and was immersed in the third. The first phase, from January 1962 until September 1963, resulted in the sale of 8,042 villages to their peasant cultivators. (Originally, it had been estimated that 13,904 villages were eligible for distribution under the first phase, but "ownership disputes" resulted in the exclusion from the land reform of some 5,862 villages.[16]) The second phase of land reform, which limited the number of hectares—from 30 to 150, depending on the quality of the land—that one owner could hold, lasted to January 1965, but seems to have seriously lagged from mid-1964. Nonetheless, at the end of 1965, the government had announced that a total of 38,792 villages had been affected by the two stages of land reform.[17] In 1966, the minister of agriculture announced twenty aims for increasing agri-

---

[15] *The Turkish Political Elite* (Cambridge: M.I.T. Press, 1965), chap. 3.

[16] The total number of villages in Iran is a matter of some uncertainty. The 1956 census gives the number of inhabited places defined as rural as 49,054 and the number of inhabited places of less than 1,000 persons as 47,116 (Ministry of Interior, Department of Public Statistics, *National and Province Statistics of the First Census of Iran: November 1956*, 2 vols. [Tehran, 1961], vol. 1, *Number and Distribution of the Inhabitants for Iran and the Census Provinces*, p. 12). The *New York Times* claims that the Iranian government has referred to a total of 54,000 (May 11, 1963, p. 28). Minister of Agriculture Arsanjani referred to 58,000 villages (Echo of Iran, *Daily Bulletin*, 10, no. 206: 3); while the director of the land reform programs, Colonel Dr. A. A. Valian, gave the total as 65,000 (television address quoted in *Kayhan* [Tehran], Nov. 9, 1965).

[17] Echo of Iran, *Iran Almanac and Book of Facts—1966* (Tehran: Echo of Iran Press, 1966), p. 571.

cultural production and rural welfare, aims that were to serve as the third phase of the program.

Meanwhile, the former owners of entire villages had been reimbursed with interest-bearing, twenty-year bonds.[18] The owners of land subject to the second phase could choose one of three options for reaching a settlement with their peasants. They could rent their land to the peasant cultivators for thirty years with leases renewable every fifth year (and thus continue to retain ownership). The owners could sell the lands directly to the farmers on the basis of mutually agreed on and government-approved terms. Or the landlords and the peasants could establish a farm company, the ownership of which would be divided between the cultivators and the present owner on the basis of the crop-sharing ratios in the area.[19] Both the first and the third of these alternatives would not alter the distribution of agricultural profits accruing to the peasants, but would offer them stability of tenure on their lands. Nonetheless, as one Kurdestani peasant suggested to an Iranian studying the land reform, "it makes no difference to the peasant whether his landlord owns one village or 600 villages; he will still have to pay rent and be at the landlord's mercy as before."[20]

Whatever its economic shortcomings, the land reform has been a source of profound political change. First, "land reform has weakened and alienated a considerable part of the shah's traditional allies: the landlords."[21] The loss or weakening of this base of support, however, has become relatively unimportant to the monarch. He no longer need rely on this social group for either the support or guidance that he required in the past, particularly on his accession to the throne in 1941 and his return to it in 1953. Moreover, the pace of social and economic change in Iran has bypassed many of these older aristocrats. Their relative lack of education and traditionally conservative *weltanschauung* make them less relevant to the kind of Iran that is emerging in the last quarter of the twentieth century.

[18] The bonds can be discounted in the financial markets of Tehran at thirty to thirty-five cents on the dollar—an indication of the value that those shrewd traders attach to the bonds. A great deal of excitement greeted the government's announcement that land reform bonds could be exchanged at par value for shares in government-owned factories. The interest withered when the shares were issued, however. It appeared that the shares were being issued only for those industrial enterprises that were losing money for their former owner—the government!

[19] For information on crop-sharing practices in Iran, see Ann K. S. Lambton, *Landlord and Peasant in Persia* (London: Oxford University Press, 1953). For complete details of the land reform, see Professor Lambton's *The Persian Land Reform, 1962–1966* (London: Clarendon Press, 1969).

[20] Hossein Mahdavy, "The Coming Crises in Iran," *Foreign Affairs*, Oct. 1965, pp. 139-40. Dr. Mahdavy's article is an excellent critique of the social and economic effects of the land reforms and possible political consequences.

[21] *Ibid.*, p. 142.

Also, the land reform has disassociated many of the present elite from what had been a major source of their wealth. After a period of some adjustment, however, this is likely to be a meaningful consequence of land reform only in indirect ways. Unlike feudal aristocracies, Iran's political elite have not been attached to their estates from generation to generation. Moreover, their power, with the exception of tribal leaders and the owners of exceptionally large holdings, was based on bureaucratic position bought through the practice of *modakhel* (perquisite) with money derived from agricultural income.[22] Once the positions were obtained, they were self-generating—the positions themselves producing the funds for retaining the post or acquiring higher office. More important, with the reforms of Reza Shah, new opportunities for amassing wealth appeared. Importing, commerce, manufacturing, and new public projects such as the Trans-Iranian Railroad vastly expanded the size of the money sector. The relative decline in the value produced by agriculture was vastly accelerated by the wartime occupation and the postwar oil production that has continued to the present. Being dedicated not to their lands or peasants, but to the wealth produced by them, the elite were quick to seize the opportunities to amass the wealth that the new economic boom presented. Their holdings have by now been diversified to include urban land and real estate, commerce and light industries, or even foreign securities. Thus, many are exposed to relatively slight financial danger by the land reform.

While disassociated from land-based wealth, however, the landlords do become more dependent on these other sources of riches. And those sources of wealth in turn tend to be directly controlled by the government. That is, the land reform has not destroyed the financial power of this one segment of society—no social revolution has been effected. Rather, land reform has altered the importance of the elite's sources of wealth (and ultimately their bases of political power) to those that are under the control of the government.

An example from one well-known member of the political elite may illustrate this point. Shortly after World War II, his family took advantage of the burgeoning development of Tehran to begin to manufacture consumer products. Their success was beyond their imagination and

[22] Tribal leaders are an exception to this generalization, for they constituted, in Qajar Iran, a cohesive political entity with a military force more mobile, disciplined, and powerful than those commanded by the central government. Reza Shah's political *savoir-faire* and armed forces reduced the tribes from a meaningful threat to an occasional nuisance. An example of owners of exceptionally large holdings would be the Alams of the Qaenat in eastern Iran. Formerly virtual rulers of the Qaenat, Sistan, and Baluchistan, the Alams' private army guarded the Iranian heartland from the marches of Afghanistan and British India. The present minister of the Imperial Court, Assadollah Alam, is a direct descendant.

growing profits were reinvested in expanded capacity and eventually urban real estate and foreign stocks and bonds. All the while, the family retained the ownership of a number of agricultural villages that had originally produced the funds for the manufacturing facilities. They remained profitable, although less so than the new investments, and no additional funds were put into them. With the land reform, the family lost its villages, without great fuss. Their response was to construct a new manufacturing plant with the most modern machinery available. The plant is operating today, resembling more an American or West German experimental unit than a facility in a developing country supposedly making use of labor-intensive production processes. A handful of well-trained and white-cloaked workers watch the dials and supervise the plant where hundreds would have worked before automation. The owner explained that his family realized that their factories were now their principal source of wealth. The high-priced equipment, he continued, was necessary because it eliminated the need for workmen. Eliminating the workers also eliminated the chief entrée that the government could claim in order to control his factory. And keeping out the government was necessary if he were to remain an independent producer and retain a substantial proportion of the profits.

He explained how the Ministries of Labor (concerned with worker guilds and wages), Interior (worker political organization), Information (worker propaganda), and Health (worker welfare) were now far less likely to intervene in the affairs of his company. In their absence, some hope existed that the owners could devote themselves to production rather than to politics.[23]

But ultimately, of course, entrepreneurs such as this one will be proven wrong. It is impossible to escape the control of the government irrespective of the ruses employed. The increased reliance of this class on industry or trade rather than agricultural land to produce wealth will put them under the control of the government—if not through the ministries mentioned, then through the Ministry of Water and Power for electricity, the Ministry of Economy for import licenses and permits to engage in manufacturing, the Ministry of Finance for income and profits tax, the Ministry of Development for permits to expand production, and so on. Through the enforcement of a multitude of regulations pertaining to all phases of commercial and industrial processes, the government and the shah are able to exert control over these more modern sources of wealth. This degree of control was never possible when wealth was based

[23] The prevalence of automated production facilities in Iran is not limited to this one factory but is increasingly widespread. While it may lessen the likelihood of government intervention in the production processes and supply status among industrialists to its owners, the practice seriously exacerbates the problems of under- and unemployment that the country faces.

on rural holdings, separated by vast distances and poor communications from the capital (although such holdings, especially under Reza Shah, were subject to confiscation by the monarch—a fate suffered by no industrial firms to the present).

But in addition, the shah possesses even more direct levers for control. Few industrial or commercial undertakings are launched in Iran without the blessing of the shah. To secure those blessings, the shah is often made the gift of a share in the ownership of the venture, just as Reza Shah was the recipient of estates from favor-seeking elites. In other instances, the shah or other members of the royal family will invest their personal funds in indigenous commercial ventures. The result is that at least some member of the Pahlavi family has a direct and legitimate voice, by dint of ownership, in the operation of nearly all commerce and industry in Iran. The government of Iran and the shah and royal family, then, have become privy, either directly or indirectly, to the nonagricultural economy of Iran. As the land reform eliminated that area of the Iranian economy that stood outside the surveillance of the government, the elites who now must rely on new sources of wealth to maintain their power bases do so under the control of the government.

If land reform has antagonized a segment of the traditional elite and removed a source of wealth from the hands of the former owners, it has also eliminated a base of votes or the electoral support with which the former landowners could control the Parliament. By marshaling the peasants in his villages, an owner could assure his receiving enough votes to be elected, with the result that His Imperial Majesty had to resort to countless stratagems to assert his own control over the elections. From the Mossadegh period, he urged the Majles to pass legislation limiting the franchise to the literate. Realizing that the mass illiteracy of the countryside would result in the elimination of their electoral support, the legislators withstood the imperial pressures year in and year out.

Subsequently, in 1957, His Majesty responded by convening the upper house of the Parliament. The Iranian constitution of 1907 specified provisions for a Senate but it had never been organized. The constitution empowered the king to appoint half of its sixty members. With that power he was able to set up a second parliamentary body that could at least serve as a check on what he considered the excesses of the first. But even with control of the Senate, the shah had insufficient influence in the lower house to assure his control over the government as a whole. Control over the Majles, therefore, was also necessary. One measure facilitating this process was to cut the links between the elite and the peasant voters, some 65 per cent of the population. The land reform did this.

This control over the Majles is even more pervasive: the cooperative movement is replacing the landlord-peasant links by shah-government-peasant links. The government cooperatives, where organized and functioning, are meant to fulfill the services provided, at least theoretically, by the landlord: finance, seed, fertilizer, technical assistance, and marketing.[24] The peasants, then, have also been brought under the control of the political center and the shahanshah as a result of the land reform. Not only have the landlords been denied a source of "independent" wealth and electoral support, but the peasants are being denied an existence independent of the government.

A specter that will undoubtedly yet harass the government as a result of land reform will be the frustration of peasant expectations in years of poor agricultural production. Whereas these expectations were formerly nonexistent or were directed at the landlord, they now definitely exist and are directed towards the bureaucracy. As one member of the elite put it, "The shah has eliminated the owners of thousands of villages and, in the eyes of the farmers, replaced those *rejal va khassa* [elites and lords] with his own person." In the event of poor governmental performance or poor harvests, the ire of the peasants will be aroused. Each passing year of reform in Iran has tended to raise the standards of acceptable bureaucratic performance. With the greater capacity of the political system will come greater demands for its satisfactory employment.[25]

EDUCATION AS A POWER BASE

The principal power base for access to elite membership other than wealth is education.[26] A high level of formal education has become not

[24] In the first phase of land reform, membership in a cooperative was a theoretical requirement for receiving land. This provision was waived in the second stage of the program except in the case of endowment lands. (There, the government was eager to wrest the land and the peasants from the grip of the ulema.) In 1960, before the initiation of land reform, there were 711 cooperatives in Iran. The government claimed that 6,828, with 850,000 members, were in operation by the end of 1966. Thus only a small fraction of the new landlords were included, although the formation of nearly 7,000 even partially functioning cooperatives is an impressive feat. See Shahpour Rahbari, "Land Reform's Five Eventful Years," *Kayhan International* (Tehran), Jan. 9, 1967.

[25] No attempt has been made here to detail the other, not immediately political, effects of the land reform. The failure to supply the poorest peasants with land, the heightened exodus to the cities, the growing power of the rural moneylenders and urban food wholesalers, and the embourgeoisification of rural elements will all profoundly affect the politics of Iran in the future.

[26] Education had been a principal means of mobility in earlier times. With rigorous and thorough religious training a young man of humble origin could attain elevated religious status, even that of a *mojtahed* (a high religious authority), giving command of both wealth and power. But such training rarely provided access to formal positions within the government, of which there were previously far fewer and, in any case, such positions were considered not especially respectable (Nikki R. Keddie to author, personal communication, Feb. 2, 1969).

only the hallmark of the younger aspirants to the political elite, but a sine qua non. There are a number of indications that this is widely recognized in the society. A recent survey, for example, asked a sample of four hundred Tehrani literates, "Which one particular field of development is of greatest importance to Iran?"[27] Responses are given in table 2.1.

TABLE 2.1

Field of Development Important to Iran
According to Tehrani Literates

Field of Development	Percentage Responding
Education	40
Agriculture	32
Industry	17
Finance	3
Administration	0
Other	1
No answer	7
Total	100 .

As education is viewed as a prerequisite for national development, so is it viewed as a necessary and even sufficient condition for personal mobility. Such is the concomitant of the publicly iterated rationale of educational policy in Iran: "to train an intellectual elite who will then occupy the directing positions in society."[28] This yearning is held with such fervor that the "education suicide"—a person's taking his own life after finding that additional education is denied him or his children—is not an infrequent occurrence. One poignant case made headlines in Tehran recently when a mother of four realized that she could not afford the tuition fees and books to send her children to primary school. She threw herself from the roof of an apartment building.[29] As education has become a prerequisite for mobility and as the realization of this has spread, the government and the shah have asserted their control over the educational system. This control is manifest in a number of ways.

The *maktab* and *madresseh* have been virtually eliminated. Representing primary and secondary levels in the traditional religious educational system, these institutions were formerly the sole means of formal education available to Iranians. *Maktab* schools were the product of the

[27] National Institute of Psychology, Marketing, and Public Opinion Research Division, *A Preliminary Survey of Literate Iranians' Attitudes* (Tehran: National Institute Press, 1962), table 10(a).

[28] Herbert H. Vreeland, ed., *Iran* (New Haven: Human Relations Area Files, 1957), p. 269. Cf. Issa Sadiq, *History of Education in Iran: From Earliest Times to the Present Day*, 3rd ed. (Tehran: Teachers College Press, 1963 [in Persian]), especially chap. 11.

[29] *Tehran Journal*, Aug. 8, 1963.

individual *mullah* (Moslem clergyman) who sought commissions from parents eager to have their children cognizant with the skills of literacy, calligraphy, poetry, and religious rules and principles. The *madresseh* was a more formalized school, usually attached to a mosque or religious shrine, and training *maktab* graduates in *hekmat* (Islamic law), *'erfan* (philosophy and gnosticism), theology, logic, geography, and Arabic grammar.

The first modern primary school was not established until the late nineteenth century. But following its introduction, a network of privately sponsored, and later public, primary schools sprang up. As recently as 1936, there were 55,650 boys and girls studying at *maktab*s versus 177,000 in modern primary schools.[30] The *madresseh*s were rather less widespread, being valued primarily for the training of future members of the ulema. Nonetheless, in 1924, before the inception of the Pahlavi dynasty, 4,980 males were studying at the *madresseh*s in comparison with only 3,320 boys *and* girls at modern secondary schools.[31]

But Reza Shah's policies of educational development sounded the knell of these traditional schools. By 1935, the number of *madresseh* students had dropped to 2,900, while the number of pupils in modern secondary schools rose to 16,200. The "secularization" of the school system was established and proceeded steadily through the remaining years of Reza Shah's rule to the present. Table 2.2 reveals the decline and elimination of the traditional educational institutions, beginning in a relative sense with the anti-Qajar coup of 1921 and in an absolute sense with the last five years of the rule of Reza Shah. Following his abdication, there was a letup in antireligious sentiment as the new shah sought support where he could find it and the British and Americans urged him to strengthen the religious elements as a counter to Communist penetration from the Soviet occupation. One result was a rise in the number of *madresseh* students. But the rise was short-lived, their numbers having declined to below one thousand and no longer reported by the government as of 1950.

The elimination of the traditional educational system went hand in hand with the growth of the Ministry of Education and a Government bureaucracy capable and eager to supervise the educational process. As the *maktab*s and *madresseh*s declined, a modern, private, educational sector grew. But unlike the former schools, the modern private institutions are always under the supervision of the Ministry. Their textbooks are supplied by the Ministry, their courses of instruction and teacher qualifications are subject to Ministry rules. But whatever the independ-

[30] Empire de l'Iran, Ministère de l'Instruction Publique, Service de la Statistique, *Annuaire, 1935–1936* (Tehran: Imprimeur Madjles, n.d.), pp. 70–71.
[31] *Ibid.*, pp. 69, 72.

TABLE 2.2

Enrollment in Traditional and Modern
Primary and Secondary Schools in Iran,
1922-1962 (in 100s)

Year	Primary School		Secondary School	
	Traditional	Modern	Traditional	Modern
1922-23	2.1	-	.6	-
1923-24	22.9	64.9	5.0	3.3
1928-29	35.9	100.6	5.5	7.0
1931-32	51.0	130.6	3.7	12.5
1935-36	55.6	177.1	2.9	16.2
1940-41	37.3	287.2	.8	28.2
1945-46	22.1	293.7	3.1	29.4
1950-51	-	481.2	-	-
1955-56	-	824.0	-	142.1
1960-61	-	1,431.6	-	279.7
1962-63	-	1,719.4	-	326.9

Sources: Ahmad Fattahipour Fard, "Educational Diffusion and the Modernization of an Ancient
Civilization--Iran" (Ph.D. diss., University
of Chicago, 1963). Statistics for the 1962-
1963 school year from Ministry of Education,
Office of Studies and Programs, Amar-e Farhang-e
Iran [Educational statistics of Iran] (Tehran,
1964), p. 11.

ence of the schools from the government, they too have been relatively
overwhelmed by the burgeoning public sector, although there has been
an absolute increase in their numbers (see table 2.3).

With this dual expansion—in the number of modern primary and
secondary school pupils and in the influence of the government in the

TABLE 2.3

Proportion of Students Enrolled in Modern Schools
by Sponsor, 1935 and 1960

Year	Primary Enrollment		Secondary Enrollment	
	Private	Government	Private	Government
1935-36	36%	64%	51%	49%
1960-61	8	92	16	84

Source: Compiled from the files of the Ministry of
Education.

modern educational process—the government is able to exercise control over access to educational facilities. One basic feature of the educational system, more a pattern of social forces than conscious policy but nonetheless the responsibility of the government, is the exclusion of rural students from secondary schools. At the present time, there are some six secondary schools in towns and villages of less than five thousand persons, in which some 68.6 per cent of the total population resided in 1956.[32] The poorer, rural students are virtually restricted to an education ending at the primary level.

Another factor that serves to weed out pupils in the advance up the educational ladder is a series of nationally administered examinations. For the urban and wealthier rural pupils who aspire to a secondary school education, an "11-plus" type of exam must be surmounted at the end of the sixth grade. A similar exam separates the first from the second cycle of secondary school, another must be passed for graduation from secondary school, and yet another for admission to the university.

In addition, education is not inexpensive. Indirect costs for the family of the pupil consist of the lost income that even the young child can earn from an apprenticeship in the bazaar, rug weaving, or odd jobs. The direct costs are more formidable, however. Even in government schools, education is not free and the tuition must be paid. While tuition fees do not appear high, the eight to twenty dollars per term are beyond the means of most urban families in Iran. In addition, text books are not given away, they are sold; and regulations specify the wearing of school uniforms that are costly to lower class pupils.[33]

The result of these direct and indirect costs, the location of the secondary schools, and the system of examinations is an educational pyramid with sharply angled slopes, i.e., with a high dropout rate restricting enrollment at each level to a progressively smaller number of students (see table 2.4).

But these primarily implicit factors, whose effects are to reduce the number of children receiving educations, are augmented by more explicit means for restricting access to education, especially at higher levels. Statistics on applications and acceptances issued by all Iranian universities illustrate this contention. In 1964, 29,335 individuals received permission to take university entrance exams. This group was made up of 11,825 individuals graduating from secondary school in June of that year

[32] Ministry of Interior, Department of Public Statistics, *National and Province Statistics of the First Census of Iran: November 1956*, 2 vols. (Tehran, 1961), vol. 2, *Social and Economic Characteristics of the Inhabitants for Iran and the Census Provinces*, p. 5.

[33] In 1964, the shah ordered the minister of education to distribute without charge books for the first to the fourth grades of primary school. See "Shah Orders Free Books for Grade Students," *Kayhan International* (Tehran), June 30, 1964.

TABLE 2.4
Number of Students Enrolled by
Grade in Iran, 1962-1963

Primary school					
1	2	3	4	5	6
410,066	361,752	295,557	248,446	213,028	190,504

Secondary school					
7	8	9	10	11	12
81,578	57,789	51,828	35,104	25,721	23,954

Source: Ministry of Education, Office of Studies and Programs,
Amar-e Farhang-e Iran [Educational statistics of Iran]
(Tehran, 1964), p. 11.

Note: The progressively smaller classes can in some measure
be attributed to the annual expansion in the total number
of primary school students, which created a bulge in the
earlier years. It is the author's opinion that this
accounts for only a small fraction of the sharply de-
creasing number of students in each grade.

and 17,150 who had previously graduated and had been denied access
to universities in former years. Of the thousands of aspirants, less than
4,000 were accepted.[34] But this did represent a slightly greater percentage of acceptances than in the previous year when 18,000 took the
exams and 2,050 were accepted.[35] (All ten Iranian universities counted
only 24,459 students at undergraduate and graduate levels in the 1963–
1964 academic year.[36])

An Iranian who has been influential in the formulation and administration of higher education policy indicated that the failure of Iranian
universities to expand and accept more students was not a haphazard
consequence of an inefficient educational bureaucracy. He related that
"orders had come from above" to restrict entrance to Iranian univer-

[34] *Kayhan International* (Tehran), July 31, 1965; Aug. 11, 1965; Sept. 6, 8,
1965. The desire for admission to the universities is so great that applicants tend
to take entrance exams for more than one faculty. Thus the 30,000 would-be students took 54,840 exams.

[35] *Tehran Journal*, July 18, 21, 30, 1964; Aug. 5, 12, 1964; and Sept. 24, 1964.
But the percentage of acceptances has not improved appreciably since. In June of
1970, 64,000 high school graduates were examined in competition for 8,990 places.
Tehran Journal, June 11, 12, 1970.

[36] Ministry of Education, Office of Studies and Programs, *Amar-e Farhang-e
Iran* [Educational Statistics of Iran] (Tehran, 1964), p. 56. In more recent years,
enrollments at universities have increased markedly although a considerable lag in
comparison to secondary schools remains. See this author's "Higher Education and
Social Change in Iran," in *Iran in the 1960's*, ed. J. C. Hurewitz (New York:
Columbia University Press, forthcoming).

sities. He was to make higher education more expensive while raising the minimum entrance examination grade considered necessary for admission. Thus access to higher education would be limited to those students "who had the most at stake" in maintaining the present system.[37] It was clear that children of the elite were those considered committed and, thus, acceptable.

As an alternative to their inability to gain entrance to universities within Iran, many Iranians contemplate study abroad. In 1964, there were 19,500 Iranian students studying in twenty-three foreign countries. In 1968, the figure rose above 25,000. More Iranians were studying at universities outside their country than were enrolled at the universities of Tehran, Tabriz, Meshed, and Ahwaz and the National Teachers' College and the National University.[38] But while this option is available and is obviously used, it remains available primarily to the scions of the upper and upper middle classes who can afford the high costs involved.

The result is that those students who do receive modern educations through university levels or postgraduate studies tend to represent only a narrow segment of the total society. That is, those who receive the higher degrees and can thus lay claim to a key power base, tend to be the children of present-day elites. In other words, the political elite of today are enhancing the likelihood of the succession to power of their children by providing these children with higher educations while excluding the children of the nonelite. This would conform to the observation that among "modernizing traditional elites," the well educated do not rule solely because they are the well educated. On the contrary, they rule because "they are educated members of other ruling groups in the society."[39]

Increasingly, the shah has come to exercise greater control over the distribution of these most important bases for elite status in Iran. At least part of His Majesty's success in maintaining his own power must be attributed to this very control. By judiciously administering the allocation of key values, the shah has been able to fashion an elite whose mem-

---

[37] Personal interview.

[38] "19,499 Iranians Studying Overseas," *Kayhan International* (Tehran), June 28, 1964.

[39] Harry J. Benda, "Political Elites in Colonial Southeast Asia: An Historical Analysis," *Comparative Studies in Society and History*, 7 no. 3 (April 1965): 234. Vide idem, "Non-Western Intelligentsias as Political Elites," in *Political Change in Underdeveloped Countries: Nationalism and Communism*, ed. John H. Kautsky (New York: John Wiley and Sons, 1962), pp. 235–51; Harry J. Benda, "Intellectuals and Politics in Western History," *Bucknell Review*, 10 (1961): 1–41; Edward Shils, "The Intellectuals in the Political Development of the New States," in *Political Change in Underdeveloped Countries*, ed. Kautsky, pp. 195–234; and H. Schelsky, "Technical Change and Educational Consequence," in *Education, Economy, and Society*, ed. A. H. Halsey, Jean Floud and C. Arnold Anderson (New York: Free Press of Glencoe, 1961), pp. 31-36.

ber's remain fundamentally loyal to his throne. Simultaneously, the king strives to co-opt all individuals who have captured or been allowed to capture the power bases. For the recalcitrant, the potential counterelites, the techniques of seduction are employed, the basic relationship between the king and his elites being one of inclusivity. But there are those who refuse to succumb to the blandishments of the court. An elaborate system for coping with such persistent independence has been established, a system that is the subject of the next chapter.

:*3*:

THE SHAHANSHAH OF IRAN

AND THE COUNTERELITE

Where the word of a King is, there is power,
and who may say unto him, What doest thou?
Ecclesiastes 8:4

---

*W*hat of these potential counterelites who persist in their opposition formulations and refuse to repent, be seduced, or be co-opted? Counterelites who continue their political activities are ipso facto considered opposed to the present elite. Inasmuch as the structure of the elite is predicated on the notion of inclusivity, opposition to the elite is equated, by the regime, with opposition to the regime itself. And the regime, to the present, has refused to tolerate persons who, by its own definition, are in opposition to it. The result is that the active unassimilated or unassimilatable are subjected to continued pressure from the regime.

A variety of instrumentalities exist to supervise, control, and, if necessary, repress such real or potential opposition. The State Security and Intelligence Organization (SAVAK) is surprisingly efficient and pervasive. Not only do its agents infiltrate counterelite organizations, but more modern means of electronic surveillance are not unknown.[1] Furthermore, the discipline, power, and mobility of the armed forces and national police have been increased. Control over the mass media has been enhanced so that opportunities for the public expression of counterelite positions are negligible. Finally, the regime has successfully demoralized

---

[1] While SAVAK is "efficient and pervasive," it is fallacious to attribute omniscience to it as do many of the demoralized elite. The presence of the security agents makes counterelite activity much more difficult, but not impossible, as the successful assassination of Prime Minister Mansur in January 1965 demonstrates. Nonetheless, it is true that with their Israeli and American advisers, SAVAK is becoming increasingly more efficient.

many of these groups by broadening its own support among foreign nations. In the past, opposition elements have perceived United States policy as the principal obstacle to their achieving power. Continuing American support for the monarch has affirmed this belief. But, in addition, that country which has supported opposition to the shah in the past now seems to have made a volte-face. The Soviet Union (and East European nations) have made their peace with the monarch and ply him with steel mills, grants-in-aid, and even weapons. The reaction of many in the opposition seems to have been spelled out by an Iranian proverb. "Enemies," the saying goes, "are of three kinds—enemies, friends of enemies, and enemies of friends." The results have been confusion and demoralization among many—seeming to approximate the response of many Europeans and Americans to the Soviet-Nazi pact of 1939.

By relying on its greater political capacity at home and this more widespread support abroad, the regime has continually restricted the limits of acceptable counterelite behavior. Where street demonstrations were common occurrences in the past, a clandestinely printed and distributed pamphlet is now a rarity. What can be legitimately done or said is narrowly circumscribed. As a result, the unassimilated or unassimilatable counterelites have few options—the most likely are demoralization or depoliticization. For the individuals beset by the former of these two options, political activities continue to be pursued, but with a deep sense of pessimism, inefficacy, disarray, and hence, a lack of effectiveness. The depoliticized, on the other hand, have entirely withdrawn from politics to pursue personal interests at the expense of any broader concerns. Counterelites who fail to succumb to these common resolutions of their dilemma, i.e., who indicate that they can act and act with dispatch in a political fashion, are subject to stringent regime measures. Exile (either government- or self-imposed), assignment to foreign posts, removal from office, or ultimately, imprisonment may well be their fate.

DEMORALIZATION OR DEPOLITICIZATION

The most frequent resolution of the counterelite dilemma in Iran is an extreme demoralization resulting in nearly total ineffectiveness as a political actor. As a result of the shah's present policy, individuals who have insisted on pursuing counterelite strategies appear to have lost their confidence and their discipline, and, as a result, a sense of direction. Small groups of the co-depressed will gather in weekly *dowrehs* (circles) to complot once again the gaining of political power. And once again there are the realizations: "The shah is too strong. The shah cannot be pressured or cajoled into following our plans. Perhaps we should meet again next week after more thought. Be so kind as to have more tea. May your shadow never grow less. God be with you."[2]

Perhaps the most effective political activity in which the demoralized but still active counterelite engage is subscribing to newspaper clipping services in Europe.[3] These services scan American and European publications for reports of oppositional activities and forward them to subscribers in Iran, while the subscribers survive by the vicarious satisfaction and stoked hopes from reports of antiregime activities (usually "pseudo events") that exist in the mass media of the West.[4] They pursue little tangible activity of their own and bide time.

Exclusion from the political process may result in depoliticization. This phenomenon resembles demoralization but shows added symptoms of political withdrawal. The demoralized counterelite lack the psychological or organizational means to be effective but continue to participate in politics. The depoliticized segments of the counterelite also lack the means to be effective but recognize their deficiencies and respond by turning their backs on the political process. Many intellectuals, for example, "have returned to the sullen quiescence which is their tradition whenever a hostile regime is in power. They participate in the economic life of the state, but without enthusiasm."[5] Others have withdrawn from fear of the consequences of sedulous counterelite activities.

With the small, private sector and the pervasive presence of the government, locating a sanctuary for withdrawal from the political process

[2] After having had the privilege of sitting through a particularly agonized session of this kind, I asked why they didn't gather arms, destroy the government, and take power? After considerable thought, these members of the counterelite agreed that such a move would only result in the imposition of a military dictatorship with a fascist general at its head. "Better to keep what we have," they agreed.

[3] There are adequate precedents for similar practices. Naser ed-Din Shah Qajar (1848–1896) subscribed to two such clipping agencies following his trips to Europe. He insisted that each agency compile all articles in any European publication which related to Iran. Each agency sent its clippings to a different court official. Thus Naser ed-Din attempted to prevent either official from merely removing clippings unflattering to the sovereign and so enhancing the king's perception of his own worth in the eyes of the farangis. See Naser ed-Din Shah Qajar, *A Diary Kept by His Majesty, the Shah of Persia, During his Journey to Europe in 1878*, trans. A. H. Schindler and Baron L. de Norman (London: Richard Bentley and Son, 1879); and also Naser ed-Din Shah Qajar, *The Diary of His Majesty, the Shah of Persia, During His Tour Through Europe in AD 1873*, trans. T. W. Redhouse (London: John Murray and Sons, 1874).

[4] In this sense, the seemingly futile antishah and antiregime demonstrations of Iranian students in the United States and Europe are efficacious. While the shah, as the target of these demonstrations on his trips abroad, is nonplused by them, publicity generated by them feeds the demoralized and crippled opposition within Iran.

[5] Richard W. Cottam, *Nationalism in Iran* (Pittsburgh: University of Pittsburgh Press, 1964), p. 42.

can be a difficult task. Here again, the regime's preference for inclusivity is salutary, for as a counterelite becomes depoliticized to the point where he can function in a political setting without expressing his intense alienation from the elite, he will be allowed a position within the bureaucracy. At present, the University of Tehran serves as such a haven for depoliticized Iranians. A number of professors and directors of research institutes at the university were ardent supporters of Mossadegh and, in fact, served as ministers under his premiership. One well-known professor served not only as Mossadegh's home minister but also as his supporter to the very end. Together with six others of the faithful, he spirited the beleaguered Mossadegh over the back wall of the prime minister's home, then under siege by promonarchy army troops. Despite these acts, once viewed as high treason, he and others of similar stamp retain their posts—partly because some are outstanding scholars; partly, no doubt, because of the need for trained faculty members; but basically from a desire to undercut the formation of counterelites by holding out the possibilities or realities of co-optation.

One result of this policy for the regime, however, is that the fidelity of the university's faculty must be suspect. This appears to be a principal explanation for the refusal of the regime to expand the University of Tehran. Despite the regime's control over the social backgrounds of the entering students, it is harder for the regime to control the instruction that those elite children receive. Thus, the response of the shah has been to expand the university system, where necessary, by building completely new institutions outside the capital city with a younger and previously uninvolved faculty.[6] (Presumably, the recent Ph.D.s from America and Doctorates from France have matured in the more pacific, post-Mossadegh period.)

Others of the depoliticized withdraw from politics to journalism. But here they also threaten the regime's efforts to control the mass media. A particularly talented and prolific journalist withdrew from the making of political news to the reporting of foreign events. Even this proved too upsetting to the regime, which forbade his further writing; he now publishes books.

The regime's concept of an ideal sanctuary for the depoliticized, then, is a position where some contribution to Iranian development can be made, that provides no opportunity for communication with sizable numbers of politically active or influential persons or to the urban

[6] The major new university is the Pahlavi University of Shiraz. Modeled after an American institution, it has a number of cooperative arrangements with the University of Pennsylvania. The second new higher education facility is still in the inceptive phase. Originally scheduled for construction in Tehran, the Arya Mehr Technical University is being built in Isfahan.

masses, but that is not totally isolated from the scrutiny of the elite. Various ministerial departments and university research posts have been found to fill these desiderata. Whatever the occupations of the demoralized or depoliticized, it appears that these potential counterelites are rarely successful in completely eliminating their political alienation. With the loosening of political control in Tehran, counterelite activity could reassert itself. But the years following the overthrow of Mossadegh witnessed a steady growth in the power of the regime and the control it exercised over national political expression. Political parties were banned and replaced by the *Melliyun* (Nationalists) and *Mardom* (Peoples) parties, which were created by the shah and led by two of his most trusted elite. Press laws were decreed and censorship instituted. The Senate was convened (which gave His Majesty more control over the legislature). The State Security and Intelligence Organization (SAVAK) was established with American aid. And the Imperial Iranian Armed Forces were vastly strengthened.

With this newly created capability, the government moved to eliminate the support and popularity once enjoyed by its most serious opponent, Dr. Mohammad Mossadegh. Yet, 1960 and 1961 were years of growing political turmoil, culminating in the overthrow of a cabinet, the appointment as premier of Dr. Ali Amini (although he was personally mistrusted by the shah), and the holding on May 16, 1961, of a public congress of the formerly outlawed National Front. This entire period was not the result of an anomic outburst reflecting the desperation and fervor of the urban poor and Moslem clergy, as was the making of the June 1963 riots. (The response to the latter was uncomplicated—mobilize the army and put down the rioters by force.) The 1960–1961 turmoil was far more perturbing to His Imperial Majesty, for it represented the resurgence of the supposedly demoralized and depoliticized. At present these demoralized and depoliticized groups are again dormant in Iran. How long this stagnation of political activity will remain is uncertain. What is certain, in the context of Iranian politics, is its artificiality.

Some say that the emotions blocked from expression by the quiescence and widespread depoliticization have been displaced elsewhere in Iranian life. The nearly perpetual grumblings and other verbalizations of discontent are one outlet for these tensions. And as long as they remain at the verbal level and out of the mass media, they are tolerated by the regime. The shah has publicly acknowledged this toleration. He has said, "I believe in balancing toughness towards subversive organizations with leniency as to expressions of individual viewpoints."[7]

[7] Mohammad Reza Shah Pahlavi, *Mission for My Country* (New York: McGraw-Hill, 1961), p. 129. Lucian Pye has observed in personal communication to the author (Nov. 2, 1967) that the types of verbal hostility to the regime so prev-

One Iranian social scientist has even accounted for the appallingly dangerous Tehran traffic in this manner. Aggressive driving, he argues, provides a release to emotions thwarted from political expression. Automobile and traffic infractions provide a politically discreet means of acting out counterelite sentiments.[8] And, finally, the automobile represents a tremendous democraticizing force, removing the power and status considerations otherwise operative in the social structure. Once behind the wheel, more Iranians are more nearly equal.[9]

GOVERNMENT-IMPOSED EXILE

Elites who refuse co-optation and fail to succumb to demoralization or depoliticization are subjected to yet another regime response, exile, a response that results in their exclusion from the political process. While this method of isolating one's opponents has a long history, its full development is a product of the twentieth century.[10] At present, it has a number of variants, the most notorious form being the banishment of individuals whom the regime deems politically undesirable. In 1964, for example, Ayatollah Khomeini was swooped upon by the Iranian police, put aboard a plane at a military airport, and taken to Turkey, where, with the cooperation of Turkish authorities, he was kept under house arrest.

Khomeini's fame and popularity is such that SAVAK took the unusual step of issuing the following public statement: "Since according to reliable information and sufficient evidence, Mr. Khomeini's attitude and provocations have been considered contrary to the interests of the people and to the security, independence, and territorial integrity of the State, he has been exiled from Iran effective November 4, 1964."[11]

Ayatollah Ruhollah al-Musavi al-Khomeini. Khomeini, an influential Shi'a *mullah* of the theological center of Qum, first came to public atten-

---

alent in Iran, if heard in Indonesia in the days of Sukarno, would have resulted in jail terms for the disgruntled complainers.

[8] Personal interview, Feb. 8, 1965.

[9] After a trip to Persia, John Fischer, the editor of *Harper's*, related how his Iranian driver accounted for that nation's hair-raising traffic: "Iranians . . . do not believe in traffic rules, which were not mentioned in the Koran and anyhow were an outrageous restriction on individual liberty" ("The Land of the Charming Anarchists: A Report from Iran, Part I," *Harper's*, March 1965, p. 24).

[10] Reza Gholi Mirza was a royal prince who passed a good part of the nineteenth century in exile. He wrote a memoir of European and Iranian life at the time, soon to be published by the University of Tehran Press. See Hafez Farman Farmayan, "The Forces of Modernization in Nineteenth Century Iran," in *Beginnings of Modernization in the Middle East*, ed. William R. Polk and Richard L. Chambers (Chicago: University of Chicago Press, 1968), p. 135.

[11] *Kayhan International* (Tehran), Nov. 5, 1964.

tion in 1961 following the death of Ayatollah Borujerdi. Khomeini was one of several principal contenders to succeed the venerated leader of the Shi'ites, and he began to issue public statements in opposition to governmental decisions. He branded the plan to enfranchise women as violating their station in Islam and was arrested in 1962 for fiery speeches against the Local Council Election Bill. In January 1963 (before the national referendum that was to pass on the shah's Six-Point White Revolution) he was arrested for allegedly issuing pamphlets asserting that land reform was contrary to Islam, which guaranteed the sanctity of private property. In March of the same year, theological students at Qum held public demonstrations that resulted in the arrest of their leaders and the occupation of mosques, shrines, and theological schools by members of the security police.[12]

The religious holidays of Moharram were a time of increased passions as the devout anguished over the martyrdom of Hossein and Hassan, the sons and, according to the Shi'ites, the rightful successors of Ali to the caliphate. Khomeini's picture covered the bazaars of Iran as a symbol of the type of opposition to illegitimate authority offered by Hossein and Hassan. The authorities waited until the early morning hours of June 4, after the end of the holy days, and arrested Khomeini at Qum. Within two hours, crowds of protesters began to form before the bazaars of Tehran and by 10:00 a.m. the troops had opened fire. The rioting spread to Meshed, Qum, Isfahan, and Shiraz but was finally put down with a heavy loss of life over the course of three days.

Khomeini was detained until August 3, when he was released to house arrest. SAVAK again issued a public statement: ". . . understanding has been reached between security authorities on the one side and Their Eminences Khomeini, Qumi and Mahallati on the other according to which the gentlemen will cease to interfere in political matters; and since this understanding has given full assurance that the gentlemen will not act contrary to the interests and law and order of the State, they have now been transferred to private houses."[13] Whatever the nature of the

[12] Following these events, Ayatollah Milani, a leading theologian from Meshed, sent a widely circulated letter to Ayatollah Khomeini protesting the government's actions in the following terms: "You are aware, and certainly know better than myself, that at the present, religious and national interests are threatened and violated by the corrupt Ruling Body and *agents of the offices which cannot be held responsible*. It would be strange for a Moslem to allow himself to remain silent under such circumstances and fail to defend Islam." A showdown between the ulema and the government was imminent. The confrontation occurred in the June riots and resulted in thousands of deaths. (Text of letter in possession of author, also translated by Echo of Iran, "Religious Demonstrations and Clashes," *For Your Information*, no. 386 [June 8, 1963], p. 4.)

[13] Echo of Iran, "The Case of Mr. Khomeini," *For Your Information*, no. 457 (Nov. 18, 1964), p. 3.

"understanding" reached, few of the faithful were convinced that the three Ayatollahs would refrain from involvement in politics. SAVAK's attempt to eliminate their popularity by associating the three ulema with the government was a failure. And so was SAVAK's attempts to isolate Khomeini from future political participation.

On the eve of the elections for a new Parliament in October 1963 (to replace the session that was dissolved by His Imperial Majesty in May 1961), Khomeini was again taken from his home. Having charged government interference in the elections, he ordered his followers to boycott the vote. This time, Khomeini was held until May 1964, when SAVAK announced that yet another "understanding" had been reached. Upon his release, Khomeini denounced the understanding, claiming that as a good Shi'ite, he was entitled to the use of *taqiyah* (dissimulation) to conceal his true feelings, inasmuch as the agreement was extracted under "duress." Nonetheless, His Eminence remained silent for some five months.[14]

In October 1964, the Majles passed, in a matter of hours after its first submission by the government, a bill to grant diplomatic immunity to American military personnel. In the ensuing days, the Majles passed another government bill, to accept a loan of $200 million from the United States for the purchase of military equipment. The connection was too blatant and too reminiscent of the capitulations that had limited Iran's national sovereignty until their abolition in 1928. The Ayatollah responded with vitriolic censure.

. . . the Majles approved . . . this most disgraceful decree . . . thus placing the Iranian people under American bondage.
. . . Why? Because America is the land of the Dollar and because the Iranian Government needs dollars. . . .
. . . Today, when colonial territories are bravely freeing the bonds that have chained them, the so-called progressive Majles . . . votes for the most shameful and offending decrees of ill-reputed governments.[15]

The circulation of this speech in pamphlet form was a threatening indignity to the government, and its response was Khomeini's exile. Of interest to us is (a) the total unwillingness of the regime to allow Khomeini to serve as a critic of the government's policies and thus a focus for counterelite sentiment; (b) the dogged persistence of Khomeini in pursuing a course that he must have realized was intolerable to the regime and likely to lead to retribution; (c) the enduring forbearance of

[14] Some organs of the press claimed that Khomeini was not totally silent. Rumor had it that the Ayatollah was making tape-recorded sermons from the sanctuary of his home and dispatching copies to important religious centers.
[15] From a clandestinely printed and circulated pamphlet stating the Ayatollah's position, in the author's possession.

the government over a period of some three and a half years, in hopes, undoubtedly, of co-opting the Ayatollah; (d) the relatively nonviolent and mild punishment—exile—that was administered when regime efforts to seduce and co-opt had failed; and (e) that through the entire period of detention, imprisonment, and, ultimately, exile, Ayatollah Khomeini was never officially charged with any wrongdoing and never brought to trial.

SELF-IMPOSED EXILE

In addition to government-imposed exile, which might be described as manifest, punitive banishment, there are other forms that the practice assumes in Iran. A common means of excluding counterelites from the political process is what might be considered a self-imposed exile. The process consists, basically, of the individual's leaving the country before the eruption of an open conflict with the regime.

General Teimur Bakhtiar. A well-known example of self-imposed exile is the case of General Teimur Bakhtiar. Bakhtiar was the son of a leading khan of the Bakhtiari tribes who served as governor of the Bakhtiari regions as well as several terms in the Majles. Educated at French schools and St. Cyr, Bakhtiar entered the Iranian army and rose through the ranks. With the marriage in 1951 of Soraya, also a Bakhtiari, to His Imperial Majesty, the outlook for the young officer improved. After the overthrow of Mossadegh (in which he played no role), he was promoted to general and, in short order, to military governor of Tehran and director of army intelligence.

In 1957, when the State Security and Intelligence Organization was established with American aid, Bakhtiar was the logical choice as its director. From 1957 to 1961, he strengthened the organization and his own position within the Iranian elite. But he was unable to prevent the political disquiet that began in the summer of 1960, resulting in the cancellation of the Majles election in September. That autumn was a period of increasing turmoil with demands for new elections, free of the control of the secret police.

The second round of elections for the twentieth session of the Majles began in January 1961, but were as poorly managed as the previous ones. By the time of the shahanshah's inauguration of the Majles on February 20, the National Front, Dr. Ali Amini (Iranian ambassador to Washington and former minister of finance for Mossadegh), Dr. Mozaffar Bagha'i (an ex-Tudeh and head of the *Zahmat-keshan* or Toiler's party), and other groups had boycotted the elections. Students closed the University of Tehran with widespread demonstrations, and the

National Front sponsored an ominously successful general strike in Tehran.

His Majesty responded to the mounting political chaos and the growing power of the counterelites (and many Iranians claim to the inauguration of President John F. Kennedy in January) in characteristic fashion. He made overtures to the dissident counterelites by taking a number of apparently liberalizing steps, without, however, allowing any fundamental diminution in his own power.

As in the turmoil following his accession in 1941 and the threat from Mossadegh in 1951, the shah responded to counterelite pressures in 1961 by manipulating his opulence. In 1941, the shah had offered the crown lands to the state. In 1951, he had offered to distribute the crown lands to the peasants. In 1961, he renewed the distribution of these lands and placed the Pahlavi Foundation on a solid financial footing. He gave up to the foundation assets that he personally owned and that were valued at $135 million.[16] Oil tankers, hotels, a toll bridge, banks, factories, and even orphanages were included in the capital of the foundation.[17]

In the royal decree that transferred the assets to a perpetual endowment, His Majesty specified the purposes it would serve:

In view of our constant endeavour and firm belief in seeking Almighty God's blessing, the welfare of our nation, for the peace of the soul of our great father, His Late Majesty Reza Shah the Great, for the glory and happiness of the noble Iranian people and country, it has been our constant effort since our accession to the throne to raise the level of knowledge, to improve health and sanitation, to develop agriculture, and to give help to the needy and contribute to other charitable works.[18]

The *shah-parastis* (promonarchists) and the foreign press viewed the gesture as one of magnanimous devotion to the welfare of his people.[19] The more cynical and the dissident counterelites wondered how His Majesty had accumulated such sums to begin with. They charged that,

[16] *Kayhan* (Tehran), Sept. 28, 1961. The valuation must be considered highly approximate, given the political considerations and the lack of recent appraisal by trained auditors or accountants.

[17] The shah publicly claimed that these assets represented "90 per cent of the whole of my private fortune" ("Address of His Imperial Majesty, The Shahanshah of Iran" [Speech delivered at the National Press Club of the United States, Washington, D.C., April 13, 1962], p. 2). There is no one with whom the author has discussed His Majesty's wealth who accepts a figure remotely approaching 90 per cent.

[18] "Royal Decree of the Pahlavi Foundation Endowment," *Kayhan* (Tehran), Sept. 28, 1961.

[19] The shah was hailed by foreign observers, the *New York Times* reporting that the foundation was His Imperial Majesty's "plan to give away a $132,720,000 fortune to the Iranian people" (Oct. 8, 1961, p. 20).

48

in any case, the assets turned over to the foundation were only a tiny fraction—in the neighborhood of 10 per cent—of the shah's personal fortune, and that by the shah making himself guardian of the endowment, there was little likelihood that the funds would be used for their stated purposes.[20]

In addition to subjecting the entire nation to the same type of material seduction with which individual elites or potential counterelites were co-opted, His Majesty responded to the political pressures in other ways. General Abdollah Hedayat, chief of the supreme commander's staff and number two man in the armed forces after the shah; General Alavi Kia, chief of army intelligence; a number of lesser military personnel; and General Bakhtiar were simultaneously removed from their posts.

The dismissal of General Bakhtiar was particularly satisfying to all parties in the turmoil, save the general. Apparently, the shahanshah was furious with the performance of SAVAK's chief for his inability to hold pacific elections and, basically, to fulfill his principal responsibility, the maintenance of "state security." The counterelites held Bakhtiar chiefly responsible for the increasing terrorism and violence in Iranian political life. And, finally, His Imperial Majesty is likely to have assumed that Bakhtiar's dismissal would please the incoming, liberal, American president. Whatever the ultimate reasons, the dismissal of the generals quieted public unrest, at least temporarily.

Nearly two months later, however, on May 2, 1961, Tehran teachers struck for higher salaries and demonstrated in front of the Majles. On the next day, demonstrations continued and clashes broke out between the teachers and security forces. Almost immediately, one of the striking teachers was killed. His death galvanized the waverers, and schools throughout Tehran were shut down as the body of the newly created martyr was paraded through the streets. His Majesty again responded. Prime Minister Sharif Emami, an engineer with service in the Iranian railways and Plan Organization, was dismissed and Dr. Amini, popular with the demonstrators (and with American officials), was asked to form a government.

General agreement exists that the appointment of Amini could have come about only as a result of the shah's perception of intense disquietude. Amini was, and remains, deeply mistrusted by the monarch. He is known to favor limitations on the power of the throne. He had served under Mossadegh, and although no member of the National

---

[20] It is difficult to assay the effects of the Pahlavi Foundation. It is unquestionably true that the foundation plays a crucial role in all areas of Iranian public life. After the government itself, it is the most powerful economic force in the country. It seems certain, however, that a great deal of its resources are spent in maintaining and enhancing that economic power. Resources devoted purely to charity rather than commercial undertakings appear relatively slight.

Front, was not viewed as hostile to it.[21] He was reputed to be devoted to general civil liberties, and he was a man known for profound personal integrity as well as great forcefulness. (A story widely circulated at the time of Amini's cabinet concerned Reza Shah. Looking back over the entire one hundred and thirty years of Qajar rule, Reza Shah is reputed to have claimed that the only "man" in the entire Qajar family—the only Qajar with the manly virtues of integrity, energy, and vigor—was Fakhr ol-Dowleh, the daughter of Mozaffar ed-Din Shah and Amini's mother.)

If the shah had misgivings and the National Front expectations, both were proven wrong by subsequent events. Amini was unable to shake the power of the shah or to alter the priorities that the shah had for national political and economic life. The National Front, initially buoyed by the printing of Mossadegh's picture in Tehran's newspapers, for the first time in seven years, was soon disenchanted.[22] A mass meeting scheduled for July 21 was closed down by army troops and the leaders were arrested.

By the end of 1961, Amini had antagonized all major sectors of the elite. The landed aristocracy and members of the Majles and Senate, led by Sardar Fakher Hekmat, six times speaker of the lower house, and Mohsen Sadr (Sadr ol-Ashraf), president of the Senate, expressed intense hostility to the closing of the Parliament, the failure to hold new elections, and the Land Reform Program being vigorously pursued by Amini's minister of agriculture. The clergy and religiously oriented politicians and *bazaaris* (merchants and traders) had as their spokesman Seyyed Jaafar Behbehani, the son of an Ayatollah and grandson of the widely revered Seyyed Abdollah Behbehani, one of the two leading "liberal" clerics in the struggle to wrest a constitution from the Qajars. They also protested the land reform and lack of elections. In addition, they were concerned with an alleged burgeoning of Baha'i influence within the upper reaches of the government and deviation from the principles of Islam. The National Front and other opposition groupings expressed their animosity through Allahyar Saleh. Minister in numerous cabinets, ambassador to Washington, and an ardent supporter of Mossadegh, Saleh's ardent nationalism bridled at the alleged growth of American influence in Iran and the severe curtailment of civil liberties that prevented opposition politicians from functioning. Finally, a strong

---

[21] After serving briefly as Mossadegh's minister of finance, he was dismissed by Mossadegh in 1952. After the latter's overthrow in 1953, he regained the Finance portfolio under General Zahedi. Later he concluded the agreement with the International Oil Consortium, which "denationalized" Iran's petroleum, at least in the eyes of the National Front. Thereafter, most members of the Front considered him at best suspect. Nonetheless, his known devotion to civil liberties induced the Front to greet his premiership with considerable hope.

[22] See *Kayhan* (Tehran) or *Ettela'at* (Tehran) of May 20, 1961.

military clique made up of the deposed generals was led by Teimur Bakhtiar. The generals were incensed by their dismissals and the allegations of corruption and incompetence with which their dismissals were explained.

Not surprisingly, although the shah continued to offer support publicly, time was running out for Amini. In the summer of 1962, he was faced with a budget crisis. The shah's refusal to reduce military expenditures and the unwillingness of the United States to bridge the deficit proved insoluble. Amini tendered his resignation. In a move totally unexpected by Iranian politicians and, apparently, by the prime minister himself, the shah accepted the resignation. Assadollah Alam was asked to form a new government.

Meanwhile, however, General Bakhtiar was reputed to have been politically active in the capital. Rumors circulated that the teachers' demonstrations had emanated from the intrigues of Bakhtiar, hoping to seize power. When he failed in this, he carried on increasingly intensive clandestine activities against the prime minister. Manifestations of the underlying tensions soon became obvious. At a press conference, Prime Minister Amini presented his and the regime's official disapproval of the recent Indian occupation of Goa. Some days later, Bakhtiar convened his own press conference to congratulate Prime Minister Nehru on India's assertion of her national sovereignty.[23]

Amini responded by pressing the shah for cuts in the military budget and drastic reductions in the size of the armed forces and officer corps. Rumor had it that three hundred senior officers were placed on permanent retirement. Bakhtiar's response was to step up his antigovernment activity. It is even reported that Bakhtiar planned to engineer a *coup d'état* against the shah himself. In early January 1962, Bakhtiar was reported in contact with the National Front. He was subsequently implicated in clashes between university students and the army that led to the closing of the University of Tehran.

Whatever the bases for these outpourings from Tehran's rumor networks, His Imperial Majesty took them to heart. On January 26, 1962, the shah confronted Bakhtiar in a face-to-face showdown, whereupon the general left immediately for Europe.[24] Bakhtiar established his residence in Europe, presumably enjoying the resources placed there for this very eventuality when he was director of SAVAK. He maintained indirect contact with segments of the Iranian polity but never returned to Iran, at least openly. During the 1963 riots, he was observed flying from

---

[23] For reports of the prime minister's press conference and the official position, see *Kayhan* (Tehran), Dec. 20, 1961. For Bakhtiar's conference, see *Peighame Emruz* (Tehran), Dec. 27, 1961.

[24] *Manchester Guardian*, Feb. 1, 1962.

Switzerland to Baghdad—undoubtedly to be closer to the seat of power should his opportunity arise.

On August 15, 1967, the Office of Military Prosecution announced that General Bakhtiar had been under investigation for "amassing a vast fortune illegally" while head of SAVAK. In addition, he was charged with "engaging in illegal activities . . . to further his own personal ends." In the nature of Iranian justice, "orders have been issued to confiscate all his properties while the relative case is passing through judicial channels and charges are being investigated against him in court."[25] In June 1969, Bakhtiar's properties were confiscated and in September of that year, he was tried in absentia by a military court and sentenced to death for treason. In August of 1970, Tehran newspapers reported that the General was accidentally killed by a member of his hunting party while searching for game in the mountains of Iraq, only 20 miles from the Iranian border! In December of that year, SAVAK announced that it had uncovered a massive plot, originally masterminded by Bakhtiar, to overthrow the regime. Hundreds of arrests followed. Bakhtiar is dead, but he clearly remains a force in the politics of Iran.

While General Bakhtiar is a particular instance of self-imposed exile, there are entire classes of persons who receive the encouragement of the regime for the self-same resolution of their counterelite postures. Tribal khans and politicians espousing what the regime considers to be radical ideologies, who decide to live abroad, are not discouraged in their resolve. This same phenomenon is responsible for a large proportion of the Iranian students remaining abroad. It has been estimated by an Iranian government official that approximately 50 per cent of the privately supported students from middle-class families, 60 per cent of government and foundation supported students and an equal percentage of privately supported upper-class students, and 90 per cent of students who have failed academically do not return to Iran from Europe and the United States.[26] It is unquestionably true that higher wages, better living conditions, and the pleadings of foreign spouses all coalesce to keep the student away from his country. But the widespread political disaffection

[25] Echo of Iran, *Daily Bulletin*, 15, no. 180 (Aug. 16, 1967): 1. In 1969 Bakhtiar was arrested in Beirut and sentenced to jail for arms-smuggling. The failure of the Lebanese government to extradite him to Iran on the completion of his jail sentence led Iran to break diplomatic relations.

[26] Dr. Habib Naficy (supervisor of Iranian students in the United States), "The Brain-Drain: The Case of Iranian Non-Returnees" (Paper presented at the annual conference of the Society for International Development, Washington, D.C., March 17, 1966), pp. 6-8. Senator Walter F. Mondale has placed Iran in the ranks of those countries with the highest rate of non-returning students ("The Brain Drain from Developing Countries," *Congressional Record*, 89th Cong., 2nd sess., vol. 112, no. 146, Aug. 31, 1966, pp. 21477–80).

of the students in Europe and America, heightened by National Front agitation, is an important factor. It becomes highly relevant when the government openly discourages the more active and vocal of Iran's critics from returning. Inability to find any but the most menial of jobs in Tehran (except for student leaders who are frequently offered high posts) discourages many of those activists who fail to heed the government's advice.

ASSIGNMENT TO FOREIGN POSTS

If government-imposed exile or self-imposed residence abroad exclude many of the unassimilated or unassimilatable potential counterelites, a third variant for excluding these elites most resembles the American corporate practice of "demotion to chairman of the board." In Iran the variant takes the form of assigning the persona non grata to a diplomatic post abroad. In this fashion, the banished person is not only removed from the local political scene, but he is also offered a glamorous substitute, and he continues to receive material and status rewards from the political system that has effectively eliminated him. He continues to be in the service of the shah and his behavior may legitimately be scrutinized. Finally, while he is segregated from his power base or political following, those followers will likely be mollified by dint of his new and prestigious post.

The practice has a lengthy history in Iran but recently has been developed as a more frequently employed device. This is partly a reflection of the growing power of His Imperial Majesty but is equally dependent on the greater availability of foreign posts. The post-World War II expansion of international relations and of Iran's role in the international political system has opened myriad positions for such exiles. More than fifty Iranian embassies, the United Nations and its multitude of regional offices and special programs, the Central Treaty Organization, and a number of Iran's other international obligations all boast sizable delegations of Iranians. And His Imperial Majesty has been quick to use the new opportunities.

Dr. Hassan Arsanjani. One of the most notorious and informative of recent cases concerns Dr. Hassan Arsanjani. Dr. Arsanjani was appointed by the shahanshah as ambassador to the government of Italy in June 1963, and he served in Rome until late 1964 when he was replaced. Returning to Tehran, Dr. Arsanjani busied himself with the private practice of law. But it is not for his ambassadorship or law practice that he is remembered. Dr. Arsanjani was the "ambitious and ebullient"[27] minis-

---

[27] *Economist,* May 12, 1962, p. 557.

ter of agriculture who launched Iran's land reform during the premier-ship of Dr. Amini, continued it through the early term of Amini's succes-sor, organized a Farmer's Congress in Tehran, and then found his un-willingly submitted resignation accepted. Herein lies a lesson in Iranian politics.

Hassan Arsanjani burst rather suddenly on the Iranian political scene. In 1945, at the age of twenty-three, he founded the *Azadi* (Liberty) group and began the publication of the daily *Darya* (Sea), in which he propounded notions resembling his later land reforms. In the same year, his political group merged with the Tudeh, but Arsanjani, personally, re-fused their overtures. He was then elected to the next Majles (in 1946) but the Credentials Committee denied him membership. He was later to recall: "Before I could take my seat . . . the landlords and their stooges who were then all in the Majles sent me threats that I should either with-draw my words and theories and take my seat in the Parliament or be thrown out so that I couldn't carry on in the manner which they consid-ered most outrageous and lacking in decorum and precedent."[28] Char-acteristically, Arsanjani refused to recant and went into relative obscur-ity. While he worked for the Agricultural Bank and eventually rose to head its Rural Cooperatives branch, he pursued political activities by supporting the careers of Qavam and Razamara. The latter was made prime minister in 1951, but was assassinated before Arsanjani could secure a place of power. Qavam was appointed prime minister after the first dismissal of Mossadegh in 1952 and Arsanjani accepted the post of deputy prime minister. But Qavam fell in three days and Arsanjani was once more forcibly retired from politics.

In 1958, Arsanjani attached himself to Ali Amini. He formed an organization whose express purpose was to advance Amini to the pre-miership. This plan too collapsed, for Amini was implicated, by the re-gime, with a plot to overthrow the government. General Gharani, then head of army intelligence and the alleged ring leader, was imprisoned. Amini was dismissed from his post as ambassador to Washington. And Arsanjani was detained.

Finally, in May 1961, when Amini reached his goal as prime minis-ter, he invited Arsanjani to take the Agriculture portfolio. Although it is reported that the shah was reluctant to accept Arsanjani, who by then had a reputation for extremism and decidedly unpopular causes, Amini's urgings apparently carried His Majesty's misgivings and Arsanjani joined the cabinet. Within two weeks, he had organized and convoked a Land Reform Seminar to formulate plans for the implementation of steps that he had contemplated since 1945. At the seminar, he made his position perfectly clear: "One can no longer continue with this system from the

[28] *Tehran Journal,* June 8, 1963.

Middle Ages. . . . In these land reforms we are facing the reactionary front which has wasted fifty years of the Parliamentary regime and have now confronted us with the choice of a "red" or "white" revolution. If the country remains in its present state, it will explode."[29]

He spent the remainder of 1961 drafting legislation and experimenting with land reform and peasant cooperatives. In order to maintain the momentum that his appointment had engendered, however, Arsanjani prevailed upon the shah to renew the distribution of crown lands. The crown lands or royal domain were primarily acquired by Reza Shah and encompassed some of the most fertile land in Iran. These villages were located in a number of provinces but were primarily concentrated in the luxuriant *jangal* (jungle) bordering the Caspian Sea. By the time of Reza Shah's abdication, more than two thousand villages passed to the control of the new monarch. Using a measure of 4.8 persons per household,[30] some 235,800 persons were in the direct service of His Imperial Majesty qua landlord (see table 3.1).

TABLE 3.1

Number of Villages and Families
Constituting the Crown Lands

Province	Villages	Families
Fars	19	1,200
Kerman	191	4,250
West Azarbaijan	315	6,365
Tehran	428	4,424
Gilan and Mazandaran	1,214	32,878
Total	2,167	49,117

Source: Echo of Iran, "Distribution of Lands in Iran and Those Opposed to It," Echo Reports, no. 25-26 (Aug. 10, 1959), p. 4.

Note: These statistics do not include the agricultural holdings of His Majesty, which were not included as crown lands, nor the vast holdings of the princes and princesses of the royal blood who acquired estates, not only from Reza Shah, but also through their own acumen.

[29] *Kayhan* (Tehran), May 24, 1961.

[30] Ministry of Interior, Department of Public Statistics, *National and Province Statistics of the First Census of Iran: November 1956*, 2 vols. (Tehran, 1961), vol. 2, *Social and Economic Characteristics of the Inhabitants for Iran and the Census Provinces*, p. 398.

After the abdication of Reza Shah in 1941, a general outcry was heard in the capital over the devious and often ruthless means that the deposed tyrant had used to acquire the property that caught his eye. The peasants of Mazandaran even rose in revolt against the royal estates, beating officials and burning houses built on orders of Reza Shah. In response, the new king announced that the crown lands would be turned over to the government for return to their original owners. Apparently, a few of the estates that had been most blatantly confiscated were restored to the injured parties. But gradually, the center of power shifted back to the monarch. In 1949, after an attempt was made on his life, the shah outlawed the Tudeh party and withal silenced his principal critics. And, less than one month later, the Majles passed a law returning the royal estates to the shahanshah. When confronted with a threat to his throne in the form of Prime Minister Mossadegh, however, the shah remembered those lands.

In 1951, His Majesty announced a scheme to distribute the royal estates. Farmers working land in his villages were to receive deeds for the fields they were already tilling. Considerably reduced annual remittances would still be made, but in lieu of rents, they would be considered as mortgage payments. After twenty-five years, the new landlords would receive a fee simple title deed and would be outright owners of the land. In order to supervise the collection of the annual payments, the shah established a Development and Rural Cooperatives Bank, and directed that its assets be invested in development projects, especially those relating to agriculture.

In February 1951, the shah distributed the first of his villages at Davood Abad, Varamin, not far from Tehran. Almost immediately the plan was attacked by Prime Minister Mossadegh and his supporters. They charged that the shah was attempting to make political capital at their expense. Moreover, they claimed that by selling lands originally acquired without payment, His Majesty would obtain prodigious funds to be used for his personal welfare rather than for development spending, as the king had claimed.[31] The shah eventually acceded to pressure from Mossadegh and placed the royal domains under the supervision of the government.

[31] The Development and Rural Cooperatives Bank explained that resistance to the shah's land reform proposals was based on two points: "One, the feeling that His Majesty had taken the step under inspirations from the Americans began to be spread secretly to inspire the simple people with the illusion that the distribution of lands was inspired by the foreigners. The other argument put forward to these simple people was that this was an action against the big landlords. . . . It should not be left unsaid that the instigations initiated by the subversive elements and those averse to the progress and prosperity of the Iranian nation were not without effect on this issue" (translated from a statement shown the author by the director of the bank).

With the overthrow of Mossadegh, the lands once again reverted to monarchic control. And once again, the shah announced his intention of distributing them. By the end of 1957, however, only 107 villages had been transferred to the peasant cultivators. The next year, His Majesty announced still another plan for dealing with his villages. "His Majesty decided to establish a Pahlavi Foundation to employ for charitable purposes the profits of such Pahlavi Estates as could not be distributed or divided."[32] And so the Crown Lands Distribution Program rested until the political turmoil of 1961, when Arsanjani enlisted the firm support of His Majesty. The removal of the lands from the foundation, and their distribution (as well as the deeding of major new assets to the Pahlavi Foundation) followed. Anew, the royal personage began leaving Tehran to distribute title deeds to his own peasants.

This scheme was actually the second attempt to effect land reform in the country. Originally, Reza Shah had begun a land distribution scheme in the early 1930s, with a view to enforced habitation of the migrant tribes on public domain lands. They were to be deeded parcels of such land on condition that they agreed to reside permanently on their land and to engage in full-time farming. For want of cadastral surveys and tribal acquiescence, the plan was a total failure. Faced with the task of drafting new legislation, Arsanjani considered the experiences of these previous programs. He also had before him the text of a land reform measure already law, having been approved by Parliament in 1955, but that law he could reject out of hand as it had been passed by a landlord-packed Majles. But the situation in 1961 would be different. After Amini assumed the premiership, the new Majles was subject to almost universal charges of a rigged election. The clamor rose until His Majesty dissolved the Majles, but he did not provide for new elections.[33] The shah later provided Amini with a decree allowing him to govern by fiat. It was under this blanket authorization that on January 15, 1962, Arsanjani announced that the Land Reform Bill had become law, by royal proclamation.

The new law tried to cut through the problems of the Iranian country-

[32] Statement by Mohammad Ja'afar Behbehanian, director of the Pahlavi Foundation, while recalling its inception (*Kayhan* [Tehran], Sept. 28, 1961).

[33] Article 48, Constitutional Law of Iran (as amended May 8, 1949), states:

The King may dissolve the National Consultative Assembly or the Senate separately or at the same time. In each case when one or both Chambers are dissolved by Imperial decree, the reason for the dissolution must be mentioned in the decree, which shall also provide for new elections.

The new elections must begin within a month after the decree and the new Majles or both new Houses must convene within three months after the same date.

(From Ministry of Foreign Affairs, Information and Press Department, no. 2, p. 6.)

side. It specified that each family could retain one village irrespective of size; that the peasants in the excess villages would receive title to the land they were then tilling; that peasants would make annual payments to the government for fifteen years, after which they would own their land; that the ex-landlords would be reimbursed for their lands with fifteen-year government interest-bearing bonds; and that the government would establish rural cooperatives to assist the peasants in fulfilling this new agricultural responsibility.

Neither Arsanjani nor His Majesty lost additional time in carrying out this decree. In March, the shah traveled to Maragheh in the northwest of Iran and personally handed land deeds to peasants representing 520 new owners.[34] Arsanjani warned the landlords against obstructionism and censured them for converting the peasants into "fifteen million helpless and semi-starved people."[35] As the spring of 1962 waned, the pace of land distribution accelerated. Both the shah and Arsanjani flew from one end of Iran to the other distributing deeds to Turcomens, Qashqais, Baluchis, Mazandaranis, Shirazis. But then, in July, Prime Minister Amini resigned. To the surprise of political observers, Arsanjani was named as agricultural minister in the next cabinet, under Alam.

His reappointment confirmed the belief that his power no longer depended on Amini, but rather was rooted in the shah himself. With this new vote of confidence, the agriculture minister intensified his efforts, the program of land distribution, and the turmoil in the countryside. By the end of the year, Arsanjani could report that 500,000 hectares of land had been distributed to 35,000 peasant families and 1,080 cooperatives had been established.[36]

But Arsanjani's paramount triumph, which ironically also marked the denouement of his power, was the Congress of Rural Cooperatives, which the minister ran in early January 1963. Some 4,700 delegates gathered in Tehran to thank His Majesty and praise his minister. Most of the delegates were chairmen or officers of the rural cooperatives; as such, they represented the elite of the new owner-cultivators. After days

[34] One clue to the choice of Maragheh as the seat of the new land reform program is revealed in a dispatch from the ceremonies by Dana Adams Schmidt:

> The Shah, wearing the uniform of Commander in Chief of the army, bent to each peasant and raised him kindly to his feet. He inquired kindly in Persian about the subject's land or children. An interpreter translated the greetings into the peasant's language, Turkish.
> The Shah said that the people of the province had not benefitted in the period the area was in the Soviet sphere, or under the regime of . . . Mohammad Mossadegh, now confined to his farm near Tehran.

(*New York Times*, March 15, 1962, p. 14.) A great deal of immediate attention was also devoted to land reform in the Kurdish regions of western Persia.

[35] *Economist*, May 12, 1962, p. 557.

[36] Echo of Iran, *Daily Bulletin*, 10, no. 199 (Nov. 7, 1962): 1.

of speech-making and meetings, the delegates unanimously passed eight resolutions.

The major points of the resolutions were:

1. . . . the farmers take an oath to give their last breath to the protection of the Constitutional Monarchy in Iran;
2. We . . . resolve that the prime duty of the Government is the observance of the U.N. Charter on Human Rights; . . .
3. . . . the reconstruction of the Iranian economic and social structure in favor of the Toilers of Iran is the prime task; . . .
4. . . . unity of all the farmers is a necessity; . . .
5. . . . all should join the mighty class of rural cooperatives; . . .
6. . . . rural organizations should be based on the economic interests of the rural people; . . .
7. . . . We unanimously confirm and approve the six laws offered in the referendum by His Imperial Majesty; and
8. . . . thanks and appreciation for the selfless efforts and sacrifice of Dr. Hassan Arsanjani.[37]

Shortly after the congress, Arsanjani sought and received permission for a three weeks' rest trip to Europe. As soon as he had departed, a number of ominous signs materialized. Security forces disrupted the work of land reform officials. Orders contradicting previous instructions of the minister permeated through the Ministry. The cabinet was reshuffled and new ministers, inimical to Arsanjani, were appointed. Finally, a high-level conference was arranged that advocated economic programs opposed by the minister.

Arsanjani extended his stay but the shah cabled him to return, and on March 1 Arsanjani was received in audience. At the meeting Arsanjani reputedly demanded $100 million for the formation of cooperatives; centralization of finance, planning, and administration of all land reform programs under his jurisdiction; and various cabinet changes to enhance ministerial harmony.[38] The shah promptly refused and immediately "accepted" Arsanjani's resignation.

Fundamentally, Arsanjani's growing power with the peasants was clearly intolerable. But for the same reason a crude effort to destroy the man was hazardous. A too blatant showdown, with the aggrieved ex-minister left in the capital to rally his peasants, might be embarrassing. But his appointment as ambassador was ideal, because it would enforce

[37] Ministry of Agriculture, Department of Information, *Avalin Congreye Melliye Sherkathaye Ta'avaniye Rusta'iye Iran* [The first national congress of rural cooperative societies of Iran], Tehran, March 1961, p. 111. This report is a glossy, two-hundred-page report on the Congress, replete with scores of photographs of the minister.
[38] Echo of Iran, "The Resignation of Dr. Hassan Arsanjani," *For Your Information,* no. 375 (March 14, 1963), p. 4.

separation from his rural supporters and erode his power base. Simultaneously, his being co-opted by the regime, evinced by his service in the lucrative and sinecurelike post of ambassador in Rome, would defile his reputation among the alienated peasantry and urban liberals. Arsanjani was dismissed from the Agricultural Ministry. He was appointed ambassador. He left with tumult and returned slightly over a year later, unobtrusively.[39]

There were several collateral reasons for Arsanjani's dismissal, but, principally, it appears that His Imperial Majesty resented and feared the power that Arsanjani was collecting independently of the throne, based on peasants and urban liberals. The earnest support that Arsanjani had received at the congress was most telling. Also, the resolutions of the congress too strongly reflected the personal ideology of Arsanjani, underplayed the importance of the monarch, stressed the kinds of radical and divisive reforms that His Majesty had always sought to avoid, and suggested in their pleas for civil liberties that those virtues were somehow missing in Iran. The emphasis on "constitutional" and "human rights" also hinted at a major bid for the support of urban political groups. Finally, before his departure for Europe, Arsanjani had played a major role in the successful national referendum that was held on January 26, 1963. He demonstrated a capability to provide thousands of peasants at short notice for proreferendum rallies. His ability to deliver these peasants to Tehran for political purposes was especially foreboding.

Combined with his reputation for demagogy and his public performances which fed that reputation, Arsanjani left His Majesty with little choice. As the shah made every effort to co-opt him into the elite, Arsanjani seems to have fashioned a power position calculated to place himself in the elite irrespective of the wishes of the king and immune from the latter's control. But a lesson that must haunt the mind of the shah is the peril to his life and his throne posed by elites with independent power bases. For example, fears of the senior Qashqai tribal chiefs, Nasser Khan and Khosrow Khan, have plagued the shah for three decades. Their ability to influence national politics with tribal power has resulted in European exile for both. Nevertheless, in the fall of 1962, their tribal devotees were accused of following the instructions of the Khans by killing engineer Malek Abadi, a land reform official. They were also denounced for leading a tribal revolt that harassed the government for eight months in 1963.

[39] Apparently, once in exile as ambassador, Arsanjani realized what was happening to his reputation. Perhaps it was in response to this realization that he began publishing a series of documents outlining his radical social and economic views in the pages of *Bamshad* (Tehran). The series began on August 11, 1964 and ended with his recall to Tehran on August 19. With his return, Arsanjani turned to the private practice of law. He died unexpectedly of a heart attack in May 1969.

Another example of a politician using an independent power base for opposition to the shah is a man whose very name the shah refuses to mention because "it had become plain . . . soon after his appointment as prime minister that he wanted to destroy my dynasty."[40] His Majesty clearly recognizes that Mossadegh nearly succeeded in this goal because he had mammoth mass support:

How could anyone be against Mossadegh?

He would enrich everybody, he would fight against the foreigner, he would secure our rights. No wonder students, intellectuals, people from all walks of life flocked to his banner.

With such promises Mossadegh carried everything before him . . . no one could stand against him.[41]

In the final showdown, Mossadegh failed because he was unable to secure control of the army. Again, the lesson was not lost on the king.

Dr. Manouchehr Eghbal. Arsanjani is not alone in enjoying that form of exile which results in being posted to a lucrative foreign post. Nor are the roots for such exile necessarily located in His Majesty's fear of independent bases of power. Neither are its subjects necessarily under quarantine from their indigenous supporters.

Dr. Manouchehr Eghbal, for example, was sent to Europe after mishandling the first elections to the Twentieth Majles. He had been the target of severe criticism from all sections of the political spectrum for his gross and illegal interference in the balloting. Under mounting general discontent, he resigned in August 1960, after completing forty-one months in office, the longest tenure of any prime minister to serve under Mohammad Reza Shah to that time. In part as punishment for the poorly run elections, but primarily as a reward for his long service and, no doubt, in part to help Eghbal weather political opposition by removing him, the shah determined to post him abroad.[42]

The pressure on the shah, both from Amini and the political chaos following his appointment, is manifest, however, in the various posts to which Eghbal was assigned and then withdrawn. Initially, it was announced that Eghbal would go as ambassador to the Court of Saint James's. Shortly thereafter, Amini took office and widespread arrests took place. His appointment annulled, Eghbal secretly fled the country to

[40] Mohammad Reza Shah Pahlavi, *Mission for My Country*, p. 97.
[41] *Ibid.*, pp. 90–91.
[42] There was mounting public displeasure and criticism of Eghbal, not only for his gross misconduct during the elections, but also for deeds committed during his premiership. For example, on February 23, 1961, students at the University of Tehran staged a demonstration against him, although he had already been removed from office, and burned his automobile on the grounds of the campus.

avoid a similar fate.[43] From this self-imposed exile, Dr. Eghbal wrote the newspapers to announce that he had been reappointed, but as ambassador to Spain. Only a matter of days passed before His Imperial Majesty canceled this appointment. (Pressure against his entire family was mounting, and Eghbal's brother, Ahmad Eghbal, was cashiered from the Ministry of Foreign Affairs.) Then, after several months out of the news and a corresponding decline in his saliency, and the fall of Amini, the shah appointed Eghbal as Iranian representative to the European office of UNESCO, perhaps the greatest sinecure available to Iranian exiles.

That exile can have value as well as cost is attested by Eghbal's subsequent fate. The Amini government had already begun its anticorruption purge. After his flight, Eghbal was formally charged with illegal interference in the elections and with providing illegal tax concessions to a number of soft drink manufacturers, resulting in their shortchanging the public treasury of some 500 million rials ($7,300,000). But under Iranian law, an ex-cabinet minister could not be punished without a special act of Parliament. As the shah had dissolved that body, Eghbal's prosecution was hampered. Ultimately, some twenty-five minor officials were sentenced to fines and imprisonment for ballot tampering but by the time Amini could have the law amended to allow for the trial of Eghbal, the ex-prime minister was in his new post and no action was taken.

Exile, then, is one of the means that the shah employs to control elite who refuse to be co-opted or who violate the rules of the political game even after they have been co-opted. Its practice assumes a variety of forms, but it remains, relatively, a last resort when other methods for political control have failed. Nonetheless, a recent report has suggested that there are as many as five thousand Iranians who are banned from entering their own country. This figure seems incredibly high, however, even to many of the exiles themselves.[44]

REMOVAL FROM OFFICE

His Imperial Majesty has other means of limiting the power of the counterelite than these variations in what is basically the rather uncommon practice of forced or voluntary exile. One such means that is repeatedly employed is the removal of dissidents from office. There exist numerous examples whereby a member of the counterelite, persisting in attacking the government or regime, exhausts the patience and tolerance

[43] During his entire term as an exile and, subsequently, as Iranian ambassador to UNESCO, Eghbal is reported to have drawn a salary as professor of medicine at Tehran University. Holding two (or three) full-time jobs is not an uncommon practice but simultaneously holding full-time jobs in different countries is.

[44] Echo of Iran, *Daily Bulletin: Political Edition*, 15, no. 41 (Feb. 21, 1967): 5.

of His Majesty. More unusual is the case of a group of the most trusted of the elite, perceived by others in fact as *nokare dowlat* (lackies of the government), being so removed.

By the second day of the extensive rioting following the mourning of Moharram and the arrest of Khomeini in June 1963, the blood of thousands of Iranians had been spilt.[45] His Excellency Hussein Ala, then serving as minister of the Imperial Court, expressed mounting concern over the force of the military reaction to the riots. He called together a handful of Iran's most elite officials, among whom were Abdollah Entezam, General Morteza Yazdanpanah, and Sardar Fakher Hekmat. Together they agreed that the savage military response to what had begun as a simple protest against the arrest of Khomeini could only redound to the ill of His Majesty. Already the strength and determination of the rioters had grown in the face of the shooting. Disorders had spread through Iran and rumor had it that University of Tehran students were about to enter on the side of the rioters. And, increasingly, the demonstrators were not expressing their violence in random fashion. They were seeking out, looting, and burning undefended government offices.

The results, this group assumed, could be a government victory, but by bloodbath. Or the army could waiver and the government fall, perhaps with unimagined consequences for the shahanshah. In either case too many lives would be lost and too much bitterness engendered for the intrinsic importance of the riot's origins. They decided to approach His Imperial Majesty to urge him to temper the violence of the government's response.

Hussein Ala. Who were these four members of the elite who had resolved on this unusual step? Hussein Ala was then seventy-eight years of age. His father had served the Qajars as prime minister, minister, and ambassador and had been a leading constitutionalist in the 1905–1907 revolu-

---

[45] Estimates of the numbers of casualties suffered in the rioting vary widely by source. One elite respondent, sympathetic to the demonstrators, estimated that "between five and ten thousand had *died* throughout the country." Writing in *Peighame Emruz* (Tehran) on June 10, 1963, Dr. A. R. Azimi suggested that "some of the persons arrested during the June 4 disturbances had confessed that they had been paid 25 rials [33 cents] each to take part in the processions. They had been told that if killed they would go to Paradise. We are told that the number reached 10,000." Premier Alam, on the other hand, told the *New York Times* that 86 were killed and 150 injured (June 7, 1963, p. 1), while Iranian newspapers reported that "official figures put the casualties at 200" (*Tehran Journal*, June 8, 1963). The author was an eyewitness to the initiation of firing by army troops on the first day in front of the Tehran Bazaar. It is his personal opinion that actual casualty figures resemble more closely the former estimates than the latter. Whatever the actual totals, which will undoubtedly never be known, the number of dead and wounded certainly reached many thousands.

tion. Ala himself had served with distinction under Reza Shah and Mohammad Reza Shah. He had filled cabinet posts in the Ministries of Finance, Public Welfare, Science, Agriculture, Trade, and Foreign Affairs. He had been a delegate to the Paris Peace Conference following World War I (where the Iranian delegation was excluded by British pressures), and he was Iran's chief delegate to the United Nations after World War II. It was Ala who eloquently pleaded Iran's case against the USSR in the Security Council, protesting the Soviet's refusal to withdraw their troops from Iranian territory. He had also served the two monarchs as ambassador (to Spain, London, and the United States), and the present king as prime minister and twice previously as minister of court. He was considered so devoted to the monarch that Mossadegh had demanded and received his dismissal by the shah. At the time of this extraordinary meeting, Ala was once again serving as minister of court, a position to which he had been reappointed immediately following the overthrow of Mossadegh.

Abdollah Entezam. Abdollah Entezam, born in 1907, was the son of Entezam os-Saltaneh (Order of the Kingdom), who several times served the Qajars as minister. Abdollah Entezam had entered government service in the Foreign Ministry and filled a variety of foreign posts until Ala was called to form a cabinet. Entezam served as his minister of foreign affairs. After Mossadegh's overthrow, Entezam again served as minister of foreign affairs through the cabinets of General Zahedi and Ala. In 1957, he was appointed director of the National Iranian Oil Company, a position he was holding when the riots broke out.

Sardar Fakher Hekmat. In 1895, Sardar Fakher Hekmat was born into a renowned family of Shiraz. His grandfather was the most famous physician of his day while his father was a wealthy landowner. Hekmat was early a patriot, taking part in the Constitutional Revolution. Later, during World War II, he organized military resistance to the British in southern Persia. Thereafter he served as governor of numerous provinces but entered the Majles in its fourth session, inaugurated shortly after the coup staged by Zia ed-Din and Reza Khan. Hekmat continued to serve in numerous sessions of the Parliament, even rejecting a request from the shah to form a cabinet. Beginning in 1941, he was elected speaker of the Majles, a position that he held through the dissolved twentieth session. He headed the lower house from 1947 through 1961, save for the Mossadegh period, when he "retired" from politics as a result of his differences with the prime minister. At the time of the riots, Hekmat was preparing to resume his political activities in the elections for Parliament that had been promised for that summer.

General Morteza Yazdanpanah. General Morteza Yazdanpanah was the oldest and most venerated general of his time. Born in 1888, he was a graduate of the *Ghazaq Khaneh* (Cossacks' House) where officers were trained for the Russian-sponsored Cossack Brigade. At the time of the 1921 coup, Yazdanpanah was a general commanding the Northern Army. He was invaluable to Reza Shah from 1921 to 1941 as he drove his troops victoriously against the tribes in all sections of the country. With the abdication of Reza Shah, the new king leaned heavily on the experienced and devoted Yazdanpanah. The general served him four times as minister of war, as His Majesty's general adjutant, and finally as senator. With the dissolution of the Parliament in 1961, His Majesty appointed General Yazdanpanah as director of the Imperial Inspectorate (an Iranian variant of the ombudsman reporting directly to the shah), a position he was filling in June 1963.

These four devoted elite officials carried their forebodings to His Imperial Majesty at a hastily arranged audience. What actually transpired at that audience is unknown. It is reported that the shah was infuriated. That any of his servants, even these four trusted officials, should presume to instruct him in the conduct of kingship, which he had practiced since 1941, was insufferable. What is known is the aftermath. Ala was relieved of his duties as minister of court. Later, he was "promoted" to the Senate. Yazdanpanah was dropped from the Inspectorate. He was also "promoted" to the Senate. Hekmat was forbidden to campaign for the Parliament, was not appointed to the Senate, and remained in the silent isolation of an inactive politician. Entezam was retired from the National Iranian Oil Company and was "at home." (He was succeeded by Dr. Eghbal, who returned from Europe.)

These four had attempted what is never done in Iran—to volunteer suggestions of policy to His Imperial Majesty. That a member of the elite should assume that he could alter the behavior of the shah might establish a precedent dangerous to the continued autonomy of His Majesty's sovereignty. From the shah's perspective, such an assumption must be rejected out of hand, while publicly negated and invalidated. A most effective means of accomplishing these ends and destroying the assumption is to render powerless their perpetrators. In this, the shah did not hesitate, irrespective of the individuals involved.

Interestingly, these same riots witnessed a similar incident that Persians, *au courant* with court matters, consider unprecedented. Another government official offered the shah an ultimatum, and, strangely enough, succeeded. During the night between the first and second days of rioting, Prime Minister Alam roused the shah by telephone. He respectfully suggested that troops who had spent the day and evening firing on their own countrymen might refuse to continue a second day. With riots having broken out in cities around the country, no risks could be run in Tehran. If the troops of the capital refused to "shoot to kill" as the shah had ordered, forces throughout Iran might waiver. The shah is reported to have raged that as commander in chief of the Imperial Iranian Armed Forces, he knew his men. They were too well disciplined and too obedient to refuse to execute even his most inconsequential orders, he said. Alam then responded that such might be the case. But if the shah did not remove the troops that had seen action and replace them with fresh troops from outside the city by morning, he was resigning the premiership. His Majesty knew Alam as a trusted boyhood playmate who had been totally loyal his entire life. If he concurred, it would be one of the few such incidents of his rule. The shah hesitated, but agreed. On the second day, fresh troops "shot to kill."

IMPRISONMENT

Another technique used by His Majesty to exclude the potential counterelite is imprisonment. This is usually a means of final recourse in the co-optation process, to be adopted when more conventional techniques for eliminating the counterelite have failed. On the other hand, temporary imprisonment for corruption is an often used device for expressing the royal displeasure. In fact it is frequently difficult to discriminate between prisoners being held for alleged political offenses and those incarcerated for more ordinary civil and criminal offenses. Where boundaries between these types of offense are so poorly defined because of the centrality of politics and because the shahanshah is the unmistaken keystone of the political system, distinctions between civil, criminal, and political can become meaningless. Intense observation of Iranian politics will convince one that these distinctions are, in fact, spurious. Any offense is a priori a political offense.

A practice of the regime compounds this. Frequently, members of the elite will be charged with corruption and removed from office, exiled, or imprisoned when their offense was, in fact, entirely political. Such charges are advanced in order to mask the existence of the political turmoil that endures beneath the placid facade of Iranian unity and stability. In addition, instances of corruption are easily found, expeditiously adjudicated, and immediately credible, to the politically aware.

Those intimate with the workings of Iranian politics suggest that corruption among the elite is used in exactly the same way as are the resignations submitted to the president of the United States by his cabinet secretaries as they assume the responsibilities of their offices. When the chief executive determines that a secretary is no longer satisfactorily fulfilling those responsibilities, he may accept, with deep regrets, the resignation. It is alleged by some that His Majesty not only maintains a dossier pertaining to the improbity of each member of the elite, but actually countenances or even encourages their dishonesty in order to fatten their dossiers. When the proper moment arises, the elite can be confronted with the dossier and his resignation or exile demanded. Or if need be, the materials therein can be used as the basis for successful judicial proceedings. Either way, the suspect or unwanted elite official can be politically neutralized.

Abol Hassan Ebtehaj. It is impossible to ascertain with surety those corruption cases that have their roots in treasonable issues. Nonetheless, Tehran rumor networks agree on a number of recent instances. Perhaps the most notorious was the imprisonment of Abol Hassan Ebtehaj. As the former governor of the National Bank (1942–1950), managing director of the Plan Organization (1954–1959), and founder of the private Iranians' Bank, Ebtehaj is known as Iran's leading economist. More important, outside the country his reputation for integrity and professional competence is second to none, and in Iran, he is known as "first of the 'technocrats.' "[46] On November 10, 1961, Ebtehaj was taken into custody by the police.

The public reaction was sharp and critical. Prime Minister Amini felt obliged to deny any responsibility in the arrest. Ministry of Justice inspectors acknowledge that they were investigating complaints made by Ahmad Aramesh, Ebtehaj's successor as Plan Organization chief. In a speech to the Majles, Aramesh charged that under Ebtehaj, the Plan Organization had paid David E. Lilienthal and Gordon R. Clapp 7 billion rials ($100 million) since 1956 without their having accounted "for even a single rial."[47] (At the time, the two former chairmen of the Tennessee Valley Authority were directors of the Development Resources Corporation. The latter company was responsible for the planning and construction of a TVA-like scheme in the oil and water rich southwestern province of Khuzestan.)

Subsequently, Minister of Justice Nour ed-Din (Light of the Faith) Alamuti claimed that Ebtehaj had wasted vast state funds and signed contracts without the necessary approval. Nevertheless, Ebtehaj was never formally charged with these or other offenses. Seven months after his arrest, Ebtehaj was released from prison on bond, agreeing that if he left Iran, he would pay the government $171 million in forfeited bail.[48]

Ebtehaj demanded speedy resolution of his case. But Amini was dis-

[46] *Kayhan* (Tehran), Nov. 14, 1961. Also see U.S. Congress, Senate, Committee on Foreign Relations, *Activities of the Development and Resources Corporation in Iran*, 87th Cong., 2nd sess., 1962, esp. pp. 23–24, 34.

[47] *Kayhan* (Tehran), May 1, 1962.

[48] Arnold Beichman in the *Christian Science Monitor*, Sept. 26, 1962, reports that $171 million is the total spent until that time on all Khuzestan projects.

placed by Alam and with him went Alamuti; the case hung fire. Ultimately, the whole affair was dropped and Ebtehaj was acquitted. On February 13, 1964, "the Examining Magistrate ruled that the charges were unfounded. The ruling was confirmed by the Prosecutor of the Civil Service Tribunal."[49]

In assessing this bizarre series of episodes, it seems clear that Ebtehaj was not imprisoned on the basis of the published accusations. His renowned and proven integrity and the abandonment of the case argue against such an eventuality. Rather, the causes for his arrest must be sought in political affairs. Only slightly more than one month previous to his arrest, Ebtehaj had delivered an address at the International Industrial Conference in San Francisco. In his talk, Ebtehaj spoke of the need for government planning and a strong private sector in developing societies. He also urged greater multilateral assistance, criticizing bilateral aid programs of the past. He charged that country-to-country aid led to the diversion of funds from development efforts "by military and political considerations." Moreover, he said,

Even if a recipient government became convinced in all good faith of the fairness of certain bilateral programs offered by another country, it would soon be condemned in the public mind. Opposition leaders will charge the government with selling out to the imperialists, and the public will believe those charges.

No matter how false the accusation that other nations will use "development schemes" to exploit poverty and restrict freedom, it is a popular belief that must be recognized. Bilateral aid poisons the relationship between nations, frustrates the donor, and causes revulsion in the recipient.

. . . Where the recipient government is corrupt, the donor government very understandably appears, in the judgement of the public, to support corruption. . . .

The bilateral approach cannot bring about reform . . . [but] delays internal pressures toward reform by providing considerable material resources to corrupt regimes and by unwittingly fostering the fear that development aid will be stopped if the old regime is overthrown. . . .[50]

Lest there be any uncertainties in his listeners' minds about the countries he was using in this model, Ebtehaj continued,

I can think of no better summary of all the disadvantages and weaknesses of the bilateral system than the modern history of my own country. Not so very many years ago in Iran, the United States was loved and respected as no other country, and without having given a penny of aid. Now, after

[49] *Kayhan International* (Tehran), Feb. 17, 1964.
[50] Abol Hassan Ebtehaj, "A Program for Economic Growth," (Paper delivered at the International Industrial Conference, San Francisco, Sept. 1961), p. 4.

more than $1 billion of loans and grants, America is neither loved nor respected; she is distrusted by most people, and hated by many.[51]

Ebtehaj concluded his talk with a plea for ending bilateral aid with the thought that,

Social and political unrest is a manifestation of the despair and lack of faith of the people, of their distrust of incompetent and sometimes corrupt governments, and of the whole pattern of bilateral agreements that seem to support the bankrupt system.[52]

It would seem incontestable that His Majesty had resorted to imprisoning Ebtehaj not for mismanagement or corruption, but as chastisement for these aspersions against his regime, Iran, and the United States. Allegations were made to the wasted funds and misbehavior in his dealings with Lilienthal and Clapp partially because of the fortuitous raising of those charges by Aramesh some time previously. Partially, no doubt, they were made because of their very incredibility to all who knew Ebtehaj personally. And finally, they were undoubtedly a rebuttal of Ebtehaj's defense of Lilienthal and Clapp in his damaging speech.[53] But few took those charges seriously. The general belief was that the issue of corruption was being raised as the basis for a punitive response to a political offender. Some time later, the United Nations requested that Ebtehaj serve as chief economic adviser to the government of Algeria, then struggling to correct the excesses of the Ben Bella era. Ebtehaj accepted, but His Majesty refused permission.[54] The royal displeasure was still aroused.

THE NATIONAL FRONT

Finally, there are instances of imprisonment that grow out of activities perceived by the regime as direct threats to its welfare. These are fre-

[51] *Ibid.*, p. 4   [52] Ibid., p. 7.

[53] Ebtehaj said:

In my own experience the possibility of utilizing foreign planning and administrative personnel is best illustrated by the work of Lilienthal and Clapp in the development of Khuzestan (Iran). To be sure, theirs is primarily an American firm, but no one in 1956 would have accused President Eisenhower of using these two great advocates of the Tennessee Valley Authority as front men for American aid! Their reputation for integrity and imagination, not their nationality, attracted us to them. And the team they sent to Khuzestan was an international one led by men of international reputation.

. . . No mere advisors could have accomplished what they have; and no team of bi-lateral aid supervisors could have been given the hiring and firing responsibility that this foreign firm was asked to accept.

(*Ibid.*, pp. 5–6.) This rebuttal was made after Aramesh's speech.

[54] Echo of Iran (*Daily Bulletin: Political Edition*, 15, no. 41 [Feb. 21, 1967]: 5) also claimed that there were then 15,000 Iranians forbidden to leave Iran. Ebtehaj was obviously among them.

quently seen as manifestly treasonable and no attempts are made to rationalize, in terms of corruption, the deserts meted out to the offenders. In recent years, most of these imprisonments involved the most articulate and best organized opposition group in Iran, the National Front. From 1963 to 1966, the regime conducted an extensive campaign to eliminate the *Jebheye Melli* (National Front) as a meaningful political force. The Front, which came into existence as a coalition of political groupings revolving around Dr. Mohammad Mossadegh, began to fragment and collapse with the approach of the showdown between the prime minister and the shah in 1953. Many of its original and most prestigious leaders split away to form their own parties or to join the shah. Hossein Makki, Dr. Mozaffar Bagha'ee, Seyyed Hassan Ha'eri Zadeh, and Ayattolah Kashani all withdrew their loyalty. With Mossadegh's overthrow, the Front collapsed. A number of the ex-prime minister's staunchest lieutenants escaped to Europe and the United States; there they formed a new coalition, more radical than the Front, the *Moghavamate Melli* (National Resistance Movement), and began publishing *Bakhtare Emruz* (The West Today). Within Iran, the NRM was able to organize an occasional demonstration (at the trial of Mossadegh, against the negotiations with the international oil companies, etc.). Many were caught in mass arrests, tortured, and imprisoned. Still others of Mossadegh's supporters, primarily the intellectuals, remained in Iran and withdrew to faculty positions at the University of Tehran.

Mossadegh, meanwhile, had been tried and found guilty of high treason. His foreign minister, Hossein Fatemi, who went into hiding with the premier's arrest, was convicted of the same offense and executed. The prime minister, however, was too likely to be martyred by such a death—and Iran's history is fraught with martyrs who invariably serve as focuses for antiregime opposition.[55] Instead, he was sentenced to three years' solitary confinement after which he was released and he "retired to his country estate near Tehran, for he is a wealthy man."[56] Thereafter, with Mossadegh a prisoner and the army and the newly formed SAVAK apparently omniscient and omnipresent, both the National Resistance

[55] Vide Vladimir Minorsky, "Iran: Opposition, Martyrdom, and Revolt" *Unity and Variety in Muslim Civilization*, ed. G. E. von Grunebaum (Chicago: University of Chicago Press, 1955), pp. 183–206.

[56] Mohammad Reza Shah Pahlavi, *Mission for My Country*, p. 82. Richard W. Cottam relates the peculiarly Iranian ruse that converted Mossadegh from a "free man" to a detainee at his own estates. After his release from prison he visited his country estate. Suddenly his home was attacked by a large mob. The beleaguered ex-prime minister phoned for police protection which arrived, drove off the attackers, and never left. Nor did the police ever allow Mossadegh to leave. It was later revealed that the leader of this mob was the notorious Sha'aban Bi Mokh (Sha'aban the Brainless) who had led the *bazaari* mobs for the shah against Mossadegh in August 1953. Vide Cottam, *Nationalism in Iran*, p. 295.

Movement and the intellectuals were in a slough of despondency and inactivity.

With the first elections to the Twentieth Majles, however, this was to change. The shah's attempt to experiment in controlled democracy, i.e., the creation and direction of a two-party political system by the throne, in 1957, was a demonstrable failure. For as the election campaigns wore on, the party candidates took their roles seriously and began unbridled attacks on their opposite numbers. When the election results were announced, then, they were greeted with an uproar of dismay. As if the heated campaign had not been held, the shah-sponsored Prime Minister Eghbal's *Melliyun* party won 104 seats in the Majles, The *Mardom* party led by Asadollah Alam captured fifty seats and the independents but three seats.

When the shah canceled the first elections and brought Sharif Emami, once a partisan of Mossadegh's, to the premiership, hopes for a massive liberalization of political life were inflamed. The second elections witnessed even more unrestrained campaigning. A number of politicians, many of whom had been rejected by the *Melliyun* and *Mardom*, declared as independents. (Abdul Rahman Borumand went so far as to run a second time under the banner of the National Front. But for a second time this transcended even the new liberalism and Borumand was arrested.[57])

The results of these elections were more assuring. The *Melliyun* led with sixty-nine seats, the *Mardom* had sixty-four. But with neither party holding a majority, the votes of the thirty-two independents also elected would be decisive. And among the thirty-two was the name of Allahyar Saleh, the leader of the Iran party, the intellectual wing of the National Front. With Saleh's election, a resurgent Front began to operate. Rumors were rife in Tehran that the Front was being encouraged because of President John F. Kennedy's liberal philosophy. A visit by Averell Harriman was perceived as "paving the ground for the National Front."[58]

Whatever the truth to these rumors, a convention was held, a platform issued, and a new central committee elected. The Front organized public meetings, demonstrated at the university, protested the second elections as fraudulent, and went so far as to call for a general strike. With its success, the Front grew bolder. It opened a headquarters and began to register members. Symbolizing their resurgence, the Front called a mass meeting for July 21 to commemorate the return to power of Dr. Mossadegh on that date in 1952 (after he had been dismissed by the shah for a total of three days). It was this meeting that the government forbade.

---

[57] *Ibid.*, pp. 297, 301. Borumand had tried to run in the first elections but had been arrested.

[58] *Diplomat* (Tehran), May 17, 1961, expands on these rumors.

Their wishes were enforced with tanks, and a number of the National Front leaders were temporarily arrested.

Faced with this rebuff and the growing restrictions of the Amini regime, the Front turned inward to consider problems of internal organization. Engineer Mehdi Bazargan had resigned from its central committee, announced the formation of a new political grouping, the *Nehzate Azadi* (Freedom Movement of Iran), and promptly sought its recognition by the central committee as part of the National Front. With legitimacy provided by a letter from Dr. Mossadegh welcoming the Movement, Bazargan's new group was accepted. From its platform and founding members, it was clear that the Freedom Movement represented a materialization within Iran of the radical NRM still abroad. The Freedom Movement, like the NRM, was primarily a coalition of activists— bazaaris, religious leaders, and students—as opposed to the Iran party's intellectuals led by Saleh.[59] The presence of this division between the radical activists and the relatively more conservative intellectuals persisted and did not escape the regime.

The National Front was, perhaps, the unwitting party to a massive and bloody clash between students at the University of Tehran and army troops in January 1962. University students were agitated over the closing of the National Teachers' Training College following student protest there at an announced cut in scholarships. Then it was learned that three students had been expelled from the Dar ol-Fonun for outspoken criticism of the government. In protest, University of Tehran students demonstrated in sympathy with their colleagues—even offering two minutes of silence in honor of the recently martyred Lumumba.

The very next day, January 22, the university was stormed by government troops. Perhaps the best description of what happened was supplied by the university chancellor, Dr. Ahmad Farhad, in his letter of resignation to Prime Minister Amini protesting the assault:

Pursuant to our conversation, at 11:00 a.m., soldiers and paratroopers had occupied Tehran University. There was no reason or excuse for the violation of the rights or regulations of the University.

Soldiers and paratroopers after entry attacked boys and girls indiscriminately. . . . Many of the students were beaten to the point of death.

I have never seen or heard so much cruelty, sadism, atrocity, and vandalism as on the part of the Government forces. Some of the girls were criminally attacked in the classrooms by the soldiers.

When we inspected the University buildings, we were faced with a situation as if an army of barbarians had invaded an enemy territory. Books were torn, shelves were broken, typewriters smashed, laboratory equipment stolen or destroyed; desks, chairs, doors, windows and walls were vandalized

[59] Cottam, *Nationalism in Iran*, p. 293.

by the troops fighting unarmed students without interference from their officers.

Even the University Hospital was not immune from the soldiers.[60]

When the attack had subsided, the government closed the university and ordered massive arrests. Government opponents of all political coloration were detained.

The National Front leaders were the first targets; they were accused of inciting the students. But other politicians, usually considered the Front's enemies, were also arrested, including Fatollah Forud, an ex-mayor of Tehran, and his political ally, Assadollah Rashidian, a banker and known friend of the British. Seyyed Ja'afar Behbehani and S. Behdad, the editor of *Jahan*, were also taken. It was then that General Bakhtiar became implicated. As the investigation deepened, more of the guilt was reputed to center on Bakhtiar. It appeared that he had instigated the military attack in order to embarrass the shah, bring down Amini, discredit the National Front and have himself—the choice of the military—promoted to the premiership.

Following these revelations, Bakhtiar went into exile and most of the politicians were released—all but the Iran Freedom Movement leaders, who remained longer in jail. Their student wing had issued a pamphlet analyzing the attack that infuriated the regime. The students explained that:

The intention was to close down the University because the University had become the last bastion of the national struggle, it had replaced the Bazaar as a political centre. In the old days, the Bazaar could resist the Government because it was economically independent and it enjoyed clerical support. But the centralization of Government and the establishment of banks . . . robbed it of its independence. With the economic depression [beginning in 1960], the intimidation of the police finally was able to completely suppress the Bazaar voice. The clergy were similarly silenced. The civil service restricted. The press muzzled. The Majles nonexistent. They had left only the University. . . . It was this last voice that had to be silenced. The Ruling Class obviously wants a university. Their country, for propaganda sake, must have everything—even a nuclear reactor! But this university should not have living students, let alone talking ones.[61]

With the dismissal of Amini, newly installed Premier Alam paid a personal visit to Allahyar Saleh. To the utter astonishment of many within and without the National Front, Alam told Saleh that the shahanshah

[60] A copy of this letter from Dr. Farhad was read to me in a personal interview with an elite respondent. It was also translated by the Research and Information Commission of the International Students' Conference and received wide circulation abroad. (As is often the case in Iranian politics, Dr. Farhad's daughter is now married to Dr. Amini's son.)

[61] From a broadsheet entitled "The Fate of the University," signed by Students of the Freedom Movement of Iran and dated March 1962.

wished to make use of National Front views in administering the country. He was even prepared to assign cabinet seats to Front nominees and to assure the election of their representatives to the next Majles. To those aware of His Majesty's style of co-optation and inclusivity, these overtures were less surprising.

After several further meetings and an invitation from the prime minister to meet directly with the king, the Front issued a memorandum outlining three conditions for joining the government. It demanded strict observance of the constitution and "sincere" enforcement of the principles guaranteeing a constitutional monarchy. Also, it called for immediate elections to be held according to law. Finally, the Front stressed that basic legal freedoms were "necessary and essential" for carrying out any reforms.[62]

In effect, the Front was demanding an entire restructuring of the political system that the shah had fashioned since 1953. His "rule" would revert to his "reign." Political parties, including the Front, would contest free elections and dominate a Majles outside the control of the throne. The center of power would pass to the legislature. The Front clearly refused to be co-opted. Front leaders must have realized that acceptance of their conditions would be impossible for the king, and they were. Negotiations broke off and the Front returned to sub rosa polemics against the government.

Then in January 1963, in the face of the Rural Cooperative's Conference and growing publicity for the referendum, the Front held another National Congress. After electing a new central committee, the Front urged the people of Iran to boycott the January 26 referendum called to ratify the shah's Six-Point Reform Program. To fortify public opposition, the Front announced a mass meeting and demonstration on January 25 to protest the balloting and issued a manifesto that ended:

We warn the people of Iran that our country is now on the verge of being officially changed from a democratic parliamentary regime to that of reaction and despotism.

We must, therefore, say YES to the abolition of the feudal system; land and water for the farmers and better rewards for the worker; sovereignty for the nation and freedom for all; and destruction of colonialism and exploitation.

But we must say NO to the ARBITRARY RULE OF THE SHAH, HIS INTERFERENCE IN THE AFFAIRS OF THE STATE, THE RULE OF TERROR AND SAVAK ATROCITIES, COLONIAL DOMINATION OF THE COUNTRY, POLICE VIOLATIONS AND GENDARMERIE OPPRESSION AND THE OVERLORDSHIP OF GOVERNMENT OFFICIALS IN TOWNS AND VILLAGES.[63]

[62] Translated from the communiqué of the National Front as detailed by an elite respondent in a personal interview.
[63] From a manifesto of the National Front in the author's possession.

His Majesty responded with fury. From his perspective, these leaders had demonstrated their total alienation from his rule and unwillingness to be co-opted or demoralized or depoliticized. Their leader, who had nearly succeeded in unseating the shah, had not, after all, been executed and was not even imprisoned. Their second-in-command had been elected to Parliament, and the organization had been allowed to surface. A four-star general (the first in Iran's history) who commanded the army and the chief of the secret police had both been fired and replaced by officers reputed for their liberalism.[64] Finally, the shah's staunchest ally and prime minister had made overtures to the Front leaders seeking their cooperation and offering to bring them into the government. Their unwillingness to play the game of politics in Iran by the established rules must have appeared to the shah as gross obstructionism. Their widespread popularity among the mobilized segments of the urban population —students, teachers, *bazaaris*, religious leaders, and workers—made that obstructionism not merely troublesome but pernicious and, perhaps, lethal.

National Front leaders were rounded up and their scheduled meeting was banned. The shah went to Qum, the hub of religiously inspired opposition to his rule, and distributed land reform deeds in the face of the hostility of the ulema and *ruhanis* (clergymen). He blasted his opponents in a speech there, branding them "100 times more treacherous than the Tudeh":

... the "Black reactionaries" and "the destructive red elements" will not sit quietly. They cannot see the implementation of the six bills which insure the prosperity and glory of Iran and make it an advanced Modern Iran. ...

Now these very persons whose flesh and blood belongs to the aliens present themselves as patriots merely to serve their own ends though the whole record of their lives is marked with black and dirty acts. They do not wish to see the country make progress and be prosperous. These people hold meetings and issue resolutions and communiques in order to serve their own ends. They have chosen the Egyptian government as their leader and want Iran patterned on Egypt.

... We shall pity these people if they do not mend their ways and do not make use of our generosity.[65]

With the opposition muzzled, the government announced overwhelmingly popular support for the referendum. According to official figures, 5,593,826 Iranians had cast their votes for the land reform, the nationalization of forests, the sale of state-owned factories, a profit-sharing

[64] The new head of SAVAK, General Hassan Pakravan, whose name translates "pure soul," was known as a soft-spoken, pipe-smoking intellectual.
[65] From the official text of the speech as published in *Ettela'at* (Tehran), Jan. 24, 1963, p. 1.

scheme for factory workers, the enfranchisement of women, and the establishment of a Literacy Corps. Only 4,115 voted "no."[66]

A quiescence descended on Tehran after the referendum. But it dissolved in April as the National Front detainees went on a hunger strike. Students at the university then demonstrated in sympathy while families of the prisoners paraded before the Ministry of Justice and a delegation delivered a letter to the United Nations secretary general at the UN offices in Tehran. Indications of a new direction in Iranian politics were immediately evident. Buoyed by his success in the referendum and still smarting from his rebuff at the hands of the Front, the shah gave orders for the immediate suppression of these demonstrations.

While the National Front leaders remained in jail, the rioting of June 1963 occurred. More arrests followed and the government turned its attention to prosecuting prisoners charged with these crimes. As the investigations progressed, additional arrests were made and the last four months of 1963 took on the character of a mass roundup of opposition politicians throughout Iran: controlling the opposition through imprisonment became more prevalent. It is estimated that at least 250 persons were arrested, including other National Front supporters, members of the Tudeh party's Revolutionary Committee and Provincial Committee, religious leaders throughout Iran, and, once again, General Gharani and his supporters.

Finally, one year after their original arrest, in January 1964, a number of National Front leaders were brought before a military court-martial and charged with activities against the security of the state. But of all the detainees, only the leaders and founders of the Freedom Movement were put on the docket. The government was clearly striking at the activist and more radical wing of the Front—the reinstituted National Resistance

---

[66] *Ettela'at* (Tehran), Jan. 31, 1963, p. 1. The newspaper compared the figures pertaining to Iran's referendum with a then recent referendum sponsored by de Gaulle in France.

TABLE 3.a

Comparison of Referendum Results
in France and Iran

	Iran	France
Number of eligible voters	6,098,777	26,603,264
Actual voters	5,593,826	22,598,850
Number voting in favor	5,589,710	17,668,889
Number voting against	4,115	4,624,511
Number abstaining	0	303,449
Percentage of voters	91	89.9
Percentage of "yes" votes	99	77.3

Movement. Engineer Bazargan and his coleader, Seyyed Mahmud Taleghani, were sentenced to ten years' imprisonment. Other members of the group were jailed for terms of one to six years. The intellectual wing of the Front was treated more liberally—perhaps to hold open the promise of an ultimate reconciliation with the Front's more conservative members. Allahyar Saleh was eventually released, but in poor health, he retired to his home in Kashan.

The years 1965 and 1966 witnessed other arrests and other trials in Iran. Numerous suspects were detained after the assassination of Prime Minister Mansur in January 1965 and after the abortive assassination attempt on the life of the shah in April of that year. A general roundup of members of the political opposition was conducted on the eve of the anniversary of Mossadegh's overthrow. Fifty-five persons were taken into custody at the end of the year and charged with plotting the overthrow of the regime and the establishment of an "Islamic Government." Fourteen leaders of the Tudeh were tried in absentia and sentenced to death.[67]

Speculating on the number of political prisoners who remain in Iranian jails is a highly tenuous affair. One foreigner commented, "By Middle East standards, the 100 to 200 political prisoners now in jails is a relatively small total."[68] It is by no means certain that the number is between one hundred and two hundred, although it does appear that the number is, in fact, substantially below the numbers prevailing in other countries of the Middle East. (This, of course, is no consolation to a determined member of the Iranian opposition.)

In spite of these measures for dealing with potentially threatening elites, the government of Iran resorts to "the specific means peculiar to it . . . the use of physical force" only when other means of implementing the wishes of His Imperial Majesty have failed.[69] Except in instances that

[67] The fortunes of the National Front have remained at a low ebb to the present. Continued government pressure has hindered efforts to reorganize and government reforms have stolen much political thunder from the Front. Finally, the death of Dr. Mossadegh at the age of eighty-six in 1967 removed a great symbol of opposition and the only unifying factor of the Front. An unusual index of his popularity, and perhaps of the Front itself, was manifest at his death. It is the custom in Iran for family members and close friends of the deceased to place small condolence-type advertisements in newspapers. Within a week of Mossadegh's death, Tehran papers were adding extra pages to carry an extraordinary number of such messages. The printing of all further condolence notices for the late prime minister was shortly banned by the government.

[68] Alfred Friendly, "Shah's Image Established, His Program Accepted," *Washington Post*, July 6, 1966.

[69] Max Weber, "Politics As a Vocation" in *From Max Weber: Essays in Sociology*, trans. and ed. H. H. Gerth and C. Wright Mills (New York: Oxford University Press, 1958), p. 78.

constitute a direct physical threat to the regime, every effort is made to seek a resolution of political controversy through nonviolent means. The attempted seduction of counterelites is the technique most universally applied by the regime to co-opt and thus disarm its opponents. If these efforts are successful and the dissident is brought into the system, then the techniques of seduction must be continually maintained, both to prevent backsliding on the part of the newly co-opted and to appease those partisans of the regime who would resent not sharing in the largesse and recompense because of their loyalty. Consequently, the regime confronts (and satisfies) persistent demands for new bureaucratic positions bearing high prestige, high salaries, luxury imports, and the like, all necessary to maintain the status quo. Greater resources are needed merely to stand still.

If the efforts at seduction are not successful and the counterelite persist, then the regime hopes for a resolution through demoralization or depoliticization. These solutions are ultimately less acceptable than co-optation because they have proven to be only temporary adjustments to immediate political realities. Too often in the past, the university professors, bureaucrats, and *bazaari*s have devoted themselves to their professions when counterelite activities were dangerous. But with the removal of regime pressures, they renewed their political activities. Thus a slight letup in regime control frequently has led to widening and ultimately massive political agitation, emanating from what had appeared as a stable polity and society.

Only when the counterelites fail to adopt one of these means for coping with their hostilities to the regime or its programs are more decisive countermeasures employed. Exile for the more powerful or those with a political base, retirement for the older or less powerful, and imprisonment for the most threatening are the three most commonly employed techniques for excluding those who refuse either to change their ways or to exclude themselves. This pattern is revealed in the continuing efforts by the shah—extending over some six years—to keep the door to National Front co-optation open. If Front leaders would only accept him and renounce their manifestly complete alienation, he would welcome them. Each arrest of Front leaders was followed by his retreat and their release. Government posts were offered the Front, as were ministerial portfolios. But to the Front, the shah qua ruler, i.e., tyrant rather than constitutional monarch, is anathema and to accept a cabinet post under his rule would be "patriotically suspect."[70] Only when the shah felt that their alienation was total and that they would persist in attempts to act out that alienation did he move against them in a decisive fashion.

The regime, then, is reluctant to suppress counterelites before they

---

[70] Cottam, *Nationalism in Iran*, p. 300.

have been given several opportunities to "reform." This is partly responsible for the often noted phenomenon that arrests of elites for corruption or political misdeeds are never petty matters but involve millions of rials or crimes of high treason. An Iranian folk story puts it succinctly: A Persian once claimed to know Arabic. When asked what the Arabs called a cow, he offered their word. He was then asked what the Arabs called a calf. The man did not know but, typically, did not wish to admit his ignorance. He replied, "Well, the Arabs are patient people. They wait until the calves grow up and then they call them cows."[71] So it is with His Majesty's response to the political opposition.

[71] "Purge of the Corrupt Officials," *Mehre Iran* (Tehran), Dec. 30, 1964.

:4:

THE SHAHANSHAH OF IRAN

AND THE ELITE

Imperious, diligent, and fairly just, the Shah is in his own person the sole arbiter of Persia's fortunes.
Lord Curzon, *Persia and the Persian Question*

We have discussed the efforts that the shah makes to control demands for elite membership. By attempting to manage access to the resources that serve as the main power bases, he is able to regulate the numbers and types of persons who can present legitimate claims for inclusion into the political elite and, in turn, the types of demands that the elite will make of the political system. We have also noted the means he employs to deal with incorrigible elites who persist in making demands that he has defined as illegitimate. But how does he maneuver those who are members of the political elite? What is his type of governance vis-à-vis the khans, sheiks, emirs, mirzas—those who are the "governing class"?

DIVIDE ET IMPERA

The monarch's basic style can be described simply as *divide et impera* —a policy with a long and honored history in Iran. Perhaps the first Iranian to develop the technique to a sophisticated level was Darius the Achaemenid (who ruled 521–485 B.C.). He feared the concentration of power in the hands of his governors and the rebellion of distant provinces. To prevent this, Darius appointed a satrap, a general, and a secretary of state in each satrapy. All three officials were independent of each other and reported directly to Darius's court. Sykes suggests that "under this system of divided powers, the three great officials would be hostile to one another and consequently most unlikely to organize a rebellion.

As a further precaution, inspectors of the highest ranks were sent out at irregular intervals, supported by strong bodies of troops, and armed with full powers to investigate and punish any abuses and to report on the Satrap and other officials."[1] The extent of Mohammad Reza Shah's debt to Darius will become manifest in the course of the following discussion.

This policy of *divide et impera* was developed to still more refined levels by Shah Abbas, the great Safavid monarch (1587–1629). Shah Abbas feared the machinations of three sets of his subjects, and for each he applied a variant of the divide and rule policy. Safavid kings before him had learned to fear the *shahzadehs* (the royal princes and princesses) and even their ambitious sons. Shah Abbas set one against the other and nurtured their jealousies and rivalries, hoping to dissipate their energies in mutual conflict and to prevent their combining against him.[2] In addition to the children of the royal blood (whom he either blinded or executed), the shah feared the power of the tribal chiefs. In the first years of his reign, Shah Abbas had been a puppet in the hands of two of the Qizil-bash nobles, one of whom actually placed him on the throne.[3] He devoted considerable energies thereafter to playing off the chiefs of the Qizil-bash tribes. Those whom he could not neutralize in this fashion were eliminated by exile or death. He also created a new tribal military force, the Shahsevens, whose ranks were filled by recruiting from each of the seven Qizil-bash tribes. Their subsequent campaigns against the very tribes from which they were recruited eliminated the possibility of further tribal threats.

Finally, Shah Abbas devised an ingenious and apparently original scheme for applying his maxim among the politically unreliable city

[1] Sir Percy M. Sykes, *A History of Persia*, 2 vols. (London: Macmillan Co., 1921), 1: 162.

[2] Sykes relates the actions of Shah Abbas when the policy failed. He murdered the mistrusted:

> Safi Mirza, his eldest son, was the first victim. . . . The second son, Tahmasp Mirza, fortunately died a natural death; but shortly after the murder of Safi Mirza, the two remaining sons became objects of their father's dreadful jealousy. Khudabanda, the elder, had acquired much credit in an expedition to Arabia, and owing to his "affability, bounty, loyalty, courage and experience in arms, at home and abroad," was hailed as a promising successor to the throne. The Shah showed his displeasure by putting to death the Prince's tutor. Khudabanda hastened to court and expostulated wildly, going so far as to draw his sword. Thereupon his father had him blinded. The Prince became half insane, and in order to avenge himself killed Farima, a daughter on whom the Shah doted, and then himself took poison. The eyes of the fourth son, also, were put out, and by this act Shah Abbas cut off the last of his sons from the throne. (*Ibid.*, 2: 182–83.)

[3] The *Qizil-bash* ("red heads," from an unusual red headgear they fancied) was the name applied to the Turkish tribes in Iran who supported the early Safavids. See Edward G. Browne, *A Literary History of Persia*, 4 vols. (Cambridge: Cambridge University Press, 1953), 4:48.

dwellers who had proved a threat to previous Safavid kings. Shah Abbas countenanced factions within each town who were set against each other and encouraged to maintain high levels of tension and even conflict. The Jesuit Père Krusinski reports their names as Pelenk and Felenk and their conduct,

so opposite, and so much enemies one to the other, that people in different States, in arms against one another, do not push their aversion and enmity farther. . . . Though they fought without arms, because they were not supposed to make use of anything else but stones and sticks, it was with so much fury and bloodshed that the King was obliged to employ his guards to separate them with drawn swords. . . . At Ispahan in 1714 they were under a necessity, before they could separate the combatants, to put about three hundred to the sword on the spot.[4]

Sir Percy Sykes comments that while Shah Abbas's policy of divide and rule "greatly strengthened the power of the Crown, it undoubtedly conduced in the end to the weakening of the nation and the degeneration of its rulers."[5]

This was by no means the last instance whereby a Persian monarch created or stimulated dissensions among the leaders of groups perceived as menacing. A similar practice was the pillar of Qajar policy towards the tribes. Fath Ali Shah and subsequent Qajars made the creation of "tribal feuds into instruments of State policy."[6] And the artificial bifurcation of the politically aware urban population was fostered by the Qajars into the nineteenth century.

But if Iranian history is replete with elegant examples of this means for dealing with internal opposition or checking potential opposition, the present form of the policy constitutes a new level of sophistication. Its basic purposes are to prevent the formation of coalitions among the political elite that might challenge the supremacy of the king, and to prevent the rise to prominence of any single individual who could attempt to impose limits on the shah's power.

[4] As reported by Browne (*Literary History of Persia*, 4: 119–20), from *History of the Revolution of Persia*, 2 vols., by Father Krusinski, trans. Father du Cercea (Dublin, 1729), 1: 91–92. A later work on Persia (Jonas Hanway, *An Historical Account of British Trade Over the Caspian*, 4 vols. [London: Sold by Mr. Dodsley, 1753], 3: 32–33) refers to the two groups as Peleuk and Feleuk. They were later known as Haydari and Ni'mati.

[5] *History of Persia*, 2: 118. Sykes is undoubtedly correct in speaking of the degeneracy of later rulers. Lord Curzon mentions that "the later Safavi sovereigns . . . divided their existence in about equal proportions between the chase, the harem, and the bottle" (Lord George N. Curzon, *Persia and the Persian Question*, 2 vols. [London: Longmans, Green and Co., 1892], 1: 395.

[6] Ann K. S. Lambton, "Persian Society under the Qajars," *Journal of the Royal Central Asian Society*, 48 (April 1961): 130.

APPOINTMENT POLICIES

This *divide et impera* policy, whose overriding purpose is to prevent any diminution in the power of the monarch, has several components. One basic aspect is the appointment of personally antagonistic individuals as directors of major organizations within the Iranian government. The central institutions within the civil bureaucracy are the cabinet, the Senate, and the National Iranian Oil Company, powerful because of its control over Iran's petroleum wealth. Frequently these will be headed by personal enemies. A most notorious example of this was the recent period in which Assadollah Alam was the prime minister, Dr. Manouchehr Eghbal was head of the National Iranian Oil Company, and engineer Sharif Emami was president of the Senate. (With the premiership of Hoveyda, the relationships do not appear to have grown more cordial.) All three individuals represented widely varying social background and education. Eghbal and Emami were ex-prime ministers, and all, reputedly, nursed deep and mutual hostilities.

Previously, these mutual hostilities were introduced into the cabinet itself. But in recent years, efforts have been made to establish "party" governments. Beginning with the *Melliyun* party under Prime Minister Eghbal and, since 1964, the Iran Novin (New Iran) party under Hassan Ali Mansur and Amir Abbas Hoveyda, the prime ministers have been allowed to staff their cabinets with party men—a united "team."[7] Save for the Ministries of War and Foreign Affairs, which the shah continues to reserve for his sole jurisdiction, the factionalism formerly produced by appointments to the other posts has been reduced. Increasingly, the cabinet has begun to act as a more unified agency and conflicts now tend to exist between the cabinet and other parts of the bureaucracy, rather than within the cabinet itself.

A second component of the divide and rule policy is His Majesty's seeming penchant for shaking up personal relations within the administration by making surprise appointments. The king appears to delight in appointing individuals of low status to positions associated, in the minds of the elite, with high power. Conversely, high-status individuals are frequently assigned to posts not known for their importance. Several examples of this practice might be cited, although a most notorious example of the latter was the seconding of Assadollah Alam to Shiraz after his premiership. From 1962 to 1964, Alam had served the king by converting the turbulence of the Amini period to one of relative tranquility. He

---

[7] Perhaps because of the past glaring failures of Iranian organizations which required "team" spirit and cooperation, the mass media have taken to referring to the cabinet as the "prime minister's team." For an earlier study of the cabinet, see Leonard Binder "The Cabinet of Iran: A Case Study in Institutional Adaptation," *Middle East Journal*, 16 (Winter 1962): 29–47.

conducted the successful referendum and elections for the Majles and Senate which were unparalleled for their orderly and predictable outcome. When he was replaced by Mansur, Alam assumed the chancellorship of Pahlavi University. There, Alam was several hundred miles from the seat of power and in charge of an institution with slight connection to the bureaucracy and no prestige within it. But Alam still remained powerful. In fact, at the time the power attributions for this present study were made by the panel of ten, Alam had left Tehran for his new post. Yet he was one of only four individuals from a general elite of three thousand whom all ten rankers dubbed "politically very powerful."

The principal effect of this practice is that the individual so appointed intervenes in the administration at a level more commensurate with his personal power than his organizationally derived influence.[8] As a result, personal relationships within the bureaucracy are disturbed as administrators find their orders ignored and lower echelon personnel going over their heads. Formal communication and authority relationships—as defined by the organizational charts so assiduously constructed by the High Council on Government Administration—dissolve and organizational effectiveness is diminished. But from the perspective of His Imperial Majesty, these results are not necessarily untoward. While the capability of the bureaucracy is reduced and with it the efficiency with which the shah's reforms are effected, the ability of any bureaucratic agency to amass independent power or to combine with other agencies for the same purpose is reduced. The overlapping and nonsequential relationships seriously impede the development of unity that the bureaucracy would need to challenge the wishes of the king.

OVERLAPPING BUREAUCRATIC RESPONSIBILITIES

A third major component of the shah's style of rule is his penchant for "hedging his bets." Thus, responsibility for the performance of any task considered vital to the regime is never assigned to a single agency. No one bureaucrat or administrator will ever be allowed to amass power by dint of the fact that he alone can supply some wanted service or effect a desired end. The task of supplying intelligence to the regime is a relevant example. Accountability for gathering and interpreting intelligence on

[8] Individuals who are unusually powerful will frequently retain their high statuses even when dismissed from their important positions. If subsequently placed in a relatively minor post, they may demand and receive deference on the basis of their status rather than bureaucratic position. For a similar development in an American bureaucratic structure, see Philip Selznick, *TVA and Grass Roots: A Study in the Sociology of Formal Organization* (Los Angeles: University of California Press, 1953). Selznick details how the "agriculturalists" in TVA, by working with a local base of support and representatives on the board, were able to exert influence out of proportion to their organizational power.

internal and external political matters is not assigned to a single organization. Rather, a multiplicity of agencies are charged with gathering intelligence on similar matters.

The *Sazeman-e Ettela'at va Amniyate Keshvar* (State Security and Intelligence Organization) bears principal responsibility for general intelligence. (Established in 1957 with American aid and technical assistance, SAVAK has since developed closer collaboration with the Israelis.) The three directors of the organization all have been known for their unswerving loyalty to the king. But the first, General Bakhtiar, was dismissed amidst rumors of inciting rebellion. The second, General Pakravan, was assigned as ambassador to Pakistan amidst rumors of royal dissatisfaction with his leniency towards suspected traitors. The third and present chief, General Ne'matt'ollah Nassiri, might well succeed where each of his predecessors has failed. Nassiri was a classmate with the crown prince at the Military Academy and received his officer commission with the future shah. He demonstrated his loyalty and toughness by serving as commander of the Imperial Guards from 1950 and by carrying on activities against Prime Minister Mossadegh. It was Nassiri, then a colonel, who carried the shah's orders of dismissal to Mossadegh on August 16, 1953, and who ultimately found and arrested him after his escape from the armed forces besieging his house.

But even with these credentials, Nassiri is not entrusted with sole responsibility for intelligence. Nominally within the organizational framework of the *Sazeman* is a Special Intelligence Bureau, which is physically separate and financially independent. It is assigned the task of duplicating the work of SAVAK with regard to potentially serious threats to the regime. It is headed by General Hossein Fardust, who was not only a classmate with the future monarch and Nassiri, but was one of the Persian boys whom Reza Shah dispatched to Switzerland with his son. The shah has described him as a "special friend" during his childhood.[9]

Finally, the J-2 branch of the Imperial Iranian Armed Forces is charged with duplicating the function of both these organizations. Its head is General Azzizollah Kamal. Although not an early companion of the king, Kamal is generally regarded as totally loyal to the shah.

These men and their organizations duplicate each other's efforts. There is little likelihood that any important internal or external threats to the regime will escape unnoticed. Moreover, with at least three independent agencies, it is unlikely that any intelligence of importance will be held back from the ears of the monarch. In order to lessen this probability even further, His Majesty has regularly scheduled personal

[9] Mohammad Reza Shah Pahlavi, *Mission for My Country* (New York: McGraw-Hill, 1961), p. 54.

audiences with each of his intelligence chiefs. Thus, the overlapping of responsibility means that no one officer can become indispensable. No one officer can exert influence over the king because the responsibilities that he fulfills are unique or essential. The dismissal of any of the three would not submit the regime to any "intelligence gap."

And this overlapping of function is not restricted to the gathering of information vital to the survival of the regime. Similar practices exist elsewhere in the bureaucracy. There is a Ministry of Economy and another for Development and Housing. Labor unions are the concern of the minister of interior and the minister of labor. Responsibility for the Literacy Corps is assigned to the armed forces and the Ministry of Education.

THE SINGLE-PARTY SYSTEM

The vaunted single-party system for Iran was doomed to inevitable failure. Those who recognized the shah's desire for redundancy also realized that any single-party system would be anathema to him. And as it was unwelcome to him, its future was ominous. Shortly after the referendum of 1963, rumors percolated through Tehran political circles that a single-party system would be the logical outcome of the Rural Cooperative's Congress and the overwhelming unity demonstrated in the balloting. Further, the royal experiment with a controlled two-party system had been disastrous. What more logical, then, than a single, mass party? These rumors reached new heights when an article appeared in the press entitled, "A Single Party System for Iran," which was written by a foreigner conducting political research in Iran known to have met with the shahanshah and other political notables during that time.[10] Given the political cynicism and mistrust so widespread in the capital, it was generally assumed that the single-party plan had been devised in the offices of the United States State Department and the CIA, which then transmitted the plan to Iran by this specially delegated foreigner.[11] What-

[10] Richard H. Pfaff in *Echo of Iran—Monthly Review*, 1 no. 2 (Feb. 28, 1963): 19–24.

[11] The "fallout" resulting from American researchers becoming too involved in local politics was only too evident to this author. Arriving to conduct my research after the appearance of the article, I was initially taken as a replacement for the recently departed Dr. Pfaff. Several Iranian politicians assured me that American sponsorship for the generally unpopular Mansur and his party was "proven." They claimed to have been sounded out by various American diplomats, including, in one case, the United States ambassador himself. The Americans were reported to be investigating Iranian sentiments toward Mansur as prime minister as early as the spring of 1963, although he did not assume that office until March 1964. (Because my formal interviewing did not begin until December 1964, however, I believe that my credibility as a legitimate student of Iranian politics had been thoroughly established.)

ever the substance to these rumors, subsequent developments did not discredit them.

Hassan Ali Mansur, future leader of this party, like many of his fellow political aspirants, was then a member of a *dowreh* (circle) composed of contemporaries and familiars. The *dowreh* met regularly to discuss Iran's social and economic problems. Unlike other such groups, however, this one had been publicized as a study group and been dubbed the Progressive Center. Shortly after the appearance of Dr. Pfaff's article, this *dowreh* was further distinguished by being royally chartered as the Economic Research Bureau to the Imperial Court.[12] Earlier, Mansur had specified that his colleagues would play no role in Iranian politics. He insisted that his Progressive Center develop a "proper foundation and become naturally popular."[13] Apparently, the "foundation" that Mansur sought was not to be found in mass support. For mass support or even a firm base among the political elite would bear no relation to the fundamental source of political power in Iranian society—the shahanshah. Thus Mansur changed his attitude toward political activity with the granting of the royal charter. At a rally of the Progressive Center held shortly thereafter, Mansur announced that members of the Center could enter the coming elections of the Majles. He "hoped" that his candidates would "enjoy the support of . . . all those who believe in its aims."[14]

Late in the summer of 1963, the Congress of Free Men and Free Women of Iran was called, ostensibly to nominate candidates for the Majles. The candidates were to be broadly representative of the newly enfranchised female population, the recently landed peasantry, and workers scheduled to receive shares in the profits of factories. What transpired was three days of laudatory speeches followed by the submission of a list of nominees. This slate had been prepared by negotiations between Mansur and the Ministry of Interior.[15] Of the 193 candidates,

---

[12] The following is the text of the royal *Farman* (Charter) concerning the Progressive Center:

The body called the "Progressive Center" and composed of educated men, experts, intellectuals, and persons interested in deep and accurate studies in economic and social affairs for the welfare, comfort, progress, and prosperity of the Iranian people and homeland, enjoys our pleasure and satisfaction. In order to express our special favour and attention by This Charter, we hereby proclaim that the said Center has been appointed our Economic Research Bureau and that its members enjoy our special favour and attention.

(Text from *Peighame Emruz* [Tehran], June 5, 1963.)

[13] *Kayhan* (Tehran), Feb. 21, 1962.

[14] *Kayhan International* (Tehran), July 10, 1963.

[15] See Echo of Iran, "The 'New Iran' Party—Part I," *For Your Information*, no. 414 (Dec. 27, 1963), p. 5; and Echo of Iran, "The Progressive Center," *For Your Information*, no. 400 (Sept. 16, 1963), p. 5.

thirty-eight (including Mansur) were members of the Progressive Center. And in the subsequent elections, all were elected.[16]

The Majles held its first session in October, and although Alam retained the premiership, the Progressive Center had clearly captured the momentum. Its leader had already confidently declared, "When the Progressive Center forms the Cabinet, all the key posts in the Government will obviously go to Party members."[17] Majles members flocked to join the Progressive Center. Within two months, the Center boasted that 150 of the deputies had joined. And by December 15, Mansur announced the conversion of his Center into a New Iran party. In March 1964, Mansur was called by the king to form a new government. As Mansur had predicted, party members did hold all cabinet portfolios, save the ministers of war and foreign affairs.

Thus, only months after its founding, the Iran Novin party was in control of the cabinet and the Majles. The shah received the party Executive Committee in audience and Mansur reported to the press that the shah would assume "overall leadership" of the party.[18] Tehran was in an uproar. Not only had the vaunted single party been created; not only had the government devoted its resources to advancing the interests of that party; but the monarch himself would assume its direction. As in Egypt, Iraq, and Syria, and a host of other developing societies, Iran was to have a single, national political party. How, after all, could any opposition challenge a party whose leader was the king?

But both the uproar and a single-party system were apparently more than His Imperial Majesty intended. On the very next day, the Ministry of the Royal Court reported that there had been a "misunderstanding." An official transcript of the shah's statement was issued:

I am entrusted with leading the Iranian people, and without doubt, the large organization of the Iran Novin party . . . which has been mobilised to execute these high aims, has my support and interest.

I feel there is a bright future for the Iranian people, and will watch the prosperity of the liberated farmers, workers, women, and intellectuals in the framework of the new and just political organization.[19]

Clearly, His Majesty had backed off from unconditional support of Mansur and from willingness to lead the Iran Novin. A single party

---

[16] Critics of the elections argued that the slate of 193 candidates was almost unanimously elected because the balloting was held under the martial law imposed after the June riots. The martial law was not abrogated until October 23, 1963, after the elections and the convening of Parliament.

[17] Echo of Iran, *Iran Almanac, 1964–1965* (Tehran: Echo of Iran Press), p. 190. It is telling that Mansur was already talking of a "party" although he did not head such a group.

[18] *Kayhan International* (Tehran), May 31, 1964.

[19] *Ibid.*, June 1, 1964.

would be incompatible with his perpetual inclination to provide himself with a fallback position. The support of a single party, for example, would constrain him in a choice of prime minister and cabinet. Under such a system, it would be necessary to select his executive officials from amongst the secretary-general and deputy leaders of the party. But if he were to do this, His Majesty would no longer be a free agent in staffing his government. Also, the party would be unchallenged in its recruitment and the leaders of the party unencumbered by competition from other parties. But the competition and personal animosities of the leaders are essential for preventing any cohesion of opposition sentiment or resistance to the wishes of the shah.

The result was the communication to the leaders of a number of moribund political groupings that their political activities would once more be sanctioned. The *Melliyun* party immediately revised its platform to give the party "a more progressive program."[20] The *Mardom* party tightened discipline over its twelve-man Majles faction and announced a committee to draft a new party platform.[21] Subsequently, a new political party was founded with the shah's and managed to get a handful of its members elected to the Majles. The *Khak va Khun* (Land and Blood) party is now the principal vehicle for advancing Iran's irredentist claims over the Persian Gulf island of Bahrein and for protecting the rights of the Shi'ites and Kurds living in Iraq. None of these parties, however, was allowed the encouragement or resources accorded to the Iran Novin party. It was not His Majesty's goal to restore Iran to the political chaos of 1960–1961. These parties would be allowed to function—but only at a level insufficient to generate the turmoil of those earlier years when the experiment in a competitive two-party system had collapsed.

By supporting one major political party and encouraging a number of minor parties, the monarch has accomplished diverse ends. The governing party is always confronted with a viable alternative to its rule. They well appreciate that what is but an alternative at present would actually become their replacement were the shah displeased. By offering a number of legitimate channels for the expression of political interests (admittedly, a highly circumscribed set of political interests), the available loci for co-opting elites are enhanced. That is, there are now political parties as well as administrative positions into which potential counter-elites can be co-opted. Finally, by being allowed legitimate participation in the political system—in the Majles and the Senate, if not the cabinet—the opposition becomes sullied. These opposition parties collaborate with the government and "bargain with it while constantly jockeying to obtain

[20] *Ibid.*, June 15, 1964.
[21] For a report on this platform, see *ibid.*, Nov. 1, 1964.

more power."[22] As a result, while the National Front, the major opposition force, remains totally alienated and totally uninvolved, the active opposition has become discredited for its participation in the system. Corrupted by their very participation, they too are held responsible. And for their responsibility their utility as a focus for opposition to the regime is lessened. Thus, the Front has been forced to a position of quiescence while other opposition groups have been discredited for their involvement with the regime. As a result, no meaningful focus for grouping opposition activities remains.

THE SHADOW CABINET

Yet another means that His Imperial Majesty employs in order to divide and rule is that of the shadow cabinet. Just as institutions are assigned overlapping responsibilities and the directors of those institutions, ipso facto, have overlapping duties, so this is yet another way in which the king may "hedge." A member of the political elite will be asked to follow the activities of an organization or ministry within the bureaucracy. He will be provided with information on the finances and policies of that agency, its personnel, and the intentions of its chief. With this information, he will be expected to pass on the advisability of the policies and future plans being pursued by the actual director. Moreover, he is expected to be thoroughly familiar with the entire operations of the agency or ministry.

Dr. Manouchehr Eghbal is reputed to have filled this post of shadow director at the National Iranian Oil Company (NIOC) before he actually assumed formal office. As such, he was received in regularly scheduled audiences with the king, frequently having to return from Europe to do so. As the shadow director, he accomplished several important functions. He was able to offer His Majesty another educated, but hopefully less biased, opinion on the conduct of NIOC affairs than could the actual director. This facilitated the king's supervision of the oil company and his making key policy decisions regarding the exploration, production, and sale of petroleum and Iran's relation to the international oil consortium. The director's knowledge that another individual had the ear of the monarch with regard to his own responsibilities was thought to keep him alert, honest, and more conscientious. A more important result of this policy is that the director could be replaced and the shadow director brought from the wings with minimal disruption of the agency's affairs. Given the frequent personnel changes that the king imposes on

[22] This point about oppositions is made in a general way by Andrew Shonfield, "Politics and Poverty—On Professor Shils' 'Tutelary Democracy,'" *Encounter*, no. 133 (Oct. 1964), p. 58.

the bureaucracy, any contribution to continuity is beneficial. It complements the continuity provided by the king and conduces to the stability of the political systems.

THE RISE OF EXCEPTIONAL INDIVIDUALS

Another major component in the shah's divide and rule style is based on the uneasiness induced in him by the rise to prominence of institutions or individuals. He maintains constant supervision over the political process to allay that uneasiness. Individuals who become too powerful will be reduced in stature, by being reassigned, discredited, criticized in public, or, if need be, excluded from the political elite. Institutions that manifest the same characteristics will be subject to the same fate. The directors may be dismissed, the organization itself relieved of certain responsibilities, and under extreme conditions, the entire institution dismantled.

His Imperial Majesty is especially attentive to the rise to power of exceptional individuals. In this regard, exceptional can be defined as any member of the political elite possessing or potentially possessing an unusually high degree of charisma, personal popularity, or hostility towards the regime. It would be an exaggeration to suggest that the king followed the recommendation of Thrasybulus, ruler of Miletus, by discarding those who stand above their peers.[23] But His Majesty certainly deals with leaders or elites in an approximately similar spirit. Any self-styled censor of the shah can reel off the names of individuals dismissed from office and isolated from political currents. Invariably it is explained that many were subject to this fate because they were too "smart" or too "aggressive" or too "popular." What is meant is that they refused to remain in the penumbra of the imperial presence and were accorded, or at least sought, a personal following among significant numbers of Iranians. A feature of these lists, which any researcher into Iranian politics will uncover, is their overlap. On a surprising number appear the names of Dr. Mossadegh, Dr. Amini, Ebtehaj, Arsanjani, Allahyar Saleh, Engineer Mehdi Bazargan, Ayatollah Khomeini, and Dariush Foruhar, leader of one wing of the National Front. The names of others turn up with sufficient frequency to consider them as members of the same group. Abdol-

[23] Herodotus, *The Histories*, trans. Aubrey de Selincourt (London: Penguin Books, 1961), pp. 347-48. Periander ruled in Corinth and corresponded with Thrasybulus of Miletus:

Periander sent a representative to the court of this despot, to ask his opinion on the best and safest form of political constitution, and Thrasybulus invited the man to walk with him from the city to a field where the corn was growing. As he passed through this cornfield, continually asking questions about why the messenger had come to him from Corinth, he kept cutting off all the tallest ears of wheat [sic] which he could see, and throwing them away, until the finest and best-grown part of the crop was ruined.

lah Entezam, Ahmad Farhad, Dariush Homayoun, Mohammad Darakh-shesh, Khaleel Maleki, and Shoja ed-Din Malayeri are also reputed to have been demoted or isolated for being "exceptional" individuals.

Mohammad Darakhshesh. Mohammad Darakhshesh, for example, had been minister of education in Amini's cabinet. With Amini's fall in 1962, he too was dropped from formal office. Although he retains the title of member of the High Council of the Ministry for Education (and receives remuneration for that office), he has never been invited to a meeting of that august body—if such a meeting has been held. But he has been arrested since 1962 and his house has been kept under surveillance. Why should a minister of education be accorded this unusual treatment?

Darakhshesh was more than an ordinary civil servant. After graduating from the Tehran Teachers' Training College and Tehran University, he entered government service as a secondary school teacher. He formed the Association of Teachers' Training College Graduates and used it successfully in a teachers' strike for higher wages in 1949. Later in the year, the association and its magazine, *Mehregan*, were banned, along with other political parties, after the abortive assassination attempt on the life of the shah. But this was not the end for Darakhshesh. With the *sholugh* (turmoil) preceding the oil nationalization, the group was back, switching its affiliation from the Tudeh party to Khaleel Maleki's socialists.

In the early years, Darakhshesh sided with Mossadegh, but later broke with him and threw in his lot (and that of his association) with the shah. Not surprisingly, Darakhshesh's name was among the successful candidates to the Eighteenth Majles, the first elected after Mossadegh's overthrow. To the amazement of many, however, he refused a passive role in the Parliament. Darakhshesh gave several impassioned speeches from the floor of that chamber, opposing the prospective agreement with the international oil consortium. He supported the National Front and castigated the landlords for their reactionary political policies. Thus, as might be expected, his failure to be re-elected to the Majles naturally followed. Darakhshesh went back to teaching, to publishing his journal, and to organizing the teachers. In the chaotic spring of 1961, it was the teachers' organization that demonstrated before the Majles. And it was the killing of one of the teacher-demonstrators that resulted in the fall of Sharif Emami and the investiture of Amini.

To placate this well-organized and aroused group of teachers, the shah agreed to Darakhshesh's inclusion in the cabinet. It ought to have been obvious, however, that with the return of political autonomy to the throne, the "exceptional" individuals would be dismissed. Darakhshesh was one of those individuals, primarily because he had been able to construct a base of power distinct from the throne. Moreover, that base—

the teachers' organization—was sufficiently vigorous to permit his demanding and receiving a cabinet portfolio. With Amini's fall, therefore, the regime struck back. The Association of Teachers' Training College Graduates was disbanded. Its club house was closed and shuttered. The publication of *Mehregan* was suspended. Characteristically, though ruined as a political figure, Darakhshesh was not ruined as an individual. He received a new post at the Ministry and was allowed to return to his home. Insofar as he shuns political activity, he is permitted this relative freedom. But allegations of his political involvement and the detention of the mass of political figures following political disturbances have resulted in his periodic arrest. Nonetheless, there is no reason to assume he will continue to be harassed if he can but learn, at the age of fifty-two, to live the sedate life of a retired homebody.

Shoja ed-Din Malayeri. Other individuals have tried to have it both ways. They have tried to build a power base other than the graces of His Imperial Majesty while retaining his support by constantly professing their loyalty and fidelity to the throne. Shoja ed-Din Malayeri is such an individual. Malayeri was born and educated in Tehran, receiving a degree from its university. After graduation, he entered the bureaucracy and held a variety of posts, including director of the Translation Department of the Ministry of Agriculture, chief inspector of the Ministry of Interior, member of the High Council for Electricity, and finally deputy minister of interior.

With that title, he was appointed director of the *Sherkate Sahamiye Vahede Autobus* (United Bus Company) of Tehran. The UBC was established by the Majles in 1952. Its charter specified that the owners of existing buses were to place these vehicles under government ownership in return for shares in the new corporation. The fierce resistance of Tehran's independent operators kept the law a dead letter until 1956. Then a new law was passed and General Alavi Moqadam, chief of the national police, assumed the additional duties of organizing the UBC. Under his aegis, the new company commenced operations in June 1963, "amidst appropriate ceremonies."[24] After taking shape under its powerful chief, the job was passed to Malayeri, who imported new buses and expanded their routes while raising fares. But the more relevant program that he undertook was the political organization of the bus drivers. As the reforms from the throne were publicized and their implementation begun, more and more rallies were held—to mobilize and inform public opinion and to demonstrate public solidarity with the shahanshah. And when the initial preoccupations of 1963 were transformed to the zealous-

[24] Safa Haery, "Drastic Changes Needed in Tehran Bus Service," *Kayhan International* (Tehran), Aug. 3, 1964.

ness of 1964, Malayeri's bus drivers were ever more in evidence. They were ideally suited for the role of public demonstrators. Being dependent on the UBC for their incomes, they were easily marshaled to attend meetings. Being bus drivers, they were able to provide their own transportation. (Caravans of buses loaded with bus drivers going to yet another welcoming ceremony or parade became commonplace.) Finally, the income of the UBC allowed Malayeri to employ more than two thousand bus drivers, a substantial surplus being available to serve as vociferous *shah-parastis*. The result was that the director of the UBC had constructed a disciplined force of highly mobile, able-bodied male demonstrators. They were frequently used in the service of the regime and aided the regime's efforts to generate public support for its reforms. But professions of loyalty and demonstrated support of the throne were insufficient to overcome the shah's profound distrust of political figures who possess independent bases of power. As with Arsanjani and Darakhshesh, Malayeri was suspect because of his leadership of organized followers available for political purposes. While the first led peasants, the second, teachers, and the third, bus drivers, all presented fundamentally the same dilemma to the king. All were dealt with accordingly. Malayeri was appointed as director of the Iran Fisheries Company, charged with developing the caviar of the Caspian and the seafood of the Persian Gulf.

The above is not to suggest that no individuals of unusual talent are allowed to function in the bureaucracies. There are numerous examples of capable, well-trained, and efficient civil servants. But these so-called technocrats must pay a price in order to serve—the price of becoming depoliticized or apolitical. Some individuals have demonstrated their ability to withdraw from political activities to fill technical positions in the bureaucracy. Others have firm reputations for the apolitical pursuit of their responsibilities. In this latter category, Mehdi Sami'i and Dr. Khodadad Farmanfarmaian may be mentioned. As director of the Central Bank and director of the Plan Organization, the two have been most successful in remaining outside many of the political currents of the capital. While they are both regarded as followers and supporters of Ebtehaj, neither has allowed that relation to interfere with his responsibilities for directing the planning and fiscal fates of Iran. In return both have been rewarded by their successes in building their organizations to unchallenged positions of expertise and competence as well as by the statuses and other rewards that are their due.

It needs to be made explicit that "depoliticized" and "apolitical" are actually misnomers. In the Iranian context, these two concepts refer to the withdrawal from any activities that the shah would consider actually or potentially injurious to his regime. Failure to pursue those activities while filling key posts in the bureaucracy is certainly not being "nonpolitical," therefore. Rather, they are highly political acts in the sense that the satisfactory management of a central bank, for example, is an important contribution to the longevity and security of the throne. They are only "nonpolitical" in the sense of not challenging that throne with regard to the distribution of values in Iranian society.

DECISION MAKING

There are a number of additional techniques that the shah employs to complement the divide and rule tactics that remain the basis of this governing style. One such technique is the effort to force communications within the bureaucracy in vertical rather than horizontal lines. Both intra-agency and interagency communications are meant to be basically hierarchical—between levels—rather than horizontal—between divisions. Even the most petty information, intelligence, and problems are communicated upwards for decision making while orders are communicated downward for execution.

Whenever possible, decisions are made at the apex of each bureaucratic structure. While the efficiency of the bureaucracy is thereby diminished, so are the possibilities that decisions considered perverse by the shah will be made. Similarly, there is a greater likelihood that His Majesty may thereby play a personally decisive role in the decision-making process. To abet this likelihood, the king is physically present for the making of major administrative decisions whenever possible. This is accomplished in two ways.

As often as is feasible, the cabinet of ministers meets in the imperial presence.[25] The king often takes charge of these meetings both to remain abreast of developments in each ministry and to be able to participate in the making of decisions. The decisions, having been pushed up the bureaucratic hierarchy, must be settled at the interministerial level, rather than by consultations between lower level officials of the different ministries. And it is at sessions of the cabinet that the principal interministerial decisions are taken.

Having already been made aware of many relevant issues through audiences with the shadow ministers and through the reports of SAVAK, the king is at no disadvantage in terms of information. On the contrary, because communication within the bureaucracy tends to remain within vertical lines, a minister is frequently unaware of important affairs occurring outside his own bailiwick. When confronting the shahanshah, then, the ministers are not only cognizant of the constitutional power of

[25] Leonard Binder (*Iran: Political Development in a Changing Society* [Berkeley: University of California Press, 1962], p. 118) relates that the shah meets with the cabinet only once out of three weekly meetings. While this was true for earlier periods, the king has attempted to be present more frequently in recent years.

the monarch to dismiss them but also of his superior information. He possesses knowledge of factors outside their own agencies that bear on them as well as factors internal to their agencies and thus central to their concerns.

An example of the shah's intervening in a session of the cabinet to retain his decision-making capability—an atypical instance of such intervention, for it proved disastrous—occurred in late 1964. As the year passed, it became obvious that Iran was entering a financial crisis. A burst of renewed economic activities spurred by government spending was meant to pull the country out of the economic depression of 1960. The result, however, was that:

Pressure on domestic resources and considerable increase in the demand for consumer goods led to an unprecedented increase in imports and a sharp rise in prices. Expansion of bank credit to the private sector resulted in a "liquidity squeeze" for the banking system. . . .

Government's fiscal operations failed to mop up the extra purchasing power in the hands of the public.[26]

By the month of November, it was clear that a dangerous monetary crisis was imminent. In the preceding three months, the price of flour, bread, and rice—staples of the Iranian diet—had risen 10.1 per cent.[27] Meanwhile, the government found that its receipts in the first nine months of the year had fallen 4.6 per cent, while its disbursements had risen 2.5 per cent over a similar period a year previous.[28] Rather than the predicted budget surplus of $34 million, a $60 million deficit loomed. The deficit for the next year was predicted at $233 million.[29] And finally, there was a decline in government holdings of foreign exchange of $38 million, versus an increase of $24 million in 1963.[30] Meanwhile, throughout the year, the Plan Organization had heightened the crisis. While the Third Plan had covered 41 per cent of its life span by the end of November 1964, the Plan Organization had spent only 23 per cent of its budgeted outlays. But as 1964 had progressed, the Plan Organization was spending greater and greater sums on nondevelopment spending, aggravating the trends.

His Majesty's response was not untypical. He established several committees to study the question. Within the Plan Organization, the Central

[26] Bank Markazi Iran (Central Bank of Iran), *Bulletin*, 3, no. 16 (Nov.-Dec. 1964): 690. Also see George B. Baldwin, *Planning and Development in Iran* (Baltimore: Johns Hopkins Press, 1967) for a detailed examination of the origins of this crisis.

[27] Bank Markazi Iran, *Bulletin*, 4, no. 17 (Jan.-Feb. 1965): 719.

[28] Plan Organization Director Engineer Safi Asfia in the *Tehran Journal*, Dec. 3, 1964.

[29] Bank Markazi Iran, *Bulletin*, 3, no. 16 (Nov.-Dec. 1964): 723.

[30] *Ibid.*, p. 727.

Bank, and the Ministry of Finance, study groups were at work. An inter-cabinet group surveyed the same problem. By November, the reports were in and, as might be suspected, a wide variety of policies was suggested. All centered about the need to diminish the purchasing power of the private sector while raising government revenues and limiting the spending of the public sector to essentials and developmental outlays. At a four-hour cabinet session on November 23, 1964, the ministers voted to raise the prices on a number of products over which the government had a monopoly.

The shah is reported to have intervened and demanded a firmer stand. He specified that the 40 per cent rise in gasoline prices urged by the ministers on the basis of their studies was too lenient. "Let them pay double," he is reported to have commented. Gasoline went from 5 to 10 rials per liter. Whereas the cabinet had urged a modest hike in the price of kerosene—the fuel used by the vast majority of Iranians for heating, lighting, and cooking—the king set the rise at 1 rial per liter, from 2.5 to 3.5 rials.[31] And so it was with a number of other commodities. When the concerted conclusions of the experts had not satisfied the king, he demanded and was accorded the more radical action he favored.

It was for the hapless prime minister to announce the new price rises to a silenced Majles. Mansur declared:

I must unfortunately say that the increase in our national income is very inadequate and has not kept pace with the population increase. . . .

Our economic course is an inflexible one. . . . When Governments are engaged in the execution of . . . a White Revolution . . . they have to take basic decisions and apply drastic measures. . . . We must have a great motto for building a new Iran. This motto should be a "National Crusade for Progress."[32]

But the price rises for gasoline and oil were not the sole changes. New taxes were announced for Iranians wishing to travel abroad, on soft drinks, and on alcohol. The Ministry of Finance ordered a pay freeze and the rescinding of salary increases. The Majles imposed new municipal taxes on diesel motor vehicles and other services. Government ministries, as so often in the past, were forbidden to hire new personnel.

The public reaction was immediate and vehement. A general strike was called, and taxi drivers pulled their taxis off the streets and refused to work. But 1964 was not 1961, and vigorous police measures brought all but the most recalcitrant taxi drivers back to the streets. A more

[31] It is interesting that the price of diesel fuel was not raised. The government was attempting to placate the private sector into increasing its investment for industrial development.

[32] Hassan Ali Mansur, speech to the Majles delivered November 24, 1964, quoted from *Kayhan International* (Tehran), Nov. 25, 1964.

devastating public response occurred, however—a marked drop in public consumption of gasoline and kerosene.[33] Not only had sales fallen off, but they had plummeted to the point where revenues of the NIOC were expected to decline, despite the doubling in the price of gasoline and the 40 per cent rise in the kerosene price. Whereas the shah had counted on an additional 7 billion rials per year in new revenues, NIOC officials began to predict a drop in their annual income from domestic sales of 500 million rials.[34]

Seven weeks after the price rises, on January 13, 1965, Mansur went before the Majles and reported that a new agreement with the oil consortium would supply Iran with additional revenues. As a result, the government was rescinding the price rise on kerosene and dropping the price of gasoline from 10 rials to 8 per liter. While a new agreement had been signed for offshore oil production, it was the decline in revenues and the profound public dissatisfaction that motivated the shah to relent on the price rises. But his decision was too late. Eight days later, Hassan Ali Mansur was assassinated on his way into the Majles. And in April, an abortive attempt was made on the life of the shah. While there was no direct link between the two events, it was unquestionably the milieu of discontent and malaise permeating all Tehran, but especially the poorer sections surrounding the bazaar, that spawned the assassins. The driver of a Tehran taxi spoke for many Persians when he responded to a question from the author about the late Mansur: "What is it to me? Bread! Bread to eat every day is what matters. This prime minister, that prime minister. We must eat!"

The fuel price hikes were one example of the intervention of the king in the decision-making process of the bureaucracy. Lucian W. Pye has

[33] This form of political pressure is not uncommon in Iran. It resembles the response to Naser ed-Din Shah's granting a concession for a tobacco monopoly to an English company. With the issuance of a religious decree forbidding the consumption of tobacco, consumption fell off to the point where the shah was forced to cancel the concession. (See Nikki R. Keddie, *Religion and Rebellion in Iran: The Tobacco Protest of 1891–1892* [London: Frank Cass and Co., 1966].) The closing of their shops by bazaar merchants is a similar policy. But with the relative decline in the economic importance of the bazaars, this has recently proved inefficacious. Thus, following the June 1963 riots, the government gave all merchants twenty-four hours to reopen their shuttered shops. After the expiration of the deadline, noncompliers found that the army had entered the bazaars and completely bricked up their storefronts. Another recent example of these passive techniques was a consumer strike in Isfahan which protested the rise of electricity rates by illuminating homes with lamps and candles. Such passive means of protest are not only safe but seem in accord with a general cultural disdain for violence.

[34] *Khushe* (Tehran), Jan. 3, 1965. Within a week government economists were explaining the drop in revenues succinctly. Some 30 per cent of all gasoline used within Iran was estimated to be consumed in government-owned vehicles. The government agencies do not pay the posted prices, however. Therefore the drop in private consumption was truly phenomenal (*Donya* [Tehran], Jan. 9, 1965).

offered an explanation for such behavior of the shah, which appears to the outside observer as nonrational as this action. Pye explains that an absolute monarch must occasionally behave in an illogical fashion to demonstrate that it is he, the monarch, who rules and not logic, not rationality, and certainly not the dictates of "planning and programming and budgeting."[35] Whatever the explanation, it seems certain that the decision was unwise and ill-conceived. The regressive nature of the price rises and the depths of public passions resulted in a highly elastic demand for fuels. Consequently, none of the crises that originally prompted the price rises were allayed and new measures had to be taken in 1965, primarily another approach to the oil consortium.

In addition to the cabinet meetings over which the shah presides, he fosters his dominant role in the decision-making process by maximizing the number of face-to-face communications he has with key individuals in the bureaucracy. The shah maintains a calendar that establishes regular weekly audiences with ministers and directors of key institutions within the government, like the NIOC, the Central Bank, and the University of Tehran. These officials are received in private audience to report their activities over the week and to discuss key decisions with the king. But his many private audiences are not limited to these responsible officials, for the king also regularly sees his shadow administrators and a number of personal acquaintances. Assadollah Alam, for example, would be seen regularly on this basis. Seyyed Jalal ed-Din Tehrani is reported to be a frequent visitor to the palace. The Seyyed is a senator, but more relevantly, an astrologer, and it is claimed by some that he is occasionally consulted. A select few venerated, aged members of the political elite are also regularly received by the king. Until his death recently Seyyed Zia ed-Din Tabatabaie, who staged the 1921 coup with Reza Khan, was reported to discuss contemporary political affairs with the king two and three times a week. The shahanshah also sees a group from the political elite for recreation. He is fond of social card games and a clique of elite members are his fellow players. Dr. Jamshid A'alam is perhaps the most known of His Majesty's gaming associates. Finally, the king sees a number of the princes and princesses on a regular basis, especially for social events and movies at the palace.

[35] Personal communication to the author, May 12, 1968. Also, Gerschenkron has made the same point: "When Stalin, during his night vigils in the Kremlin used to telephone–in the small hours of the morning–factory managers and party bureaucrats throughout the huge country, inquiring, commanding, and threatening, he knew well that incessant and arbitrary intervention of dictatorial power is one of the conditions of its stability" ("On Dictatorship," *New York Review of Books*, 12, no. 12 [June 19, 1969]: 4). For two perceptive analyses of dictatorship see his "The Changeability of Dictatorship," and "The Stability of Dictatorships," in his *Continuity in History and Other Essays* (Cambridge: Harvard University Press, 1968), pp. 281–343.

There are, then, a variety of types among the political elite who share the honor of frequent meetings with His Imperial Majesty. His ministers, administrators, advisers, friends, and relatives all explicitly or implicitly serve to keep His Imperial Majesty at the very nucleus of the Iranian political system. Astride the formal and informal channels of communication, he is party to the information on which that political system operates. By integrating that information and by maintaining frequent and periodical personal contact with the government elite, the shahanshah is able to dominate the decision-making processes of the government.

CORRUPTION

There are, however, two additional components to His Majesty's style of rule that complete the picture of his dominance: the tolerance or even encouragement of corruption and the possession of a monopoly over the means of physical violence. Corruption is not a latter-day phenomenon in Persian politics. Herodotus and Plutarch both mention early instances of corruption, especially in the conduct of foreign affairs.[36] Its presence and durability are even celebrated in Persian poetry:

> In Persia will bribes ever go out of fashion, O Kablay?
> Will the mullas for justice develop a passion, O Kablay?
> From magic and murshids can Islam win free?
> Bid the dead come to life, for 'twill easier be,
> You limb of the devil and son of a gun, O Kablay.[37]

Indeed, there are many members of the elite who argue that corruption has always been endemic in Persian society, but only recently have the venality, unscrupulousness, and turpitude that were once accepted been considered evil. As one person put it: "What was an accepted administrative practice in the past is now branded corrupt."

While these practices may be branded corrupt at present, there is no

---

[36] Plutarch, for example, explains a victory of Artaxerxes in such a fashion. Artaxerxes, surnamed the "Thoughtful," ruled from 404 to 358 B.C. and defeated Xenophon and his legions of Ten Thousand. Of another campaign, Plutarch writes: "Artaxerxes, perceiving what was his wisest way of waging the war, sent Timocrates the Rhodian into Greece, with large sums of gold, commanding him by a free distribution of it to corrupt the leading men in the cities, and to excite a Greek war against Sparta. So Timocrates following his instructions, the most considerable cities conspiring together, and Peloponnesus being in disorder, the ephors remanded Agesilaus from Asis" (Plutarch, *The Lives of Noble Grecians and Romans*, trans. John Dryden [New York: Random House, Modern Library, n.d.], p. 1263).

[37] By the Persian poet Dakhaw (Deh Khoda) of Qazvin. The poem first appeared in the weekly *Sur-E Israfil*, one of a number of publications that sprang up at the time of the Persian Revolution. See Edward G. Browne, *Press and*

doubt that they continue to exist. But there has been a major metamorphosis in the form of their occurrence. As with so many other features of the society, corruption has been brought under the control of the center and is now used as a major counter in the co-optation process, that is, in the seduction of the elite.[38] The immense enlargement of government revenues and resources over which the monarch has control has facilitated that process. Combined with the growth of central political power, these resources have made it possible for the government to dominate totally the economic as well as the social life of the nation. As a result, there are a greater number of extensive projects with vast cash flows in the control of the government. If the opportunities for rewarding friends have been prodigious, the occasions for silencing enemies are no less Cyclopean.

But concurrent with the availability of these immense resources, there has come a reduction in the need for the shah to sanction such corruption. The throne is far more powerful and secure than it has ever been before. While Reza Shah's hold over the crown, for example, was relatively firm, he was able to exercise less power than his son as the instruments for the exercise of such power—the civil and military bureaucracies—were less developed, while other institutions outside kingly control—the tribes and the Islamic clergy—were far more powerful. Thus the need for that ruler to seduce more of the members of his elite and counterelite was in all probability far greater than at present.

In short, the need for the shah to sanction corruption has been reduced while his capabilities for doing so have been enhanced as the relative and absolute value of his largesse to the corrupted is greater than in the past. The results of these conflicting pressures are difficult to assess. What appears to have happened is a general diminution in the rewards allowed the counterelite. The shah no longer *needs* to accord deference to those opposition elements to preserve his rule. The Persian poet Sa'adi had counseled otherwise:

Poetry in Modern Persia (Cambridge: Cambridge University Press, 1914). Kablay refers to one who has made the pilgrimage to Karbala and is used here as a general expletive.

[38] Apparently, various forms of corruption have been used for years in the co-optative process, but especially co-optation by foreign powers. In 1920, the British were burdened by the size of the monthly payments they were making to co-opt Ahmad Shah Qajar and the Iranian government. The British ambassador cabled to Lord Curzon that "if certain kinds of expenditures (especially mensualities [monthly bribes paid to critics of the government to silence their opposition]), which are in fact illegal had not been sanctioned, deficit and amount of British subsidy required would be *pro tanto* decreased" (Rohan Butler and J. P. T. Bury, *The Near and Middle East, January 1920–March 1921*, Documents on British Foreign Policy 1919–1939, 1st series, vol. 13 [London: Her Majesty's Stationery Office, 1963], p. 532).

A vicious fellow's mouth must utter words.
If thou desirest not bitter words, sweeten his mouth.[39]

The shah no longer must "sweeten mouths" to silence opponents.

There appears, on the other hand, to have been no lessening in the willingness of the shah to reward members of the elite. Although there has been a precipitous decline since 1962–1963 in reported incidents of corruption, this is generally assumed to reflect a lack of interest in uncovering such occurrences rather than a lack of suitable cases. We have mentioned above that allegations of corruption are frequently used to dismiss and even prosecute officials suspected of political disloyalty. With the renewed political calm of the Alam era, the need for such prosecutions has diminished. It is far more likely, and generally accepted, that many officials enjoy the cream from the top of government expenditures. If they do, their conduct is tolerated by the regime as one of the prices of political stability.

THE ARMED FORCES

Perhaps the final and most obvious means available to the king for manipulating the behavior of his subjects is the use of physical force. The British officials who complained in 1920 of the "mensualities" being paid to the Qajar monarchs also noted that "the present system of Government, in absence of moral and material force, relies on bribery and repression."[40] It would be incorrect to suggest that His Majesty continues to "rely on repression." The "moral" and "material" foundations of his regime are more secure than ever before and physical repression is not a manifest part of his style of governance. Rather, a twofold process has been occurring in Iranian politics since 1960. On the one hand, there has been a marked reduction in the physical presence of the armed forces in their role of defender of the regime, while the intervention of members of the armed forces in the civilian political process has increased. On the other hand, the king has developed unchallenged control over the instruments of physical violence while those instruments have, in turn, asserted their claims of unassailable physical power over other institutions in the society.

As recently as fifty years ago, the armed forces of Iran consisted primarily of a Cossack Brigade staffed with Russian officers operating in the northern provinces and a Household Guard for the court. There also existed, on paper, a regular standing army of forty thousand men, but one observer described that force as "beneath contempt. At least a dozen

[39] *Gulistan* [The rose garden], trans. Edward Rehatsek (New York: Capricorn Books, 1966), p. 91.
[40] Butler and Bury, *Near and Middle East*, p. 537.

different patterns of rifles constitute their armament, consisting of match-locks, flintlocks, sniders, Martinis, obsolete Russian guns, and a portion of a cargo of nondescript description that was seized some years ago in the Persian Gulf. When it is added that there is not a round of ammunition to fit any of the above weapons, some idea of the value of these 40,000 men may be formed."[41] In fact these troops were useless to the Qajar regime and to the Nationalists in the Constitutional Revolution and its aftermath. The two most powerful military forces in the country at that time proved to be Bakhtiari tribesmen under the command of Samsam ol-Saltaneh and a troop of volunteers led by the Armenian Ephraim Khan, of Tabriz. To the honor of both groups, and especially the latter, is their responsibility for preserving the constitutional regime and preventing the return to power of the deposed tyrant, Mohammad Ali Shah Qajar.

But other military forces were soon created. A Treasury Gendarmerie was established by the American treasurer general of Iran, Morgan Shuster, in 1911. With Russian pressures and British acquiescence, however, Shuster was dismissed in 1912 and a new gendarmerie was formed with Swedish advisers.[42] Then, during World War I, the Persian government succumbed to British demands. The cabinet agreed to a British-organized and -officered force, the South Persia Rifles, to protect British trade routes in the south as well as to act as a quid pro quo for the military presence of other nations. The ever-tenuous internal security of Iran rested, then, on Swedish-led gendarmes, British-led Persia Rifles, and Russian-led Cossacks.[43] When the officers commanding this last force

---

[41] Donald Stuart, *The Struggle for Persia* (London: Methuen and Co., 1902), pp. 183-84. Stuart describes a victorious campaign conducted by this "army" as follows:

> That the general efficiency of the army is not of a high order may be instanced. On the last occasion on which its services were required, it took twenty days to mobilise and then only 20,000 men rallied to the standard. This was during the Kurd rebellion when that warlike tribe ravaged the country for miles around; nor was the advance made for a further period of three months, as every general insisted on taking his division by a different route until sanction was given for a "go as you please" advance! Meanwhile the Kurds having concluded their business, had returned to their homes, and the army on arrival, finding no enemy to confront, returned to Tehran. Medals were lavishly distributed to commemorate this glorious campaign.

(*Ibid.*, p. 177.)

[42] For Shuster's own provocative account of his ultimately unsuccessful mission, see his *The Strangling of Persia: A Record of European Diplomacy and Oriental Intrigue* (London: T. Fisher Unwin, 1912). See also Robert A. McDaniel, "The Shuster Mission and the Culmination of the Persian Revolution of 1905–1911" (Ph.D. diss., University of Illinois, 1966).

[43] For various accounts of the inauguration and operations of the South Persia Rifles see Christopher Sykes, *Wassmuss: "The German Lawrence"* (London: Longmans, Green and Co., 1936); Sir Clarmont Skrine, *World War in Iran* (London:

were recalled to Russia during the 1917 Revolution, a Persian colonel, Reza Khan, achieved command. But under him neither the military nor Iran itself was to be the same.

For Reza Shah, as he was later known, was the first ruler of Iran "who instinctively understood the lesson of European history—the emergence of a unified national state coincides with the development of a standing national army."[44] Putting aside the preferences of past rulers for armed forces composed of separate fighting units, Reza Shah's policies of national development created a Westernized, unified army.[45] "This army was capable of maintaining the absolute authority of the central government throughout Iran—a condition that had not existed in the country for centuries."[46] The military proved unable to defend Iran against the foreign aggression of 1941, however. Invading British and Russian troops effectively destroyed Reza Shah's hard-won military gains in a matter of days.

Nonetheless, the new shah was quick to appreciate the importance of the army, both to himself as a ruler and to an Iran subject to centrifugal pressures. Immediately upon taking office, he devoted himself and the resources of his country to rebuilding the shattered army. In 1943, for example, a budgetary crisis forced the shah to spell out his priorities. The American financial adviser Arthur Millspaugh urged a reduction in size of the ninety thousand-man standing army. Millspaugh relates: "I told the Shah that if the Army budget were increased we could do little if anything for agriculture, education, or public health. He said: 'Very well, then; we'll have to postpone those things.' "[47]

The priorities for the expenditure of Iran's national wealth have remained relatively stable since that time. The shah has resisted the pressures exerted by Dr. Mossadegh, other opposition politicians, and the Americans, as well as those of subsequent financial crises. His public position has also been remarkably consistent. In a major statement of his policies broadcast throughout Iran immediately after the death of Mansur, the shah succinctly stated his views towards the military:

Constable and Co., 1962), pp. 1–67; and Sir Percy Sykes, *History of Persia*, 2: 451–540. Sir Percy Sykes, the historian, is none other than Brigadier General Sykes, the commander of the South Persia Rifles. For information on the early years of the Cossack Brigade, see Firuz Kazemzadeh, "The Origin and Early Development of the Persian Cossack Brigade," *American Slavic and East European Review*, 15 (1956): 342–53.

[44] Amin Banani, *The Modernization of Iran, 1921–1941* (Stanford: Stanford University Press, 1961), p. 54.

[45] For an indigenous account of Reza Shah's military policies, see Malek ol-Sho'ara Bahar, *Tarikh-e Azab-e Siasi* [A history of political parties], 2 vols. (Tehran: Amir Kabir Publishers, 1944), vol. 2, passim.

[46] Banani, *Iran*, p. 57.

[47] Arthur C. Millspaugh, *Americans in Persia* (Washington, D.C.: Brookings Institution, 1946), p. 105n.

In any case, God willing, our future is so bright that we should not neglect even for a moment the means of attaining it. Despite all the confidence we have in our political alliances, we must not, even for a moment, neglect to strengthen our defense forces until the day when there is a reliable general disarmament in the world, especially because we occasionally note some weakening and wearing off of the United Nations Organization and also because we hear of certain insolence against our interests.[48]

As a result, the Imperial Iranian Armed Forces have consistently grown in size, been equipped with modern weapons, and been charged with the performance of vital nonmilitary functions.

When in 1921 Reza Khan led his Cossack troops from Qazvin to the capital, his columns numbered between 1,500 and 3,000 men.[49] Several hundred troops formed a Royal Guard. Perhaps an additional few thousand Iranians armed as border guards and gendarmes were loosely under central control. With this, Reza Shah began his reforms. He unified all the disparate forces, dissolved the Cossacks and South Persia Rifles, and increased the number of men under arms. In the first year following his accession to the throne, he devoted 43 per cent of his government's expenditures to the Ministry of War,[50] a proportion that was to remain nearly as high during his entire rule. With these funds, he enlarged the army in successive stages to a force of 100,000 men by 1941.

Following the invasion, Millspaugh sought to persuade the new king that the collapse of the army before the foreign invaders demonstrated the utter prodigality of maintaining a large force. While Millspaugh argued, however, the shah insisted on "at least 90,000."[51] The number has never diminished since. By the time of Amini's premiership, Iran could boast a standing army of 200,000 men, larger than the armies of either West Germany or Japan, although the dictates of the country's

[48] From the official text of the royal message delivered on January 26, 1965, the day of Mansur's death and the second anniversary of the national referendum (Ministry of Information, *Facts About Iran*, no. 209, p. 18). The shah has made more specific references to the "insolence" against Iran's interests. He has denigrated Nasserite and Arab nationalist claims to Khuzestan (advanced most often by Syria). See his speech at an audience granted to Majles deputies on March 1, 1966, as reported in *Kayhan International* (Tehran), March 3, 1966.

[49] General Hassan Arfa, who was at the time a captain in the Imperial Guards, recalls that the Cossacks had "perhaps 1500 men." See General Hassan Arfa, *Under Five Shahs* (London: John Murray, 1964), p. 108. British Foreign Office documents of the time state that "Kazvin and Hamadan detachments of Cossack brigade, numbering from 2500 to 3000 men, with 8 field guns under command of Colonel Reza Khan, marched from Kazvin to Tehran, and entered the town 21st February shortly after midnight" (Butler and Bury, *Near and Middle East*, p. 730).

[50] E. R. Lingeman, *Report on the Finance and Commerce of Persia, 1925–1927* (London: His Majesty's Stationery Office, 1928), p. 12. Lingeman had been in charge of Commercial Affairs at the British Embassy.

[51] Millspaugh, *Americans in Persia*, p. 155.

economic recession and the government's financial crisis suggested a reduction in military expenditure. The new Kennedy administration urged the same program. Indeed, the shah announced that he had determined to reduce the size of the armed forces by 15 per cent.[52] But in spite of his announcement, it was the shah's refusal to lessen military expenditures that prevented Amini from balancing the budget. There is no evidence that the size of the Iranian armed forces was ever altered except for purposes of expansion, and by 1965 the force was estimated at 220,000 men.

The quality of the equipment of the armed forces has improved at a rate greater than its size. Originally the troops could boast a motley assortment of makeshift weapons. Reza Shah modernized these and constructed munitions plants and arsenals. Machine gun and rifle assembly plants were established by Brno of Czechoslovakia. Heavier artillery was imported from Sweden. Faced with the budgetary difficulties of World War II, however, it was obvious to Mohammad Reza Shah Pahlavi that Iran could never afford to equip a modern army by self-generated funds. The shah turned to the United States. After a long courtship beginning with the first American military mission to the Iranian gendarmerie in 1942, significant levels of aid were finally obtained from President Dwight D. Eisenhower following the overthrow of Mossadegh. In the two postwar decades, Iran received nearly a billion dollars in military assistance from the United States—in the forms of grants, loans, direct shipment of surplus stocks, and technical training (see table 4.1).

The initial American rationale for providing these supplies stemmed from the dictates of its containment policies. The Pentagon hoped to be able to strengthen the Iranian military to the point where it could resist a massive Soviet land invasion. With the passage of time, the importance of this goal was progressively diminished. Secretary of Defense McNamara spelled out the more recent American rationale for military aid to Iran before the House Foreign Affairs Committee:

With respect to Iran, our objective has been to help build up its military forces to the point where they can ensure internal security and provide at least an initial defense against an overt Soviet attack. Although the Iranian military forces, with our aid, have improved significantly during the last decade, they are still not, and never can be, a match for Soviet forces presently deployed along the Iranian borders, even though the terrain favors the defense.

In Iran, as elsewhere in the world, the best defense against the spread of communism is a steady improvement in economic and social conditions which is the primary aim of our economic assistance efforts. In this connec-

[52] *Kayhan* (Tehran), Aug. 28, 1963, summarizes reports of the *New York Times* about American pressures through its military aid missions in Iran.

tion the assurance of a continued substantial level of military assistance support has enabled the Shah to concentrate on reforms leading to economic and social progress throughout the country.[53]

Following this presentation of America's views for such support, a new military aid agreement was concluded between Iran and the United States. Using the revolving credit, "Country-x" authorization of the Export-Import Bank, the United States agreed to guarantee a loan of $200 million to Iran for the purchase of arms. In addition, an outright grant of $50 million was made for the purchase of spare parts.[54]

But these same premises of economic determinism and the use of foreign aid to reduce Iranian dependency on the United States are apparently also shared by the USSR.[55] It has made frequent overtures to Iran and made its opposition to the United States presence unambiguous: "Situated as she is on the borderline of the two systems, Iran is doomed if she lets herself be turned into a base of imperialist aggression. No two opinions are possible about that."[56] Iran has not become such a base. The cooling of His Majesty's relations with the United States—evident since the election of the Democratic party in 1960—and his firm efforts at internal reform must have impressed the Soviets. Almost in causal fashion, more cordial relations with the USSR accompanied the worsening relations with the United States. By 1965, the shah and Soviet leaders "declared their readiness for still further expansion of friendly and good neighborly relations . . . as well as for the substantial expansion of economic, scientific, technical, and cultural cooperation beneficial to both nations."[57] Few foresaw the area in which the most dramatic expansion in "good neighborly relations" would occur. While presenting his annual budget message in early 1967, the prime minister declared that Iran had "clinched" a $110 million arms deal with the Soviet Union. Iran would receive weapons in return for which she would supply the USSR with local products and natural gas.[58]

In addition to the foreign aid that Iran has received—massive for a nation of 25 million—a striking level of internally generated funds has

[53] Statement by Secretary of Defense McNamara before the Committee on Foreign Affairs, U.S. Congress, House, *Foreign Assistance Act of 1964*, 88th Cong., 2nd sess., March 25, 1964, p. 90.

[54] "$200 Million for Arms," *Kayhan International* (Tehran), Oct. 26, 1964.

[55] Vide Leo Tansky, *U.S. and U.S.S.R. Aid to Developing Countries—A Comparative Study of India, Turkey, and the U.A.R.* (New York: Frederick A. Praeger, 1967).

[56] A. Leonidov, "Iranian Tragedy," *New Times*, no. 23 (June 1960), p. 11.

[57] Official communiqué released simultaneously in Tehran and Moscow following the shah's visit to the Soviet Union, as printed in *Kayhan* (Tehran), July 5, 1965.

[58] *Kayhan International* (Tehran), Feb. 20, 1967. Prime Minister Hoveyda also explained that the loan that the USSR was advancing would bear interest at 2½ per cent per year.

TABLE 4.1
United States Aid

	U.S. Overseas Loans and Grants -					
Program	Postwar Relief Period	Marshall Plan Period	Mutual Security Act			
	1946-48	1949-52	1953-57	1958	1959	1960
AID and predecessor agencies - total	-	14.9	303.4	51.4	46.0	37.5
Loans	-	-	65.0	40.0	37.7	-
Grants	-	14.9	238.4	11.4	8.3	37.5
Social Progress Trust Fund	-	-	-	-	-	-
Food for Peace - total	-	0.1	14.7	0.5	0.9	0.7
Title I - (total sales agreements)	(-)	(-)	(12.4)	(-)	(-)	(-)
Less: (planned for U.S. uses)	(-)	(-)	(4.0)	(-)	(-)	(-)
Title I - planned for loans and grants	-	-	8.4	-	-	-
104c - grants for common defense	-	-	5.9	-	-	-
104e - grants for economic development	-	-	-	-	-	-
104e - loans to private industry	-	-	-	-	-	-
104g - loans to governments	-	-	2.5	-	-	-
Title I - ass't from other country agrmts.	-	-	-	-	-	-
Title II - emergency relief & econ. dev.	-	-	3.4	-	-	-
Title III - voluntary relief agencies	-	0.1	2.9	0.5	0.9	0.7
Title IV - dollar credit sales	-	-	-	-	-	-
Export-import bank long-term loans	-	-	48.7	-	-	-
Other U.S. economic programs	25.8	1.5	-	-	-	-
Total economic	25.8	16.5	366.8	51.9	46.9	38.2
Loans	25.8	-	116.2	40.0	37.7	-
Grants	-	16.5	250.6	11.9	9.2	38.2
Military Assistance Program - (chg. to app.)[b]	-	16.6	133.9	73.0	90.9	89.1
Credit assistance	-	-	-	-	-	-
Grants	-	16.6	133.9	73.0	90.9	89.1
(Additional grants from excess stocks)	(-)	(0.7)	(21.1)	(1.8)	(6.0)	(7.0)
Other military assistance (grants)	-	-	-	-	-	-
Total military	-	16.6	133.9	73.0	90.9	89.1
Total economic and military	25.8	33.1	500.7	124.9	137.8	127.3
Loans	25.8	-	116.2	40.0	37.7	-
Grants	-	33.1	384.5	84.9	100.1	127.3

Source: U.S. Office of Statistics and Reports, International Cooperation Administration, Foreign Assistance and Assistance from International Organizations, July 1, 1945 through June 30, 1966 (Washington, D.C.: U.S. Government Printing Office, 1967), p.12.

[a] Represents loan under Section 104(c).

[b] Annual data represent deliveries; total through 1966 is the cumulative program.

To Iran, 1945-1966

(U.S. Fiscal Years; Millions of Dollars)

Net Obligations and Loan Authorizations								
Period	Foreign Assistance Act Period					Total 1946-66	Repayments and Interest 1946-66	Total less Repayments and Interest
1961	1962	1963	1964	1965	1966			
62.0	53.0	22.0	4.3	2.5	6.9	603.8	85.0	518.8
37.2	19.7	17.4	1.3	-	4.9	223.1	85.0	138.1
24.8	33.3	4.6	3.0	2.5	2.0	380.7	-	380.7
-	-	-	-	-	-	-	-	-
23.9	13.9	21.7	11.8	23.0	11.6	122.8	6.6	116.2
(19.5)	(6.6)	(6.9)	(5.4)	(11.5)	(-)	(62.4)	(-)	(62.4)
(5.8)	(1.7)	(1.7)	(1.6)	(5.8)	(-)	(20.6)	(-)	(20.6)
13.7	5.0	5.2	3.8	5.8	-	41.8	3.0	38.8
-	4.6[a]	-	-	-	-	10.5	0.4	10.1
-	-	-	-	-	-	-	-	-
1.6	0.3	1.0	0.3	1.2	-	4.4	0.4	4.0
12.1	-	4.2	3.5	4.6	-	26.8	2.2	24.6
-	-	-	-	-	-	-	-	-
8.6	6.0	13.1	2.2	1.4	-	34.7	-	34.7
1.6	2.9	3.4	5.8	0.2	2.2	21.3	-	21.3
-	-	-	-	15.6	9.4	25.0	3.6	21.4
21.3	-	-	8.7	18.5	-	97.2	71.6	25.6
-	0.4	0.2	1.1	1.4	2.6	33.0	2.4	30.6
107.2	67.3	43.9	25.9	45.4	21.1	856.8	165.6	691.2
72.2	24.6	22.6	13.8	39.9	14.3	406.9	165.6	241.3
35.0	42.6	21.3	12.1	5.5	6.8	449.8	-	449.8
49.2	33.3	66.0	27.3	49.9	44.7	895.2	-	895.2
-	-	-	-	-	3.6	139.0	-	139.0
49.2	33.3	66.0	27.3	49.9	41.1	756.2	-	756.2
(10.1)	(1.1)	(2.7)	(4.0)	(1.0)	(1.0)	(57.1)	(-)	(57.1)
-	-	-	-	-	-	-	-	-
49.2	33.3	66.0	27.3	49.9	44.7	895.2	-	895.2
156.4	100.6	109.9	53.2	95.3	65.8	1,752.0	165.6	1,586.4
72.2	24.6	22.6	13.8	39.9	17.9	545.9	165.6	380.3
84.2	75.9	87.3	39.4	55.4	47.9	1,206.0	-	1,206.0

also been devoted to defense. Iran's defense budget constitutes some 25 to 30 per cent of each year's steadily mounting government budget.[59] And this percentage understates actual defense expenditures. Wherever possible, major military expenditures, e.g., the construction of bases and barracks, are assigned to nonmilitary accounts in the budget. The development expenditures of the Plan Organization are a favored home for such expenses. Finally, in the face of growing unrest in the Middle East, Iran has sought to generate new funds. In late 1965, the Majles authorized the government to supplement the defense budget by further borrowings of $200 million. In presenting the bill, the prime minister told the Majles that the measure was necessary to secure Iran's "frontiers and territorial integrity against outside threats."[60] It was clear that the threats to which he referred emanated from Egypt and Syria. These threats were not perceived as less when Iran announced in early 1967 that her defense spending was still inadequate, although it was running at an annual rate of at least $485 million.[61] To further strengthen defense, the shah announced that for the first time in their history, Iranians would be "invited" to "subscribe to defence expenditures through the floating of 3,000 million rials [$40 million] worth of defense bonds."[62] Since 1967, at least two additional borrowings of $200 million have been authorized.

With the funds and outright gifts of equipment provided by the United States and the Soviet Union as well as the resources generated by Iran's own economy, the shah has been able to insure the adequate supply of his troops. For example, in fiscal year 1962, the United States supplied the Iranian gendarmerie, which has an authorized strength of 30,000 men, with the following equipment: 2,000 tear gas grenades, 1,602 quarter-ton trucks, 1,040 jeeps and miscellaneous motor vehicles, 29,960 weapons, and 15 aircraft.[63] Aside from these rather prosaic sup-

---

[59] U.S. Army, *Area Handbook for Iran* (Washington, D.C.: Special Operations Research Office, American University, 1963), p. 606.

[60] "$200 Million Arms Loan Sought," *Kayhan International* (Tehran), Nov. 10, 1965. The full text of the bill as approved is as follows:

Article: In order to stre[n]gthen the defense forces of the country, the Government is hereby authorized to seek credit facilities in foreign exchange equivalent to the rial value of 15 billion rials, in one lump sum or in several instalments, from any sources it may choose at its own discretion, and at a rate of interest not to exceed the customary level. The agreement concerning the period and other conditions of the loan shall become valid after approval by the Council of Ministers. The expenditure of the said credit will not be subject to the Law of Public Accounting and Audit or the Government Transactions Regulations.

(Echo of Iran, *Daily Bulletin: Political Edition*, 13, no. 246 [Nov. 10, 1965]: 2–3.)

[61] "Soviet Arms Agreement Is Announced in Tehran," *New York Times*, Feb. 20, 1967, p. 8.

[62] *Kayhan International* (Tehran), Feb. 20, 1967.

[63] Daniel Newberry, "GENMISH—United States Army Military Mission with the Imperial Iranian Gendarmerie" (Tehran: mimeo, n.d.), table D, inclosure 5. In

plies, however, Iran can boast more sophisticated weapons. In 1966, Iran was equipped with Hawk antiaircraft missile battalions.[64] The year before, Iran became the first foreign nation to receive America's highly advanced supersonic jet tactical fighters, the F-5. General Khatami, the brother-in-law of His Imperial Majesty and commander of the air force, announced that a total of one hundred F-5 fighters would be received by 1970.[65] Later the United States agreed to sell Iran "at least one squadron of F-4 Phantoms, the most advanced jet fighter in the American inventory."[66] In addition, Iran bolstered her naval forces. In late 1966, the shah placed orders totaling $63 million in Britain for five destroyers, a number of other naval vessels, and more ground-to-air missiles.[67]

But a military force is more than weapons alone. With her military resources, Iran has also been able to develop a network of modern military installations. For example, in 1965, the Iranians officially opened the Shahrokhi Air Base near Hamadan. The base boasts one of the longest runways in the world, as well as advanced radar systems.[68] Naval bases on the Persian Gulf and defensive forts around Iran's borders have

---

summarizing the over-all effectiveness of GENMISH, Mr. Newberry commented, "It is estimated that the Gendarmerie is disaffecting fewer people these days than formerly" (*ibid*).

[64] "U.S. Hawk Missile Going to Iran," *New York Times*, Feb. 8, 1966, p. 20.

[65] *Kayhan International* (Tehran), Feb. 2, 1965. Khatami described the plane as flying at 900 miles per hour while carrying 6,200 pounds of bombs in addition to 420 pounds of ammunition for its 20 mm. cannons. Many were surprised at the dispatching of these advanced supersonic planes to the Iranian air force. Only a few years before, *Time* had commented that "an Iranian mission has just asked Washington for an additional loan to balance the badly out-of-whack Iranian budget and the military minded Shah grumbles that he is not getting any supersonic century series jet fighters, even though there are only a handful of Iranian pilots skillful enough to fly the F-86's he already has" (*Time*, July 18, 1960, p. 25).

[66] "Iran to Get F-4's Top U.S. Fighters," *New York Times*, Dec. 14, 1966, p. 15. History seemed to be repeating itself. As the *Times* commented: "There is concern in US military circles that the Phantom may prove too advanced for the 10,000 man Iranian Air Force. Only recently did the Iranian Air Force acquire a supersonic capability with the purchase from the United States of two squadrons of F-5's. The United States was believed to have urged Iran to buy more F-5's, but it was understood that Shah Mohammad Reza Pahlavi insisted upon the F-4's" (*ibid.*). It was generally assumed that the F-4's were the shah's price for not turning to the Soviet Union for military supplies. See the *New York Times*, July 14, 1966, "Iran Said to Consider Buying Soviet Missiles;" and Sept. 19, 1966, p. 8, "U.S. Dissuades Iran from Seeking Soviet Arms." Only four months later, the shah announced his Soviet arms deal. There may have been some consolation in the fact that the Soviets are expected to supply Iran only with "unsophisticated" equipment, such as armored personnel carriers and military trucks.

[67] *Kayhan International* (Tehran), Sept. 1, 1966. The same newspaper of Feb. 20, 1967, in analyzing the budget items, mentioned that $63 million represented only a "down payment" for these weapons.

[68] *Kayhan International* (Tehran), Aug. 17, 1965. At the dedication ceremonies, the U.S. ambassador said that the base " 'symbolizes the dramatic progress' the Iranian Government and people are making in the development of their country" (*ibid.*).

recently been under construction. Nor have the noncombat needs of the military been neglected. New housing projects and apartments have been built by the Ministry of Housing and the Plan Organization and reserved for military personnel. The new Officers' Club of Tehran seems to the uninitiated more a palace for the commander in chief himself. Finally, the government has not been remiss in satisfying the more direct material aspirations of military leaders. His Majesty has consistently stressed the need to raise military salaries and he has more consistently done so. In the midst of the economic crisis of late 1964 and the accompanying extraordinary price rises and tax hikes, for example, the king announced his intention of raising the salaries of army and gendarmerie officers. It was estimated that the raises would cost the government an additional $2 1/2 million per year.[69] In addition, the government allows officers in the military to import such luxuries as automobiles without the payment of customs duties, as well as occasionally providing outright bonuses for their purchase.[70]

The shah, then, has increased the size and fighting efficiency of his armed forces. He has also, apparently, succeeded in satisfying their material aspirations. But he does not risk this eventuality as he has consistently striven to eliminate the possibility of losing direct command of the forces. This has traditionally assumed two dimensions. On the one hand, the shah has closely supervised the personnel who comprise his officer corps. On the other, he encourages the inculcation of loyalty to his person and the institutions of the monarchy.

In the first regard, no promotions above the rank of major can be made without the shah's explicit perusal of the officer's dossier. The shah personally examines the records of all these officers to determine the advisability of their promotion. He has forbidden any of his generals to visit the capital or to meet with any other general without his personal, case by case, permission. Finally, His Majesty frequently meets with his commanders and deals with them in the same fashion with which he treats his civilian bureaucrats.

But as well as satisfying the commanders, the shah also makes stringent efforts to build loyalty among the troops. Certainly the rewards he accords the army are one such method. But the shah does even more. He frequently appears in full military regalia surrounded by a coterie of important generals—even at totally civilian functions, such as the distribution of land reform deeds or supervising a Boy Scout encampment. (At such times, he is referred to as the commander in chief of the Imperial Iranian Armed Forces.) The first order of duty each morning at all

[69] Echo of Iran, *Daily Bulletin*: *Political Edition*, 12, no. 264 (Dec. 14, 1964): 6.
[70] Personal interview.

Iranian military camps is the mass recital of a prayer for the welfare and longevity of the shah. The slogan *Khoda, Shah, Mihan* (God, Shah, Fatherland) is a byword in the military. And the shah does not demur in publicly lauding the military for its help in carrying out the White Revolution. A recent Armed Forces Day provided the shah with a suitable occasion for thanking the army. "It is our hope," the shah concluded, "that with the help of Almighty God, the Army will gain even more success in the path of greatness of the beloved nation."[71]

This treatment has not gone unnoticed by the less favored civilians. An unusual editorial in one of Tehran's daily newspapers verbalized the citizens' growing indignation:

Perhaps it is time for our military leaders to give a second look to the unfair and unnecessary privileges which some of our military personnel have obtained in past years. Such privileges . . . should be reappraised by the military leaders of the country in view of the growing public disapproval of such privileges.

Indeed, the Imperial Army should be rightly concerned about the unfavorable public attitude in this regard . . . at a time when the majority of the country's population is experiencing many financial and social frustrations and at a time when everyone is urged to tighten his belts, public jealousy is too natural to overlook.

The fact that our army officers are receiving "most favored" treatment and constitutes a privileged class—in fact, the "upper class" of those on the government payroll, is a by-product of the past when the government had little support among the populace and had to build support for itself by lavishly feeding the armed forces.[72]

The response of His Imperial Majesty was to order the military to shed its uniforms in public places and to refurbish its image by performing more immediately useful tasks.[73]

Since 1963, the armed forces have responded to the shah's plea with startling rapidity. The army has assumed responsibility for an ever-widening number of nonmilitary functions. Civil action programs under the tutelage of American advisers have witnessed army battalions building roads, primary and secondary schools, and public baths as well as distributing food and medical supplies to famine, epidemic, and earthquake areas. In addition, the military has organized its new recruits into a series of noncombat "corps"—the Literacy Corps, Health Corps, Development and Rural Extension Corps. To staff these new groups, the army conscripts additional men, above its military requirements. The

[71] "Shah Gives Armed Forces Day Message," *Kayhan International* (Tehran), Jan. 8, 1964.
[72] *Tehran Journal*, Dec. 2, 1963.
[73] "No Military Uniforms in Public Places," *Kayhan International* (Tehran), Feb. 19, 1966.

recruits are given basic military training and then special instruction relevant to their future assignments. The remaining two years of their duty are spent entirely as members of a given corps.

It is generally agreed that these civic corps have been immensely successful. By January 1969, some 44,000 recruits had served or were serving the Literacy Corps in some 22,000 villages. By contrast, in the entire fifty years' existence of the Ministry of Education, only 16,000 teachers had been dispatched to rural areas.[74] Moreover, more than 6,000 of these corpsmen became regular teachers under the Ministry upon completing their military service. The more recently formed Health Corps and Development Corps (January 1964 and September 1964) have nonetheless managed to post more than 6,000 trained physicians, medical assistants, and extension workers to rural areas.

With the intervention of the military in these traditionally civilian matters, there has been a steady accrual in the power of the armed forces at the expense of the civil bureaucracy. One contributory factor has been the allocation to the military of additional resources for filling its new roles. The entire costs of the Literacy, Health, and Development programs are borne by the Plan Organization and the ministries of Education, Health, and Housing and Development. The armed forces have not been required to reapportion any of their regular funds for these purposes.[75] Moreover, the assumption by the military of these traditionally civilian responsibilities has at least partially relieved the civilian ministries from the need to improve their own efficiency. The civil bureaucracies have been relatively weakened as a swelling list of services comes to be performed by the armed forces.

The armed forces, moreover, have assumed wider responsibilities for the administration of justice. Enabling legislation for martial law in Iran was originally passed by the Majles to deal with the threat posed by the deposed Mohammad Ali Qajar's attempt to regain his throne. It was used frequently thereafter to deal with government opponents. Martial law was called upon by the Allies throughout World War II to eliminate alleged Nazi sympathizers. The shah used it as a means of dealing with the Tudeh after the 1949 assassination attempt. General Razmara relied on it for authority to deal with Mossadegh's supporters in 1950. And that nationalist prime minister dealt with many of his opponents under its legitimation. With Mossadegh's overthrow, martial law remained in effect to the mid-1950s as General Bakhtiar, then military governor of Tehran, eliminated Mossadegh's partisans and Tudeh members from positions of power. Martial law was again declared following the June 1963 riots and remained in effect until after the elections that fall.

[74] Echo of Iran, *Almanac—1969*, p. 482.
[75] *Kayhan International* (Tehran), June 2, 1964; and personal interviews.

But even when explicit military rule is not in effect, the armed forces continue to play a judicial role. All alleged treasonable offenses are tried before military courts and the definition of treason has steadily widened. Since 1965, a number of key trials have been held before military tribunals. Fourteen Tudeh leaders were tried in absentia and thirteen sentenced to death. A second group of alleged Tudeh leaders was also tried and sentenced. Twelve young men charged with complicity in the 1965 attempt on the life of the shah received jail terms and death sentences (later commuted to life imprisonment by the shah). Members of a group accused of *Feda'ine Islam* (Sacrificers or Devotees of Islam) tendencies were sentenced to death and prison for the killing of Prime Minister Mansur. The clandestine Islamic Nations party was judged treasonable and fifty-five of its members were given lengthy jail terms. Leaders of the Iran Freedom Movement were sentenced by such a court, as was Khalil Maleki, the leader of the Socialist League. Maleki and two associates received sentences up to three years. In 1966, Ahmad Aramesh, former chief of the Plan Organization and leader of the Progressive group, was also sentenced to three years, for publishing pamphlets "enciting unrest and rebellion." Most recently, the jurisdiction of the military has been broadened to the extent that even currency forgers are brought to justice by such tribunals.[76]

But the presence of the armed forces in civilian life is not restricted to these corps or to the judicial functions of the military. Recent years have also witnessed a marked increase in the number of individual military officers assigned to traditionally civilian posts. SAVAK, the national police, and the Passport Service remain in the hands of the military. A recent minister of agriculture was General Esma'il Riahi. His successor is a colonel. A minister of information was a general. The governors of sensitive and disturbed areas are generals. The director of Civil Aviation is a general. And the recent mayor of the nearly ungovernable Tehran is a brigadier general. This mayor, taken aback by the problems he faced, reportedly requested the shah to assign him "ten high ranking officers" to head each of Tehran's ten districts, for "only men with military discipline will be able to overcome all the difficulties."[77] Numerous other officers on active military service fill positions throughout the civil bureaucracy.

[76] An armed forces prosecuting attorney, Captain Saleh Kameli, justified the military trial of the forgers as follows: "The security of the country rests upon its economic, military, political, and social strength. If any of these pillars of the state were tampered with, the integrity and national security of the nation would be threatened. The Bank Melli [National Bank] has given written testimony that since the discovery of the gang, public confidence in certified checks has been damaged" (*Ettela'at* (Tehran), Aug. 22, 1967, p. 1). The gang was found guilty for forging $67,000 of such checks and sentenced to long terms of imprisonment.

[77] Echo of Iran, *Daily Bulletin: Political Edition*, 15, no. 141 (July 1, 1967): 1.

With these achievements, the military has become by far the most efficient bureaucratic organization in Iran. Capitalizing on their efficiency and loyalty, the shah has encouraged the armed forces in two endeavors. Their first task—the establishment of a monopoly over the means of physical violence—has already been accomplished. Its achievement was heralded by the ability of the armed forces to repress the urban discontent that exploded into widespread riots throughout Iran in June 1963, while simultaneously extinguishing a tribal uprising in Fars.[78] The second task has perhaps been less explicitly encouraged by His Imperial Majesty. Nonetheless, the military's assumption of civil power seems to have been pursued with vigor. In a private audience with this researcher, the shah emphasized that "We in Iran have one invariable rule—the complete and unalterable separation of the armed forces from politics." In its implementation, this rule seems to have taken a different form— the rigid exclusion of Iranian politics from the military bureaucracy. Events have demonstrated that the converse, the intervention of the military into the political sphere, is pervasive.

But it should not be concluded that Iran is ruled by a military government. The shah realizes the ultimate futility and inevitable debacle that military rule invites. He has told highly critical students that "A country cannot be ruled by the force of the bayonet and secret police. For a few days, this may be possible, but not for all times. Only a majority can rule a society."[79] With his programs of distributive justice based on the six-point referendum, the shah appears to be struggling to unite that majority behind his rule. The land reforms and economic development based on mounting oil revenues will abet his goal. In the process, however, His Imperial Majesty recalls the caveat of Sa'adi that a kingdom is based on people, a king, *and* an army.

What we have demonstrated in the last three chapters are the ways in which His Imperial Majesty controls his political elite. He manipulates the channels of wealth and education through which aspirants for membership in the general elite must pass. He controls the patterns of recruitment from this elite into the elite of elites—the nucleus of the most politically powerful individuals. The entire recruitment process has been described as one of co-optation through seduction. With surprising

[78] To some, the year 1963 appeared as a fulfillment of then Senator Humphrey's warning of 1961: "Do you know what the head of the Iranian Army told one of our people? He said the army was in good shape thanks to U.S. aid—it was now capable of coping with the civilian population. That army isn't planning to fight the Russians. It's planning to fight the Iranian people" (*Newsweek*, 57, no. 21 [May 22, 1961]: 19).

[79] From a speech by His Imperial Majesty to Iranian students in Vienna, delivered in June 1960 and reported by M. Behsaz, "The War of Ideologies," in *Tehran Mosavvar* [Tehran Illustrated], July 31, 1964.

toleration, His Majesty is willing to give what members of the elite want, so long as those demands are not directly political.

Once the elite is constituted, the shah seeks to control political behavior. We have detailed some of the means employed by the monarch to accomplish this. His style of rule—assessed as one of *divide et impera*—has proven efficient as a means for manipulating the elite and assuring their loyalty, or at least, their ineffectiveness in challenging the autonomy of this position.

Finally, we have described the keystone in the shah's rule—his control over the armed forces. Their loyalty to him and their unparalleled position of institutional power vis-à-vis other organizations within the political system are central characteristics of Pahlavi power.

It remains to investigate the consequences that these royal policies partly nurture—consequences that in turn feed back to His Imperial Majesty and affect his reign, his rule, and the success of political development in Iran.

A HISTORICAL PERSPECTIVE

ON THE ELITE NATURE OF IRANIAN SOCIETY

Over every authority, God has placed a higher authority.
Nizam ul-Mulk, *Siyasat-Nama*

---

e have examined the central position of the shah in contemporary Iran. Although his particular style of rule sets the tone of politics in that country and establishes patterns of behavior that animate the political process, there are other important actors in that process. Before turning to their styles of behavior or "code," we wish to describe the social and political milieu in which they and their monarch operate.

The quotation that begins this chapter was no idle speculation, but accurately reflected both the nature of political organization in Persian society in the days of its author, Nizam ul-Mulk of the eleventh century, and in most periods of Iranian history. After arguing for the hierarchical nature of Iranian society, Nizam ul-Mulk went on to issue a warning to his ruler, Sultan Malik-Shah of the Seljuk dynasty, to know and respect society's ranks:

God, be he exalted, has created the king to be the superior of all mankind and the inhabitants of the world are his inferiors; they derive their subsistence and rank from him. He must then keep them in such a position that they always know their places and do not put off the ring of service from their ears nor loose the belt of obedience from their waists. At all times, he must let them know how they stand whether in merit or demerit, so that they do not forget themselves. . . . He should know the measure and rank of everyone, and be constantly enquiring into their circumstances lest they deviate from the letter of his commands or overstep the limits which are set for them.[1]

---

[1] Nizam ul-Mulk, *Siyasat-Nama* [The book of government or rules for kings], trans. Hubert Drake (London: Routledge & Kegan Paul, 1960), p. 192.

118

Persian society, then as now, was viewed as a progression of ranks, the members of each possessing successively more authority than the ranks below. While all societies can be viewed as a hierarchy of ranks, few people have been as consistent as the Persians in delineating and identifying intrasocial ranks or broad social classes or in having those perceptions of the social structure remain so constant over time.

The Achaemenids (550–330 B.C.), the first of the Iranian national dynasties, united the Medes and Persians and spread Iranian hegemony from the Indus in the east to Egypt in the west. Achaemenid rulers divided their subjects into four classes: (1) princes of the royal blood and military commanders; (2) religious officials and keepers of the Zoroastrian fire temples, the Magi; (3) learned men including scribes, astrologers, physicians; and (4) cultivators of the soil and menials. The "first" class (as the elite are known in Iran today) was further subdivided by the rulers. After himself, the shahanshah counted members of the royal family on the next level of rank. Below them were the personal companions of the king who were entrusted with the execution of special missions. The commander of the king's bodyguard and other important military chiefs were next in authority. Local rulers and the satraps of the major conquered territories constituted yet another level of the elite. Finally, six noble families, who, with the royal family, were known as the Seven Princes, "generally filled the great offices and formed a permanent council."[2]

The second of Iran's great national dynasties, the Sassanians, once again expanded the empire and succeeded in the previously unimagined feat of capturing a Roman emperor—Valerian. And once again, the ideal society of the Sassanians was conceptualized in four gross categories: religious leaders; warriors; bureaucracy (including biographers, poets, astronomers, and physicians); and peasants, shepherds, merchants, and artisans.[3] As in Achaemenid times, the elite were further divided into subranks that were manifest by the proximity to the monarch allowed the group at functions of the royal court. Closest to the king sat the ministers of the crown, followed by the *Mobed*s and *Hubed*s (the

[2] Sir Percy M. Sykes, *A History of Persia*, 2 vols. (London: Macmillan Co., 1921), 1: 140, 175. Also see Richard N. Frye, *The Heritage of Persia* (London: Wiedenfeld and Nicolson, 1962), pp. 97–99; and Herodotus, *The Histories*, trans. Aubrey de Selincourt (London: Penguin Books, 1961), p. 70. The tradition of the "Seven Great Families" may have stemmed from the heads of seven Persian tribes forming the basis of the Achaemenids and was certainly strengthened by the participation of Darius the Great and representatives of the six other families in the slaying of Gaumata the Pseudo-Smerdis of the Greeks, who usurped the throne in 521 B.C. In any case, it was a tradition that remained vital through the subsequent Parthian (249 B.C. to A.D. 226) and Sassanian (A.D. 240 to 640) dynasties.

[3] Arthur Christensen, *L'Iran sous les Sassanides* (Paris: Gennther, 1936), pp. 93 ff.

chiefs of the Magi and the judges). This entire assembly was circled by the *Sepahbad*s, or commanders in chief of the armies of the empire, who in turn were flanked by singers, musicians, and men of science and learning.[4]

These divisions of society in terms of relative status levels were frequently and publicly made in Sassanian times, with even the *Avesta* suggesting the propriety of such a quadripartite ordering of mankind. Scholars, however, have questioned the actual meaning of these groupings or classes. Richard Frye asks whether these were "theory, tendency, or reality."[5] But confirming these divisions is the report that Artaxerxes, or Ardeshir, the exalted Sassanian monarch, kept his subjects "rigidly in their separate divisions, for the reasons he explained, that nothing more swiftly leads to the destruction of empires than the transfer of one class to another, whether it be the elevation of the humble into a higher class or the degrading of the nobles into a lower one."[6] If the quotation attributed to Ardeshir is not apocryphal, we can assume that this division was more than theoretical and represented a castelike social structure with horizontal rather than vertical mobility and recruitment, as a general rule, being intraclass rather than interclass.

The lengthy interregnum between the Sassanians and the Safavids witnessed great social and political turmoil in Iran as Arab, Seljuk, and Mongol invaders pressed their suzerainty on the Persians for ten centuries. At least for the first of these conquerors, the Arabs, it appears that the social structure retained its distinctive identity. Many sources attest to the alacrity with which the Sassanian-Zoroastrian elite went over to the "enemy" by quickly adopting Islam, in the process failing to provide leadership for the remainder of society, who remained Zoroastrian for much longer, or to demonstrate a sense of social consciousness that might have alleviated the hardships brought about by the conquest. But "the old Persian aristocracy and landed proprietors did . . . succeed in preserving much of their power and wealth by embracing Islam and throwing in their lot with the conquerors, to whom their services were needful, and their local influence and knowledge indispensable."[7] Undoubtedly, their success in retaining power mitigated the early Arab proclivity for a simple division of society between believer and infidel,

---

[4] George Rawlinson, *The Seventh Great Oriental Monarchy or Geography, History, and Antiquities of the Sassanian or New Persian Empire*, 2 vols. (New York: Dodd, Mead and Co., 1882), 2:302.

[5] *Heritage of Persia*, p. 54.

[6] Jahiz, *Kitab Al-Taj*, ed. Ahmad Zeki Pasha (Cairo: 1914), as quoted in *The Social Structure of Islam*, by Reuben Levy (Cambridge: Cambridge University Press, 1962), p. 69. Jahiz was a ninth-century sage of Basra.

[7] Edward G. Browne, *A Literary History of Persia*, 4 vols. (Cambridge: Cambridge University Press, 1953), 1:233.

and preserved not only the pre-Islamic structure of Iranian society, but even continuity of personnel (other than the Magi, of course).

The Safavids (1500–1722) resurrected the tradition of great national Iranian dynasties which had collapsed with the fall of the Sassanians. With them was also reinstituted the four-class division of Iranian society. This class structure was maintained under the Qajar dynasty (1789–1925), but was augmented to reflect the heightened importance of the tribes (on which Qajar military strength was based) and the commercial sector.[8] At the apex of society sat the Qajar Shah, and then members of the Qajar family. Next in importance came the *Ilkhan*s and *Ilbeigi*s of the great Persian tribes, the Bakhtiaris, Qashgai's, Kurds, Baluch, Afshars, Qara Gozlus, Arabs, and Turkomans. (The military officers, recruited almost entirely from the tribal chieftains, made up another group conceptually distinct but socially identical with the preceding group.)

The Qajar monarchs expanded and organized the civil bureaucracy by appointing officials charged with specific administrative responsibilities. The *sadri-e a'zam* served as a prime minister to supervise the activities of other officials. The *mustawfi ol-mamalik* (finance), *vazir-e lashkar* (war), *munshi ol-mamalik* (chief secretary), *sahib divan* (signer of official documents), *mu'ayyir ol-mamalik* (master of the mint), *khatib ol-mamalik* (reader of the *khutba*), and *minajjim bashi* (chief astrologer) composed the king's cabinet. By 1850, Naser ed-Din Shah eliminated these officials and established six "ministries" on "modern" lines: finance, war, interior, foreign affairs, justice, and *awqaf* (religious endowments).

Below the bureaucracy were the religious leaders, the *mujtahed*s, the *shaykh ol-Islam*, in the towns, and the *imam jum'eh* in the cities. Counted after the spiritual heads were the merchants and owners of large numbers of villages, appearing for the first time in the explicitly articulated social structure. Their identification as a distinct group with greater status than the mass of peasants and menials undoubtedly reflects

[8] For information on the Qajar period, see Ann K. S. Lambton, "Persian Society under the Qajars," *Journal of the Royal Central Asian Society*, 48 (April 1961): 130; idem, "Islamic Society in Persia" (Lecture delivered at School of Oriental and African Studies, University of London, March 9, 1954); Lord George N. Curzon, *Persia and the Persian Question*, 2 vols. (London: Longmans, Green and Co., 1892), vols. 1 and 2, chaps. 7, 13–15, 17, 18, 28–30; Sir Harford Jones Brydges, trans., *The Dynasty of the Kajars* (London: J. Bolin, 1833); Sir Thomas Edward Gordon, *Persia Revisited, With Remarks on H.I.M. Mozaffar ed-din Shah* (London: E. Arnold, 1896); Ali Akbar Siassi, *La Perse au Contact de l'Occident* (Paris: E. Leroux, 1931); R. G. Watson, *A History of Persia* (London: Smith, Elder and Co., 1886); Edward G. Browne, *A Year Amongst the Persians* (London; Adam and Charles Black, 1893); and Nikki R. Keddie, *Religion and Rebellion in Iran: The Tobacco Protest of 1891–1892* (London: Frank Cass and Co., 1966).

economic development in the eighteenth and nineteenth centuries, the growing economic interdependence of formerly disjunct regions, and an increase of foreign trade.[9]

Finally, at the nadir of the social hierarchy were the masses—the town and country peasants, laborers, menials, domestics, and artisans. Under the Qajars as in a score of previous centuries, the principal function of these masses was to pay taxes to government officials, local landlords, or both. No wonder they remained "illiterate, ignorant, and inarticulate," showing "a common feeling, that of distrust and fear, directed, on the one hand, toward the privileged and powerful above them, especially the officials of the government, and on the other hand toward the foes from without and the bandits and rebels from within. No one ever closed or bridged the chasm."[10]

Such, then, was the nature of traditional Iranian society: the ruling family, leaders of the tribes, civil bureaucracy, religion, commerce, and the peasants and menials. From the earliest days of Iranian greatness to the time of Reza Shah Kabir and his drive for modernization, there has been a highly articulated social structure whose divisions were always well defined and recognized. Moreover, an explicitly identified elite group has existed for the same period, an elite group which was differentially rewarded as, it was assumed, was their rightful desert. This was also reflected in the counsels of Nizam ul-Mulk, who reminded the monarch that:

One of the principles which kings have observed in all ages is to preserve ancient families and honor the sons of kings, not allowing them to be neglected and debarred from their rightful position and power. Rather did they give them a portion for their substance so that their families continued to flourish; other deserving persons too were given allotments from the treasury, such as learned men, descendants of Ali, guardians of the frontiers and expositors of the Quran.[11]

[9] The introduction of commercial elements to the class structure also indicates the possibility for group mobility within the Iranian system. For information on economic change in Qajar Iran, see Marvin L. Entner, *Russo-Persian Commercial Relations, 1828–1914*, University of Florida Monographs, Social Sciences, no. 28 (Gainesville: University of Florida Press, 1965); Ali Amini, *L'institution du monopole du commerce extérieur en Perse* (Paris: Rousseau and Co., 1932); Mustafa Khan Fateh, *The Economic Position of Persia* (London: P. S. King and Son, 1926); Abbas Chams-ed Din Kia, *Essai sur l'histoire industrielle de l'Iran* (Paris: M. Lavergne, 1939); Ann K. S. Lambton, *Landlord and Peasant in Persia* (London: Oxford University Press, 1953), esp. chaps 6–8; G. R. G. Hambly, "An Introduction to the Economic Organization of Early Qajar Iran," *Journal of the British Institute of Persian Studies*, 2 (1964): 69–82; L. E. Frechtling, "The Reuter Concession in Persia," *Asiatic Review*, 34 (July 1938): 518–33; and Curzon, *Persia*, esp. vol. 2, chaps. 28, 29.

[10] Arthur C. Millspaugh, *Americans in Persia* (Washington, D.C.: Brookings Institution, 1946), p. 12.

[11] *Siyasat-Nama*, p. 144.

Despite the differential rewards and the apparent rigidity of the classes themselves, however, the personnel who composed these classes were less rigidly assigned to them than might be supposed. Social mobility was always a possibility in Iran, and class divisions could at least occasionally be broken. The fictitious but now legendary Hajji Baba of Isfahan is a personification of an almost cyclical progression between "the heights of prosperity and the depths of penury and ignominy" in traditional Persian society.[12] From illiterate barber to wandering *mullah*, to the counselor of kings, he crossed class lines, for better and worse, with alacrity.

Iranians themselves are fond of citing actual Persians whose lives exemplify the possibilities for mobility. Perhaps the most widely noted example is the mid-nineteenth century vizier of Naser ed-Din Shah, Mirza Taghi Khan. The Amir Kabir (the Great Amir), as he is now known, was "truthful, incorruptible . . . and placed the finances of the country on something resembling a business-like footing."[13] In addition, he established the first school with a modern curriculum in Iran, the Dar ol-Fonun. Yet in spite of his exalted position, the Amir Kabir's father had been a cook and steward.

Other examples of great mobility may be cited. Hajji Muhammad Hussayn Khan, Amir ol-Dowleh, was a grocer who became *beglerbeg* (governor) of Isfahan by dint of a large gift to the king, and in 1806, the *mustawfi ol-mamalik* (minister of finance) under Fath Ali Shah.[14] Mobility through marriage is illustrated by the third wife of Naser ed-Din Shah, and his favorite, Anis ed-Dowleh, who was originally a miller's daughter from a village near Tehran. As he was passing on horseback, she lifted her veil before the Shadow of Allah, the Pivot of the Universe. The shah is reported to have been so fascinated by this brazen act that he brought her to the palace, where she gained such influence that "she has secured lucrative positions at Court for all her relations."[15]

---

[12] Reuben Levy, "Introduction" to *Qabus Nama* [A mirror for princes], by Kai Ka'us Ibn Iskandar, trans. Reuben Levy (London: Cresset Press, 1951), p. xvi. See James Morier, *The Adventures of Hajji Baba of Ispahan* (London: Oxford University Press, 1959). Hajji Baba himself relates: "There is a reaction in misfortune which frequently produces increased prosperity. Thus when the smith sprinkles water upon his burning charcoal, it is extinguished for a moment, and smoke takes the place of flame; but again, at the slightest blast of his bellows, the fire breaks out with redoubled brilliancy" (*ibid.*, p. 360).

[13] Sykes, *History of Persia*, 2: 340.

[14] Lambton, "Persian Society," p. 134.

[15] Curzon, *Persia*, 1: 409. Another interesting case of rapid mobility is reported by F. A. C. Forbes-Leith, *Checkmate: Fighting Tradition in Central Persia* (London: George G. Harrap and Co., n.d.), pp. 69–70. He mentions that the chief tax collector and private secretary for all ninety-six villages in the Hamadan area owned by Sardar Akram (shortly after World War I) had been a groom for the Sardar's father only seven years previously.

123

The most startling example of rapid mobility, however, is provided by the rise of new ruling families. The Pahlavis, to take only the most recent example, descend from an undistinguished line of petty military leaders from the province of Mazandaran bordering the Caspian Sea. Reza Khan, as the father of the present shah was known before his coronation, had but poorly mastered the skills of literacy even "as a grown man."[16] Reza Shah's accession to power not only supplied an entire new ruling family but also made room at the top for numerous officials who had abetted his rise.

Coupled with such examples of mobility may be mentioned the general lack of esteem associated with lineage or pedigree. Other than certain members of the ex-ruling house, the Qajars, who relish their descent from kings, the Seyyeds who trace their lineage to the Prophet, and various tribal leaders who boast family trees that lead back, rather mysteriously, to heroes such as Chingiz Khan or Tamerlane, few Iranians take the subject at all seriously. "If the word *najabat*, 'nobility,' and *najib*, 'noble,' are heard, they refer to the rank which an individual may hold, there is no allusion to birth."[17] Thus mobility was never hindered by a high regard for pedigree.

Another factor that historically facilitated mobility in Iran was the almost universal practice of selling offices. Through a system known as *modakhel* (perquisite), nearly all official positions in the realm were available to the highest bidder. The principal offices were, in effect, auctioned at the annual *No Ruz* (New Year's) ceremonies. Lord Curzon described the practice as it existed at the end of the nineteenth century: "From the Shah on downwards, there is scarcely an official who is not open to gifts, scarcely a post which is not conferred in return for gifts, scarcely an income which has not been amassed by the receipt of gifts. Every individual with hardly an exception in the official hierarchy . . . has only purchased his post by a money present either to the Shah or to a Minister or to the superior governor by whom he was appointed."[18]

---

[16] Mohammad Reza Shah Pahlavi, *Mission for My Country* (New York: Mc-Graw-Hill, 1961), p. 36. The extent to which Reza Shah was illiterate as the shahanshah is a moot point but it seems probable that he was never wholly comfortable with the skill.

[17] Levy, *Social Structure*, p. 70; see also Jakob Edward Polak, *Persien: das land und seine bewohner*, 2 vols. (Leipzig: F. A. Brockhaus, 1865), 1: 35 ff.; and Sir Arnold Wilson, *Persia* (London: E. Benn, 1932), p. 9.

[18] *Persia*, 1: 438. Another perceptive observer commented that:

The Shah at the head, farms out the provinces of his realm at *No Ruz* to the highest bidders; and the man who has hired a province hurries to his miniature kingdom and extorts money on his arrival from all the rich inhabitants under his rule. Some intrigue at the capital may oust him from his position before the year is out, therefore, his great aim is to recoup himself and make a handsome sum over and above his outlay in the shortest possible time . . . his suite do their share in extorting money from the townsfolk. These latter probably

The consequences of this practice for mobility were striking. Scarcely a post existed that was not available to the interested subject willing and able to pay. Meanness of birth or social status was no more an obstacle to high position than was a surfeit of mendacity or venality or a lack of ability or intelligence.[19] Wealth and power in Qajar Persia were in a symbiotic relationship. Wealth was frequently a necessary and sufficient requisite for political office. The latter was, in turn, a sufficient condition for attaining wealth, which in turn led to a more elevated political position with greater political power. In this way Iranians have continued to confound theorists who suggest that wealthy officials would prove to be honest. One such Persian theorist, Kai Ka'us Ibn Iskandar, had long since equated officials of the realm with an irrigation channel and the monarch with a garden: "If the canal supplying the field or garden is moist and well soaked, it conveys water quickly to field and garden; but if the earth in the canal is dry and water has not for a long time passed through it, then, when water is admitted, until it is itself saturated with moisture, it will not deliver water to the garden or field."[20] Max Weber has made a similar point in suggesting that "only economically independent officials, that is, officials who belong to the properties strata can permit themselves to risk the loss of their offices."[21] But in Persia, even well-soaked canals had a penchant for absorbing water and propertied and nonpropertied officials of the bureaucracy, faced with the risk of loss of position, resorted to the *modakhel*.[22]

One final factor affecting social mobility in traditional Iranian society was a general willingness to accept the *nouveau arriviste*. Ibn Iskandar, in the *Qabus Nama*, warns his son that "There is no fool greater than he who sees a man of lowly state risen to greatness and continues to regard

---

"grind the faces" of their apprentices in their turn; and the lowest servant in Persia will make his *modakhel* on the smallest article purchased from his employer. . . . In short, practically every office is sold in Persia, and practically every official is corrupt.

(Ella C. Sykes, *Persia and Its People* [London: Methuen and Co., 1910], pp. 58–59.)

[19] Curzon, *Persia*, 1: 444.

[20] *Qabus Nama*, p. 216.

[21] *From Max Weber: Essays in Sociology*, trans. and ed. E. H. Gerth and C. Wright Mills (New York: Oxford University Press, 1958), p. 235.

[22] While this practice facilitated mobility, it also contributed to the near total ineptitude of the Iranian bureaucracies. Curzon explains the disastrous condition of the armed forces of his day in just such terms: "It may safely be averred that no general officer obtains his post without a substantial money equivalent. His own profit consists in what he can extract from the colonels and majors under his command. They, in turn, squeeze the captains and lieutenants, and these, not behind hand in resourcefulness, extract moisture from what one would, prima facie, imagine to be the flinty consistency of the Persian infantry soldier, by selling to him the privilege of furlough or leave to work as an artisan in the bazaar" (*Persia*, 1: 442).

him as lowly."[23] An Arabic proverb is occasionally cited at similar appropriate moments:

> Honor lies in the mind and acquired worth,
> Not in origin and noble birth.

The lack of value accorded genealogy, the rise of new ruling dynasties, a general appreciation of the fluctuations inherent in human existence, a willingness to welcome the socially mobile, and vaunted examples of mobility all served to make interclass movement a possibility. But despite these factors such mobility was difficult at best and by no means common.[24] For while there existed the possibility, the means that would make that possibility a reality were generally lacking. Primarily, of course, Persians of low status lacked wealth, for by definition in Iran, "high and low rank depend upon riches or poverty."[25] They also lacked the means that would facilitate the acquisition of wealth. Formal education, access to persons of power, military command posts, and marriage with social betters were normally explicitly or implicitly restricted to the members of the "first" class, the elite. Thus, while the Amir Kabir has earned a high place in Persian history, it is less frequently noted that his father had been the chief steward to the chief vizier of Mohammad Shah, the monarch preceding Naser ed-Din. (That he met his end by having his veins opened on order of the shah only three years after he had been elevated to the vizierate is even less cited.)

Basically, despite a fairly common nineteenth-century practice of appointing as vizier "a man of no family, for it was deemed impolitic to appoint to this post a prince of the blood or great noble," examples of rapid or far-reaching mobility in Iran have become fewer.[26] Those examples of such mobility that do exist serve primarily to justify the ideology of an open-class system—an ideology that serves several important functions. Firstly, one of the geniuses of the Iranian system, a genius that has made a particular contribution to its survival, is that the system approximates a "flexible autocracy."[27] The ideology of upward mobility has made it possible for the ruler, in times of threat, to accede or grant power to nonelite, nonaristocratic elements. On numerous occasions, Iran has found "the right man" who led the nation out of what appeared at the time to be certain destruction or loss of identity. Two kingly exam-

---

[23] P. 46.

[24] Lambton, "Persian Society," p. 134.

[25] Nizam ul-Mulk, *Siyasat-Nama*, p. 203.

[26] Sykes, *History of Persia*, 2: 383.

[27] James H. Meisel, *The Myth of the Ruling Class: Gaetano Mosca and the "Elite"* (Ann Arbor: University of Michigan Press, 1962), p. 201. Meisel discusses the possibility of the ruler's breaking the grip of the "aristocratic clique" and the flexibility of the "autocratic principle . . . in times of trouble."

ples are Reza Shah and Nadir Shah, but there are many ministers and military leaders who have been accepted or co-opted into the political elite in times of danger.

Another function that the ideology of an open-class system performs is to strengthen the position of His Imperial Majesty vis-à-vis the elite. By its explicit rejection of the notion of any "innate" superiority or virtues possessed by the *kelass-e avval* (the elite), the open-class system denies to the elite any claim over the shah. In turn, his dependency on the elite is reduced, for only his system is "closed," being based on the innate virtue of primogeniture from the late shahanshah. All others of the elite, with the exception of certain tribal leaders, can lay claim to no such native attributes.

This potential for mobility also served to mitigate the evils of the government and social system for members of the lower class. The ideology of the open-class system was a sop to the disadvantaged and debased. For if no criterion for mobility existed save wealth—no attributes inherent to the individual—then as long as the possibility of acquiring wealth existed, mobility would certainly follow. The consequence was a dearth of social conflict defined on class terms, and a peculiarly pacific quality to social relationships in general. Finally, Iran's rather rigidly defined social structure in which mobility was always, nonetheless, a possibility gave a highly "democratic" tinge to the society, "for every man sees a chance of someday profiting by the system of which he may for the moment be the victim and as the present hardship or exaction is not to be compared in ratio with the pecuniary advantage which he may ultimately expect to reap, he is willing to bide his time and to trust to the fall of the dice in the future."[28]

The ideology of an open-class system, then, was primarily an ideal. It served a number of useful purposes for Iranian society, but was mirrored in reality only to the slight extent which allowed that ideology to remain vital. In concert with a set of articulated social classes featuring an explicitly defined elite group, the history of Iran has shown "elitism at its crudest, the notion that The Few should rule because they do in fact rule, for The Many do not and never will."[29] As this has been true for two thousand years of Iranian history, the contemporary period, not surprisingly, provides us with a situation not grossly disparate.

The elitist nature of Iranian society is reflected in the inordinately great benefits that members of the elite derive from the system. We have already discussed the distribution of these benefits, in the process of recruitment by co-optation. The fruits of those benefits will be evident in our discussion below of the social backgrounds of the elite. One such benefit that deserves special treatment, however, is political power. As

---

[28] Curzon, *Persia*, 1: 444. [29] Meisel, *Ruling Class*, p. 3.

politics is a central feature of Iranian life, so is political power the prime value for most educated and involved Iranians. This is yet another value that is disproportionately allocated in Iran.

But a gross view of Iranian politics in the contemporary era seems to belie its elite nature. For that view reveals a scene of almost unmitigated political turmoil. Frequent and sweeping alterations of personnel appear to be the complement of political violence and change. Even the monarchy itself has not been immune from the apparent chaos. Since the inauguration of the Qajar dynasty in the late eighteenth century, only one Persian king has relinquished his throne through natural death at old age. More recently, the three monarchs preceding the present shah were each deposed: Mohammad Ali Shah was banished in 1909 by the Nationalists who supported the newly inaugurated constitutional regime against his despotism; his successor, Ahmad Shah, was deposed (along with the entire Qajar dynasty) by Reza Khan; and in turn, Reza Shah Pahlavi, as he was thereafter called, abdicated in response to the British and Soviet occupation. While Mohammad Reza Shah has successfully maintained his grip on the throne, he too has been the intended victim of assassinations and coups. Wounded by a would-be assassin in 1949, he was saved from a similar or more serious fate in 1965 by two personal bodyguards, who gave their lives to a machine gun-wielding Imperial Guardsman. Other attempts have also been formulated to oust the king. In August 1953, the shah even abandoned Iran and flew to Europe when Mossadegh refused his order of dismissal. And since that time a number of alleged plots against the throne have been uncovered.

If the monarchy has been subject to the pressures of violent change and political chaos, how much more were those pressures directed against the political elite. Assassinations have been one manifestation of such license. Prime Minister Mansur, shot before the Majles, is only the most recent victim of such tactics. Prime Minister Hossein Ala was saved from a similar attempt in 1957. Less fortunate were Prime Minister, General Haji Ali Razmara in 1951; Minister of Court Abdul Hossein Hazhir in 1949; the chief of Mossadegh's police, General Mahmud Afshartus in 1953; a noted newspaper correspondent, Ahmad Dehghan in 1950; and a score of other prominent officials in earlier years.[30]

A more pacific symptom of this seemingly chaotic system of politics may be found in the shah's predilection for the periodic investiture of new cabinets. The power attributions of present-day cabinet ministers leaves no doubt that the cabinet is the most powerful formally consti-

---

[30] The periodicity of twentieth-century assassinations is another measure of political chaos. Those times in which the prime ministers served the fewest number of months and headed the greatest number of cabinets also witnessed the greatest number of attempts on the lives of political figures.

tuted group of civilians. This contention bears out the observations of Professor Leonard Binder that the cabinet is "the principal coordinating body in the Government."[31] Yet the ministers remain utterly dependent on the royal prerogative for their continuation in office, and with great frequency the king has exercised his power by dismissing his ministers. Since the advent of the constitution in 1907, some 117 distinct cabinets have been designated by the shah. Year in and year out over this sixty-year period, after an average of six months' tenure in office, yet another set of officials were called to ministerial portfolios.

But a more penetrating analysis of these statistics reveals another view, one of more meaningful political order. Over the life of the 117 cabinets, only thirty-eight different individuals served as prime minister (see table 5.1). These prime ministers averaged nineteen months in office, despite the fact that any given cabinet that they might have headed served for less than a half year.

The number of different cabinets and individual prime ministers who have served per decade from the advent of constitutionalism to the present provides an index of the considerable political stability of Iran (see table 5.2). In terms of the average number of months served by each prime minister, the fewest number of different prime ministers, and the smallest number of different cabinets, one decade is paramount. It is the period of 1927 to 1937 that corresponds most closely with the height of Reza Shah's autocracy. Indeed, that cabinet with the second longest tenure of the twentieth century served in this period, that of Ahmad Matin Daftari. Taking office as the youngest prime minister in Iranian history in October 1935, he served continuously as prime minister over one cabinet (with some personnel shuffles) until June 1940.

Similarly, the most recent decade in Iran's history has witnessed the second fewest number of cabinets and prime ministers and the third longest tenure, as His Imperial Majesty has been able to re-assert his control over the political process following the Mossadegh period. The cabinet and prime minister of Dr. Manouchehr Eghbal served from April 1957 to September 1960, the third longest tenure in this century. The unparalleled political order of the contemporary era is indicated by the present prime minister, Amir Abbas Hoveyda, who has served in office continually since 1965, by far the longest tenure of any Iranian premier.

Conversely, the periods of recent Iranian history that witnessed the least stability also possessed the greatest number of cabinets. The two decades following the granting of the constitution, 1907 to 1927, were

[31] *Iran: Political Development in a Changing Society* (Berkeley: University of California Press, 1962), p. 125. See also Binder, "The Cabinet of Iran: A Case Study in Institutional Adaptation," *Middle East Journal*, 16 (Winter 1962): 29–47.

TABLE 5.1

Prime Ministers of Iran and Total Number
of Cabinets Headed, 1907-1968

Name of Minister	Cabinets Headed
1. Ahmad Qavam	11
2. Mostaufi ol-Mamalek	11
3. Sepahdar-e Azam	9
4. Samsam ol-Saltaneh	7
5. Mohammad Sa'ed	6
6. Mohammad Ali Forughi	5
7. Moshir ol-Saltaneh	5
8. Vosuq ol-Dowleh	4
9. Sardar Sepah (Reza Khan)	4
10. Nasir ol-Molk	3
11. Nezam ol-Saltaneh	3
12. Ala ol-Saltaneh	3
13. Moshir ol-Dowleh	3
14. Ali Soheili	3
15. Ibrahim Hakimi	3
16. Hossein Ala	3
17. Assadollah Alam	3
18. Amir Abbas Hoveyda	3
19. Ain ol-Dowleh	2
20. Seyyed Zia ed-Din Tabatabaie	2
21. Ali Mansur	2
22. Abdul Hossein Hazhir	2
23. Mohammad Mossadegh	2
24. Ja'afar Sharif Emami	2
25. Ali Amini	2
26. Hassan Ali Mansur	2
27. Afkham	1
28. Mirza Ali Asghar Khan, Atabek Azam	1
29. Farman Farma	1
30. Sepah Salar-e Azam	1
31. Mokhber ol-Saltaneh	1
32. Mahmud Jam	1
33. Ahmad Matin Daftari	1
34. Morteza Qoli Hedayat	1
35. Mohsen Sadr	1
36. Lt. Gen. Haji Ali Razmara	1
37. Maj. Gen. Hassan Zahedi	1
38. Manouchehr Eqbal	1
Total	117

periods of political chaos, internal revolution, and foreign invasion, but were ended by the assertion of Reza Shah's central control. The two decades following the abdication-overthrow of Reza Shah by the Allies were similarly characterized by foreign invasion, economic disruption, and political chaos. Not until the assertion of decisive control by the present shah did relative stability come about, at least as manifested in the number of different cabinets and individual prime ministers.

These relations can be demonstrated more decisively by compressing these six decades of Iranian history into four periods, as shown in table 5.3: 1907 to 1926 (the initiation of "constitutional" government under the Qajars to the establishment of the Pahlavi dynasty); 1926 to 1941 (the rule of Reza Shah); 1941 to 1953 (the period of foreign occupation

TABLE 5.2

Number of Cabinets and Prime Ministers
per Decade in Iran, 1907-1968

Decade	Number Different Prime Ministers	Average Number Months Served	Number of Cabinets	Average Number of Cabinets per Prime Minister
1907-17	14	8.8	35	2.5
1917-27	11	10.9	28	2.5
1927-37	5	24.0	6	1.2
1937-47	9	14.3	18	2.0
1947-57	10	12.0	17	1.7
1957-68	6	22.0	13	2.1
Total	55[a]		117	

[a] The total number of prime ministers is greater than the actual 38 because an individual who served in this capacity was recorded separately for each decade in which he served.

TABLE 5.3

Number of Cabinets and Prime Ministers
in Four Historical Periods, 1907-1971

Period	Number Different Prime Ministers	Average Number Months Served	Number of Cabinets	Average Number of Cabinets per Prime Minister
1907-26	17	14.0	61	3.6
1926-41	6	31.3	9	1.5
1941-53	12	12.0	31	2.6
1953-71	8	26.7	16	2.0
Total	43		117	

to the overthrow of Mohammad Mossadegh); and 1953 to the present (the rule of Mohammad Reza Shah).

It may be hypothesized that: (1) periods of centralized government in Iran are marked by little political turnover and infrequent alterations of personnel among the political elite; (2) the opening of the government to greater bargaining and political give and take is marked by an increase in the turnover of the political elite; and (3) a breakdown in central control and the advent of relative political chaos results in rapid turnover of cabinets and prime ministers.

The seeming chaos of rapidly interchanging cabinets was increased by the previous practice of dismissing a prime minister for a period of months only to recall him to office again. In past decades, relatively few men alternated in controlling the premiership. For example, in the decade 1940 to 1950, twenty-seven cabinets were formed by His Imperial Majesty. But only nine men served him as prime minister and these men tended to replace each other in that office over the entire period. They served in the following order:

Mansur	Sadr
Forughi	Hakimi
Soheili	Qavam
Qavam	Hakimi
Soheili	Hazhir
Sa'ed	Sa'ed
Hedayat	Mansur
Hakimi	

Only in recent years has there arisen the principle of having individual prime ministers head contiguous cabinets and then be permanently displaced from the premiership.

As with the *nakhost vaziri*, so with the *vozara*. The ministers tended to replace themselves in office just as did the prime ministers. In his study of the "Role of the Cabinet in the Government of Iran," Leonard Binder notes that from 1941 to 1952, some 400 cabinet positions were filled. But these 400 positions were actually held by only 144 persons.[32]

The usual statistics of personnel changes are misleading. The reality of the most recent sixty years of Iran's political history is of far less dramatic changes—of far fewer individuals manning the political "command posts." Rather, the image Iran presents is of a pool of politically active individuals into which the shah, or perhaps the Majles in time of more decentralized political power, dip periodically for political leaders. This game of "musical prime ministers," as it has been described, whereby the "years come and go but the faces in Iran stay the same" helps account for the peculiarly elitist nature of Iranian politics.[33] Put differently, above a cutoff point in a hierarchy of political power, individuals move into positions of greater or lesser importance with fair rapidity. Mobility up *and* down this hierarchy, within the elitist universe, is common. It is less common, however, for individuals to move below the elite cutoff point, even when they lose their official positions, which appear to be the bases of their power and hence political elite status.

[32] *Iran*, p. 115. Another observer, commenting on an earlier period, has noted that "The 300 odd vacancies in some 24 cabinets between August 1941 and November 1948 were filled with few exceptions from a clique of 70 or 80 politicians, all over fifty years of age, and many over sixty" (L. P. Elwell-Sutton, "Political Parties in Iran, 1941–1948," *Middle East Journal*, 3, no. 1 [Jan. 1949]: 46).

[33] Quotations from interview with an elite respondent.

Thus, for example, all living ex-prime ministers ($N = 11$) were ranked in the 10 per cent of the "general elite," which we have considered to consist of the most politically powerful individuals in Iran, and hence within the Iranian power elite as we have defined it. Indeed, all ex-prime ministers fell within the top 3 per cent of the general elite (the *least* powerful had a rank of 102), with a mean rank of 29 (when ranking the general elite from 1 to 3,100 on the basis of reputed power).

Of similar interest are the sources of recruitment into the prime ministership. Of the last ten individuals to have served in this post, not one was not already considered a member of the political elite before assuming office. Through the holding of other important governmental positions, extraordinary wealth, or personal friendships with important members of the elite and especially with His Imperial Majesty, these individuals were counted "politically very powerful" before assuming the highest political office of Iran.[34]

As with the prime ministers, so with others of the political elite. Social background data indicate that the overwhelming majority of present-day members of the elite boast parents with social and personal attributes characteristic of the elite of their own day. The system, in other words, may be thought to constitute a "modernizing traditional regime" which consists of "elite groups predominantly recruited on an ascriptive basis, from among established, not to say vested, social classes, strata, or groups."[35] Those less politically elite (than the top 10 per cent of the general elite) also supply members to the ranks of the politically powerful, but to a relatively slight degree. Mobility from the "powerless" to the "powerful" occurs with relative infrequency in these higher strata of Iranian society, as will be demonstrated in Chapter 6 in an examination of the backgrounds of the contemporary elite.

In sum, then, the members of the elite have been allocated the rewards of political power and other values available in their society in proportions beyond which the populations of more equalitarian societies are likely to tolerate. If government in the United States is *in theory* "of the people, by the people, and for the people," and *in practice*, "of the people, by a political elite, for the people," as all governments to some degree must be, then the government of Iran historically has been and continues to be "of, by, and for the elite."

[34] While the reputational analysis to determine membership in the political elite was conducted only in regard to the contemporary period, the ten individuals on the power attribution panel were asked to supply rankings of certain historically key political figures. It was recognized that attempts to identify an individual's actual political power, before that individual assumed his most important political position, through a reputational method was, at best, extremely suspect. Thus this line of research was not carried out for any large segment of the general elite.

[35] Harry J. Benda, "Political Elites in Colonial Southeast Asia: An Historical Analysis," *Comparative Studies in Society and History*, 7, no. 3 (April 1965): 234.

:6:

AN ANALYSIS OF THE SOCIAL BACKGROUNDS

OF THE CONTEMPORARY POLITICAL ELITE

*T*he shah and his elite together elaborate the political process of Iran and, as a result, have disproportionately allocated the outputs of their political system in a mutually beneficial fashion. But who are these members of the elite? What are their social backgrounds? What distinctive characteristics identify them from their twenty-five million countrymen?

The questionnaire with which the 167 members of the political elite were interviewed contained a vast array of items pertaining to social background. In addition, wherever possible, biographical data for the 140 members of the elite not so interviewed were collected.[1] By combining these data sources, the social backgrounds of the elite as a group could be analyzed.[2]

BIRTHPLACE AND RESIDENCE
Isfahan is a paradise full of luxuries;
Were there but no Isfahanis in it . . .
Iranian proverb

The members of the political elite have less diverse backgrounds than did their fathers, and their fathers had less diverse backgrounds than the

---

[1] Published registers of biographical data are unfortunately rare in Iran. The most adequate sources for such material are the Echo of Iran's annual almanacs (Tehran: Echo of Iran Press), which contain a "Who's Who in Iran" section. In addition, the Echo of Iran publishes two biographies per week of prominent Iranians. Those were kindly made available to me by Mr. Jahangir Behrouz, publisher of the Echo. In addition, the *Kayhan* and *Ettela'at* newspapers have published a certain amount of biographical data.

[2] For a separate analysis comparing respondents to nonrespondents, see Appendix II.

population at large. There are many indicators of this diminution of social variety and accompanying diminution of the bases from which mobility to political power is possible. One such indicator may be found in the places of birth of the members of the elite. In many technically advanced societies, birthplace has been assumed to be relatively uncorrelated to attitudes and behavior. Even in those countries with the most developed and integrated communications networks, however, behavioral and cultural differences attributed to regional variations may be found.[3] Where the development of internal communication has been less pronounced, regional peculiarities are far more likely to exist.

Such regional peculiarities are widely recognized in Iran. The nation's folklore is replete with aphorisms of the personality characteristics associated with birth and life in her various cities. Bakhtiaris and Luris are known as simpletons; Qazvinis as rustics; Yazdis as braggarts; and the inhabitants of Shah Abdul Azim (Rey), the shrine of pilgrimage a few miles south of Tehran, not surprisingly, as inhospitable.[4]

Similar thoughts are often voiced in poetry—the most widely employed satirical device in Iran. Some samples of what constitute a very large body of literature are as follows:

> A dog of Kashan is better than the noble of Qum,
> Although a dog is better than the native of Kashan.[5]

> From a Tabrizi, thou will see naught but rascality,
> Even this is best, that thou shouldst not see a Tabrizi.[6]

A series of maxims in proverbial form are also used to describe the alleged weaknesses of the inhabitants of various regions. The people of Isfahan, for example, have been widely viewed as avaricious. As the saying goes, "He is as mean as the merchants of Isfahan who put their cheese in a bottle and rub their bread on the outside to give it a flavor."[7]

A striking finding of our data is the relative isolation of the political elite from these variations based on birthplace and residence. In gross terms, whereas 5.1 per cent of Iran's total population of 18,954,704

---

[3] For a classic, fictional treatment of regional variation in England, see Mrs. Elizabeth Gaskell, *North and South* (London: Chapman and Hall, 1855). Also see Merrill Jensen, ed., *Regionalism in America* (Madison: University of Wisconsin Press, 1951); Howard W. Odum and Harry Estill Moore, *American Regionalism: A Cultural-Historical Approach to National Integration* (New York: H. Holt and Co., 1938); Richard E. Engler Jr., *The Challenge of Diversity* (New York: Harper and Row, 1964); and, of course, Karl Deutsch, *Nationalism and Social Communication* (Cambridge: M.I.T. Press, 1953), esp. chap. 2.

[4] These and other urban peculiarities may be found in the general travel literature of Iran, as well as in S. Khaim, *Zarb Al Masalhaye Farsi va Englisi* [Persian-English proverbs] (Tehran: B. & D. Beroukhim Booksellers, 1956).

[5] Edward G. Browne, *A Year Amongst the Persians* (London: Adam and Charles Black, 1893), p. 184.

[6] *Ibid.*, p. 84.   [7] *Ibid.*, p. 214.

TABLE 6.1

Birthplace by Province of the Political Elite
and Total Population of Iran

Province	% of Elite Born There	% of Fathers of Elite Born There	% of Total Population of Iran Born There
City of Tehran	54.1	35.5	5.1
Other than Tehran	45.9	64.5	94.9
Central Province	2.2	4.4	5.6
Khorasan	7.2	9.3	10.8
Azarbaijan	6.7	9.3	16.3
Gilan	6.7	7.3	9.5
Esfahan-Yazd	6.7	7.9	9.0
Fars-Banadar Jonub	4.5	6.9	7.3
Mazandaran-Gorgan	3.2	6.9	9.0
Kermanshahan	2.3	2.0	7.8
Baluchistan-Sistan	.9	1.0	2.3
Kerman	.9	2.0	4.3
Kurdestan	.9	1.0	2.9
Khuzestan-Lorestan	.5	2.5	9.9
Outside of Iran	3.2	4.0	0.2
Total	100.0	100.0	100.0
N	(222)[a]	(203)	(18,954,704)

Source: Percentages for the total population of Iran were calculated from data given in Ministry of Interior, Census
Statistics, 2:162-64 (table 13).

Notes: It is not surprising that the least represented of the four
provinces among the birthplaces of the political elite are
Baluchistan-Sistan, Kerman, Kurdistan, and Khuzestan-Lorestan.
Collectively, they are the poorest regions of Iran as measured
by the welfare of the indigenous inhabitants; the homes of
Iran's major ethnic groups (Arabs, Kurds, and Baluchis); and,
with the exception of Khuzestan, the most sparsely inhabited
provinces of Iran.

For information on ethnic distribution in Iran, see U.S.
Army, Area Handbook for Iran (Washington, D.C.: Special
Operations Research Office, American University, 1963),
pp. 85-93; Herbert H. Vreeland, ed., Iran (New Haven: Human
Relations Area Files, 1957), pp. 37-55; Richard W. Cottam,
Nationalism in Iran (Pittsburgh: University of Pittsburgh
Press, 1964), esp. chaps. 3-8; and articles on the tribes of
Iran by V. Minorsky and others in The Encyclopedia of Islam,
4 vols. (Leyden: E. J. Brill, 1913).

[a] The number of nonrespondents plus the number of respondents
does not always total 307 because biographical data for all
140 nonrespondents were unavailable. The situation is con-
founded because the number of nonrespondents for whom data
are available varies with the nature of the biographical
variable. Data for elite occupations, for example, were more
readily available than data for elite birthplaces.

persons had been born in Tehran as of 1956, some 35.5 per cent of the fathers of the members of the political elite had been born there. And some 54.1 per cent of the political elite themselves had been born in Tehran.[8]

More significant than the gross figures on the birthplaces of the members of the elite is an examination of the proportion of the political elite born in Tehran at differing age levels (see table 6.2). The relationship is inverse, that is, the younger are the more likely to have been born in

TABLE 6.2

Age of Members of Elite by
Place of Birth

| Age | Place of Birth | | Total | N |
	Outside Tehran	In Tehran		
39 or younger	36.8%	63.2%	100.0%	19
40-49 years	40.4	59.6	100.0	42
50-59 years	46.8	53.2	100.0	47
60-69 years	50.0	50.0	100.0	40
70 or older	78.9	21.1	100.0	19

Note: x^2 = 9.258; df = 4; p = .055; gamma = .281.
The strict statistical requirements for the use
of the x^2 have not been met in this work. Nonetheless, the statistic has been included in all
cross tabulations as an indication of the strength
of the relationship.

Tehran. With the passage of time, moreover, the representation of Tehranis among the political elite will continually increase, as no set of factors has appeared or is likely to appear that would alter the dominance of the capital and the access it provides.

But if the younger members of the elite tend increasingly to begin their lives in Tehran, the older members have not been lax in escaping the rudeness of the provinces for the capital. The vast majority of the 45 per cent of the elite born outside the capital migrated to Tehran and took up permanent residence there during or before World War II (see table 6.3). Only five members of the elite do not live in Tehran, all five being religious leaders who reside in Najaf (Iraq), Qum, Meshed, and Shiraz.[9]

[8] An interesting finding on place of birth of Iranian political elite is made by G. Hossein Razi, "Social Change and Political Leadership in Iran: A Case Study of the Politics of Transition" (unpublished manuscript, n.d.). Razi, in analyzing the places of birth of forty-three "government leaders" and twelve "opposition leaders" mentions that 64.3 per cent of the former were born in Tehran versus only 16.8 per cent of the latter. Unfortunately, our data do not permit a similar comparison.

[9] Actual statistics on the population of the birthplaces of the elite and the percentage of the total population of Iran residing therein, by size of place in 1956, are given in table 6.a. Unfortunately, data for the size of the birthplace for the total Iranian population are not available. As a standard of comparison, size of

The preponderance of the elite in the capital city is matched by the obvious and immense dominance of Tehran in the life of Iran. Binder, for example, has commented that:

The urban-rural division in Iran, as in many underdeveloped countries, places the bulk of the population in the countryside and concentrates political power in the capital city . . . the fate of the nation being decided in Tehran. By any yardstick, it would seem that the political action of Tehran street sweepers is more significant for the future of the regime than the pains and pleasures of the elite of a host of provincial towns.[10]

If this holds for the street sweepers of Tehran, how much more relevant for the national political elite! That all but five of the political elite make their permanent residence in the city, or that 54 per cent of the present elite were born there; or that of the elite born elsewhere, 70 per cent

TABLE 6.a

Population of Birthplaces of the Elite and
Percentage of the Total Population
Residing Therein, as of 1956

Size of Place	Political Elite Born There		Percentage of Total Population of Iran Residing There
	Number	Percentage	
1,000,000 or more	120	55.3	8.0
300,000-999,999	0	0.0	0.0
100,000-299,999	48	22.1	8.5
25,000-99,999	24	11.1	6.6
10,000-24,999	12	5.5	4.5
5,000-9,999	5	2.3	3.8
1,000-4,999	7	3.2	17.3
999 or less	1	.5	51.3
Total	217	100.0	100.0

Source: Ministry of Interior, Census Statistics,
1: 12 (table 9).

place by residence was used. It has been assumed that differences in internal migration will tend to cancel out and result in the approximately relevant proportions used here. Where this is not the case, data on percentage of population residing in a given place will understate the differences in proportion of persons born in a given size of place because migration in Iran has been from smaller towns of birth to larger cities of residence. That is, this comparison probably underemphasizes the disproportionately greater birth of the political elite in large cities. For example, while 8.0 per cent of the population of Iran resided in the city of Tehran in 1956, only 5.1 per cent of the population was actually born there (Ministry of Interior, Department of Public Statistics, *National and Province Statistics of the First Census of Iran: November 1956*, 2 vols. [Tehran, 1961], vol. 2, *Social and Economic Characteristics of the Inhabitants for Iran and the Census Provinces*, pp. 162–64 [table 13] [hereafter cited as *Census Statistics*, 2]).

[10] Leonard Binder, *Iran: Political Development in a Changing Society* (Berkeley: University of California Press, 1962), p. 161.

TABLE 6.3
Migration to Tehran for Members of the
Elite Born Elsewhere

Date Settled in Tehran	Percentage
Not yet permanently settled	6.0
1955-present	2.8
1945-54	8.9
1935-44	12.7
1925-34	27.8
1924 or earlier	41.8
Total	100.0
N	(79)

Note: A handful of the political elite live in the
capital but maintain their official residences outside Tehran. Nevertheless, one need not fear for
their welfare as they have assured themselves the
ability to return to the luxuries of the capital as
efficiently as possible. Thus one of the most powerful of the elite has had the government construct an
airport with modern lighting in the seat of his
family domains, a town of 13,000 people, where he
maintains his official residence. (There are only
four other civilian airports in all of Iran that can
boast of such lighting facilities. See Government
of Iran, Department General of Civil Aviation,
Aerodrome Directory [Tehran, 1963].)

migrated permanently to the capital at least thirty years previously all
attest to this fact.

While this is decidedly the case for political affairs, the dominance of
Tehran is no less manifest in other areas. The 10 per cent of Iran's population who live in the city and among them virtually the entire political
elite enjoy inordinately disproportionate amounts of the values of Iranian
society, and in the process give form and content to all areas of Iranian
life:

EDUCATION

33 per cent of the nation's secondary school students study in Tehran.[11]

34 per cent of all Iranian literates live in Tehran.[12]

69 percent of all those who have any college education live in Tehran.[13]

73 per cent of all university students in Iran are studying in the capital's
institutions of higher learning.[14]

[11] Ministry of Education, Office of Studies and Programs, *Amar-e Farhang-e
Iran* [Educational Statistics of Iran] (Tehran, 1964), p. 11. Of a total of 326,856
secondary school students, 109,281 were studying in Tehran and Shemiranat.

[12] Ministry of Interior, *Census Statistics*, 2: 45–76 (table 7). Of the 1,910,630
total of literates over the age of 10 in Iran, 644,478 lived in the Tehran census
province.

[13] *Ibid.*, pp. 80–142 (table 9). Of the 32,471 Iranians of both sexes with any
university training at all, 22,465 resided in the Central census province.

[14] Ministry of Education, *Amar-e Farhang-e Iran*, p. 98, table 5. Of 24,456
students in institutions of higher learning in Iran (1964), 17,736 were studying
in Tehran.

139

HEALTH

48 per cent of all licensed physicians live in Tehran.[15]

77 per cent of all beds in medical hospitals are in the capital.[16]

79 per cent of all beds in mental hospitals may be found in Tehran.[17]

In 1955, infant mortality was estimated at 71 per 1,000 live births in Tehran and 217 per 1,000 in villages adjacent to Tehran.[18]

COMMUNICATIONS

43 per cent of all cinemas in Iran are located in the capital. All cinemas rated first class are in the city.[19]

62 per cent of all the nation's passenger automobiles are owned and driven by Tehranis.[20]

71 per cent of Iran's telephones are operating in the capital.[21]

83 per cent of Iran's television receivers may be found in Tehran and its suburbs.[22]

95 per cent of all daily newspapers are published and read in Tehran.[23]

ECONOMY

37 per cent of all workers in the electricity, gas, and water industries are employed in Tehran.[24]

56 per cent of all workers employed in factories of ten persons or more work within the city limits.[25]

[15] Speech by Dr. N. Rahnavardi, member of the Public Health Committee of the Iranian Majles, before the Health Committee of the Tehran Chapter of Lions International, Tehran, December 21, 1964. The figures that he gave were 1,796 physicians of a total of 3,722.

[16] From a speech by Majles Deputy Maku'si to the lower house as reported in the *Tehran Journal* of November 16, 1964. 14,000 of 18,000 medical hospital beds are concentrated in Tehran.

[17] Echo of Iran, *Almanac—1964–1965*, p. 498. 1,750 of 2,200 sanatoria beds are in Tehran.

[18] U.S. Army, *Area Handbook for Iran* (Washington, D.C.: Special Operations Research Office, American University, 1963), p. 146.

[19] Echo of Iran, *Almanac—1964–1965*, p. 639. The statistics are that 82 of the 190 cinemas of Iran are located in the capital.

[20] *Ibid.*, p. 486. The figures for 1964–1965 are 75,833 of a total for all of Iran of 122,745. This ratio has remained constant in recent years. Similar figures for 1960–1961 were 57,868 automobiles of a national total of 93,079, or 62 per cent.

[21] *Ibid.*, p. 444. Of a total of 118,000 telephones, 84,000 operate in Tehran.

[22] *Idem, Almanac—1966*, p. 515, gives the statistics, 100,000 of 120,000 television sets.

[23] *Ibid.*, pp. 219–21. Press circulation statistics are not aggregated and reliable figures are notoriously impossible to gather. The government's Press Law of 1963 specifies that newspapers with circulation of less than 3,000 and magazines of less than 5,000 could no longer be published. A commission was established by the terms of the press law to ascertain circulation figures for all printed media. The commission has never met (personal interview).

[24] Ministry of Interior, *Census Statistics*, 2: 326–39 (table 23).

[25] Government of Iran, Department General of Publications and Broadcasting, *Bulletin* (Tehran, April 1961), pp. 2 ff. (statistics exclude the oil industry). Tehran dominates the industrial sector to a large degree and in surprising ways. Thus the undersecretary of agriculture in a speech reported in *Kayhan Inter-*

100 per cent of all banks, insurance companies, and other fiduciary institutions have their headquarters in Tehran.[26]

Thus the elite tend to be immune from the variations of regional residence and birth. But, in addition, the very concentration of those factors that serve to minimize such variations tends to enhance the relative unity of the elite, while exacerbating the urban-rural, capital-hinterland, and elite-mass bifurcations of the society. In short, while those traditional regional variations are being reduced by the dissemination of the mass media, education, and modern means of communication, the concentration of these in the capital is contributing to new forms of social discontinuities.

While Tehran dominates the life of the nation, large cities in general play an increasingly dominant role vis-à-vis smaller centers of population. If we compare the birthplaces of the elite with those of their fathers, we note that in 63.5 per cent of the cases, the places of birth of the two generations were identical. Of the remaining elite who were born in cities different from the birthplaces of their fathers, some 90 per cent were born in cities that were larger in 1956 than were the birthplaces of their fathers *in 1956*. That is, the use of identical census data for determining the size of places of birth for both generations revealed that the elite not born in the birthplaces of their fathers were born in larger cities. What is at work here is not that cities have grown larger over the years between the birth of father and son (which is generally true), but that the process of urbanization that has beset much of the developing world and Iran in particular has enhanced the importance of the larger cities in the nation's political life.

Urbanization in Iran, however, has been peculiar in at least two senses. Firstly, it has not been a general, nationwide phenomenon. And secondly, where it has occurred, it has persisted doggedly in a steady and often rapid compounding of urban populations. It is impossible to establish with certainty the rate of population growth in Iran, but most demographers would put the total annual percentage increase somewhere between 2.5 and 2.9. But urbanization represents a different pattern. Certain cities show a net annual decline in population over the fifteen-year period (1941–1956) for which rudimentary data are available: e.g., Bandar Pahlavi, —1.0 per cent; Meshed, —0.6 per cent; and Hamadan, —0.2 per cent. Other cities indicate growing populations, but at a rate slightly below or approximately correspondent with the average annual population growth for the country as a whole: e.g., Isfahan, 1.5 per cent; Shiraz, 2.1 per cent; and Tabriz, 2.2 per cent. One city, Tehran,

---

national (Tehran) (Nov. 2, 1964) related that tractor motors from rural areas all over Iran must be brought to Tehran for overhaul.

[26] Echo of Iran, *Almanac—1966*, pp. 465, 467.

dominates statistics on population growth just as it dominates all other statistics in Iran. Its annual average growth rate from 1941 to 1956 was some 11 per cent.[27] In the period from 1956 to 1964 a special study revealed that the rate of growth increased and hovered at 15 per cent per year.[28]

The dominance of the capital city over the life of Iran, its population growth, and its "production" of the political elite is paralleled by and reflected in the life chances of the elite themselves. The members of the elite born in Tehran are eligible for "the best of everything" and they usually get it in proportions greater than their country cousins. Furthermore, Lerner has argued that "cities alone have developed the complex of skills and resources which characterize the modern industrial economy."[29] Being born in Tehran usually meant that the elite were born into households already amenable to the contemporary world.

For one thing, their fathers were more likely to have had modern, rather than traditional or *maktab*, educations. Whereas only one-seventh of the fathers of elite born outside Tehran had studied in modern educational institutions, nearly two-fifths of the fathers of elite members born in Tehran had been so educated. Similarly, the fathers of the Tehranis are more likely to have been government employees and primarily highly placed officials.

In addition to having fathers in government service, elite members born in Tehran had other family assets. Iran is a society for which "nepotism, where possible under modern conditions, is a strict family

TABLE 6.4
Fathers' Employment by Birthplace of the Elite

Fathers' Employment	Birthplace of Elite	
	Tehran	Not Tehran
Government	64.0%	46.2%
Nongovernment	36.0	53.7
Total	100.0%	100.0%
N	(86)	(80)

Note: $x^2 = 5.258$; df = 1; p = .022; gamma = $-.347$.

[27] Ministry of Interior, Department of Public Statistics, *National and Province Statistics of the First Census of Iran: November 1956*, 2 vols. (Tehran, 1961), vol. 1, *Number and Distribution of the Inhabitants for Iran and the Census Provinces*, p. 5 (table 6) (hereafter cited as *Census Statistics*, 1).

[28] From a continuing demographic study by Professor M. Ecochard of Paris University, as reported in *Kayhan International* (Tehran), Nov. 16, 1964.

[29] Daniel Lerner, *The Passing of Traditional Society: Modernizing the Middle East* (New York: Free Press of Glencoe, 1958), p. 60.

obligation."[30] As such, the power of one's extended family can be of crucial significance in determining one's career. Members of the political elite born in Tehran are much more likely to be related to the Pahlavis and to the former ruling dynasty, the Qajars (interestingly, however, neither ruling family originated in Tehran, the founders of both having been born in the province of Mazandaran).[31] All of the political elite related by blood to His Imperial Majesty are Tehranis by birth. Of the forty-seven members of the elite who count themselves Qajars, some 11 per cent were born in towns of less than 100,000 persons. Another 21 per cent were born in the provincial cities. But 68 per cent, or thirty-two former princes or princesses, are from the capital. Aside from membership in the extended families of Iran's ruling dynasty or preceding kings, the Tehranis are also more likely to be from nonroyal families whose members, nonetheless, were politically influential. Two and one-half times as many of the elite born in Tehran, compared to those born in cities of fewer than 100,000 persons, could claim such influential relations.

Tehranis, then, have had a number of advantages affecting their life chances vis-à-vis those of the elite born outside Tehran. Fathers with modern educations; fathers with positions within the royal court, the civil or military bureaucracies; and families with ties to the ruling families or other influentials provide access to the values in Iranian society over which they had control. For example, a combination of political and intellectual influence at home and the greater educational opportunities of the capital made it possible for members of the elite born in Tehran to pursue their educations to high levels (see table 6.5).[32]

There are other advantages that accrue to Tehranis. One of them is the chance to travel abroad with greater frequency than is true for non-Tehranis. While 37.1 per cent of the elite who were born in Tehran had made ten or fewer trips outside their native land, the comparable figure for those born in towns of less than 100,000 is 57.1 per cent. Conversely, only 23.8 per cent of the small-towners have made more than twenty trips, while 45 per cent of the native Tehranis have done so.

But foreign travel and higher education are only intermediate to a more highly sought-after value in Iran—political power. Once again, there is a positive (albeit weak) relation between birth in Tehran and

[30] Binder, *Iran*, p. 159.

[31] For information on the Qajars, see Sir Percy M. Sykes, *A History of Persia*, 2 vols. (London: Macmillan Co., 1921), 2: 277, 289 ff.; for the Pahlavis, see Mohammad Reza Shah Pahlavi, *Mission for My Country* (New York: McGraw-Hill, 1961), pp. 35-36.

[32] This is an interesting example of the problems of differential access and unbalanced development of educational facilities. See, for example, James S. Coleman, "Introduction" in *Education and Political Development*, ed. James S. Coleman (Princeton: Princeton University Press, 1965), pp. 30-31.

TABLE 6.5
Elite Education by Place of Birth

| Highest Education Level | Place of Birth | | | |
	Tehran	Not Tehran	Total	N
Maktab or secondary school	31.2%	68.8%	100.0%	28
University	43.1	56.9	100.0	51
Postgraduate	62.5	37.5	100.0	88

Note: x^2 = 9.891; df = 2; p = .007; gamma = -.409.

reputed political power. Education, travel, power—these and other values accrue disproportionately to those of the elite born in Tehran. They also accrue disproportionately, but to a lesser extent, to those born in the larger provincial cities. (While 75 per cent of the elite were born in major cities and only 6.0 per cent in towns of less than 10,000, the comparable figures for the rest of the nation are 16.5 per cent and 73 per cent, respectively.) The townspeople and peasants—most of the population—are born into an environment that has less to offer, and they receive less.[33] The traditional regional variations, in the process, become secondary to new types of variations represented by the great proportion of the elite born in Tehran (or early migrating there) and by the inordinately disparate distribution of resources to the capital. One danger in these new discontinuities may well be a growing disinterest in national development as the elite seek to preserve their special privileges, if necessary at the expense of that development.[34]

[33] The "country cousins" do manage to receive a greater share of certain desired items than would be expected from their numbers alone. One such item is landownership, another is children as shown in table 6.b.

TABLE 6.b
Number of Children by Size
of Elite Birthplace

| Number of Children | Size of Birthplace | | |
	Tehran	100,000-999,999	99,999 or less
0-2	55.4%	48.5%	41.5%
3 or more	44.6	51.5	58.5
Total	100.0%	100.0%	100.0%
N	(83)	(33)	(41)

Note: x^2 = 2.195; df = 2; p > .20; gamma = .201.

[34] Mary Jean Bowman and C. Arnold Anderson ("Concerning the Role of Ed-

AGE

Send not an old man to buy an ass, nor a young man to choose a wife—
the one is satisfied with any speed, the other with any beauty.
Iranian proverb

As is true of any political elite, the age distribution of the most politically powerful Iranians is considerably different from that of the Iranian population of similar age limits (see table 6.6). Members of the political

TABLE 6.6

Age Distribution of the Iranian Political Elite
and the Population of Iran 30 Years and Above

Age in Years	Political Elite	Population 30 Years and Above
30-39	8.5%	37.9%
40-49	26.0	25.1
50-59	29.3	18.7
60-69	25.6	11.2
70 and older	10.6	6.8
Total	100.0%	100.0%
N	(246)	(6,518,981)

Source: Ministry of Interior, Census Statistics,
2: 1-2.

elite are considerably older than the total population of Iran over the age of thirty; the median age of the former is 54.0 and of the latter, 43.8 years.[35] Insofar as longevity and age are valued in Iranian society, it is obvious that the political elite are disproportionately rewarded in this area as in so many others.

Numerous observers have made the point that in more traditional, non-Western societies power is a concomitant of age.[36] That association has been even more vociferously claimed in Iran.[37] Our data bear out these generalizations, albeit to a very slight extent. Of the elite under the age of fifty, 23.5 per cent were at the lowest levels of reputed power, with reputed power scores of 6 or less. Of those sixty years of age or over, the

ucation in Development," in *Old Societies and New States*, ed. Clifford Geertz [New York: Free Press of Glencoe, 1963], p. 277) make this point also.

[35] Ministry of Interior, *Census Statistics*, 2: 5–18.

[36] Kusum Nair, *Blossoms in the Dust* (New York: Frederick A. Praeger, 1962), pp. 153–55. Miss Nair also discusses the tensions in India which arise from a conflict over these values. The aged continue to expect deference from the young, but, increasingly, the young expect deference from the aged because of their higher levels of formal education.

[37] U.S. Army, *Handbook*, p. 134. Herbert H. Vreeland writes: "Since it is also a period of maximum power, influence, and wealth, old age rather than youth is often regarded as an ideal time of life" (*Iran* [New Haven: Human Relations Area Files, 1957], p. 236).

percentage in the lowest rating of reputed power is a similar 27.1 per cent. At the higher levels of power, however, the differences are slightly more pronounced. Of the younger elite, 37.6 per cent had found access to the most powerful group, with reputed power scores of 10 to 20; whereas 43.8 per cent of the older elite were among that group. Put differently, whereas the elite sixty years of age or older constitute 36.2 per cent of the entire elite, they make up 40.6 per cent of the most powerful group. Conversely, 34.6 per cent of the politically powerful are under the age of 50 but only 33.3 per cent of the most powerful are in that age group.

But while the association between age and power is positive, the relationship is not especially powerful. We would suggest that whatever positive association exists is not that between power and age qua chronological longevity. Rather, the older elite tend to be more powerful because age tends to be correlated with the length of one's active political life which is, in turn, correlated with mobility to positions of political power. Put more simply, the older elite would be expected to be more powerful because they have spent more time gathering and controlling bases of political power.

But why, then, is the association not more significant for these older elite? The answer lies in the course of recent political history in Iran. With the advent of Hassan Ali Mansur to the premiership in 1964, a group of younger "technocrats" were brought into the cabinet. In most cases, these ministers had never previously held a major post within the bureaucracy. (One of these men was even younger than the Constitutional age level for ministers of thirty. When questioned, he abruptly raised his age to the minimim.) But despite the youth of these "new" elite, their formal positions served as sufficiently important bases of power to thrust them, literally overnight, to high levels of reputed power. Table 6.7 reflects this development. The most distinctive feature of this

TABLE 6.7
Ages of the Elite by Formal Occupational Position

Age in Years	Occupational Position			
	Cabinet	Director, Ministerial Dept.	Senate	Majles
Less than 50	53.6%	39.3%	4.3%	57.9%
50-59	21.4	39.3	21.6	26.3
60 or more	25.0	21.4	76.1	21.1
Total	100.0%	100.0%	100.0%	100.0%
N	(28)	(28)	(47)	(20)

Note: $x^2 = 34.364$; df = 6; p < .001; gamma = .253.

table is the high proportion of cabinet ministers in the youngest category and the even greater proportion of senators in the oldest age group. The members of the Senate most nearly approximate the conventional model between age and power. For the Senate itself has little institutional influence (being a captive of the royal prerogative) and membership in the Senate, while conferring status, confers no political power. The high levels of reputed power achieved by its members are based on their past positions and lengthy careers in the service of Iran. The cabinet represents the reverse side of the coin. For the bureaucracies that its members direct control and expend huge budgets and employ tens of thousands of persons. There, power is associated with position (and not vice versa, as is the case with the former group).

The remaining positions represent a middle ground. The directors of ministerial departments are more nearly equally divided among the three age categories and such a position is one to whose holders intermediate levels of reputed power were assigned. The members of the Majles, like the cabinet ministers, are predominantly younger men. But like the Senate, the Majles has little influence over the political process. Consequently, its members who lacked lengthy service were accorded low levels of power.

Thus within the political elite, at least, there is no simple relationship between age and power. While the latter seems to accompany the former, the influence of formal positions appears to override the importance of age. And as His Majesty has demonstrated an increasing penchant for technical competence rather than experience among the elite, age will continue to decline in importance. One member of the elite violently disagreed with this prediction. "Science," he argued, "is the basis of our government and science is the fruit of experience." But he clearly spoke for a dwindling minority.

RELIGION

Free thought and faith—the upshot's one; they wrangle o'er a name:
Interpretations differ, but the dream is still the same.[38]

The political elite are basically unified in their professions of religious belief. Ninety-seven per cent of the respondents noted that Islam was their preferred religion. The remaining five individuals counted one Christian, one Baha'i, and three who refused to answer on the grounds of "invasion of privacy." This overwhelming preponderance of Moslems among the responding elite is matched by the preponderance of Mos-

[38] Browne, *Year Amongst the Persians*, p. 133. The poem is by the Persian poet Sa'ib.

147

lems in the population at large. The 1956 census indicated that some 98.4 per cent of all Iranians considered themselves Moslems.[39]

Once past this rather indiscriminate tally of Islam versus non-Islamic religions, however, more interesting divergencies appear. The elite were also asked to relate the extent to which they actively pursued the dictates of their religion (see table 6.8). The distribution of approximately

TABLE 6.8

Extent to which Elite Respondents Execute the
Duties of their Religion

Degree	Percentage
Very much, completely	24.0
To an extent	18.0
Little	22.2
None at all	19.2
Other answers, miscellaneous	16.6
Total	100.0
N	(167)

equal answers across the various categories of degree of religious observance may be surprising to students of American politics familiar with the readiness with which leading politicians fulfill the public requisites of religious observance. It is similarly unexpected to those who are schooled on the allegedly pervasive qualities of Islam.

But the willingness of 41.4 per cent of the respondents to admit that, at best, their religion sat lightly on them is not particularly remote from the secular trends evident throughout Iran. Be it in the area of reduced political leadership provided by members of the Islamic clergy or the diminution of clerical influence on the educational system of Iran, it is obvious that secularism in the form of "a-religiousness" rather than "antireligiousness" is growing. The efforts of groups and individuals to "purify" or "regenerate" Islam tend to fail, unheeded.[40] Religion is not

[39] Ministry of Interior, *Census Statistics*, 2: xvii, 146–59 (table 11). Census data on religious preferences were glaringly inadequate, as Baha'ism was not considered an officially recognized religion but a heretical and deviant Islamic Schism. "Baha'i" does not appear in census code categories under religion. The category for "other" religions contains 59,256 individuals (0.3 per cent of the entire population) which is vastly below even the most conservative estimates for the number of Baha'is in Iran. One is forced to conclude that Iranians who were so rash as to report their religion as Baha'i were counted under Moslems. The remainder, perhaps yielding to the traditionally approved *taqiya* (dissimulation or bending to the inevitable), undoubtedly announced to the census takers, "Islam."

[40] The efforts of the followers of Ahmad Kasravi to make Islam meaningful for our times have, by and large, been greeted by derision from religionists and the ulema and neglected by the rest of the population. (Cf. the forthcoming book by

so much frontally challenged as a system of beliefs by the political elite, as it is peripherally ignored. Where religion is accorded deference by the elite, it is most often as a political force.

Additional insight into the relevance of religion for the elite may be gained from a closer examination of their stated religious preferences. Elite respondents specified their preferences for Islam in three ways. One group of respondents replied that they were Shi'ites ($N = 63$). Another group replied that they were Moslems by birth ($N = 24$), and yet another group identified themselves as Moslems ($N = 74$).[41] A breakdown of these preferences by the extent of religious practice is shown in table 6.9.

TABLE 6.9
Claimed Execution of Religious Duty

Stated Religious Preference	Yes Completely or To an Extent	No Little or Not at All	Total	N
Shi'ite	81.5%	18.5%	100.0%	63
Islam	37.5	62.5	100.0	24
Islam, by birth	0.0	100.0	100.0	74

Note: x^2 = 42.402; df = 2; p = .001; gamma = .848.

Those of the elite for whom religion means Shi'a Islam find that religion salient and practice their religion. Those members of the political elite who profess the faith of Islam or Islam by birth are those who tend *not* to practice their religion. (But only 37 per cent of the elite explicitly considered themselves to be Shi'ites.) This phenomenon of the majority of the elite considering themselves "Moslem" while that designation bears with it little personal saliency has additional significance as it lies at the root of the foreign relations dilemma of Iran in the Middle East. The country is an Islamic nation whose interests would be assumed coincident with the Islamic bloc, but the very root of the connection, Islam, is of little salience among many present members of the political elite. When religion does become salient for the elite, it is Shi'a Islam, which by its very nature and by the tradition of its longstanding doc-

---

William Staley [Ph.D. diss., Princeton University, 1967] on Ahmad Kasravi and his followers, the *Azadegan* [the Partisans of Freedom].) Groups such as the Society for the Propagation of Islam or the Society for the Regeneration of Islam do exist, but without tangible effects.

[41] Actually, one Moslem respondent specified his preference as "Sunni Moslem." Given that he represents but one individual of the 97 per cent who are Moslems, he will not be included in these calculations.

trinal and political disputes with Sunni Islam, tends to isolate and segregate Iran from her Islamic brethren.[42]

The historical development of Shi'ism and its differences with Sunni Islam amplify these findings. For the adoption of Shi'ism as the official state religion of Iran by the Safavids in the sixteenth century had the major effect of defining the nation of Iran and of isolating Iran from her Sunni Arab and Ottoman neighbors to the west and Afghans to the east. The doctrines, which are essentially similar to those of Sunni Islam, differ in conceding to Ali, the son-in-law of the Prophet Mohammad and the fourth Caliph, and his descendants the sole legitimate claim to the Caliphate. "Shi'ism began as a purely Arab and purely political faction" following the death of Ali and "appealed with great success to the discontented masses and especially to the Mawali [Moslems converts who were not full members by descent of an Arab tribe]."[43] With its original home in present-day Iraq, the sect spread to Iran and "served as a cloak for the introduction into Islam of all sorts of old oriental beliefs, Babylonian, Persian, and even Indian."[44] From its very inception, then, Shi'ism served as a divisive force within the *umma* (Community of the Faithful).

Another effect of the lack of saliency that religion bears for the majority of the elite is a domestic one. In contrast to the nonreligious elite, the majority of the population of Iran, or at least the urban, mobilized segment of the population, are allegedly committed Shi'ites.[45] Cer-

---

[42] It is not meant here to suggest that there exists any unidimensional or unicausal phenomenon to explain Iran's relations with other Islamic countries, but rather to raise what certainly must be considered one of the central factors in those relations.

[43] Bernard Lewis, *The Arabs in History* (New York: Harper and Brothers, 1958), p. 71.

[44] H. A. R. Gibb, *Mohammedanism: An Historical Survey* (London: Oxford University Press, 1957), p. 121.

[45] Empirical evidence on the saliency or meaning of Islam is sadly lacking and our data bear no relevance to this point. Observation of mass participation in religious mourning and festive days and the ability of the Ayatollahs and *mullah*s to bring "their" people out onto the streets in huge numbers do suggest the correctness of this assumption. Similarly, rare has been the diplomat, author, or traveler in Iran who, feeling able, or more likely, obliged, to write on his Iranian experience, has failed to mention the importance of Shi'ism for "the people." These indications notwithstanding, this author prefers to reserve final judgment in the absence of better evidence. It may be appropriate, however, to relate my assumptions. The burden of Shi'ism is, I would suggest, carried as easily by the majority of the people as by the elite. There is indeed a great deal of popular emotion generated on religious holidays and religious leaders do exert a considerable influence over the faithful. Popular behavior reflects cultural or political phenomena rather than religion, however. Shi'ism as an ordered body of earthly and transcendental doctrine is far less important than Shi'ism as a cultural and political phenomenon. It is of great aid and comfort to the regime and the majority of

tainly there exists a highly vocal (albeit privately highly vocal) cadre of religious leaders and activists who have immense influence with the urban population and who are unalterably hostile to the elite in this regime. Moreover, there is a long and revered tradition of religious officials leading mass movements into the midst of major political controversy. The activities of principal *mullah*s in the Tobacco Concession controversy of 1891–1892, the Constitutional Revolution of 1905–1907, and the initial resistance to Reza Shah are well remembered.[46] Thus, the failure of the political elite to accord great seriousness to their religion—insofar as that is perceived—results in the further estrangement of the defenders of the faith. Major, violent, antigovernment demonstrations in cities throughout Iran in June 1963 are but the latest testament to that estrangement. Coming, as it did, on the heels of the passionate Moharram ceremonies, touched off by the untimely arrest of prominent Ayatollahs, and led by religious fanatics, it suggests that religious leadership of political movements is not a curious relic of past history. The more recent arrest and exile of the Ayatollah Khomeini suggests that the government is also fully aware of this phenomenon.

These blatantly antireligious acts in concert with the perceived lack of personal relevance that Shi'ism apparently holds for the elite exacerbates antiregime sentiment and the reputed illegitimacy of the present regime. In recognition of this, His Imperial Majesty and the elite frequently manipulate religious symbols in an attempt to make credible their publicly expressed concern for religion. The shah invites religious dignitaries to formal and highly publicized court audiences. At a recent *salaam* ceremony, for example, the "official" religious leaders (the only ones invited to such functions) paid homage to the king as "herald-bearer and defender of the Shi'a world."[47] In addition, the shah offers financial support for the repair and maintenance of religious shrines; religious dignitaries are on hand to bless the safety of His Majesty on his foreign travels; the shah and political leaders make pilgrimages to holy places in Iraq and Meccah and Medina; and finally, the bureaucracy, at least

---

the political elite that the institutional embodiment of the religion is weak and unstructured. Accordingly, the religion as a political force cannot bring sustained and serious pressure to bear on the government.

[46] See Nikki R. Keddie, *Religion and Rebellion in Iran: The Tobacco Protest of 1891–1892* (London: Frank Cass and Co., 1966); Firuz Kazemzadeh, *Britain and Russia in Iran, 1864–1914* (New Haven: Yale University Press, 1968); Ann K. S. Lambton, "The Tobacco Regie: Prelude to Revolution," *Studia Islamica*, 22: 71–90; and Peter Avery, *Modern Iran* (London: Ernest Benn, 1965), pp. 266–67.

[47] *Kayhan International* (Tehran), May 2, 1964, reports these remarks on the occasion of an audience for the Shi'a celebration of Id-e Ghadir (to commemorate the day when Mohammad allegedly designated Ali as his true successor).

halfheartedly, does enforce Islamic laws during the Moharram and Ramazan mourning and fast days.[48]

But despite the frequency of these efforts, there is a failure to overcome the bifurcation between elite and mass stemming from the secularism of the former. For one thing, the official religious leaders who publicly perform Shi'ite rituals or appear at court functions are widely viewed as "kept" *mullah*s. Their stock in the knowledgeable community at large is nil. For another, even profound acts of piety by the elite cannot overcome the hostility that popular religious leaders acting in both their religious and their political capacities bear for the elite.

Our data show little likelihood that these untoward foreign and domestic consequences of elite "a-religiousness" or outright hostility to Islam will abate on account of changes in elite attitudes. In fact, in the absence of significant secular trends among Iran's neighbors and people, these patterns are likely to worsen in the future. For younger members of the elite are less likely than their elders to take their religious duties seriously.

TABLE 6.10
Elite Execution of Religious Duties by Age

Execution of Religious Duties	Age of Respondents		
	49 or Younger	50-59	60 or Older
Yes, completely, plus to an extent	28.8%	54.1%	70.0%
No, little, plus not at all	71.2	45.9	30.0
Total	100.0%	100.0%	100.0%
N	(52)	(37)	(50)

Note: x^2 = 17.545; df = 2; p = .001; gamma = .543.

In Iran, as in other countries, one frequently hears the argument that "the youth will return to the fold" and that one need not fear their transitory lack of religious fervor. In fact, the data do not show whether Iranians become more religious as they grow older or whether younger people in Iran are less religious than their fathers were at the same ages.

[48] "No Films During Mourning Period" (*ibid.*, April 25, 1965) goes on to relate that cinemas would be closed for five days, liquor stores for seven days, and that all secular music would be banned from the mass media for the full month of Moharram. *Kayhan* (Tehran), Dec. 11, 1966, related that "The General Police Administration requested the public yesterday to refrain from eating, drinking, or smoking in public throughout the month of Ramazan." These and other articles go on to elucidate the dire consequences to flow from violating such codes. In fact, they remain unenforced in all but the most traditional sections of Iran's cities.

But there is evidence that suggests that the latter is more nearly true. Religious performance is compared with education level in table 6.11. While the few cases make analysis difficult, it seems clear that for all but the oldest of the elite, higher levels of education are associated with the

TABLE 6.11

Elite Execution of Religious Duties by
Education Level and Age

Religious Execution	Age of Elite								
	Less than 50			50-59			60 or Older		
	M-S[a]	U[b]	PG[c]	M-S	U	PG	M-S	U	PG
Yes	33.3%	42.9%	22.9%	66.7%	83.3%	35.3%	68.7%	57.1%	80.0%
No	66.7	57.1	77.1	33.3	16.7	64.7	31.2	42.9	20.0
Total	100.0%	100.0%	100.0%	100.0%	100.0%	100.0%	100.0%	100.0%	100.0%
N	(3)	(14)	(35)	(3)	(12)	(17)	(16)	(14)	(20)

[a] M-S = education at the maktab or secondary level.

[b] U = university.

[c] PG = postgraduate.

lower performance of religious obligations. We can expect, then, that as the political elite become better educated, they will be increasingly non-religious irrespective of the age level. And there is ample evidence that age and highest level of formal education achieved are inversely corre-lated among the elite.

That the younger elite are unlikely to grow in religious fervor as they gain in years is also suggested by table 6.12. Holding education level constant, we can compare knowledge of the Arabic language with lack of it for each age group. (Inasmuch as the "liturgy" for Shi'ite religious

TABLE 6.12

Knowledge of Arabic by Age Group, Given
Various Levels of Elite Education

Claimed Knowledge of Arabic	Elite's Highest Education Level								
	Maktab-Secondary School			University			Postgraduate		
	To 49	50-59	60 or more	To 49	50-59	60 or more	To 49	50-59	60 or more
Yes	0.0%	50.0%	50.0%	16.7%	29.4%	50.0%	25.0%	40.7%	54.2%
No	100.0	50.0	50.0	83.3	70.6	50.0	75.0	59.3	45.8
Total	100.0%	100.0%	100.0%	100.0%	100.0%	100.0%	100.0%	100.0%	100.0%
N	(4)	(4)	(4)	(18)	(17)	(20)	(40)	(27)	(24)

observances is given in Arabic, it might be assumed that familiarity with Arabic would be essential for absolutely proper conduct of religious ritual.) The table shows us that, indeed, knowledge of Arabic does increase with education level, irrespective of the age of the elite. But while familiarity with Arabic increases with education, knowledge of Arabic is vastly different within similar educational levels according to age level. Thus of all elite forty-nine or younger, 20.9 per cent claim a knowledge of the holy language. Fifty-one per cent of those sixty years or older do so. On the assumption that Arabic is not something learned late in life, then, this is another indication that even in the future the better educated, younger elite of today are likely to manifest even less genuine religious interest than the older elite do at present. In secular thought as in any other value area, the elite will always lead the remainder of the population. Whether they will remain as perilously out of line with popular sentiment and with Arab states' policies as they are at present is an open question. Our data suggest no reason to assume otherwise.

ELITE FATHERS, ELITE SONS

Granted that your father was learned; but of what use is that to you? . . .
The offspring of a cruel man becomes a tyrant.
Iranian proverb

Members of the political elite had disproportionately higher opportunities for access to their positions in Iranian society and especially to the governmental bureaucracy than did other members of the society, positions that served as the principal base value for gaining political power and thus consideration as members of the political elite. One of the fundamental issues in elite studies is the degree to which access to an elite is restricted to descendants of members of that elite. The issue centers on the extent to which the "power elite" is, in fact, a "ruling class."

Popular mythology about Iran's powerful families suggests that such is the case. The "One Thousand Families" reputed to rule Iran are also alleged to deny political power to others. Indeed, the family connections of the current political elite usually do spread to other members of the elite. To take but one prominent example, the late Hassan Ali Mansur was related by blood or marriage to the following prominent Iranian families: Amini, Qavam, Farmanfarmaian, Vossuq, Pirnia, Moshiri, Vakil, Teimurtash, Malek, Varasteh, Qaragozlu, A'lam, Emami, Zia'i, Azodi, Mo'tamed, Loqman, Naficy, Loqman-Adham, Vahabzadeh, Mo'aven, Nasr, Mojtehi, Ashtiani, Esfandiary, Ebtehaj, Ghavam ol-Saltaneh.[49] Those familiar with the history of contemporary Iran will

---

[49] Echo of Iran, "Hassan Ali Mansur," *For Your Information*, no. 467–68 (Jan. 30, 1965), p. 2; augmented by personal research.

recognize the names of prime ministers, cabinet ministers, senators, aides and adjutants to the Imperial Court, and so on. Evidence from these family ties alone would suggest that one thousand would be a grossly inflated estimate of the number of ruling families.

Although Mansur had an unusually large number of influential relatives, others of the 307 Iranians we have defined as the political elite also could boast of important family ties. Looking at the closest blood relationships within the elite itself, one may find fifteen pairs of brothers, two sets of three brothers each, and one group of four brothers. There are eight members of the elite who can also count ten of their sons within that elite. As a group, 75 per cent of the elite claimed to have at least one influential relation (although not necessarily among the 307). They claimed 18 prime ministers, 48 cabinet ministers, 20 senators, and 21 members of the Majles as such relations. That fully one-quarter of the elite ($N=40$) claimed no influential relationships whatever seems to indicate that this group does not form a totally closed ruling class. Access to its ranks is not limited solely to the scions of its present members. But if this elite group does not form a ruling class, neither is it composed primarily of *nouveau arrivistes*. Perhaps the most striking demonstration of this point is through an examination of the fathers of the elites (see table 6.13). Despite the relatively recent burgeoning of the civil service,

TABLE 6.13

Highest Position Held by Fathers of the
Political Elite

Position	Percentage
Prime minister or minister	9.2
Provincial governor-general or governor	8.4
Department chief (civil service)	6.8
Parliamentarian (Majles or Senate)	5.6
Imperial Court (aide, adjutant, or secretary)	4.8
Ordinary civil servant	4.4
Child of Reza Shah Kabir	3.2
Officer of the Imperial Iranian Armed Forces	2.8
Ambassador	1.6
Total	46.8
Nongovernment posts	25.6
No data	27.6
Total	100.0
N	(250)

some 64.4 per cent of the elite for whom data are available had fathers who held posts in the government or Imperial Court.[50]

[50] That some two-thirds of elite fathers were government civil servants is an astoundingly high proportion. This is true, not only because of the recent explosion in the size of the government bureaucracies, but because of the generally wide-

It is possible that the fathers of the present political elite held posts in the civil and military bureaucracies because of the intervention of their sons. But the implausibility of this notion is revealed by data on the number of years ago that the elites' fathers held their most important positions (see table 6.14).[51] The father of only one member of the

TABLE 6.14

Number of Years Ago that Elites' Fathers
Held their Most Important Positions

Number of Years Ago	Percentage
Holds post now	1.1
1-5 years ago	3.2
6-10 years ago	3.2
11-19 years ago	7.5
20-24 years ago	7.5
25-44 years ago	35.3
More than 45 years ago	42.0
Total	100.0
N	(93)

political elite is now serving in the government. In fact, both this father *and* his son are included in the political elite. It is widely recognized that the father prevailed upon higher authorities to place his son within the civil service (and not vice versa). One other case of a father-son inclusion in the power elite and in government service should be noted, that of Ali Mansur and his son Hassan Ali Mansur. The elder Mansur held the post of prime minister in 1940 and again in 1950. His son held that post from 1964 to 1965. The elder Mansur was reputedly instrumental in obtaining political power and position for his son. Nonetheless, this pair has been excluded from these data due to the untimely assassination of Hassan Ali Mansur in 1965. Aside from these two examples, however, almost 80 per cent of the fathers of the elite who did hold government positions held those posts twenty-five or more years previous. And not only were the fathers likely to have held their government positions prior in time to their sons, but, more importantly, almost all of the fathers held high positions within the civil service.

Because the fathers of present members of the political elite held important and influential government positions, they thus were themselves likely to have been members of the political elite of their day. So

spread disdain which the population as a whole held for such "servants" until recent years. Nikki R. Keddie reports in a personal communication, for example, that government service has been traditionally disparaged (Feb. 2, 1969).

[51] For lack of other data, we have here considered that the date at which the father of a member of the elite held his most influential position was as relevant to the question of father to son or son to father influence as would be the date of the father's last position.

were they members of the intellectual elite of their day. Ninety-five per cent of the fathers of members of the political elite are reported by their sons to have been literate. This literacy figure compares with data for all Iranians over the age of seven, of whom only 15.4 per cent were literate in 1956, and for all Iranians over the age of 55, of whom 93.5 per cent were illiterate in 1956.[52]

These elite fathers are not merely literate, however. One quarter of them have had modern educations, twenty-one having studied outside Iran. Given the relatively recent introduction of secular, modern institutions of learning, this appears all the more striking. As recently as 1923–1924, there were only 227 Iranians studying above the secondary level at institutions that were clearly *établissements supérieurs* and not merely secondary schools with lengthened curricula.[53] A school of law, established by the Ministry of Justice and meant to prepare its students for the judiciary, boasted 69 pupils. And a school of medicine, run by the Ministry of Health, claimed 158 students at all stages of medical training. Only 3,300 pupils were studying at modern secondary schools throughout the country, 2,000 of whom were in Tehran.[54] Secular, modern education appears to have been an important base value in contributing to the acquisition of influential government positions for the fathers of the present elite.

TABLE 6.15

Fathers' Type of Education by Fathers'
Position in the Government

| Type of Education | Highest Position Held | | | | | |
	Prime Minister	Department Chief	Court Officials	Majles/ Senate	Lower Position	No Government Position
Modern-secular[a]	58.8%	53.3%	41.7%	33.3%	9.1%	12.2%
Traditional-religious[b]	41.2	46.7	58.3	66.7	90.9	87.8
Total	100.0%	100.0%	100.0%	100.0%	100.0%	100.0%
N	(17)	(15)	(10)	(12)	(20)	(74)

Note: x^2 = 11.428; df = 4; p = .02; gamma = .536.

[a] Modern-secular education is here defined as formal schooling at public or private elementary, secondary, or higher institutions of learning in Iran or abroad.

[b] Traditional-religious education refers to study at maktab schools and all other institutions for Islamic education.

[52] Ministry of Interior, *Census Statistics*, 2: 77–79 (table 8).
[53] Ministère de l'Instruction Publique, Service de la Statistique, *Annuaire, 1935–1936* (Tehran: Imprimeur Madjles, n.d.), p. 68.
[54] *Ibid.*, p. 69.

For the fathers of the contemporary elite, a striking positive association clearly existed between modern, secular education and influential
government positions. This emphasizes the original relationship between
these structures, to be noted below: the educational system being developed to meet the personnel needs of the bureaucracy. Table 6.15 also
highlights the relevance of education for political power, a phenomenon
clearly operative at present, but obviously important in the previous
generation.

Not only were the fathers of the political elite disproportionately
powerful and well educated, they were also disproportionately wealthy—
at least as measured by the conventional standards of Iran. Some 77.1
per cent of the respondents' fathers or mothers owned land and at least
one-fifth of the respondents' parents owned more than five villages (see
table 6.16). Data on the landholding of the elite and their parents were

TABLE 6.16
Parents' Agricultural Holdings

Number of Whole Villages Owned					
1 or less	2 to 4	5	Undetermined or Urban Land Alone	No Land	Total
20.5%	11.8%	22.4%	22.4%	22.9%	100.0% (N=170)

most difficult to acquire, for at the time of the interviews, land reform
was being pursued vigorously. Even those of the elite whose properties
had already been distributed were wary of association with the "Black
Reactionaries," as the shah was then branding those who opposed the
land reform. One means of avoiding that charge was to deny any association with agricultural land at all. Therefore, the percentage of elite parents owning large holdings has undoubtedly been underemphasized.
Nonetheless, a startling connection among a number of variables is beginning to appear. Wealth, power, knowledge among fathers are all
associated with power among sons.

But wealth and power are also clearly associated among the fathers
themselves. Our data do support the frequently noted observation that
connects landownership and positions of power within the government
(see table 6.17). Of the fathers of the elite who owned land, 61.9 per
cent were employed by the government. But of those who did not own
land, only 38.5 per cent held government posts. But this rather gross relationship masks a more significant finding: the higher the father's position within the bureaucracy, the greater is the likelihood of that father's
owning land. That members of the Majles and Senate (in previous gen-

TABLE 6.17
Fathers' Position in the Government by
Fathers' Landownership

Position	Landownership			N
	Yes	No	Total	
Majles or Senate	100.0%	0.0%	100.0%	12
Ministry or court	88.9	11.1	100.0	12
Prime minister or minister	88.2	11.8	100.0	17
Dept. director, officer of armed forces, or governor	84.2	15.8	100.0	38
Lower level position: govt. clerk, etc.	45.5	54.5	100.0	11

Note: $x^2 = 14.687$; df = 4; $.01 > p < .001$; gamma = .638.

erations of government officials) universally owned land is not surprising. These parliamentarians used a local power base to assure their being returned to office in Tehran. And they used the ownership of land to assure their control over the local power base. But the preponderance of land ownership among other government officials suggests the acute interconnection between the possession of wealth and the possession of political power in Qajar Iran.

As discussed above, however, it is fruitless for us to attempt an assessment of causality. Surely, many of the fathers of the present-day elite acquired political power and elite membership through their large holdings of agricultural land. And as surely, others of the previous generation acquired lands through their government positions or commercial wealth to add elite status to their elite power positions. Possession of land conferred a not inconsiderable economic benefit upon the holder. It also justified the maintenance of a body of armed retainers to protect the holdings from bandits or marauding tribesmen and, in turn, gave the landlord considerable power. In effect, it meant that the government had often to defer to the larger landowner in the areas in which he held land. This again gave the landowner social prestige as well as political power. The fact that land offered both a profitable field of investment and conferred social prestige meant also that the ranks of the landowning classes were increased, not only by government officials who made use of their official position to buy up property in the areas to which they were appointed, but also by merchants and others who had money to invest.[55] Possession of land and political power had additional benefits: the landlord could demand and often receive high-level posts as his price for cooperating with rather than obstructing the government. Or, such posts

[55] Ann K. S. Lambton, *Landlord and Peasant in Persia* (London: Oxford University Press, 1953), p. 140; see also *ibid.*, chap. 13.

might be offered by the government as a form of pre-emptive co-opta-tion.[56] However accomplished, with land came political power and social status.

The fathers of the political elite were radically unrepresentative of Iranian society in other significant ways, and in the process were able to provide their sons with greater access to values useful for the acquisition of power. We have already mentioned that some 30 per cent of elite fathers were born in Tehran, when but twenty-five years previously, in 1940, the population of the city had been merely 540,000, in all prob-ability not more than 5 per cent of the total population.[57] Of the fathers not born in the capital, the vast majority were from the larger cities. A detailed breakdown is shown in table 6.18.

TABLE 6.18
Size of Birthplace of Fathers of Elite

Population of City	Percentage of Fathers Born by Place Size	Number of Places in Iran[a]	Percentage of All Iranians in Resi-dence by Place Size
1,000,000 or more	32.5	1	8.0
300,000 to 999,999	0.0	0	0.0
200,000 to 299,999	16.0	2	2.9
100,000 to 199,999	8.0	7	5.6
25,000 to 99,999	17.8	30	6.6
10,000 to 24,999	10.4	55	4.5
5,000 to 9,999	3.7	91	3.8
1,000 to 4,999	10.4	1,938	17.3
500 to 999	0.6	4,314	15.5
0 to 499	0.6	42,802	34.6
Total	100.0	49,240	98.8[b]

[a] Source: Ministry of Interior, Census Statistics, 1: 12 (table 9).

[b] The percentage of total Iranian residents by size of place does not add up to 100 per cent because 1.2 per cent of the population is officially considered to have "tempor-ary residences," undoubtedly some meager concession to the country's migratory population.

[56] Sir Clarmont Skrine (World War in Iran [London: Constable and Co., 1962], pp. 100–101) details the fate of the Shaukat ul-Mulk, Amir Mohammad Ibrahim Khan Alam. Reza Shah alternately forced Alam to reside in the capital or offered him cabinet or ambassadorial posts, all to keep him away from his large estates in the Qaenat. (Alam's son, Amir Assadollah Alam, partly as a result of his father's enforced residence in Tehran, became a boyhood playmate to the present shah.)
[57] Ministry of Interior, Census Statistics, 1: 5 (table 6), 12 (table 9).

In addition to being born in larger cities, fathers of the present-day political elite pursued urban-based occupations. Table 6.19 represents a distribution of principal occupations of fathers of the members of the elite for whom information is available. Of the 328 occupations repre-

TABLE 6.19

Principal and Secondary Occupation
of Fathers of Elite

Occupation	Percentage
Government service[a]	39.6
Landlord	26.2
Merchant	11.9
Religious leader	8.5
Professional	7.6
Unskilled and miscellaneous	6.2
Total	100.0
N	(328)

[a] Data on percentage of fathers with government occupations differ from data given in table 6.13 because the former refer to all occupations, while the latter refer to principal occupation alone. An individual might hold a succession of official posts and still consider himself, or be considered by his son, as primarily a "landlord," "merchant," etc.

sented, only seven refer to manual occupations such as baker, agricultural laborer, peasant proprietor, craftsman, or herder. In one respect, this surprisingly low percentage might represent an attempt on the part of elite respondents to magnify the memory of their fathers and, in the process, their fathers' importance, by inflating the status of their occupations. On the other hand, the paucity of lower status or manual jobs represented so well correlates with other evidence on social backgrounds presented here that this phenomenon is assumed to dramatize the low level of mobility from nonelite to general or political elite positions.

The remaining occupations in the table pursued by the fathers of the elite—*karmandane dowlat* (government employees), *sahebane malek* (landlords), *tajerat* (merchants), *ulema* (Moslem clerics), and *ahaliye herfe* (professionals)—are specifically those that would provide the greatest physical mobility and access to diverse intellectual currents and experiential stimuli in the performance of the tasks of that occupation. Government officials represent a group whose locale of service frequently required movements to different areas of Iran, or at least inspection tours of the country. The landlords of Iran are widely recognized as an absentee landlord group who make their home in the capital, periodically visiting their estates and indulging in a vast amount of travel for pleasure. The fathers of the elite in commerce represent primarily just that—the import-export or wholesale trade rather than production or industrial enterprise. A great deal of foreign travel has traditionally been associated with this trade. At the least, its successful pursuit requires one to be familiar with foreign developments and markets. Similarly with religion, where pilgrimage is one of the five cardinal duties of a proper Moslem. Moreover, the Shi'a sect, overwhelmingly preponderant in Iran, is especially devoted to pilgrimages in connection with visits to shrines and tombs of especially revered religious figures, the Imams. The chief focuses of Shi'ite pilgrimages are the Iranian cities of Meshed and Qum, Nejef and Kerbela in Iraq, and the centers of Mecca and Medina in Arabia. As such, religious leaders in Iran have always been especially well traveled within the country and much of the Arab world. These pilgrimages result in a cross-fertilization and communication of ideas and information. As Sir Richard F. Burton described one caravan outside of Mecca: "And nothing stranger than the contrasts: a band of half naked Takruri marching with the Pasha's equipage, and long-capped, bearded Persians conversing with Tarbush'd and shaven Turks."[58] Finally, the professional groups in Iran have frequently traveled in the retinue of important political figures, as aides to branches of the Iranian armed forces, or as Iranian representatives to international forums and meetings.[59]

What the generation of Iranians who fathered the political elite of today represents, then, is a group of individuals who have, in manifest ways, been subject to those experiences that result most directly in the development of "empathy." As Professor Lerner has argued, such "high capacity for identification with new aspects of [the] environment" is the

[58] *Personal Narrative of a Pilgrimage to Al-Madinah and Meccah*, 2 vols. (London: Tylston and Edwards, 1893), 2: 66. A scholar of Islam has described this function of the pilgrimage as follows: "Islam has acted strongly . . . to unify in the same culture as much as possible the populations who have adopted it as a religion; the Pilgrimage to Mecca remains . . . the living symbol of this monistic drive" (Robert Brunschvig, "Perspectives" in *Unity and Variety in Muslim Civilization*, ed. Gustave E. von Grunebaum [Chicago: University of Chicago Press, 1955], p. 56). No less an authority than His Majesty King Faisal of Saudi Arabia has noted this same phenomenon. In addressing leaders of the various national pilgrimage delegations, he commented: "Muslim Brothers: God Almighty has imposed the pilgrimage on the Muslims to realise noble benefits and objectives, such as the exchange of views and acquaintanceship among themselves to promote their religious and worldly interests" (Echo of Iran, *Daily Bulletin: Political Edition*, 15, no. 69 [April 3, 1967]: 3).

[59] See, for example, the retinue of professionals that accompanied His Imperial Majesty Naser ed-Din Shah on his visits to Europe in the nineteenth century. Naser ed-Din Shah Qajar, *A Diary Kept by His Majesty, the Shah of Persia, During His Journey to Europe in 1878*, trans. A. H. Schindler and Baron L. de Norman (London: Richard Bentley and Son, 1879).

predominant personal style only in modern society."[60] Better educated, physically mobile, urban-based, relatively wealthy, and working in occupations with decision-making responsibilities that facilitated an exposure to diverse currents, these fathers were already the "new men" of their time.[61] In all likelihood, they provided a relatively cultured and wide-ranging home atmosphere for their sons. This socialization to wider and more modern horizons in combination with the resources and opportunities that they could make available to their sons, would almost insure the inclusion of their offspring in the subsequent generation of the elite.

That those who disproportionately possess that which a society values should have sons who do likewise is not surprising. That the present-day political elite of Iran is so overwhelmingly composed of such sons of elite fathers is, however, rather unexpected after the events of the past seventy years, especially in the face of a Constitutional Revolution; the forced abdication of monarchs; a change of dynasties; two world wars in which Iran was occupied by the United States, Russia, and Britain; tribal uprisings; and all the sordid and not so sordid political machinations to which Iran has been subject from foreigners and Iranians. Thus, while the present political elite of Iran do not constitute a ruling class—access is not restricted solely to children of the elite—there is a marked continuity whereby elite fathers are able to make available the tangible and not so tangible factors that would help insure their sons' membership in the political elite of their own day.

EDUCATION

Oh Ahuramazda, endow me with an educated child.[62]

So begins an early Zoroastrian prayer, a prayer that illustrates the dominant wish of parent for child in early Iran. From these first fragments of ancient evidence, this high value placed on education has been a continual theme in Iranian culture. Herodotus and Xenophon both noted and commented on the importance accorded education in Achaemenid times.[63] Education was still an important priority fifteen hundred years later when a prince of the South Caspian provinces composed a set of guides for living and ruling for his son and eventual successor. The author, Kai Ka'us Ibn Iskandar, remonstrated with the future ruler to "accustom yourself to acquiring wisdom and merit and learn those useful

[60] *Traditional Society*, pp. 49–50.

[61] William R. Polk, "The Middle East: Analyzing Social Change," *Bulletin of the Atomic Scientists*, 23, no. 1 (1967): 12–19.

[62] Reza Arasteh, *Education and Social Awakening in Iran* (Leiden: E. J. Brill, 1962), p. 2.

[63] See, for example, Herodotus, *The Histories*, trans. Aubrey de Selincourt (London: Penguin Books, 1961), p. 70; and Xenophon, *The Cyropedia* (London: Henry A. Bohm, 1924), p. 14, as quoted in Arasteh, *Education*, p. 4.

arts of which you are ignorant. Socrates says that there is no treasure better than virtue, no honor more glorious than knowledge, no ornament more beautiful than modesty, and no enemy worse than an evil disposition."[64] The prince reminded his son that knowledge was not only for oneself but must be passed on to subsequent generations and, moreover, that learning possessed utility other than prestige: "You must . . . teach your children all that needs learning in various acts and accomplishments in fulfilment of your duty as a father and the exercise of your loving kindness as a parent. One can never be secure against the accidents of fate nor foresee what can occur to men whether of good or ill. Every art and accomplishment is of service some day."[65] Education, then as now, was valued as an intrinsic good worthy of honor and prestige and as an important instrument for self-protection, self-gain, and social mobility. Indeed, the foundation of Iran's modern educational system was constructed from just such principles. In 1851, the Dar ol-Fonun (House of Learning) was founded in Tehran as the first government-sponsored institution of learning and the first school in Iran to be operated on contemporary Western lines.[66] This school was established, and the reform of an antiquated and practically nonexistent educational system begun, in response to a series of deleterious encounters with foreign governments. In a manner reminiscent of the American response to Sputnik I, the Iranians came to accept the notion that the infidels were not necessarily barbarians and that one antidote to their successes would be found in the reform and development of education in Iran.

Beginning in 1797, Iran had suffered fifty years of increased contact with Western powers—contact that proved almost totally disastrous to Iran. This fateful half century was initiated by the assassination of Agha Mohammad Khan Qajar, the Eunuch-Shah, who secured the throne for the Qajar dynasty through pursuit of his three passions—power, avarice, and revenge.[67] There followed a series of missions from Napoleon seeking to draw Persia into alliance against the British in preparation for a French march on India. And equally rapidly, a series of British missions made their way to Tehran to prevent such an occurrence. Despite the

[64] *Qabus Nama* [A mirror for princes], trans. Reuben Levy (London: Cresset Press, 1951), p. 28.

[65] *Ibid.*, p. 122.

[66] For information on the Dar ol-Fonun, see Arasteh, *Education*, pp. 20–21; Issa Sadiq, *History of Education in Iran: From Earliest Times to the Present Day*, 3rd ed. (Tehran: Teachers College Press, 1963 [in Persian]), pp. 332–34; idem, *Dowreye Mokhtasere Tarikhe Farhange Iran* [The contemporary era of the history of Iranian education] (Tehran: Sherkate Sahamiye Tabqe Ketab, 1961), esp. pp. 163 ff.; and Hafez Farman Farmayan, "The Forces of Modernization in Nineteenth Century Iran," in *Beginnings of Modernization in the Middle East*, ed. William R. Polk and Richard L. Chambers (Chicago: University of Chicago Press, 1968), pp. 119–51.

[67] Sykes, *History of Persia*, 2: 295.

fact that the recently crowned Fath Ali Shah was horrified at the regicide nation, Persia and France signed the preliminary Treaty of Finkenstein in 1807, pledging mutual support for an invasion of India.[68] British pressure on the shah increased. Finally, with the failure of the French to aid the Persians in their wars with the tsar, Iran abrogated its earlier agreements and signed a new mutual assistance pact with Great Britain. Besides many provisoes almost identical with the Treaty of Finkenstein, the new agreement had the added advantage of providing an annual subsidy to Iran of 150,000 pounds, to be spent under the supervision of the British ambassador.[69]

In addition to these intra-European political contests fought out on Iranian territory, Persia waged a series of debilitating and destructive wars with her more powerful neighbors to the north and west. From 1804 to 1812, Iran contested Russian pressures on Georgia and Armenia, but by 1813, in defeat, Iran recognized Russian demands on much of the Caucasus, ceded Baku and other Persian cities to Russia, and agreed to maintain no navy on the Caspian Sea. Only eight years later, Persia fought her last campaign with Ottoman Turkey. After a number of initial successes, the Iranian army was decimated by cholera and sued for peace. But Iran had yet to engage in her last major and degrading military encounters with Russia. These occurred from 1825 to 1827 and culminated in the Treaty of Turkomanchai. This document not only specified the cessation to Russia of the Persian provinces of Nakhjavan and Yerevan and the payment of an indemnity of 3 million pounds, but also marked the institution of extraterritoriality. Swiftly extended to the subjects of other European powers, these capitulations marked the end of an entirely independent Persia, an end that was dramatized by the increasing intervention of the British and Russians in the internal affairs of Iran.[70]

Other events in the later years of the first half of the nineteenth century gave dramatic witness to the decline in Iran's capacity to regulate its own internal and external affairs. A Persian expedition to wrest what it considered its rightful territory from Afghan control from 1836 to 1838 was finally suspended on pressure from the British. (As the Persians laid seige to Herat, the British landed troops in Persian Gulf

[68] Sykes reports that in his first audience with the French ambassador, Fath Ali Shah allowed himself to ask but three questions: "How are you?" "How is Bonaparte?" and "What made you kill your king?" (*ibid.*, p. 304).

[69] *Ibid.*, p. 309. The subsidy was to continue in force indefinitely, to be halted only in the event that Iran engaged in a war of aggression. Also see Ahmad Matine-Daftary, *La Suppression de Capitulations en Perse: L'ancien régime et le statut actuel des étrangers dans l'Empire du "Lion et Soleil"* (Paris: Les Presses Universitaires de France, 1930).

[70] Sykes, *History of Persia*, 2: 320. These capitulations were in force until their unilateral revocation by Reza Shah on May 10, 1928.

ports. When finally broached to the shah, this "invasion" had assumed gargantuan proportions.) Later, British and Russian "advice" resulted in the retirement of the Iranian prime minister.[71]

By the accession to the throne of Naser ed-Din Shah in 1848, it must have been clear to the young king and his vizier, Mirza Taghi Khan, that the Western powers had consistently demonstrated their superior power over Persia. Not only were they superior, but their superiority appeared to lie in advanced education. Records of the Imperial Court support this contention. In them are found such thoughts as "the Russian Government at the time of Peter the Great used modern education from the West and the teaching of the natural sciences and military skills to form an organized army using modern weapons to become powerful and attack the Empire of Iran and wrest the rich lands of the Northern Caucasus from us," and "Britain had gotten very powerful from the adoption of modern science and industry."[72]

The Dar ol-Fonun was the response. Admitting students aged fourteen to sixteen, the school was an attempt to provide educated cadres for the government's civil and military bureaucracies, cadres that would restore Iran's lost greatness and prestige. With a core curriculum of foreign languages, natural sciences, mathematics, history, geography, and drawing, students could specialize in infantry, cavalry, artillery, engineering, medicine, pharmacy, or geology.[73] Boasting foreign (mostly Austrian) instructors and textbooks, the Dar ol-Fonun set intellectual standards and social and educational precedents that hold true to the present day. Education was perceived as preparation for government service and students were to be instructed in subjects that would be of direct relevance to strengthening that service. Since education existed to fill slots within governmental bureaucratic structures, no move towards mass education was made. In fact, entrance tended to be restricted to the children of the social, economic, and political elite.

The Dar ol-Fonun remained in its isolated position—a modern innovation capping the traditional *maktab* (Islamic educational system) for some fifty years. But when other institutions of higher learning were founded, they were formed of basically the same mold. For example, a

---

[71] *Ibid.*, p. 339.

[72] Sadiq [History of Iranian education], pp. 330–34.

[73] There had been, of course, a previous tradition of state-supported educational institutions in the Islamic world. The Persian Vizier Nizam ul-Mulk completed the construction of the *Nizamiya Madresseh* in Baghdad in A.D. 1067. While certain *madresseh* had been state supported in the past, Nizam ul-Mulk was the first to regularize their financing, to strengthen markedly their training of government servants, and to appreciate their potential for the stabilization of the Seljuq Empire. Cf. Aydin Sayili, *Higher Education in Medieval Islam: The Madrasa* (Ankara: Universitesi Yilligi, 1948), pp. 50 ff. Unfortunately, this practice of state-supported education had been abandoned early in Iran.

School of Political Science was opened in 1901 under the sponsorship of the Ministry of Foreign Affairs. Initiated and supervised by Mirza Hassan Khan, Moshir ol-Dowleh, a graduate of Moscow University in political science, the school trained prospective diplomats. In fact, graduates of the five-year curriculum were obliged to serve in the Ministry of Foreign Affairs for a number of years without pay.[74] (The necessity to serve without pay was another means of insuring that only well-to-do young men would find their way into the higher educational system and the Ministry or other governmental service.)

Thus the educational system as developed in the nineteenth and early twentieth centuries in Iran had profound social effects. The gap between elite and mass was widened by the addition of yet another criterion for elite membership, another distinction that the elite would possess. Not only was the gap widened but it was made nearly unbridgeable. For with the tendency to restrict higher education to scions of elite families and the establishment of higher, or at least modern, education as a chief requirement for service in the upper reaches of the administrative or military bureaucracies and the foreign service, access to elite status through official channels was closed. Modern education became a distinguishing characteristic of the elite, but an education that it was all but impossible for children of the masses to acquire.

The political elite of today reflect this emphasis. In a country where illiteracy is paramount—some eighty-five of every one hundred Iranians can neither read nor write—the elite are astoundingly well educated.[75] Table 6.20 presents graphic evidence that members of the elite have had the benefits of formal education to a greater extent and to far higher levels than other segments of the Iranian population. In his study of Turkey's Grand National Assembly, Frederick W. Frey noted a similar phenomenon: "Within a political system or subsystem, the higher the level of formal authority of the concrete unit selected for examination, the greater the incidence of personnel of high social prestige among the members of that unit."[76] Indicating that education is a prime source of social prestige, he goes on to explain this relationship principally in terms of legitimizing the power of the influencer.

Statistics presented here are only partly relevant to Frey's work, for they contain educational levels of social or residence groups rather than occupational groups alone. Nonetheless, in the Iranian context, the same relationships between levels of prestige and of actual power are present.

[74] Arasteh, *Education*, p. 24. See also Abdullah Mostaufi, *Sharhe Zendeganiye Man ya Tarikhe Ejtema'i va Edariye Dowreya Qajariyeh* [The history of my life or a social and administrative history of the Qajar period], 2nd printing, 2 vols. (Tehran: Ketab Forushi Zavvor, n.d.), 2: 67–74.

[75] Ministry of Interior, *Census Statistics*, 2: 77–79 (table 8).

[76] *The Turkish Political Elite* (Cambridge: M.I.T. Press, 1965), p. 400.

TABLE 6.20

Highest Educational Level Achieved

Education	Elite[a]	Majles	Tehran	Iran
No formal education	0.0%	0.0%	67.6%	83.3%
Elementary	0.0	16.2	21.9	12.2
Secondary	8.2	14.5	8.4	4.1
University or postsecondary	41.1	39.7	1.8	0.4
Postgraduate	50.7	29.6	0.3	0.1
Total	100.0%	100.0%	100.0%	100.0%
N	(231)	(179)	(991,365)	(6,542,181)

Source: Statistics for Tehran and Iran are for males only in order to enhance comparability with the political elite and the Twenty-first Majles, whose members are overwhelmingly male; from Ministry of Interior, Census Statistics, 2: 80-142 (table 9). Data for members of the twenty-first session of the Majles from Zahra Shaji'i, Namayandegan-e Shoray-e Melli dar Bist-o-Yek Dowreh-ye Qanungozari [Representatives of the national assembly in twenty-one legislative assemblies] (Tehran: Institute for Social Research and Studies, University of Tehran, 1966), p. 282 (table 20).

[a] The sixteen members of the political elite who had only maktab educations (6.5 per cent of those for whom information is available) were excluded from this table for lack of comparable data in the Iranian population as a whole or the Majles.

Turning to the political elite alone we note the breakdown in their educational attainments stated in table 6.21. Where did this highly educated political elite receive their educations? Some 85 per cent of the political elite attended secondary schools in Iran. The two schools that graduated the largest number—fifty-one pupils—were the Dar ol-Fonun and Alborz College. Thus the former institution has continued to serve its original function of training its graduates for positions of responsibility. The latter school was run by the American Presbyterian Mission until World War II. Subsequently taken over by the government, it is now the largest secondary school in Iran. Together the two schools have dominated Iranian secondary education until recently, and in terms of facilitating access to the general elite serve much the same function as the Galatsaray School in Istanbul.[77]

[77] Ibid., p. 36; Issa Sadiq [History of Iranian education]. Alborz College served much the same function as did the Dar ol-Fonun, i.e., as a conduit for elite membership. An earlier observer noted of Alborz:

One of the remarkable things about this school is the class of students enrolled. While students from every grade of society and every race and creed are accepted without discrimination, an unusually large proportion are children of the

TABLE 6.21

Highest Educational Level Achieved
by the Political Elite

Level		Percentage
Maktab		6.5
Secondary school		7.7
Postsecondary institute		9.3
University		29.1
Postgraduate studies		47.4
Graduate training	6.1	
Master's degree	7.3	
Doctorate degree	25.9	
Ph.D.	3.6	
M.D.	4.5	
Total		100.0
N		(247)

Indeed, as one measure of "eliteness," the Dar ol-Fonun sent a greater percentage of its graduates who are now in the political elite to higher education than did other institutions (see table 6.22).

But the success of the Dar ol-Fonun is largely a phenomenon of the past. "Privately sponsored" has come to mean not the *maktab*, but the modern secondary school operated on the lines of the English day school.

TABLE 6.22

Sponsor of Secondary School by
Highest Education Level of Elite

Sponsor of Secondary School	Maktab or Secondary School	University	Postgraduate	Total	N
Private	45.5%	27.3%	27.2%	100.0%	33
Foreign government	11.5	30.8	57.7	100.0	26
Iranian government	7.7	34.6	57.7	100.0	26
Dar ol-Fonun	5.7	20.0	74.3	100.0	35

Note: $x^2 = 27.029$; df = 6; p $>$ .001; gamma = .336.

nobility and the aristocracy. . . . It is as if a comparatively small "prep" school in America should number among its students two brothers of President Harding, a son of Woodrow Wilson, two grandsons of William H. Taft, three grandsons of Theodore Roosevelt, and a grandson of Grover Cleveland, to say nothing of the sons of governors too numerous to mention. In addition to these there are studying in the American schools the sons of the imperial princes. . . . Seldom, if ever, has any school had such an opportunity to mould the new life of an awakening nation.

(E. Alexander Powell, *By Camel and Car to the Peacock Throne* [Garden City, N. Y.: Garden City Publishing Co., 1923], pp. 262–63.)

Government-sponsored schools have expanded rapidly and generally improved in quality. Taken together, they have deprived the Dar ol-Fonun of the status it commanded for a hundred years. The recent replacement of its name by a more "up-to-date" title has completed its denouement.

At higher levels of education, slightly more than half of the elite who attended colleges or universities studied in Iran—almost all at the University of Tehran. The 43.7 per cent of those who pursued their undergraduate education abroad did so primarily in Europe. France, with 40 per cent of the Iranian undergraduates abroad, was the most receptive of the host countries, while the United States with some 20 per cent was second. As with the elite of other developing nations, law was the most popular of the undergraduate majors (27 per cent), followed by government and the social sciences (22 per cent), natural science and engineering (16 per cent), humanities (15 per cent), military science (12 per cent), and medicine (5 per cent).[78]

The postgraduate studies pursued by the political elite accentuate patterns already noted. France now becomes that country with the largest number of Iranian postgraduate students (including even Iran itself). Some 47 per cent of all elite members who pursued postgraduate studies did so in France. Iran with 17.2 per cent and the United States with 14.1 per cent place a low second and third. Again, law was the most frequent field of specialization for postgraduate studies (35 per cent), with government and social sciences (19 per cent), natural sciences or engineering (16 per cent), the humanities (11 per cent), medicine (9 per cent), military science (6 per cent), and public administration (3 per cent) following.

The reputed predilection of Iranians for metaphysical speculations may be a valid generalization. But this predilection does not seem to have affected the elite's choice of academic specialization. Although a plurality of the elite did choose the law as their principal undergraduate or graduate major, some two-thirds pursued "practical" subjects—the social and natural sciences, engineering, medicine, military science, and public administration. This emphasis attests to the relatively low repute in which lawyers and the law are held in Iran, the weakness of judicial institutions, and the absence of a legalistic tradition, especially a colonial legalistic tradition. In no sense can legal training be viewed as a prerequisite for high posts in the civil service.

As might be expected, age and educational achievement within the ranks of the political elite are inversely related. The younger elites have the better education (see table 6.23). Whereas 64 per cent of the politi-

[78] For information on lawyers in Egyptian society, see Malcolm H. Kerr, "Egypt" in *Education and Political Development*, ed. Coleman, p. 189.

TABLE 6.23

Age of Elite by Level of Education

Age	Maktab or Secondary	University	Postgraduate
49 or younger	14.3%	35.3%	44.3%
50-59	14.3	31.4	30.7
60 or older	71.4	33.3	25.0
Total	100.0%	100.0%	100.0%
N	(28)	(51)	(88)

Note: x^2 = 20.620; df = 4; p $<$ .001, gamma = -.396.

cal elite forty-nine years of age or younger have had postgraduate studies, only 37.3 per cent of those sixty or over have had such training. Conversely, where only 6.6 per cent (N=4) of the elite under fifty have had only traditional or *maktab* education, one-third of the oldest elite have ended their educations at that level.[79]

As indeed would be expected, sons of educated fathers were themselves educated. More revealing is the extent to which present elite members are generally better educated than were their fathers, and the extent to which educational distinctions persist over the generations (see table 6.24). For members of the political elite, better educated fathers have raised heirs who can boast even higher levels of formal education. If these trends are true for the politically most powerful, how much more

[79] The inverse relation between age and education does not seem to be borne out by statistics on the number of foreign languages which members of the political elite claimed to know. In that case, the relationship is positive, as shown in table 6.c. This seeming paradox can be explained in a number of ways. Most ob-

TABLE 6.c

Number of Languages other than Persian for which Respondents Claimed Knowledge, by Age

| Number of Languages | Age | | |
	49 or Less	50-59	60 or More
One or two	67.2%	59.6%	37.9%
Three or more	32.8	40.4	62.1
Total	100.0%	100.0%	100.0%
N	(52)	(37)	(50)

Note: x^2 = 9.301; df = 2; p $<$ .01; gamma = .400.

vious is that there is no necessary correlation between formal education and a knowledge of foreign languages, which may be learned experientially. A second explanation lies in the area of religious practice. We have already noted that with increasing age there is an increase in the exercise of religious duties. (Whereas 28.8

171

TABLE 6.24

Education Level of Sons by the Education
Level of their Fathers

Highest Level of Sons	Highest Level of Fathers		
	Maktab	Secondary	University
Maktab or secondary	20.9%	0.0%	3.8%
University	30.4	35.3	23.1
Postgraduate	48.7	64.7	73.1
Total	100.0%	100.0%	100.0%
N	(115)	(17)	(26)

Notes: x^2 = 10.166; df = 4; p = .038; gamma = .439.

The marked differential between the levels
of sons' and fathers' educations necessitated
the advancement of sons' education levels by
one category. It will be noticed that we are
comparing sons' educations with fathers'
educations one category less advanced; that
is, the highest level of education for the
sons is postgraduate, while the fathers'
highest level is just university. Even
after making this categorical differentiation, the sons are far better educated than
their fathers.

applicable they must be for the population as a whole, whose fathers had such lower levels of formal education. Our data bear on this in another way. When we examine the educational levels of the elite by the occupations of their fathers, it becomes clear that the three occupational categories most closely associated with wealth and political power—through easier access to the government—produce the larger proportion of sons who have matriculated through modern higher educational institutions. Fathers whose principal occupations were the professions, government

per cent of the elite under the age of fifty reported that they did carry out their religious obligations, 70.0 per cent of those over sixty so responded.) And a knowledge of Arabic is essential for a rigorously correct execution of those duties. Thus besides knowing French and English, the standard repertoire of foreign languages, more of the older respondents than the younger also claim a knowledge of Arabic (52 per cent versus 21 per cent).

A third explanation which might be advanced is that the decline in the knowledge of foreign languages by the younger of the elite is a reflection of the lower cultural value now accorded language and linguistic ability in comparision to the recent past when verbal skills and wordplay were an important attribute of status. Cf. Edward G. Browne, *A Literary History of Persia*, 4 vols. (Cambridge: Cambridge University Press, 1953); and A. A. Brill, "Poetry as an Oral Outlet," *Psychoanalytic Review*, 18 (Oct. 1931): 357–78. For information on the importance of poetry in another society, see Donald N. Levine, *Wax and Gold: Tradition and Innovation in Ethiopian Culture* (Chicago: University of Chicago Press, 1965), esp. pp. 218–37.

service, or landlord boasted elite sons 93 per cent of whom had university or postgraduate training. Only 63 per cent of the elite sons of merchants or religious leaders enjoyed such education.

Merchants and religious leaders have long been associated in Iranian history, the coalition of the two groups at the time of the Constitutional Revolution (1905–1907) being perhaps the most manifest example.[80] In more recent times, the cooperation of the *bazaaris* and *mullahs* has ignited fundamentalist religious sentiment and hostility to the government with dire consequences. It was just such a coalition that lay at the root of the lethal urban riots of June 1963, following the Moharram ceremonies. If we assume that the merchants and religious leaders who are members of the political elite are the vanguard of all merchants and religious leaders, i.e., that they differ in degree but not in kind, then herein lies one sociological explanation for their persisting political alliance. Both groups have consistently failed to participate in the formal, Western, modern educational system in anywhere near the proportions of other groups in the society.[81]

The pay-offs to the elite for persisting in their academic pursuits come about principally in the occupational positions that they are able to attain. We have already noted that institutions of higher education in Iran owe their origin and early support to the needs of the government for trained personnel. Initially, then, these institutions were conceived as necessary fixtures for supplying skills for the government bureaucracy. But in time, the converse belief developed—that the government bureaucracy ought to be expanded to satisfy the employment needs of the graduates. A modern education had been perceived as a necessity

[80] See Edward G. Browne, *The History of the Persian Revolution, 1905–1909* (London: Adam and Charles Black, 1910); Nikki R. Keddie, "Religion and Irreligion in Early Iranian Nationalism," *Comparative Studies in Society and History*, April 1962, pp. 265–95; Ann K. S. Lambton, "Secret Societies and the Persian Revolution of 1905–1906," *St. Anthony's Papers*, no. 4, 1958; and Robert A. McDaniel, "The Shuster Mission and the Culmination of the Persian Revolution of 1905–1911" (Ph.D. diss., University of Illinois, 1966).

[81] This "national coalition" of merchants and religious leaders is demonstrable in other ways. For example, the merchant and *mullah* fathers of present members of the elite had a far greater proportion of *maktab* educations than did other fathers, as can be seen in table 6.d.

TABLE 6.d

Fathers' Education by Fathers' Occupations

| Occupation | Highest Education Level | | | | |
	University	Secondary	Maktab	Total	N
Professional	50.0%	8.3%	41.7%	100.0%	12
Government	39.4	18.2	42.4	100.0	66
Landlord	6.9	10.3	82.8	100.0	29
Merchant	10.3	3.5	86.2	100.0	29
Religious leader	0.0	0.0	100.0	100.0	20

for government service. More recently, government service has come to be seen as a necessity, or at least a rightful reward, for all those with modern educations.[82] This employment pattern is reflected in the following table:

TABLE 6.25

Employer in Present Principal Position
by Level of Education for the Elite

Employer	Level of Education		
	Maktab-Secondary	University	Postgraduate
Government	65.4%	74.0%	80.7%
Nongovernment	34.6	26.0	19.3
Total	100.0%	100.0%	100.0%
N	(26)	(50)	(88)

Note: x^2 = 2.786; df = 2; .25 p $<$.10; gamma = -.249.

Within the narrow stratum that we have identified as the political elite, the government is the chief employer. Critical observation and popular sentiment suggest that below the level of the political elite these trends are heightened to the point where government employment absorbs almost all college graduates and, with the exception of relatively menial positions in the civil and military services, almost no noncollege graduates.[83] C. Arnold Anderson has referred to the practice of filling positions in the governmental bureaucracies through the principal criterion of formal educational achievement as "occupancy by certification."[84] This practice does not necessarily lead to greater efficiency or productivity, although implicit in such employment patterns is the possibility of a government of technocrats.[85]

Another phenomenon of Iranian society is suggested by this analysis. As the political elite of Iran have disproportionately captured values in

[82] Kerr ("Egypt," p. 184) makes a similar point about education and government service in Egypt.

[83] Dr. Hassan Afshar, dean of the Faculty of Law, Economics, and Political Science at the University of Tehran, informed me that while he had no statistics about the subsequent employment of his graduating seniors, he was certain that "the overwhelming majority of them sought and soon found government employment" (personal interview, February 17, 1965). While graduates of this faculty are not representative of all university graduates, their employment patterns are not atypical.

[84] "Society and Education: An Elementary Ethnography of Formal Education" (Lecture delivered at the University of Chicago, Oct. 24, 1966).

[85] See, for example, William R. Polk, "Social Modernization in the Middle East: The New Men," mimeo, 1963.

addition to political power, and become in the process the "elite of elites," so the government of Iran is the "most elite" of institutions. The disparity in terms of the employment patterns of the public and private sectors in Iran assumes the form of a vicious circle. The less well educated its members, the less able the private sector is to compete with or challenge the public sector with its highly educated elite in a society in which education is highly valued. The less able to challenge the public sector, the weaker the private sector becomes. The weaker the private sector, the less able it is to bid for and attract the highly educated. And the vicious circle continues.

This process, moreover, is not one whereby the better educated gain their apprenticeships in the private sector and then move up to government service. The ability of the government to attract the better educated begins with the very first job a member of the elite undertakes (see table 6.26).

TABLE 6.26

Employer in First Full-time Paid Position Held by
Members of the Political Elite by Education Level

First	Education Level		
Employer	Maktab-Secondary	University	Postgraduate
Government of Iran	42.3%	75.0%	81.9%
Private sector	57.7	25.0	18.1
Total	100.0%	100.0%	100.0%
N	(26)	(48)	(83)

Note: x^2 = 15.968; df = 2; p < .001; gamma = 1.479.

The public sector has been able to challenge successfully the private sector in Iran for the employment of the better trained and educated young men. This not only enhances the appeal of government service for future job seekers but it lessens the ability of the private sector to contribute meaningfully to the development of Iran when compared to the public sector. This bifurcation may also, in some measure, account for the apparent hostility of the relatively better educated government civil servant to the less well-educated private businessman. Intraelite rivalries may, in fact, polarize about underlying issues of formal educational achievement and an innate superiority associated with that achievement.

On at least four accounts, therefore, the private sector is at a serious disadvantage vis-à-vis the public sector with regard to the contribution that it can make to Iran's development. First, the private sector has not been able to attract educated young men to its ranks in proportions comparable to government. Second, the very differences in the educational levels of the two sectors contribute to an intensification of the rivalries that would exist on other grounds and serve to denigrate the value of the private sector for the educated. Third, traditional Iranian culture has always placed a low value on commercial undertakings. Indeed, one Iranian historian notes that even the Achaemenids "regarded buying and selling in the market place as ignoble" and goes on to add that "even today, no Persian of position will condescend to enter a shop."[86] This aspect of traditional culture has persisted to the present and is reinforced by the development ideology emanating from the socialist countries. And finally, with no command over the oil resources of the nation and the annual dollar flow that it produces, the private sector cannot hope to compete with the government in bidding for resources or undertaking development projects.

Not only are the better educated of the elite more often found in government service to the detriment of the private sector, but those officials are by far the most active in the social life of their nation. While three-fourths of the elite with postgraduate education are members of three or more organizations, only one-third of the *maktab* or secondary school graduates belong to as many organizations ($p < .001$). The greater activity of the better educated of the elite may indicate that the talents of the educated, in a society that is underendowed in this regard, are more fully utilized.[87] But it also attests to the extent to which the educated elite are able to dominate the life of Iran and the importance of the acquisition of educational qualifications for inclusion in the elite.

FOREIGN LANGUAGES
The ass driver understands the ass's tongue.
Iranian proverb

Knowledge of a language different from one's native tongue is frequently viewed as the mark of a cultured man. This is especially true in Iran. By this criterion, the members of the Iranian political elite are cultured men: only one member of the elite did not know a language other than Persian. The 166 persons who did claim to know foreign languages averaged 2.5

[86] Sykes, *History of Persia*, 1: 171.
[87] This finding is similar to findings from voting and other studies in the United States which have identified a positive relation between level of education and participation in extrafamilial activities. See Bernard Berelson and Gary A. Steiner, *Human Behavior: An Inventory of Scientific Findings* (New York: Harcourt, Brace and World, 1964), p. 379. Also see Charles R. Wright and Herbert H. Hyman, "Voluntary Association Memberships," *American Sociological Review*, 23, no. 3 (June 1958): 284–94.

languages among them. Almost one-fifth of the respondents claimed to know four or more languages (see table 6.27).

TABLE 6.27

Number of Foreign Languages Claimed

Languages Known	Percentage of Elite Knowing
None	0.6
One	16.2
Two	38.9
Three	26.3
Four or more	18.0
Total	100.0
N	(167)

The predilection of Iranian political elite members for foreign languages is in some measure a reflection of the national cultural bent for language and wordplay in general. Iran has long been known for the richness of its language, as its people have been known for their facility with it. But of more direct relevance than the linguistic facility of the entire elite is the relation between the languages known and other variables. As mentioned above, age and number of languages known is positively correlated ($r = .267$; $p = .001$). But the correlation between level of reputed power and knowledge of foreign languages is not statistically significant. Whereas 81.8 per cent of the elite in the lowest power category know more than one language, 84.5 per cent of the medium power group and 86.0 per cent of the most powerful elite claim such knowledge. Clearly, members of the elite at all power levels know a variety of languages (see table 6.28).

TABLE 6.28

Languages other than Persian for which Respondents Claimed Knowledge

Language	Percentage Knowing
French	86.8
English	81.4
Arabic	34.1
German	21.6
Turkish, Turki	13.8
Russian	8.4
Other language	10.2
N	(166)

The overwhelming number of individuals who know English or French suggests the extent to which this group can maintain personal, firsthand contacts in Europe and the United States. These contacts, which are maintained through foreign travel, the foreign press or other media, and personal communication with foreigners within and without Iran, serve to keep the elite apprised of events relevant for their country and its development. But this intimate familiarity with foreign cultures also serves to feed and facilitate the elite's propensity for making the invidious comparisons that are so harmful to Iran. That the percentage of the elite claiming French is slightly greater than that claiming English is a reminder of the predominant role that French culture assumed in earlier times. This is definitely a phenomenon of the past, however. Table 6.29 reveals a decline in the younger group's percentage claiming to

TABLE 6.29

Percentage of Iranian Elite Claiming English
or French as their Best-Known Language
other than Persian, by Age

Language	39 or Less	40-49	50-59	60 or More
English	61.1	42.1	29.7	29.3
French	38.9	57.9	70.3	70.7
Total	100.0	100.0	100.0	100.0
N	(18)	(38)	(37)	(41)

Note: $x^2 = 6.774$; df = 3; $.01 > p < .05$; gamma = .304.

know French best and a corresponding rise in the percentage claiming to know English best. Note that at all age levels, the elite continue to know both French *and* English in overwhelming proportions. It is striking, however, that the proportion of the elite feeling most at home in a given foreign language alters so radically over the age groups.

The dominance of French and English together vis-à-vis any other or all other foreign languages is an indication of the traditionally preponderant cultural and educational position of France and Great Britain, and more recently, the United States. All other languages fall far behind. That only one-third of the political elite know Arabic suggests the extent to which Iran is a distinct entity in what is loosely known as the "Muslim World."[88] The elite who knew German tended to have received technical training in Germany before World War II. The relatively few Persians who claimed to know Russian were, similarly, older men—an

[88] Charles F. Gallagher, *Contemporary Islam: The Plateau of Particularism—Problems of Religion and Nationalism in Iran*, American Universities Field Staff Reports Service, South West Asia Series, Iran, vol. 15, no. 2, 1966.

indication of the extent to which Iran has insulated herself from her neighbor with whom a common border of some 1,100 miles is shared.

But the elite are linguistically isolated from domestic populations as well as from foreign neighbors. The tiny fraction of the elite who know any contemporary Iranian language other than Persian indicates the extent to which this narrowly based, Tehran elite is divorced from vast sectors of their nation. While accurate statistics on the size of linguistic minorities within Iran are notoriously difficult to obtain,[89] table 6.30 is representative.

TABLE 6.30

Major Languages of Iran by Number
of Individuals Speaking the Language

Language	Individuals Speaking	
	Number	Percentage
Turki	3,900,000	20.6
Gilaki	1,160,000	6.1
Luri-Bakhtiari	1,080,000	5.7
Kurdi	1,060,000	5.6
Mazandarani	920,000	4.9
Baluchi	430,000	2.3
Arabic	380,000	2.0
Turkomeni	330,000	1.7
Armenian	115,000	0.6
Assyrian	70,000	0.4
Total	9,445,000	49.8
Persian	9,509,704	50.2
Total	18,954,704	100.0

Source: U.S. Army, Area Handbook for Iran (Washington, D.C.: Special Operations Research Office, American University, 1963), p. 87; and Echo of Iran, Iran Almanac and Book of Facts--1962 (Tehran: Echo of Iran Press, 1962), p.772.

Almost 10 million persons, or nearly half the total population, speak a language other than Persian. The medley of linguistic and ethnic groups that are governed by the shah and his elite attests to the aptness of the official name for the country, *Shahanshahiye Iran*, the Empire of Iran.[90] But only 17 per cent of the elite (N = 28) speak any one of

[89] "The government has acknowledged that the only nationwide census—that of November 1956—under-reported the (ethnic) population by almost ten per-cent" (U.S. Army, *Handbook*, p. 772). A second census, completed in 1966, has not yet been sufficiently analyzed to clarify this point.

[90] George K. Schueller has demonstrated that the Politburo was more "representative" of the Soviet population as a whole than the Iranian elite is of that country. This is all the more surprising because the total membership of the Polit-

these languages (other than Arabic). Of the vast diversity of ethnic groups that make up Iran, only those that are variants of Turkish are represented by any number of the wielders of political power, for twenty-three of the elite speak Turkish or its local variant, Turki. Only five of the elite claim any fluency in other languages indigenous to Iran.

In yet another way, then, this elite is by no means representative of the population as a whole in relation to which it is elite. Individuals with strong regional bases of power or provincial, rural, or tribal constituencies are relatively rarely found in this group of the national elite. To some extent, this is a function of the selection procedures initially used to identify them. To a greater extent, however, it is an accurate reflection of the conditions of political power in Iran today. Local, regional, tribal, or ethnic bases of political power are of little consequence in the game of politics now played in Tehran. And unlike past decades and centuries, that game is now initiated and played out in Tehran. No longer do the outlying centers play the roles they did in the past. The Tabriz of the days of the Constitutional Revolution; the Shiraz and Isfahan of the tribal uprisings; or the Abadan of the prenationalization days have now lost their potency and political import. With the diminution of their power, the practice of local heroes assuming key roles in national politics has also disappeared. No longer would a Samsam from the Bakhtiari, who parlayed Bakhtiari tribal military strength into leadership of the Nationalists after the deposition of Mohammad Ali Shah; nor Taghizadeh of Tabriz, who won prominence throughout Iran for his association with the heroic defense of Tabriz from the anticonstitutionalists; nor Alam of the Ghaenat, whose private army was the dominant military force in eastern Iran before Reza Shah, be able to claim national political stature from a local base.

Such centralization of recruitment into the national political elite is the logical and quite natural culmination of the processes initiated by Reza Shah and carried on by his son and successor, Mohammad Reza Shah. In the course of creating a truly national armed force, Reza Shah also created administrative and educational systems and an industrial base to support that force. With these instruments, he spent much of the first decade of his rule in meeting and successfully overcoming challenges to central authority. This series of military actions highlights the relationship between internal or external conflict and political development. One observer has noted, "The prevalance of war directly promoted political modernization. Competition forced the monarchs to build their military

---

buro, which Schueller considered to be twenty-seven, allowed for less ethnic diversity than would the far larger elite of Iran. See Schueller, "The Politburo," in *World Revolutionary Elites: Studies in Coercive Ideological Movements*, by Harold D. Lasswell and Daniel Lerner (Cambridge: M.I.T. Press, 1966), pp. 106–07.

strength. The creation of military strength required national unity, the suppression of regional and religious dissidents, the expansion of armies and bureaucracies, and a major increase in state revenues."[91] Such was done in Iran—indeed, it was the major focus of the political efforts of Reza Shah. With his abdication and the succession of his son, the process was interrupted. Only with the overthrow of Mossadegh in the summer of 1953 did Iranian policy once again move in that direction. Centralization was the logical outcome; a centralization mirrored in the linguistic capabilities of the political elite.[92]

FOREIGN TRAVEL

He who has seen the world is better than he
who has merely consumed its goods.
Iranian proverb

The members of the Iranian political elite have had far-ranging, frequent, and often lengthy personal and first-hand contact with diverse cultures and countries. Travel beyond the confines of Iran has been a traditionally valued pastime in that society. Virtually all of the politically powerful have been able to enjoy it (see table 6.31).

TABLE 6.31
Number of Trips Outside Iran by Members
of the Political Elite

Number of Trips	Number of Individuals	Percentage
None	2	1.0
One to five	36	18.3
Six to ten	35	17.8
Eleven to twenty	30	15.2
Twenty-one or more	94	47.7
Total	197	100.0

Not only have these elite members traveled frequently, they have also traveled recently, as table 6.32 shows. Hence, their foreign travel was not solely a concomitant of their education or youthful grand tours, but has been a continuing activity.

[91] Samuel P. Huntington, "Political Modernization: America vs. Europe," *World Politics*, 18 (Oct. 1965–July 1966): 402.

[92] The government of Iran has continued to move in that direction irrespective of the actual level or even threat of internal or external war. The consequences—extreme centralization, bureaucratic ineffectiveness, reduced or low political participation, and little reciprocity of power—argue that the relationship between war and development is not unidimensional, nor is it unidirectional.

TABLE 6.32

Recency of Foreign Travel for
Members of the Political Elite

Most Recent Trip Abroad	Number of Individuals	Percentage
Six months or less	103	49.8
Seven months to one year	50	24.2
More than one year to four years	29	14.0
More than four years	25	12.0
Total	207	100.0

If, in gross terms, the foreign travel of the elite has been frequent and recent, it has also tended to be an in-depth experience. Almost one-half of the elite have spent more than ten years outside their native home (see table 6.33).[93]

That ninety members of the political elite have lived more than ten years abroad belies the lengthier foreign residence of some. In fact, fifty-nine individuals, almost one-third of the total, have lived more than fifteen years outside their own country. The record for foreign residence among the elite is currently held by one of the wealthiest businessmen in the capital, who has lived forty-five of his sixty-odd years in the Far East, Europe, and America. The ability of certain of the elite to remain outside Iran for years but, nevertheless, to find a place among the most politically powerful, attests to the co-optation process. The elite need not pass lengthy years moving up the administrative hierarchy. Despite, or perhaps because of, their years abroad, these individuals can still capture political power.

[93] Information on all three of these variables has been presented on the assumption that some combination of the three is essential for describing the effects of personal foreign contacts. We suggest that the interaction of (a) number of different trips abroad, (b) recency of foreign travel, and (c) length of time spent abroad collectively affect individual attitudes, cognitions, etc. which contribute to the facilitation or impedance of political development. In the Iranian case, a high correlation was found among these variables.

TABLE 6.e

Correlation (R) among Foreign Travel Variables

	Number of Trips	Recency of Last Trip	Years of Foreign Residence
Number of trips	–		
Recency of last trip	.423 (p=.001)	–	
Years of foreign residence	.614 (p=.001)	.186 (p=.05)	–

TABLE 6.33

Length of Time Spent Outside Iran
by Members of the Political Elite

Number of Years Abroad	Number of Individuals	Percentage
One year or less	22	11.2
More than one to four	34	17.2
More than four to ten	51	25.9
More than ten years	90	45.7
Total	197	100.0

But what of this point? Is the power of the elite members attributable to their foreign travel? Or do they enjoy more travel as they gain greater power? Unfortunately, our data do not allow a resolution of this issue. But table 6.34 does reveal that the greater the reputed political power,

TABLE 6.34

Number of Foreign Trips by Reputed
Political Power

Number of Trips	Political Power		
	Low	Medium	High
None to ten	57.8%	48.4%	28.1%
Eleven to twenty	11.1	15.6	26.3
Twenty-one or more	31.4	35.9	45.6
Total	100.0%	100.0%	100.0%
N	(45)	(64)	(57)

Note: $x^2 = 10.585$; df = 4; $.20 \langle p \rangle .10$; gamma = .272.

the greater the amount of foreign travel ($r = .401$; $p = .001$). Viewed in another way, whereas 36 per cent of the elite who have made ten or fewer trips abroad are among the least powerful, only 22 per cent of the less traveled are found in the most powerful category. At the opposite end of the hierarchy of foreign travel, the percentages are reversed. Only 22 per cent of the most highly traveled elite are among the least powerful, while 35 per cent are among the most powerful category of the elite.

As power is related to such travel, so is education. The higher the education level of the respondents, the greater the years spent abroad; years spent, of course, primarily in pursuit of that education ($r = .335$; $p = .001$). This relationship is strengthened by the addition of another set of variables also positively associated with foreign travel—father's socioeconomic status. Those fathers who were wealthier or better edu-

183

cated or more frequently employed by the government had sons who were more widely traveled (even holding education constant).

Statistics that indicate a positive correlation between the status and power of elite families of orientation and foreign travel are but an additional indication of the agglutination of values in Iranian society. More specifically, there is not a simple additive quality to these relations, but a geometric one. Not only does the possession of a given value lead more easily to the acquisition of other values, but still other values are acquired at an even faster rate. Family status and family power lead to more power in the future and also lead to greater foreign travel, but status plus travels lead to even higher levels of power.[94]

These data also support one of the charges frequently leveled against the political elite by its opposition. The elite are often branded, in the words of two respondents, as being "oriented to the foreign" or as having "left the customs of Iran for the ways of the *farangi* [European]." Insofar as the powerful have spent so many years of their lives away from their own land and insofar as their contact with foreign lands remains frequent and recent, these charges gain widespread credibility.[95] The saliency of this charge is supported, in fact, by an examination of the countries visited by members of the elite.

Several interesting facts emerge from the statistics in table 6.35. Those areas that have been visited by the largest numbers of elite have been the capitals of *farangistan*—Western Europe and the United States. Oppor-

[94] One value, at least, is not positively associated with foreign travel—those of the elite who travel outside of Iran have fewer children than those who remain closer to home.

TABLE 6.f
Number of Children by Number
of Trips Outside Iran

Children	Trips		
	0-10	10-20	21 or More
0-2	43.9%	50.0%	55.9%
3 or more	56.1	50.0	44.1
Total	100.0%	100.0%	100.0%
N	(66)	(30)	(59)

Note: x^2 = 1.794; df = 2; .50 $\langle$ p $\rangle$ .30; gamma = -.180.

[95] Unfortunately, we have no data that would allow us to compare the elite considered to be "in the opposition" with the nonopposition elite with regard to foreign residence or education. One might suppose that alternative patterns of foreign experience would result in alternative political orientations. We would hypothesize, however, that there is little actual distinction in the amount or locale of foreign experiences among all the elite (aside from the religious leaders) and that the roots of political opposition are to be found elsewhere.

TABLE 6.35

Percentage of Political Elite Having
Visited Foreign Areas

Foreign Area	Percentage	N
Western Europe	97.9	233/238
Turkey	64.6	124/192
United States	64.3	153/238
India	60.7	111/183
Iraq	58.8	107/182
Eastern Europe or USSR	49.7	94/189
Japan	45.4	83/183
Egypt	45.1	82/182
Pakistan	41.1	79/192
Saudi Arabia	36.3	66/182
Afghanistan	17.7	34/192
Africa (Sub-Saharan)	13.5	23/171
South or Central America	8.4	20/233
Australia or New Zealand	3.5	6/171
Communist China	1.1	2/189

Note: Because a variety of data bases was used to
gather and compute these statistics, the number
of the elite having visited the area and the base
used to calculate the percentages are given
separately for each area. Percentages do not add
up to 100, as almost all of the elite have
visited more than one area.

tunities for primary enculturation were certainly present. The elite may very well have learned European or Western styles through travel and residence in the West, and they certainly developed a cosmopolitanism manifest in many of their life styles.

The large number of elite who have actually visited Western Europe and the United States may account for another Iranian phenomenon. When a member of the political elite seeks a yardstick against which to measure the accomplishments or shortcomings of his own country, the yardstick is not likely to be a neighboring developing society. Almost always, Iran is compared to the United States or western Europe.[96] A primary result of these invidious comparisons is to minimize the achievements of Iran and maximize her weaknesses. Irrespective of what it does, Iran can never win. A chief result of using the West as the "reference figure" for Iranian development, therefore, is a widespread sense of

[96] An example of such an invidious comparison was written by Mr. A. A. Amirani, editor of *Khandaniha* (Tehran), in that newspaper on October 9, 1965:

No other country in the world offers citizens as many causes for anger and frustration as our country does. Ordinary people are constantly annoyed, frustrated, and exasperated by everything from unnecessary hooting of car horns, to the ill-manner of drivers and bad driving of taxis, to the delays in cashing checks; from the high cost of education to the high cost of bank loans; to the unscrupulous rivalry between capitalists and between the Government and the people. *Any one of them would be enough to drive an average Swede or Englishman or American stark, raving mad.* [italics added]

185

national backwardness, incessant criticism over the pace of change, and efforts to locate a scapegoat to displace blame for perceived failure.

The Iranian elite have had relatively little personal contact with their immediate neighbors. A natural basis for closer political or economic ties does not exist to the same extent as is true with some European countries.

Only half the political elite have ever visited a country under Communist rule, and these are primarily men in their fifties and sixties who passed through the USSR en route to Europe in the earlier days of poorly developed transportation. The majority of the elite have never been able to witness at firsthand the accomplishments or shortcomings of these regimes. This appears to be the result of regime pressures against such travel, pressures based on the assumption that familiarity breeds friendship. (No recognition is accorded the possibility of familiarity breeding contempt.)

Iran's failure to play any significant role in the affairs of the "third world" of Asia, Africa, and Latin America is mirrored by the dearth of elite visits to those continents.

All of these factors lend credence to the charges of the non-Iranian or Western nature of the elite. Such charges are supported and even reified by a set of statistics ostensibly unrelated to this issue. Elite respondents were asked to report the frequency of conversations or discussion they had with various groups in Iranian society (see table 6.36). Of eleven

TABLE 6.36

Frequency of Elite Communications
with Key Groups in Iran

Group	Less than a Few Times per Week	More than a Few Times per Week	No Answer	Total
Cabinet	35.6%	50.9%	3.5%	100.0%
Businessmen	48.6	47.9	3.5	100.0
Foreigners	51.3	45.2	3.5	100.0
Students	55.8	40.8	4.4	100.0
Workers	56.4	40.0	3.6	100.0
Military	59.4	36.5	4.1	100.0
Peasants	65.9	30.6	3.5	100.0
Royal family	74.3	22.2	3.5	100.0
Union leaders	78.1	18.6	3.3	100.0
Ulema	85.1	11.4	3.5	100.0
				(N=167)

such groups, foreigners were the third most frequently contacted group (on the basis of the number of members of the elite who reported discussions with these groups a few times per week or more often). Members of the elite communicated more frequently only with members of the cabinet and big businessmen. Since communication with these last two groups would entail intraelite communication, it appears even more surprising that of all the groups in Iranian society not composed primarily of members of the political elite, the foreigners are the group with whom the most politically powerful members of the society most frequently communicate.

OCCUPATIONS
A man's profession is his identification.
Iranian proverb

A variety of professions are represented among members of the political elite—physicians and soldiers, tribal leaders and ladies-in-waiting, even astrologers and riding masters are to be found in their ranks. Whatever their particular areas of vocational competence, however, one general characteristic is salient: they constitute an official, governmental elite. Some four-fifths of the political elite were employed by the government —the civil or military bureaucracy or the royal household. What is considered the private sphere of free professions, business, religion, or tribal affairs is represented by only one-fifth of the elite (see table 6.37).

TABLE 6.37

Employers of Members of the Iranian
Political Elite

Employer	First Occupation or Position		Second Occupation or Position[a]	
	N	%	N	%
Government of Iran	217	71.1	95	46.1
Imperial family or royal court	25	8.9	31	15.1
Private, self	61	20.0	80	38.8
Total	305	100.0	206	100.0

Note: x^2 = 32.646; df = 1; p>.000; gamma = .443.

[a] Data on the "moonlighting" propensities of all 307 members of the Iranian elite are difficult to obtain. The 206 whose second positions are represented here refer to those for whom information is available. It cannot be assumed that 101 of the elite not listed here have but one occupation or profession and thus only one employer. Rather, the 101 represent primarily those for whom information is unavailable. Members of the elite who have two occupations but one employer, e.g., who hold two different posts within the government bureaucracy, are listed twice for purposes of this table.

Even more significant for our purposes is the fact that with the exception of a handful of individuals (less than twenty-five), all members of the elite are occupationally dependent on the government in at least one of their positions. Many of the elite in nongovernmental occupations receive incomes from the government on the basis of past employment in the form of pensions, which are granted to all ex-cabinet ministers, parliamentarians, and other high-level personnel with the termination of their employment. Others of the elite, while primarily occupied with private concerns, serve the government as members of ministerial "high councils" (the High Council of Foreign Affairs); officers of government-sponsored and operated professional associations (the Iranian Bar Association); charities (the Red Lion and Sun Society); or in a variety of consultative or advisory roles.

This overlap between the political elite and government bureaucracies is one indication of the importance of government service for attaining political power in Iranian society. And this relationship is well recognized. Governmental positions are constantly sought after by the vast majority of articulate, educated Iranians. Government service can provide one with the formal trappings of authority and assure a flow of deference on the basis of that authority. It also provides an opportunity to form and preserve a clique of bureaucrats who can act and support all other members of the clique. Most importantly, government employment institutionalizes legitimacy of access to the bureaucracy. In this society where the role of the government is dominant and comprehensive and where bureaucratic norms and rational criteria are far from universal, a position that assures participation in the bureaucratic communications net is crucial.

One of the many complements that characterize Iran may be found here. As the elite seek to hold positions within the bureaucracy, the shah operates the bureaucracy as an inclusive, rather than exclusive, body. As we have noted, he seeks to have the civil bureaucracy encompass all those who have the skills or sophistication to operationalize and express their actual or potential dissatisfactions.[97] Moreover, by constantly expanding the size of the bureaucracy, especially at the upper levels, there is an increased likelihood of being able to satisfy the demands of the elite for posts and power.[98]

One other feature of the official character of the elite is their loss of independence vis-à-vis the government. Being part of the government, they must assume some responsibility for official activities. Being respon-

[97] We have also noted above the attempts through manipulation of university entrance regulations and fees to limit the over-all number of such persons.

[98] In 1950 there were 13 cabinet-level ministerial portfolios. In 1957, there were 17; in 1964, 21; in 1965, 24; in 1969, 26. Concomitant with this increase in the size of the cabinet has been a marked expansion in the number of deputy ministers, undersecretaries, and other secondary and tertiary bureaucratic positions, all designed to make "room at the top." In addition, the size of the civil bureaucracy as a whole is now reputed to have reached 300,000 men.

sible, their value as critics of existing policy, at least in the eyes of the most ardent opposition to the shah, is reduced. So is their ability, then, to serve as foci about which that opposition might rally.

But besides the relevance of formal positions for political power, these statistics illustrate the extent to which members of the political elite occupy a variety of positions at the summit of their society. Of the 167 respondents, only 34, or 20 per cent, did not have more than one position for which they were remunerated (see table 6.38). This "moon-

TABLE 6.38

Total Number of Respondents' Positions
for which Remuneration was Received

			Number of Positions				
	1	2	3	4	5	6 or More	Total
N	34	81	31	9	8	4	167
%	20.3	48.5	18.6	5.4	4.8	2.4	100.0

lighting" not only serves the obviously beneficial purpose of augmenting the incomes of the elite, but other ends as well. The practice of holding more than one job contributes to one's power by providing additional institutions on which to count for support. Furthermore, it provides another means of ingress to the complicated morass of Iranian politics. In other words, the elite have at their command yet another lever for affecting the government in beneficent ways. But a negative effect of the intense activity that the holding of more than one full-time position entails is the great toll it exacts in time and intellectual energy. Finally, it might be mentioned that this intense elitist activity serves to keep positions in the command structure of society out of the hands of the nonelite, narrows the size of the political elite insofar as elite status is based on the holding of official or formal positions, and materially enhances the difficulties of mobility from nonelite to elite status.

Let us turn from this discussion of elite employers and numbers of posts to an examination of specific occupations. Of the 307 in the elite, some 8.5 per cent (N = 26) have retired from their life's work and remain inactive. (The political elite include 26 individuals who are seventy years of age or older.) The remaining elite are all active and employed, although 21 persons have been retired (voluntarily or involuntarily) from their principal occupations and taken on new work, e.g., army officers retired from active duty and now serving as senators. Clearly, then, this is not an elite resting on its former occupational laurels, despite its advancing age. What do the elite do? Table 6.39 shows principal occupational positions of the elite.

TABLE 6.39

Principal Occupational Positions of the Elite

Position	Number	Percentage
Senator	49	16.0
Director of ministerial department; director or member of board of government or semigovernment organization	30	9.8
Director or member of board of private company or bank	30	9.8
Cabinet minister	29	9.4
Officer in Imperial Army, gendarmerie, or national police	29	9.4
Ambassador	26	8.5
Representative of Majles	22	7.2
University chancellor, dean, or professor	19	6.2
Journalist	15	4.9
Member, Pahlavi family	14	4.6
Official of the Imperial Court or Imperial Foundation	13	4.2
Ulema	10	3.3
Governor-general, governor, or mayor of Tehran	8	2.5
Professional: M.D., lawyer	3	1.0
Landowner; commercial farmer	2	.6
Other	6	2.0
No information	2	.6
Total	307	100.0

Note: The Persian word shoghl has a dual connotation. It implies both "profession" and "occupation." A respondent who was graduated from a medical school with an M.D. might respond that his shoghl was "medical doctor," even though he practiced no medicine and saw no patients. When asked if he had another occupation he would reply "cabinet minister" or "senator." Often, the respondents referred to their occupations in terms of what their lifelong interests have been or the field in which they were educated. Therefore, they were also asked to mention a second occupation. In many cases, the second mentioned occupation was the source or arena in which the respondent exercised the greatest political power. For purposes of this analysis, then, the author made an estimate as to which of the individual's positions was likely to be most associated with his then elite status. That position has been labeled "present principal position" and is the basis of the table.

In addition, where members of the elite are retired, data are presented for the most recent principal position.

The distribution of occupations among the elite is directly relevant to much of Iranian politics. For one thing, it dramatizes an aspect of the *divide et impera* policy used by His Imperial Majesty when dealing with the political elite. No one particular occupation represents as much as one-sixth of all the occupations of the elite.[99] Eight different occupational groupings fall within ten percentage points of each other. As a result, no particular occupational group can dominate the political life of Iran. And none can ever pose a serious threat to the control of the regime in terms of its ability to impose its will on other sectors of the elite based on the number of its members within the political elite.

Correspondingly, this distribution of powerful individuals over a range of institutions helps explain the uncanny predilection of the Iranian political system for inactivity. Each institution with its coterie of politically powerful individuals is able to check the activities of every other institution. Simultaneously, it is unable to force its own policies on other groups in the society. When clearly acting within the area generally recognized as its legitimate sphere, an institution, especially a governmental institution, can, and, of course, does function to implement policy. Often, however, an institution moves to policy matters that are not generally recognized as legitimate to its sphere or that are perceived as threatening to the institutional or personal interests of another institution and its elite officials. At such times, system power blockages, which are based on the fairly widespread distribution of politically powerful individuals over the major institutional positions, can go into action. One result is institutional *immobilisme* and a failure of the bureaucracy to cope with the requirements of modernization.

Insofar as this system has been created by the shah and he has pressed for the implementation of development plans, this feature of the bureaucracy defeats his purposes. On the other hand, it serves other of his interests insofar as the *immobilisme* of the bureaucracy reduces the likelihood of any organized effort to unseat him. These very tensions—between stability and change, control and independence—are central to the dilemma of the shah in coping with Iran's political system. (We shall return to that dilemma in the concluding chapter.)

Yet another way to illustrate this same phenomenon is from the perspective of reputed political power. Table 6.40 is a rank ordering of the occupational categories by the mean reputed power of the members of each occupational category and of the sum of the reputed political power for all the members of a given occupational category.

[99] We would argue that these conclusions are not the spurious artifact of our categories. Had we grouped the elite differently, other results might conceivably have been produced. But these categories were designed to conform, as closely as possible, to the way in which the Iranian elite itself conceives of occupational groupings in terms of "natural" groupings as well as comparative power.

It is clear that the average reputed power scores for the occupations cover a far narrower range of scores than does the range for individuals. While the least powerful individual included within the political elite had a reputed power score of 4, and the most powerful, 20, these extremes have been eliminated between occupational categories. A sixteen-point range has been reduced to five. This compression of reputed power lies at the heart of the institutional blockages within the system and helps explain the failure of any single group to dominate other groups. Herein lie the institutional checks and balances that characterize the system and that reflect His Majesty's style of rule.

TABLE 6.40

Mean Power and Aggregate Power Ranks,
by Occupation

| Position | Reputed Power Score | | | | Aggregate | |
	Mean	Median	S.D.	Rank	Power Score	Rank
Pahlavi	11.93	12.50	5.11	1	167.00	7
Cabinet	11.83	12.00	3.98	2	343.01	2
Professional	11.33	11.50	3.50	3	33.99	14
Ulema	11.00	11.50	3.55	4	110.00	11
Military	9.62	8.00	4.11	5	279.01	3
Senate	9.33	9.00	2.99	6	457.02	1
Director-governor	8.73	8.00	3.05	7	261.99	4
Ambassador	8.65	7.50	2.73	8	225.00	6
Journalist	8.53	8.00	3.40	9	127.99	10
University	8.53	8.00	3.45	10	161.99	8
Governor	7.88	7.50	1.69	11	63.00	13
Business	7.80	7.00	2.11	12	234.00	5
Court	7.54	7.00	2.10	13	97.99	12
Majles	6.96	7.00	1.52	14	153.01	9

The ranking based on total reputed power for each occupational category represents a different phenomenon. What lies at the heart of the differences here is the number of the elite included in each occupational category. This suggests, quite logically, that in order for an institution to merit consideration as a significant institutional actor, it must include in its ranks some minimal number of powerful individuals. But a comparison of the two rank orderings demonstrates that this is not frequently the case. A rank order correlation (RHO) of the two lists indicates no significant relationship between them.[100] Occupations that include a greater number of the politically powerful do not tend to be those occupations with the most powerful of the political elite in their ranks.

Only the cabinet occupies the same position on both rank orderings, indicating its central position within the bureaucracy. The royal family, surprisingly, does not occupy such a position. Three factors would seem to account for this. First, the mother and stepmother of His Imperial Majesty have tended to fall in political status in recent years as their advancing age has forced a curtailment in their activities. Second, two stepbrothers of the shah have been denied official access to the royal court, with consequent lessening of their political power. And third, besides the direct issue of Reza Shah, the royal family is composed of spouses and ex-spouses of his children, and their reputed power tends to be low. If we were to consider the royal family as only the king and his brothers and sisters, their average reputed political power would be 12.10. Excluding the two disenfranchised black sheep, their average power would be 14.5, far above the mean for any other group.

The three occupations with the widest spread in their positions on the rank orderings are the professionals, religious leaders, and businessmen. Therein lies another clue to understanding Iranian politics. The private businessmen rank fifth in total power, but twelfth in mean power. In other words, businessmen are powerful as an institutional group in Iran because there are so many of them—thirty—within the elite universe. But the average individual power of each of their members is among the lowest within the political elite. The mediocre power level of each businessman weakens their ability to act as a significant institutional force within Iranian politics.

The converse is true of the other two cases. The ulema have but ten representatives within the entire political elite and an aggregate power position of eleventh. But these ten men are unusually powerful individuals, ranking fourth on mean individual power. The significance of this wide deviation centers primarily on the question of access. More than any other occupation or institution within the elite, they represent a group to which access is highly limited. A concerted and determined government campaign, certainly since the death in 1962 of Ayatollah Borujerdi, the most venerated cleric of Iran, has denied political elite status to the Ayatollahs (literally, the sign of God, a title given to a few distinguished religious authorities). Since that time, only Ayatollah Khomeini has risen to national prominence. The nine other ulema who are accorded such status have been figures of national religious and

---

[100] RHO = .270. In order to reach a significance level of .05, RHO would have had to reach .425. The correlation, note, is positive and not inverse, but, nonetheless, not significant.

political prominence for many years. It is highly significant, then, that government efforts to control the religious sphere culminated in the forced exile of Khomeini, the one *nouveau arrivé* of the lot. Only members of the ulema tested over the years and found willing to play by existing rules of the political elite game are tolerated and every effort is made to prevent the rise of other ulema. House arrest, withdrawal of *vaqf* (endowment) funds, restrictions on travel, forbidding the *mullah* in question from publicly speaking in the mosques or informing him that SAVAK agents attend his public appearances, closing religious presses, banning gatherings for religious purposes, and infiltrating the Sufi orders are all some of the more or less serious techniques available to the government in its campaign. These have restricted ulema access to elite status, prevented the rise of ulema into lower level elite positions, enhanced the relative importance of those ulema already within the elite, and resulted in the rank order disparity noted above. The religious leaders, constrained by their small numbers, assume relevance for national politics, not as a major institutional group, but as important individuals.

Finally, the members of the elite within the "free professions" demonstrate the widest disparities in the two rank orderings. That this is the result of their small numbers within the total elite is an illustration of the success of His Majesty's policy of co-optation. Those who acquire the training to join the professions and then status as outstanding practitioners within their professions are co-opted into the bureaucracies. On the one hand, their professional skills are valuable to an understaffed bureaucracy. But on the other, that their professional skills are usually not employed by the civil service implies that they are co-opted more for the threat to the regime that they represent as free professionals than for those skills. (Physicians, for example, have recently served as directors of the National Iranian Oil Company, chancellors of the University of Tehran, cabinet ministers, and members of the Majles and Senate.[101])

To summarize, then, what we have suggested is that the phenomenon of bureaucratic *immobilisme* is a common one in Iran for a variety of reasons. One reason discussed here is that frequently those parts of the political process that count highly powerful members among them tend also to have relatively few of their members within the political elite. Let us turn briefly to individual reasons for the same phenomenon. Just as bureaucratic cross checking based on similar or conflicting power ranks

---

[101] This situation, apparently, is similar to one which formerly pertained in the United States. Five physicians, for example, were among the signers of the Declaration of Independence. In a study of this phenomenon, one author suggests that as these professions become more "professionalized," their members participate less frequently in politics. See William A. Glaser, "Doctors and Politics," *American Journal of Sociology*, 66 (Nov. 1960): 230–45. This is certainly the case for Iran with the added provision that the policy of co-optation hinders that professionalization.

tends to vitiate institutional independence and initiative, so do the cross pressures on individual members of different organizations.

Of the elites for whom information is available, 204, or 69 per cent, hold at least two full-time paid positions.[102] Some of the effects of multiple job holding have been discussed above. Here we note that this practice may subject the holder of such positions to cross pressures. Certainly, the holdings of two positions does not, by definition, produce cross pressures. There is no necessary incompatibility between holding a position as cabinet minister and poet, nor between cabinet minister and director of a government department. We suggest, however, that the elite simultaneously responsible for the latter two positions would be more subject to conflicts than the former. Conflicting, and often incompatible, demands for the allocation of time, energy, loyalties, financial resources, and budgets are likely to beset a member of the elite who seeks to fulfill the responsibilities of his diverse positions. To discuss these multiple job holdings from but one occupational category—members of the elite whose principal position is in the cabinet also hold other posts as follows: two hold a second ministerial portfolio, seven are directors of government departments, two are active duty military officers, four are active in business, two hold positions in the Imperial Court, one is a member (by marriage) of the Pahlavi family, two hold professorships at the University of Tehran, and two run large-scale agricultural enterprises.

We note, then, the tendency for elite employment patterns to reflect variety, diffuseness, and potential for individual conflict based on incompatible demands made on the individual from his institutional employers. The individual is pressured by many and frequently conflicting demands for loyalty and support from the multiplicity of groups to which he belongs or by whom he is paid. The result is often a reduction of his own effectiveness in any one area and a tendency for his efforts in any given sphere to be countered or checked by his or others' efforts in other spheres.

These institutional and occupational memberships that exist in Iran have effects within elite politics that are remarkably similar to those uncovered by research on voting behavior and social conflict in other

---

[102] This percentage for the elite as a whole is considerably below that for the 167 respondents mentioned above. This may be a function of the fact that the elite happens, in fact, to be more active than nonrespondents. It appears more likely to us, however, that this difference is to be explained rather by the more concise and definitive information provided by interviews. Published biographies used to gather biographical data on nonrespondents were cursory, at best. It is likely then that the figure of 69 per cent is a gross understatement of the percentage of the elite holding more than one paid position. Furthermore, no information at all is available on the third, fourth, and other positions of the nonrespondents.

societies. Voting studies, perhaps the earliest and most developed empirical research on cross pressures, indicates that individuals are subject to cross pressures from the holding of conflicting affiliations, institutional memberships, or attitudes. Such cross pressures are likely to result in lower stability of attitudes and interest, less participation, and a tendency to "leave the field" entirely.[103] But the effects of cross pressures manifest themselves in areas other than voting research. Studies of community conflict indicate that the presence of multiple loyalties and identifications in a society—cross pressures—reduce the likelihood of conflict in that society.[104] Many studies that deal with conflict suggest that social mobility is the primary source of the multiple loyalties and identifications that reduce conflict.[105] We suggest that institutional memberships which demand that the individual simultaneously fulfill responsibilities to diverse institutions may also serve as a basis for cross pressures. The reduction of intraelite conflict would be one result, a result to be discussed in greater detail below.

In his search for a "gestalt," the individual member of the political elite can lower the cross pressures on him in at least two ways. On the one hand, he may withdraw membership from the competing institutions. This might be effective in psychological terms, but would be politically injurious. On the other hand, the individual may maintain his memberships but lessen the personal saliency of membership in any one institution, or attempt to establish some rank ordering or priority system of loyalties.

These latter techniques are most frequently used with similar results, i.e., a marked lessening in the ability of groups to function effectively. The operation of cross pressures and efforts by individuals to lessen such pressures or their attendant discomfort minimizes the saliency of institutions and the commitment of individuals to them, lessens participation in institutional affairs, and contributes to shifting attitudes and interests. All of these contribute to the growing irrelevance of institutions in Iranian politics, the individualization of the elite "game of politics" as

[103] Bernard R. Berelson, Paul F. Lazarsfeld, and William N. McPhee, *Voting: A Study of Opinion Formation in a Presidential Campaign* (Chicago: University of Chicago Press, 1954), p. 284 et passim. See also Paul F. Lazarsfeld, Bernard R. Berelson, and Hazel Gaudet, *The People's Choice* (New York: Columbia University Press, 1948).

[104] See, for example, James S. Coleman, "Community Disorganization," in *Contemporary Social Problems*, ed. Robert K. Merton and Robert A. Nisbet (New York: Harcourt, Brace and World, 1961), pp. 553–604.

[105] "In a society where movement from a lower to a higher class occurs to a great extent and where the workers are not politically subordinated, class conflicts are alternated and the ideology of the class struggle finds it difficult to gain a foothold" (Harold D. Lasswell and Abraham Kaplan, *Power and Society: A Framework for Political Inquiry* [New Haven: Yale University Press, 1950], p. 36).

it is played in the capital, and to the peculiar kind of "basic democracy" that we have suggested exists at the elite level.

Finally, these data offer graphic evidence for the low level of political development that characterizes Iran. While numerous definitions of this concept are abroad in the discipline, a central feature of many centers about the institutionalization of politics and the political. At low levels of political development, the political sphere and the nature of political participation is defined by each institutional or individual actor. This stage of "praetorian politics" is characterized by each actor's attempting to influence politics by his own chosen means: "the rich bribe, students riot, and the military coup."[106] Put another way, Lucian W. Pye has suggested that "in the non-Western political process, there is a high degree of substitutability of roles."[107] Pye offers two examples of this substitutability on the social and personal levels. Institutions and individuals both have functionally diffuse political roles: "For example, the civil bureaucracy is not usually limited to the role of a politically neutral instrument of public administration but may assume some of the functions of a political party or act as an interest group. Sometimes armies act as governments. Even within bureaucracies and governments, individuals may be formally called upon to perform several roles."[108]

The occupations of the political elite of Iran demonstrate the ill-defined and poorly articulated nature of politics in that society. Where no particularly "political" profession or occupation exists, all become so. And every individual is as prepared for political roles as every other. It should come as no surprise, then, that a physician would direct the operations of the National Iranian Oil Company, that a professor of hydraulic engineering would lead the Parliament, that a businessman would be president of the Senate, or that a military officer would be minister of agriculture. A variety of factors contribute to this condition: the centrality of politics, the shortage of trained persons, and His Majesty's style of rule. But the consequences, irrespective of the causes, are the same: ineffectiveness and inefficiencies in the bureaucracy, a quality of the pervasiveness of politics, and the absence of any distinct set of politicians or a political sphere to serve as a locus of power.

What then has been learned from studying the social backgrounds of the contemporary political elite? Such analysis not only sheds light on the men whose orientations and attitudes, actions, and activities give substance to Iranian politics. But the analysis also reflects changes occurring

[106] From a talk by Samuel Huntington delivered at the University of Chicago, February 28, 1967.
[107] "The Non-Western Political Process," *Journal of Politics*, 20, no. 3 (Aug. 1958): 479.
[108] *Ibid.*

throughout Iranian society. For the political elite both mirror those changes and, frequently, are in their forefront.

As Tehran has come to dominate all aspects of Iranian life, so have the elite tended to be born in the capital in proportions greater than their own fathers and than the society as a whole. While the median age of the political elite bears no relation to the age distribution of the population at large, political power has begun to pass from the elders of the elite to younger men. Similarly, while the elite as a whole were born of families who claim disproportionately high social status and are extremely well educated, younger men of lower social status but with equally high education have found their way into elite ranks. The far-ranging foreign travel and language abilities of the elite both reflect and foster the political ties of their country to Europe and the United States, frequently at the expense of Iran's immediate neighbors. Finally, the multiplicity and diversity of occupations pursued by the elite are central factors in the game of politics and in the ineffectiveness of the government's bureaucracy.

But our interests in analyzing the politics of Iran extend beyond the shah's style of rule and the men he has selected to staff the highest levels of his bureaucracy. We wish to note their attitudes and values and their political behaviors that ensue.

:7:

THE ORIENTATIONS OF THE POLITICAL ELITE, I

When the court is corrupt, innocence is no security.
Sir John Malcolm, *The History of Persia*

*M*embers of the political elite, as we have seen, are drawn from a narrow segment of Iranian society, commandeer the highest formal and informal positions of power, and allocate the values of their society in a disproportionately elitist fashion. But the immediate significance of the elite for us lies elsewhere. Their behavior—what they do in the course of their daily rounds—constitutes the essence of politics in Iran. It is a major assumption of this study that the attitudes held by these individuals underlie and sustain their behavior. That is, the political elite of Iran will so behave as to maximize "the fit" or resolution between their attitudes and their behavior. There are, of course, a host of influences that might cause the elite to act in other ways. The material and human resources that they can marshal, pressures from foreign nations and others of the elite, and most importantly, the wishes of His Imperial Majesty may all run counter to the attitudes that they themselves hold. Nonetheless, it is assumed that they will so act within these constraints as to minimize the disparities between their behavior and their attitudes.

In this sense, there may be some substance to the frequently leveled charges that the elite serve to temper the policies of the shah. Whereas the *shah-parastis* (shah worshippers) argue that some of the elite subvert the liberalizing and reformist policies of the monarch, the latter's critics consider the elite as protectors or buffers, guarding the nation from the king's despotic inclinations. Both charges are predicated on the notion that as a body the elite cannot block the sovereign's wishes, for that

199

would result in their dismissal or in more threatening eventualities. But they can so orient their responses that their behavior and his wishes may be considered generally congruent. While the resultant policy outcomes may not necessarily satisfy the monarch, neither would they be too distinctive from what the members of the elite would have done in the absence of royal pressures. In this sense, elite attitudes are assumed to be more reliable indicators of the elite's future behavior than information on their present behavior.[1]

There is yet another reason for dwelling on elite attitudes, however, and that is a methodological one. No valid measures of elite behavior within the Iranian political system are currently available. Votes cast by members of the elite within the Majles, Senate, or cabinet are largely irrelevant, for they reflect more the power of His Majesty to gain formal accession to his wishes than the behavior of the elite in implementing the decrees that have been submitted to them. In addition, a large proportion of the political elite are not members of these bodies. An alternate method for studying elite behavior would be an analysis of decision making outside the Parliament. Unfortunately, such an analysis proved impossible for two reasons. When pressed to discuss the actual process of decision making, elite respondents were inclined to attribute all power to His Imperial Majesty. Secondly, the tangled skeins of power and authority in the civil and military bureaucracies mask the actions of their members and diffuse responsibility to the point where none are accountable and few seem even relevant.

For both conceptual and practical reasons, then, we have concentrated more on elite attitudes than on elite behavior. The schedule used to interview members of the elite contained a variety of questions designed to elicit a spectrum of attitudes. These ranged from issues of immediate political import then agitating the entire elite to very diffuse attitudinal indexes of general characterological orientations. The continuum between these is filled by questions whose focuses become increasingly less specific. Examples of questions that mirror this continuum from the more specifically political to the more general character orientations are as follows:

In your opinion, what have been the *actual* results of land reform to this date?

---

[1] This is not to suggest that attitudes and behavior are in fact congruent. Too large and significant a body of social science research has demonstrated the ways in which behavior may differ from attitudes. See, for example, R. T. La Pierre, "Attitudes Versus Actions," *Social Forces*, 13 (Dec. 1934): 230–37; and B. Kutner, Carroll Wilkins, and Penny R. Yarrow, "Verbal Attitudes and Overt Behavior Involving Race Prejudice," *Journal of Abnormal and Social Psychology*, 47 (July 1952): 649–52. Both studies dealt with hotel and restaurant managers who expressed an unwillingness to serve nonwhite patrons while such patrons did, in fact, receive service.

Do you consider foreign military assistance as beneficial or harmful to Iran?

To what extent do you agree or disagree that the average Iranian is overwhelmingly motivated by self-interest, that is the pursuit of his own personal interests?

The present is an immeasurably small fragment of time which has taken its place in the past almost before we are aware of its existence. To what extent do you agree or disagree?

The approximately two hundred variables generated by such questions in the elite interviews were grouped into three major conceptual areas—social background data, general character orientations, and political and social attitudes. The variables in each category were subject to separate factor analyses, in order to combine the two hundred variables into a relatively few clusters on the basis of statistical compatabilities which, ideally, could then be justified theoretically.[2]

In seeking to predict the political attitudes of the elite, those attitudes assumed most immediately relevant to their behavior in the political process, it was found that the more diffuse character orientations were far more efficient than other variables. The political experiences, personal attributes, general socialization patterns or social backgrounds of the elite were all less statistically relevant predictors than were those general orientations. In turn, however, the social background variables proved to be generally adequate predictors of elite orientations. The tripartite model proposed in the introduction—social backgrounds → general orientations → focused political attitudes—was supported by the data.[3]

The general orientations, then, appear to be the most critical set of variables in predicting the political attitudes of the elite. In the factor analysis of the former variables, four principal clusters were produced.

[2] The principal components factor matrixes generated were orthogonally rotated to approximate a simple structure by the quartimax rotation, producing statistically independent factors. One of the chief difficulties with factor analyses is acknowledged here—factors are produced on the basis of the statistical relation of the variables rather than on their theoretical relation. It was to offset, at least partly, this problem that separate factor analyses were run on each category of variable.

[3] Hyman deals with the necessity to treat variables distinctly on the basis of their conceptual and analytical significance. See Herbert Hyman, "The Distinction between Developmental Sequences or Configurations and Problems of Spuriousness" in his *Survey Design and Analysis* (Glencoe: Free Press, 1955), pp. 254-57. There he warns against the hasty discounting of variables of different analytical levels by the use of statistical controls. On this point, see Fred I. Greenstein, "The Impact of Personality on Politics: An Attempt to Clear Away the Underbrush," *American Political Science Review*, 61, no. 3 (Sept. 1967): 629–41. For a discussion of these various levels of analysis, see Neil J. Smelser and William T. Smelser, eds., *Personality and Social Systems* (New York: John Wiley & Sons, 1963), pp. 1–18.

These factors have been labeled manifest insecurity, cynicism, mistrust, and exploitation, and it is to these that we now turn.

INSECURITY

Max Weber in his study of *The City* noted the connection between the prevalance of walls in urban areas of the Mediterranean world and a "centuries-long insecurity."[4] The existence of walled cities as well as walled compounds surrounding residences in Iranian cities evinces the same phenomenon. No visitor to Tehran can be oblivious to the presence of the "compound style" of architecture that prevails in urban construction in both the poorest and richest quarters, for homes built in the days of the Qajars as well as the most recent additions to the landscape.

Iranians themselves are well aware of the purposes of these walls and the individualism and familistic independence they foster. The hindrance that they offer to interresidence communication is both a symptom of and a contributory factor to the lack of social cooperation and the nepotism for which Iranian life is so justly noted. Both Iranian and foreign observers alike tend to lay the blame for these walls on a lack of "security" defined as a condition of peril, as being exposed to hazards and dangers. And both agree that the danger and personal vulnerability can be attributed to the condition of politics in Iran. Ann K. S. Lambton, for example, in commenting on the conditions in the early twentieth century, has noted that "intrigue and corruption (which Mirza Husayn Khan Mushir ud-Dowleh once called the mother of all evils) were the constant concomitants of public life. Both derived from the prevailing insecurity and both, in turn, fostered that insecurity."[5] More recently, the perceptive editor of *Khandaniha* has attacked the government of Iran for just these reasons. The American government, he claimed,

. . . fully discharges its own obligation of protecting American lives and property—both inside and outside America, whereas in Iran, the first one to violate the people's rights is the government itself. The Americans have no daily problems such as we have, like lack of security, like the enforcement of the law, the daily bread, the evening warmth, the children's schooling, the arbitrary arrests, and the very right to live—all of which pose as puzzles for us.[6]

[4] *The City*, trans. and ed. Don Martindale and Gertrude Neuwirth (London: Heinemann, 1958), p. 75.

[5] "Persian Society Under the Qajars," *Journal of the Royal Central Asian Society*, 48 (April 1961): 135.

[6] A. A. Amirani, "Sarmaghale" (editorial), *Khandaniha* (Tehran), May 4, 1965. For other specific comments on the prevalence of insecurity in Iran, the reader is referred to Leonard Binder, *Iran: Political Development in a Changing Society* (Berkeley: University of California Press, 1962); Richard W. Cottam, *Nationalism in Iran* (Pittsburgh: University of Pittsburgh Press, 1964), esp. pp.

Security, then, is a commonly recognized desideratum which has traditionally been viewed as sadly absent from Iranian life. In its most frequent Iranian usage, referring to safety from physical harm, the term evokes images of marauding nomads, invading Turks or Mongols, or depredatory government troops.[7] But with the enforcement of at least minimal levels of law and order by Reza Shah, this simplistic notion of security was elaborated. Besides being secure from physical attack, Iranians began to demand other types of security: security from arbitrary arrest, from dismissal from their occupations without due cause, from financial manipulation and economic confiscation by the government or the elite, from all the extortions and venality and instabilities for which the political system has been renowned. But these additional sources of security were more difficult to achieve, in part, certainly, because they are more difficult to conceptualize. Protection from the attacks of tribal nomads is a palpable demand in the face of equally palpable external threats to one's well-being. But with the satisfaction of that elemental, low-level need for physical safety and well-being, demands for security are advanced that prove to be a good deal more abstruse.[8]

In some general way, all demands for security appear to be based on fear, fear that is aroused by a present or anticipated external stimulus. Freud noted, however, that not all fear was free of neurotic content. "A real danger," he argued, "is a danger which we know, a true anxiety, the anxiety in regard to such a known danger. Neurotic anxiety is anxiety in

---

17–18, 96–97, 251, 255; Nizam ul-Mulk, *Siyasat-Nama* [The book of government or rules for kings], trans. Hubert Drake (London: Routledge & Kegan Paul, 1960), pp. 9, 117, 143; Reza Arasteh, *Man and Society in Iran* (Leiden: E. J. Brill, 1964), pp. 18, 54, 122–23; Ann K. S. Lambton, *Landlord and Peasant in Persia* (London: Oxford University Press, 1953); and Joseph M. Upton, *The History of Modern Iran: An Interpretation*, Harvard Middle Eastern Monographs (Cambridge: Harvard University Press, 1960).

[7] Sykes, for example, notes that from the death of Naser ed-Din Shah in 1896 to the enforcement of tranquillity by Reza Shah,

> Persia had been brought to misery and poverty by the insecurity of life and property. The nomads were the perpetrators of outrage after outrage which had materially reduced the population in numbers and wealth. To give an instance, when I first knew Sirjan about twenty years ago, some thousands of good camels were owned in the district, but all were looted, and during the Great War not even ten remained, the sheep, too, were only one-fifth of their former number. The same process had been going on almost everywhere in Southern Persia, since . . . the nomad tribes began to lose all fear of the Government. Were this process to be continued for a decade or two, the Persian villages . . . the backbone of the country, would tend to disappear, and the whole land would be given over to the flocks of tribesmen.

Sir Percy M. Sykes, *A History of Persia*, 2 vols. (London: Macmillan Co., 1921), 2:480–81.

[8] See, for example, Abraham H. Maslow, *Motivation and Personality* (New York: Harper & Row, 1954), esp. pp. 80–106, where Maslow discusses a variety of human needs, among them the "need" for security.

regard to a danger which we do not know."[9] Freud referred to "real anxiety" as fear and "neurotic anxiety" as anxiety. In these simplistic terms, one might argue that in seeking an increase in security, Iranians intended a reduction in the external stimuli we have listed, those "known dangers" producing fear. Certainly, that Iranians desire to live free from fear need occasion no surprise.

But a fundamental difficulty mars this hasty resolution. For as Freud also noted: "There are cases in which the attributes of true and of neurotic anxiety are intermingled. The danger is known and of the real type, but the anxiety in regard to it is disproportionately great, greater than in our judgement it ought to be."[10] What is at issue is a response to the external stimulus which appears, *to an outside observer*, to be incommensurate with the threat the stimulus represents.[11] This behavioral response, be it only in the form of heightened tension or anxiety, lies at the root of what, in a general way, we refer to as insecurity. Table 7.1 illustrates this.

One point that the table suggests is the possibility of an insufficient psychic response to external stimuli. Failure to come to grips with "real"

TABLE 7.1
Nature of External Stimulus
Perceived as Dangerous

		REAL	INNOCUOUS
NATURE OF PSYCHIC RESPONSE	INCOMMENSURATE (overresponse)	anxiety	anxiety
	COMMENSURATE	fear	no significant response
	INCOMMENSURATE (underresponse)	passivity	——

[9] Sigmund Freud, *The Problem of Anxiety*, trans. H. A. Bunker (New York: Norton and Co., 1936), p. 147.

[10] *Ibid.*, p. 148.

[11] There are, of course, grave tautological issues which arise here, similar to much of the research which has gone into studies of utility maximization and measurement. On a simplistic level, if people act so as to maximize their "utiles" then what they do is done because that action maximizes their utiles, thus all behavior is "rational." See Jacob Marschak, "Scaling of Utilities and Probability" in *Game Theory and Related Approaches to Social Behavior*, ed. Martin Shubik (New York: John Wiley and Sons, 1964), pp. 95–109; and Frederick Mosteller and Philip Nogee, "An Experimental Measurement of Utility," *Journal of Political Economy*, 59, no. 5 (Oct. 1951): 371–404.

challenges and dangers is a charge frequently leveled against the political elite of developing societies. When internal social, political, and economic problems are neglected, the faults may be less in the intractability of these problems than in the affective structure of the elite.

A more telling point that table 7.1 illustrates is that the removal or lessening of "real" dangers by no means frees the individual from the anxiety that we equate with insecurity. For such a reason the establishment of domestic tranquillity by the control of the Iranian tribes *and* the political process has not served to eliminate the presence of perceived insecurity among the Iranian people. The case here appears to be one in which the perception of any stimulus, no matter how innocuous it may appear to some outside observer, may elicit, for a variety of primary and secondary reasons, feelings of intense anxiety or insecurity.

But once this is said, problems associated with the concepts security-insecurity, their importance, and their relevance are by no means resolved. After an examination of some ninety-eight published sources purporting to explore the nature and effects of insecurity, two earlier students of the problem concluded that "no consistent definitions or theory have yet been developed around the concepts of security and insecurity and the prerequisite empirical testing of the hypotheses which might be derived by objective research has hardly begun."[12] A perusal of studies subsequent to that report reveals no more definite answers to the issues already raised.[13] Perhaps the recent marked decline of interest in the con-

[12] William Bruce Cameron and Thomas C. McCormick, "Concepts of Security and Insecurity," *American Journal of Sociology*, 59, no. 6 (May 1954): 561. Another survey of the literature, contemporary with that of Cameron and McCormick, attempts to demonstrate that "there is considerable agreement among many psychologists [on some of the principal definitions and usages of the concept of personal security] . . . even though the agreement has been concealed beneath systematic differences and differences in choice of vocabulary" (Andie L. Knutson, "The Concept of Personal Security," *Journal of Social Psychology*, 40 [1954]: 221). Knutson then discusses "five broad propositions" about which such agreement reputedly exists.

[13] See, for example, the following works: Bengt Abrahamsson, "The Ideology of an Elite—Conservatism and National Insecurity" (Paper read at the Working Group on Armed Forces and Society, Sixth World Congress of Sociology, Evian, France, Sept. 1966); Leonard H. Ainsworth, "Rigidity, Insecurity, and Stress"; Mary D. Ainsworth and L. H. Ainsworth, *Measuring Security in Personal Adjustment*; D. W. Ball, "Covert Political Rebellion as Resentment"; R. B. Cattell and I. H. Scheier, "The Nature of Anxiety: A Review of Thirteen Multivariant Analyses Comprising 814 Variables"; M. J. Field, *Search for Security: An Ethno-Psychiatric Study of Rural Ghana*; John P. Gillen and George Nicholson, "The Security Functions of Cultural Systems"; John C. Leggett, "Economic Insecurity and Working Class Consciousness"; Abraham H. Maslow and R. Diaz-Guerrero, "Adolescence and Juvenile Delinquency in Two Different Cultures"; Abraham H. Maslow, "Further Notes on the Psychology of Being"; idem, "Synergy in the Society and in the Individual"; Gwynn E. Nettler and James R. Huffman, "Political Opinion and Personal Security"; Franz Neumann, "Anxiety in Politics"; Morris Rosenberg, "Self Esteem and Concern with Public Affairs"; Irving Sarnoff and

cepts of security-insecurity can be traced to a failure of intellectual progress on just these problems.[14]

One fundamental difficulty in defining insecurity is the multiplicity of sources from which the concept of insecurity achieved its current notoriety:

It had its origins in the whole range of the social and humanistic disciplines—psychology, economics, sociology, anthropology, philosophy. The intricate network of the origins of the concept of personal security includes such things as the hedonistic principle, the instincts of self-preservation and gregariousness, etc., MacDougall's self-regard and emotions of desire, the self-esteem of Bain and of James, the anxiety of Freud and also his life and death instincts, the feelings of inferiority and superiority of Adler, the introversion-extroversion of Jung and his emphasis on the future, the dynamic principles of Lewin, Murray's needs, Stern's "system of purposes," etc.—to mention but a few.[15]

Partially as a result of these diverse progenitors, the concept of insecurity has tended to be used virtually interchangeably with concepts of inferiority,[16] stress,[17] anxiety,[18] fear,[19] adjustment,[20] and, more recently, national, military defense.[21]

Users of the concept of insecurity have also differed over the extent to which insecurity is specific to functional areas or is a general personality characteristic. Some have argued that while insecurity tends to be manifest in certain areas of an individual's striving, it has a more general effect on the personality by which no functional area is left totally untouched.

Philip G. Zimbardo, "Anxiety, Fear, and Social Affiliation"; Bernard J. Siegel, "High Anxiety Levels and Cultural Integration: Notes on a Psycho-Cultural Hypothesis"; Murray A. Straus, "Childhood Experience and Emotional Security in the Context of Sinhalese Social Organization"; J. A. Taylor, "A Personality Scale of Manifest Anxiety"; Maurice Zeitlin, "Economic Insecurity and the Political Attitudes of Cuban Workers." (For further bibliographic details, see Psychology section of the Bibliography.)

[14] A survey of professional journals and books in the fields of psychology, psychiatry, anthropology, sociology, and political science from 1950 to the present reveals a paucity of studies addressing these issues.

[15] Knutson, "Personal Security," p. 220.

[16] Cf. Bingham Dai, "Some Problems of Personality Development Among Negro Children" in *Personality*, ed. Clyde Kluckhohn and Henry A. Murray (New York: Alfred A. Knopf, 1953), chap. 35.

[17] Leonard H. Ainsworth, "Rigidity, Insecurity, and Stress," *Journal of Abnormal and Social Psychology*, 56 (1958): 67–74.

[18] Freud, *Problem of Anxiety*.

[19] W. I. Thomas, "The Unadjusted Girl," in *Source Book for Social Psychology*, ed. Kimball Young (New York: Crofts, 1931).

[20] J. M. Arsenian, "Young Children in Insecure Situations," *Journal of Abnormal and Social Psychology*, 38 (1943): 225–49.

[21] Abrahamsson, "Ideology of an Elite."

But if the term insecurity eludes definition, general agreement exists that the presence of insecurity is psychically unwelcome, producing a state of tension. It serves as a motive for behavior to reduce to some undefined but tolerable limit the amount of insecurity experienced. Insecurity then constitutes a need or urge or drive and "is the core of a theory of action: security becomes a motive whether one chooses to regard the organism as striving to attain security or struggling to allay the tensions attached to insecurity, environmental or intra-personal."[22] In this sense, then, the presence of some insecurity is seen as desirable, for it serves to motivate the individual to action—action that will reduce the insecurity to some tolerable level. A. I. Hallowell has suggested that "certain anxieties may be inculcated in individuals [in the course of general socialization] in order to motivate them in the performance of patterns of behavior that are socially approved."[23] Indeed, one writer has suggested that when faced with conditions of contact with an exotic culture, certain social systems respond to the psychological dimensions of this contact by "*a conscious strict control or even rejection of available anxiety reducing patterns.*"[24] It seems obvious, however, that if the existing level of perceived psychic insecurity is too great, the result will not be a positive behavioral response, but an inability of the individual to come to grips with the problem in a functional manner. Certainly there arises the specter that individual behavior, motivated by a desire to reduce psychic insecurity, will be dysfunctional for the political or social system as a whole. These are issues to which we shall return.

PRIMARY INSECURITY AND SECONDARY INSECURITY

Maslow, one of the earliest and most articulate students of insecurity, has long argued that the concept of insecurity is one that must be considered as a phenomenon of the total personality.[25] As a more precise definition of the concept, Maslow offers fourteen subaspects, or subsyndromes, of insecurity.[26] The subsyndromes are:

1. Feeling of rejection, of being unloved, of being treated coldly and without affection, or of being hated, of being despised.

[22] Knutson, "Personal Security," p. 222.

[23] "Socio-Psychological Aspects of Acculturation," in *The Science of Man in the World Crisis*, ed. Ralph Linton (New York: Columbia University Press, 1945), p. 194.

[24] Bernard J. Siegel, "High Anxiety Levels and Cultural Integration: Notes on a Psycho-Cultural Hypothesis," *Social Forces*, 34, no. 1 (Oct. 1955): 42.

[25] Abraham H. Maslow, "The Dynamics of Psychological Security-Insecurity," *Character and Personality*, 10 (1942): 331–44.

[26] Abraham H. Maslow with the assistance of E. Birsh, I. Honigmann, F. Mc-Grath, A. Plason, and M. Stein, *Manual for the Security-Insecurity Inventory* (Palo Alto, Calif.: Consulting Psychologists Press, 1952).

2. Feelings of isolation, ostracism, aloneness, or being out of it; feelings of "uniqueness."
3. Constant feelings of threat and danger; anxiety.
4. Perception of the world and life as dangerous, threatening, dark, hostile, or challenging; as a jungle in which every man's hand is against every other, in which one eats or is eaten.
5. Perception of other human beings as essentially bad, evil, or selfish; as dangerous, threatening, hostile, or challenging.
6. Feelings of mistrust, of envy or jealousy toward others; much hostility, prejudice, hatred.
7. Tendency to expect the worst; general pessimism.
8. Tendency to be unhappy or discontented.
9. Feelings of tension, strain, or conflict, together with various consequences of tension, e.g., "nervousness," fatigue, irritability, nervous stomach, and other psychosomatic disturbances; nightmares; emotional instability, vacillation, uncertainty, and inconsistency.
10. Tendency to compulsive introspectiveness, morbid self-examination, acute consciousness of self.
11. Guilt and shame feelings, sin feelings, feelings of self-condemnation, suicidal tendencies, discouragement.
12. Disturbances of various aspects of the self-esteem complex, e.g., craving for power and for status, compulsive ambition, over-aggression, hunger for money, prestige, glory, possessiveness, jealousy of jurisdiction and prerogative, over-competitiveness and/or the opposite; masochistic tendencies, over-dependence, compulsive submissiveness, ingratiation, inferiority feelings, feelings of weakness and helplessness.
13. Continual striving for and hunger for safety and security; various neurotic trends, inhibitions, defensiveness, escape trends, ameliorative trends, false goals, fixations on partial goals; psychotic tendencies, delusions, hallucinations, etc.
14. Selfish, egocentric, individualistic trends.

Maslow argues that the first three of these subsyndromes are most probably primary in the sense of being "relatively prior (causal)" while the other subsyndromes are "relatively consequent (effects)" with regard to the developmental sequence of insecurity "even though they have equal priority and 'causal' efficacy in the cross-sectional, contemporaneous, dynamic analysis of the personality."[27] Building on this dichotomy, a more recent examination of the nature and origins of anxiety gives a comparable schema that separates the primary sources of anxiety assumed to be events occurring in childhood from those secondary or manifest sources of anxiety likely to occur in later adult life. While positing that "at least theoretically, every emotional conflict has its earlier

[27] *Ibid.* For a study of the relationship of these subsyndromes to each other and to the concept of insecurity as a whole, see Abraham H. Maslow, "Dynamics of Personality Organization," *Psychological Review*, 50 (1943): 514–39, 541–58.

antecedents," it is not necessarily the case that the emotionally disturbing events of childhood will affect adult behavior without the accompaniment or intervention of the secondary sources of anxiety.[28]

On the assumption that two separate sources of anxiety or insecurity were conceptually discernible, two separate groups of questions were included in the survey instrument administered to the Iranian political elite. On the one hand, a section of the Maslow Security-Insecurity Index was included as an index of the responses that would be expected to follow from the presence of insecurity in large measure attributable to the emotionally disturbing events of earlier childhood. On the other hand, a group of questions was included that aimed at tapping insecurity attributable to secondary or adult life experiences.

It seemed especially likely that the primary insecurity that Maslow described would be widely prevalent in Iran. For the fourteen subsyndromes appear, intuitively, to describe not only the psyches of members of the Iranian elite, but also the ways in which they behave in the political system as well. The politically active segments of the population appear to be motivated by just such considerations—individualism, striving for security and status, acute self-consciousness, verbal discontent, pessimism, mistrust, and feelings of threat. Numerous examples from Iranian culture and general observations of the behavior of the political elite may be advanced to support these notions.

Feelings of rejection. The highly articulated social structure that exists in Iran can be conceived as serving the function of protecting individuals from feeling rejected. While the class structure in Iran is theoretically open—mobility is not denied individuals because of lowly social origins —positions within the social hierarchy are very well defined. Elaborate and ritualistic modes of greeting and salutation, of deferential behavior, of discourse and other forms of interpersonal interaction exist and are widely accepted. To an outside observer, these appear to allow Iranians to confront their fellow countrymen as occupiers of positions within a status hierarchy rather than as individuals. Because the social code prescribes correct behavioral patterns toward virtually all positions in the hierarchy and because that code is so generally accepted, an individual need never fear being rejected or accepted; he has a high probability of always being treated on the basis of his status position. "When Persians meet in the streets," said Herodotus some 2,400 years ago, "one can always tell by their mode of greeting whether or not they are of the same rank."[29] Of all the tales of the legendary *mullah* Naser ed-Din, one of the

---

[28] See Henry P. Laughlin, *The Neuroses* (Washington, D.C.: Butterworth, 1967), pp. 29–30.

[29] *The Histories*, trans. Aubrey de Selincourt (London: Penguin Books, 1961), p. 134.

best known, "My New Cloak Should Eat the Polou," laments this very code and the resultant failure to confront others as individuals. As the story goes:

Mullah Naser ed-Din heard that there was a banquet being held in the near-by town, and that everyone was invited. He made his way there as quickly as he could. When the master of ceremonies saw him in his ragged cloak, he seated him in the most inconspicuous place, far from the great table where the most important people were being waited on hand and foot.

Naser ed-Din saw that it would be an hour at least before the waiters reached the place where he was sitting. So he got up and went home.

He dressed himself in a magnificent sable cloak and turban and returned to the feast. . . .

The Chamberlain himself came out of the palace and conducted the magnificent visitor of high rank to a place almost next to the Emir. A dish of wonderful food was immediately placed before him. Without a pause Naser ed-Din began to rub handfuls of the *polou* into his turban and cloak.

"Your Eminence," said the prince, "I am curious as to your eating habits, which are new to me."

"They are nothing special," said the *mullah*, "the cloak got me here, got me the food. Surely my new cloak should eat the *polou*."[30]

A central feature of this ritualistic code of interpersonal behavior is also mirrored in Naser ed-Din's tale—the dictates of *mehman navazi* (hospitality). Iranians have developed and adhere to a highly formalized system of hospitality. At all levels of the class structure, visitors are greeted with tea, and except at the most humble abode, with fruits and nuts. The guest is invited to "order" the host for "this home is yours, and I am your servant." Indeed, when asked to name the outstanding characteristic of Persians as a people, 20 per cent of the political elite replied in terms of Iranian hospitality. But in terms of this analysis, this ritualized code can be seen as a social method of limiting the likelihood that any individual will feel rejected, or need fear being treated coldly.[31]

Feelings of uniqueness. An earlier student of Iranian attitudes and modernization noted the frequency with which Iranians of the "modern"

---

[30] Adapted from Idries Shah, *The Exploits of the Incomparable Mulla Nasrudin* (London: Jonathan Cape, 1966), p. 42.

[31] The code of hospitality also serves to put limits on affect in a positive direction. By specifying "proper" hospitality, much of the excitement and spontaneity of interpersonal relations is eliminated. A similar phenomenon exists in a totally different area of Iranian life—the Majles. Persians frequently boast that their constitution, which specifies guaranteed parliamentary representation for certain religious minorities, is, therefore, highly democratic. In fact the guarantee of two seats to the Armenian Christians, for example, acts as both a minimal and maximal level for Armenian representation and effectively prevents their capturing a larger number of seats. Hospitality can, of course, be interpreted in a number of other ways—reaction formation covering hostility, status establishment, etc.

middle class believe they are "personally superior, both morally and intellectually to those around [them]." He goes on to observe that "megalomaniac claims to greatness are so common in Iran as to be socially accepted as harmless."[32] These individual notions of uniqueness are matched by a cultural stress on the uniqueness of Iran itself. More or less constant reference is made to a number of these "unique" points—the continuity of Iranian history (plans have been in motion for several years to celebrate the twenty-five hundredth anniversary of the Iranian monarchy); the "greatness" of past monarchs (Darius, Cyrus, Shah Abbas, etc.); the impressively long reign of the present ruler (1941–   ); the unique national and official religion of Iran, Shi'ism—the "Ja'afariya doctrine recognizing twelve Imams" (Article One, Supplementary Constitutional Law, October 8, 1907); and, certainly, the persisting belief in the ability of Iran to "conquer its conquerors." These notions of preeminence are prevalent in circles far wider than the "popular" culture at large. Elite respondents, for example, agreed in proportions of three to one that "Iran's culture is so unique that it has always subverted would-be conquerors and 'Iranized' them."

Feelings of anxiety. Gastil has concluded that middle-class Shirazis seemed "often to live in a state of psychological isolation and generalized fearfulness."[33] This observation is supported by elite estimates of the prevalence of injustice in Iranian society. In response to one interview question, some 72 per cent of the elite ($N = 120$) felt that there is a great deal or a very great deal of injustice abroad in their land. An additional illustration of elite anxieties appeared in a different area. Iranians frequently boast of their profound devotion to literature, and this was attested to by many of the political elite who lauded the value of literary studies, even for professional politicians. One respondent explained its value in an atypical fashion which may, nevertheless, be more telling of the underlying motivations that support such pursuits than is commonly realized. He recounted how books have been a continuing significant influence on his personality and beliefs. "Books," he explained, "provide a guide for life and they are harmless—they never threaten one."

[32] Raymond D. Gastil, "Middle Class Impediments to Iranian Modernization," *Public Opinion Quarterly*, 22, no. 3 (Fall 1958): 328. The reference to megalomania is taken from Herbert H. Vreeland, ed., *Iran* (New Haven: Human Relations Area Files, 1957), p. Alp-14. It would be wise to point out the great caution that needs to be exercised in generalizing from Gastil's "findings." As he himself points out, the questions were asked informally of only his "close acquaintances" in Shiraz, with responses numbering from fourteen to seven for any given question. ("Iranian Modernization," p. 326.)

[33] *Ibid.*, p. 329.

Perception of the world and others as dangerous and hostile. This orientation appears to operate on at least two levels in Iran. On the one hand, nature is not seen as a beneficent provider. The natural world, in a way that is perhaps commensurate with Iran's climate and harsh terrain, is not recognized as intrinsically bountiful and nurturant. On the other hand, the people within that world are themselves seen as threatening. As Gastil puts it, "The westernized middle class Iranian believes that men are by nature evil and power-seeking and irrational."[34] It appears that a similar general orientation is operative among the political elite. For in a world that is perceived as threatening, the "rational" response is not only to be on one's guard but probably to act similarly in a threatening fashion.[35] It occasions little surprise, then, that 119 of the political elite (71.2 per cent) felt that "it is usually better in Iran to 'get' one's rival before he 'gets' you." Only 23 individuals (13.8 per cent) disagreed with this notion.

Feelings of mistrust. "He believes he must distrust those around him in society, no matter by what bonds they may be attached to him, nor how friendly they may seem at the moment. . . . His father continually warns him of how others are out to cheat the unaware."[36] This observation on contemporary middle-class behavior is supported by virtually all aspects of popular culture as well as by our respondents. A host of Persian aphorisms exist to warn the unsuspecting of others. The *Masnavi*, written in the thirteenth century by Maulana Jalal ed-Din Rumi, cautions:

> Chun basi iblis i adam ru'i hast
> Pas be har dasti, na shayad dade dast
>
> Since there are many devils in the guise of men
> One should not give one's hand into every hand[37]

It was on the basis of this very mistrust that one elite respondent placed responsibility for the inefficiencies that plague the government bureaucracy. He contemplated the red tape, excessive paper work, and petty rules and regulations that characterize the Iranian bureaucracy. (These

---

[34] *Ibid.*, p. 326.

[35] Schelling, Kahn, and a host of other students of military strategy appear to have reached similar conclusions when examining America's proper military posture. See Thomas C. Schelling, *The Strategy of Conflict* (Cambridge: Harvard University Press, 1960); and Herman Kahn, *On Thermonuclear War* (Princeton: Princeton University Press, 1961). Also see, for example, Morton Deutsch and Robert M. Krauss, "Studies of Interpersonal Bargaining," *Journal of Conflict Resolution*, 6, no. 1 (March 1962): 52–76.

[36] Gastil, "Iranian Modernization," p. 327.

[37] Cited in Edward G. Browne, *A Year Amongst the Persians* (London: Adam and Charles Black, 1893), p. 301.

faults are not solely in the minds of foreign advisers or the Iranian High Council on Government Administration, both of which have struggled valiantly for so long to lessen these inefficiencies. For seven out of ten of our respondents [N = 116] reported that they almost always feel surrounded and impeded by such obstacles to sound administration.) This perceptive respondent suggested, "Paper work and red tape are definitely connected with psychological factors. The greater the trust between the members of a bureaucracy, the less the paper work. The greater the attempt to escape responsibility, the more the paper work. There is a great deal of paper work being done in our offices."[38]

General pessimism. Iranian literature is especially noted for its pessimism based on an acute consciousness of the brevity of life and the imminence of death. From the poetry of Khayyam to the most contemporary literary products of Iran, themes that stress the evils of life overbalancing the happiness it affords are rife.[39] Gastil, incidentally, also notes the presence of a pervasive pessimism.

Feelings of self-condemnation. Many of the authors already listed, plus a host of others, have noted the propensity of Iranians for self-condemnation. A great deal of this appears to be part of a general cultural pattern of elevating the status of others in an exaggeratedly polite fashion in immediate interpersonal language. Phrases such as "I am your slave" or "I am the dust under your feet" are part of the standard vocabulary of everyday language and seem to have as little affective content as any of the polite idioms used frequently in English such as "it's good to see you." Nonetheless, it is significant that phrases of the former type are so prevalent in Persian, while generally being absent from the English language. Although frequently used in a symbolic way to facilitate interpersonal relations, these phrases do seem to reflect a propensity for more fundamental self-condemnation. An earlier traveler to Iran noted that "Persia's young men are very prone, nowadays, to lament their failings as a race. National self-abasement is the burden of their talk, and much fluent diction is wasted in destructive criticism."[40] The author of these remarks goes on to suggest that far more of this disparagement is di-

[38] The respondent was a member of the Senate and not then directly involved in administration.

[39] Two readily available recent novels written in English by a Persian are permeated by such sentiment. See Fereidoun Esfandiary, *The Day of Sacrifice* (London: William Heinemann, 1960); and idem, *Identity Card* (New York: Grove Press, 1966). Such pessimism is also reflected in the music of Iran. See Ella Zonis, *The Dastgah Music of Iran* (Cambridge: Harvard University Press, forthcoming), esp. chap. 1.

[40] Anthony Hale, *From Persian Uplands* (New York: E. P. Dutton and Co., n.d., ca. 1915), p. 16.

rected at Iran's political leaders than at the individuals advancing the complaints. Nonetheless, it is clear that an immense quantity of deprecation and derogation is aimed at Persians as a nation, ipso facto including the speaker. The elite respondents themselves were startlingly free in their tendency to offer gratuitous comments that constituted ridicule and derision of Iranians. A few examples will suffice:

> Injustice in Iran is great because Iranians are basically unjust.

> Iranians accord a higher value to animals than they do to human beings.

> No society in the world can be found in which as many people understand as much in Iran. All say, "I know." All are experts.

> Iranians are lazy and irresponsible. On my first trip to the United States, I waited one and a half hours at the airport and watched an unsupervised workman repair a concrete floor, put a string around the area, ask the magazine salesman to remove the string the next day, and leave. In Iran it would have taken two workmen and a foreman one week to do the job half as well.

Individualistic trends. Of all the observations one might make about Iran, it is the tendency toward individuality that seems to be mentioned most repeatedly. Plutarch described Artaxerxes' campaign in Egypt unsuccessful because of the failure of his generals to work together.[41] More recently, Sir Percy Sykes attributes Iran's defeat in Mohammad Shah's campaigns against Afghanistan in 1837–1838 partly to the same factor: "During the winter, operations dragged on month after month with no decisive results, the Persian generals working entirely independently of one another and each being rather pleased if a rival general was defeated."[42] Gobineau, perhaps the most perceptive foreign writer on Iran, saw and reported much the same phenomenon. But he was aware that this was by no means restricted to the military:

> Je ne sais si, par les détails qui précédent, j'ai suffisamment préparé le lecteur à comprendre que l'Etat persan n'existe pas en réalité, et que l'individu est tout.[43]

The "conspicuous individualism" of Iranians continues to be reported to the present.[44] And, indeed, one is struck by the relative absence in Iranian life of meaningful and functioning groups other than the family. Iranian politics is not a process in which groups play an especially rele-

---

[41] *The Lives of Noble Grecians and Romans*, trans. John Dryden (New York: Random House, n.d.), p. 1265.

[42] *History of Persia*, 2: 331.

[43] Comte de Gobineau, *Les Dépêches Diplomatiques de Perse de Comte de Gobineau*, 10 vols. (Geneva: E. Droz, 1961), 2: 167.

[44] Arthur C. Millspaugh, *Americans in Persia* (Washington, D.C.: Brookings Institution, 1946), p. 77.

vant role. Iranian political parties are primarily collections of individuals gathered about a prominent political activist or activists and effected for office-seeking purposes. These parties most often disintegrate if the office is attained or if it appears beyond reach. They play no role as a group in the policy process itself. A similar line of reasoning might be advanced for all social activities in Iran, from the operation of the government bureaucracy to more homely examples of criminal activities. Bank robberies as they are known in the United States, for example, are substantially unheard of in Iran. That kind of successful group activity appears beyond the ken of the Iranian underworld. Bank robberies, if they are committed, tend to be primarily the work of a solitary bandit. Individualism appears operative in this area of Iranian life as in others.

Certainly, a seemingly endless parade of other quotations, anecdotes, and observations might be advanced to argue for the relevance of these and the remaining subsyndromes of insecurity as advanced by Maslow to the Iranian context. Iranian society and especially its politics appear to operate in a fashion consonant with behavioral consequences expected to follow from persons who score highly on the insecurity inventory. With these qualitative observations on this presence of insecurity in Iran, the Maslow inventory appeared to be a useful means of generating the data necessary for a quantitative confirmation of the extent of insecurity.

PRIMARY INSECURITY

The testing instrument designed by Maslow is composed of seventy-five items divided into three groups of twenty-five questions. The subsets of questions were designed to be equivalent and interchangeable forms of the test. Each of these subsets correlated greater than .90 with the total score.[45] For efficiency of administration, only one-third of the entire instrument was included in our questionnaire. The individual questions, and elite responses to each, are shown in table 7.2.

To test the internal compatibility of these twenty-five items, they were included in a factor analysis of 141 attitudinal variables. Orthogonally rotated factor loadings were derived for all variables. The third factor drawn in this fashion included no variables other than the Maslow security-insecurity items. Of the twenty-five questions, nineteen had factor loadings greater than .3, a generally accepted minimal level for including a given variable in a factor. The remaining six questions had loadings on this factor of above .2.

It should be immediately obvious that this testing instrument contains rather severe limitations. Basically, of course, the test is not one whose intent is difficult to uncover. Those answers that would be most "correct"

[45] Maslow, et al., *Manual.*

TABLE 7.2

Responses of the Political Elite
to the Maslow S-I Inventory

	Question	Yes	No	Don't Know	Total
1.	Are you generally an unselfish person?	44.6%	31.8%	23.6%	100.0%
2.	Are you often self-conscious?	32.4	50.0	17.6	100.0
3.	Do you consider yourself a rather nervous person?	29.7	52.7	17.6	100.0
4.	Do you tend to avoid unpleasantness by running away?	30.4	54.8	14.8	100.0
5.	Do you feel that life has treated you with justice?[a]	58.8	12.8	28.4	100.0
6.	When your friends criticize you, do you usually take it well?	63.5	9.5	27.0	100.0
7.	Do you feel that you get enough praise?	64.9	8.8	26.3	100.0
8.	Do you think people like you as much as they do others?	67.6	6.1	26.3	100.0
9.	Do you often have a feeling of loneliness even when you are with people?	14.9	69.6	15.5	100.0
10.	Do you ordinarily like to be with people rather than alone?	71.7	18.3	10.0	100.0
11.	Do you worry too long over humiliating experiences?	14.9	73.7	11.4	100.0
12.	Are you frequently in low spirits?	8.1	76.4	15.5	100.0
13.	Do you have social ease?	79.1	11.5	9.4	100.0
14.	When you meet people for the first time, do you usually feel they will not like you?	4.1	81.1	14.8	100.0
15.	Do you often have a feeling of resentment against the world?	8.1	82.5	.9.4	100.0
16.	Are you in general a happy person?	83.8	2.7	13.5	100.0
17.	Do you tend to be dissatisfied with yourself?	13.5	75.7	10.8	100.0
18.	Do you lack self-confidence?	6.8	87.9	5.3	100.0

ORIENTATIONS: INSECURITY

Question	Yes	No	Don't Know	Total
19. Do you often feel that life is not worth living?	4.0%	89.2%	6.8%	100.0%
20. Do you get discouraged easily?	4.7	90.6	4.7	100.0
21. Do you have enough faith in yourself?	91.3	2.7	6.0	100.0
22. Are you generally optimistic?	91.3	2.0	6.7	100.0
23. Can you be comfortable with yourself?	92.6	2.7	4.7	100.0
24. Do you usually feel friendly towards most people?	94.0	2.0	4.0	100.0
25. Are you ordinarily quite sure of yourself?	94.6	2.0	3.4	100.0 (N=148)

a
Numerous pretests with the Maslow instrument indicated
that alone of the twenty-five items, only one question,
as formulated by Maslow, made little sense in the
Iranian context. Maslow's original wording was "Do you
feel that you are getting a square deal in life?" The
notion of a "square deal" was simply not present in
Iranian culture. A variety of alternative formulations
were attempted with the form finally adopted not proving
completely acceptable. A number of respondents were
puzzled by the question, asking the interviewer how it
was possible for life to treat a person with anything.
They suggested that the subject-object order was
incorrect as "persons treated life," and not vice versa.
While this response had turned up on a few of the
pretests, it was felt that no other wording that could
be devised would prove less troublesome or less in
violation of the original meaning of the question.

on social, cultural, or personality grounds are easily discernible. The willingness of the respondents to reply in a truthful manner is strained to the utmost by the patency of the questions. Furthermore, the inclination of the political elite to respond in a less than candid fashion was enhanced by the rather direct connection between the questions and a general notion on the part of some of the elite that what was being sought here was neither their political attitudes nor social backgrounds, but rather some measure of personality or, even more threatening, their mental health. While this thought was conveyed directly to the interviewer on less than a dozen cases, it is not unlikely that similar thoughts affected the perceptions of other respondents.[46]

[46] In order to maximize the candor of the responses, these twenty-five items were not administered as were the remainder of the questions. First, these questions

Another important shortcoming of these questions is that the value of their responses is based on self-knowledge. Even with complete honesty, a respondent who is not conscious of his feelings o.˙ emotions can hardly present an adequate representation of those feelings. This issue is no different, of course, for every other item in the survey. But it is assumed that questions that are manifestly oriented towards more general character orientations will be especially liable to this shortcoming.

Finally, these questions and all others in the questionnaire are subject to charges that they will be answered in accordance with the extent to which the respondents feel their answers will contribute to their own occupational success. Again, this is no less true for all other items in the survey. But the general assumption under which all data were analyzed was that while they suffered from certain inherent shortcomings, those shortcomings were not so limiting as to obviate their usefulness. It is not entirely clear that such an assumption is operative for Maslow's Security-Insecurity Inventory. While virtually all the charges that may be leveled against these items are applicable to others, the former are culpable to an extent that seriously calls into question their validity and reliability. Given these caveats, then, any analysis of these results must be treated most gingerly and any conclusions derived from such an analysis that are not strongly supported by independent data must remain suspect. I have tried to supply such alternative data but have retained Maslow's material because of the insights it offers into the nature of insecurity in Iran.

In order to establish a set of norms for the inventory, Maslow administered the test to some two thousand subjects in thirteen institutions in the United States, ranging from a Brooklyn, New York, high school to a women's prison on the West Coast. The distribution of test scores,

---

were always reserved for the very end of the interview so as to minimize the likelihood that any disquieting effects would influence responses to other sections.

In the event that the time allotted for the interview had been exhausted—not to mention the tolerance of the respondent—mailing envelopes were given to the respondents along with a two-page list of the twenty-five items. They were asked to complete these and mail them to the interviewer.

It is principally this time limitation that accounts for the fact that only 148 of the 167 interviewees completed these questions. Of the nineteen who did not respond, four refused outright on the grounds that the questions were too personal. Fifteen of those nonresponding members of the elite had taken the mail forms but failed to return them. (Some twenty others had taken forms and returned them completed.) Reasons for the failure of the fifteen to return their schedules are not known.

This section was specially treated in another fashion—by being self-administered. Upon the completion of the other items in the survey, the respondent was given a printed two-page questionnaire and asked to answer all the items by checking the appropriate boxes. Pretests had revealed that respondents felt less uneasy when confronted by these questions in printed form rather than verbally. Nonetheless, these techniques of administration were by no means sufficient to overcome the basic difficulties of the test.

means, etc. are available but, unfortunately, no similar application of the inventory has been made outside the United States.[47] Clearly, the meaning of the scores obtained in Iran should not be assumed equivalent to scores obtained in the United States. Accepting this lack of comparability based on diverse cultural factors, it is interesting, nonetheless, to compare these results. The mean score for respondents in Iran is 19.5, exactly equal to the mean score for all respondents in the United States and falling in the center of a range of means from a low of 14.5 (a Midwest state university) to 27.2 (a women's city jail on the West Coast of the United States). The median score from Iranian elite respondents (17.1) falls slightly below the median score for all respondents in the United States (17.5). While the lack of comparability in these results prevents one from suggesting that the Iranian elite manifest levels of insecurity not appreciably different from Americans to whom the test was administered, it should be mentioned that the author's working hypothesis that the Iranian elite would manifest appreciably higher scores than Americans was not borne out by test results.

What might account for the relatively low levels of insecurity revealed by the Maslow instrument? One answer is suggested by the shortcomings raised above in regards the questionnaire. But an additional answer, derived primarily from "casual empiricism" is available. This evidence centers on child rearing practices in Iran.

CHILD REARING IN IRAN

General and impressionistic observations of child rearing in middle- and upper-class urban residences in Iran suggest that children receive upbringings most conducive to developing a sense of psychic security. Children in these homes receive what appears to an outside observer as a virtually endless amount of love and succor from their parents and servants. They are rarely forced into positions whereby they need accept responsibility for their actions or make decisions independently of their parents.

In addition, children are virtually never punished for their misbehavior and physical punishment is conspicuously absent. It is assumed that being "only a child," the improper youngster cannot be expected to assume responsibility for his behavior. And if he is not responsible, he could hardly be considered accountable. It is startling to note the advanced age at which children are considered by their parents to be still "only children." For most purposes, childhood extends to the period when the "child" is married (often to a spouse selected by his parents) and leaves his parents' house to establish his own residence.

When asked how they would deal with a ten-year-old son who dis-

[47] Maslow et al., *Manual.*

obeyed his parents, fully 80 per cent of the elite respondents suggested that they would talk to the child to show him his incorrect behavior. One of the elite justified this by suggesting that "you can make a slave out of a free man by kindness . . . and it is better to enslave one man in kindness than free a thousand slaves." (It is interesting to note the parallel which it was suggested above pertains in the relationship of the monarch to his subjects. It is also revealing of family life in Iran that this respondent felt that the father-son relationship should approximate that of master-slave.) A great number of the elite (N = 5) felt that they would forget the whole thing, than felt that either spanking, confinement, or depriving the child of food (N = 3) was an appropriate response. When they were asked how they would deal with a ten-year-old son who insulted his father and struck him, their responses were immediately incredulous. "If a child struck his father, one would have to believe that the child was joking, for this is so serious an act, it could not be done," replied one typical respondent. As a group, their responses were hardly more forceful than were those for the less serious offense (see table 7.3). One patient father seemed to sum up the group's thoughts when he suggested that "force in dealing with a child is similar to force in dealing

TABLE 7.3
Favored Methods of the Elite for
Dealing with a Ten-Year-Old Son

Punishment	Son who Disobeys his Father	Son who Insults and Strikes his Father
Spanking	1.8%	4.2%
Isolation/confinement	0.0	1.2
Depriving of food[a]	0.0	0.0
Scolding	2.4	6.0
Talking to show incorrect behavior	79.0	66.5
Talking to learn reasons for misbehavior	3.6	4.8
Loving child more	2.4	1.8
Forgetting the whole thing	3.0	2.4
Other, don't know	7.8	13.1
Total	100.0%	100.0%
N	(167)	(167)

[a] When this question was asked of the respondents, the answer choices as given were read aloud. It is telling that only one alternative was never selected-- that of depriving a wayward child of food. I would hypothesize that food plays a central part in Islamic eschatology and would constitute far too serious a deprivation to be used in disciplining a child. At another level, food in the Islamic religion might be assumed to play a role similar to that played by sex in the Christian religion.

with a nation. In both cases, force is inefficacious, undesirable, and destructive." Given these orientations to childhood misconduct on the part of Iranian fathers, who are generally alleged to be more authoritarian than Iranian mothers, it would seem that children from such households would receive unconditional love. It is assumed that such an upbringing would contribute to the development of individuals with personalities manifesting high levels of personal security.

On the assumption that the present-day political elite received their earliest socialization in generally similar circumstances, results on the Maslow instrument are more comprehensible. The elite score at the secure end of the continuum because in the sense of personal security which those questions are designed to measure, i.e., underlying or primary security-insecurity, they are relatively secure.

One specific finding of our research is relevant to this interpretation of child rearing and family life. In the original factor analysis, nine items loaded highly on an orthogonally rotated factor. The items and loadings are shown in table 7.4. The items central to this factor pertain primarily

TABLE 7.4

Family Disdain Factor

	Frequency with which the respondent discusses the following with his/her spouse:	
1.	The upbringing of children	.657
2.	The education of children	.646
3.	The family budget	.453
4.	Birth control	.386
5.	Your own career and the affairs of your work	.344
6.	Apart from your immediate family, is there anyone to whom you confide your most personal and important problems?	.367
7.	How old would you think a child had to be before he could be trusted with information about family finances, i.e., the income and expenses of the family?	.356
8.	Do you feel that you get enough praise?	.340
9.	Do you think people like you as much as they do others?	.335

to low levels of intrafamilial trust and communications. As a result, the factor has been labeled "family disdain." What groups together in this factor are answers that indicate a low level of discussion within the family on a host of subjects, an unwillingness to trust younger children with information on family finance, and a failure to confide in others. It would appear that in families where these opinions of the heads of household were translated into behavioral regularities, conditions conducive to fostering insecurity would prevail. For such homes would be those in which confidence and warmth did not encompass all members of the household—in which unconditional love and other factors conducive to psychological security were absent.

It is interesting that when scores on the Security-Insecurity Inventory are compared with scores on this factor, there is a significant positive relationship. High levels of insecurity are associated with high levels of family disdain. The converse relationship also exists ($x^2 = 6.706$; df = 2; p < .04; g = .344). What would appear to be happening is another example of the oft noted phenomenon whereby the sins of the parents are visited on the children. Fathers (and the few mothers in the sample) who manifest high levels of insecurity hold attitudes that, if congruent with their own practices of child rearing, would most likely contribute to the development of high levels of primary insecurity in their children. On the other hand, elite respondents who score on the secure end of the Maslow continuum show little family disdain and, hence, would tend to raise children who also manifested higher levels of primary security.

Another tantalizing relationship appears in the comparison of security-insecurity scores with the social background factor we have labeled urban-rural factor. This five-item factor has two items that load most highly—population of respondent's birthplace (.802) and population of father's birthplace (.773). A third question, "When did you and/or your family move to Tehran?" also loaded highly on this factor (.568). The three positive high loadings indicate the propensity of the elite and their fathers to have been born in similar sized cities and for those born in the provinces to have moved to Tehran relatively early in their lives.

The relationship between security-insecurity and urban-rural scores is shown in table 7.5. We note that scores of those from the urban end

TABLE 7.5

Scores on the Maslow Security-Insecurity Inventory by Scores on the Urban-Rural Factor

Level of Security		Urban-Rural Factor	
		Urban	Rural
Secure		33.3%	16.2%
Medium		33.3	45.6
Insecure		33.4	38.2
	Total	100.0%	100.0%
	N	(68)	(81)

Note: x^2 = 5.943; df = 2; p = .05; g = -.221.

of the factor continuum—virtually all respondents born in Tehran—show no relationship with Maslow scores. The same is not the case with scores that we have designated as rural but that contain members of the elite from smaller cities as well as villages. Here a clear relationship is established with scores bunching at the more insecure end of the continuum.

These results are consistent with a good deal of evidence regarding child rearing practices in smaller cities, towns, and villages of Iran as well as in other developing societies. An investigation by Murray A. Straus of the determinancy of the adult personality by infant experiences focused on these issues. Straus noted that the personalities of adult members of Sinhalese society "seem to be marked by feelings of insecurity."[48] Yet, he notes, by all criteria of personality accepted in the West, Sinhalese children are treated most permissively, and should, therefore, develop secure personalities. The author goes on to hypothesize that this apparent paradox can be explained by postinfantile experiences. Firstly, "the withdrawal of overt signs of parental affection after about age four or five" and, secondly, "the loose structuring of Sinhalese society . . . and . . . the discrepancy between the rigid verbal expectation of children's behavior and the actual weak disciplinary control and loose supervision of children" are responsible for adult behavior patterns.[49]

The extent to which child rearing practices in rural, village, and small-town Iran conform with methods prevalent in Ceylon is striking. And it is striking that the adult insecurity patterns for Iranians raised in the less urban areas is similar to Straus's findings. While little firm data exist on this point, evidence given above, newspaper accounts, anecdotes, novels, and personal observation all suggest that children in Iran do enjoy permissive upbringing in loose social structures.

The key variable that is absent in child rearing practices for middle- and upper-class Tehran families is the postinfantile crisis when the child is expected to abruptly assume the role of adult and accept adult responsibility.[50] We have suggested that this takes place in such families only with the (arranged) marriage of the child. But such is definitely *not* the case with children raised in lower-class families or in families from smaller cities and towns.[51] For those children there appears to be an

---

[48] "Childhood Experience and Emotional Security in the Context of Sinhalese Social Organization," *Social Forces*, 33, no. 3 (Dec. 1954): 158.

[49] *Ibid.*, By "loose structuring of Sinhalese society," Straus refers to a society in which "the pattern of rights, duties, and obligations is always open to question and exception" (p. 160). See J. F. Embree, "Thailand—A Loosely Structured Social System," *American Anthropologist*, 52 (1950): 181–93.

[50] For a description of more or less typical nineteenth-century elite childhoods, see Mirza Mahmoud Khan Saghaphi, *In the Imperial Shadow* (Garden City, N. Y.: Doubleday, Doran, and Co., 1932); and Wilfred Sparroy, *Persian Children of the Royal Family: The Narrative of an English Tutor at the Court of H.I.H. Zillu's-Sultan, G.C.S.I.* (London: J. Lane, 1902). For a twentieth-century version of child rearing among the higher social classes, the Persian-language novels of Ali Dashti are of great value.

[51] Analyses of social background data for the Iranian political elite indicate that

equally permissive upbringing in a loose social structure, but a marked hiatus in childhood. Children from these social strata and from smaller sized cities are expected early to fulfill adult responsibilities, be those defined as farming tasks, shepherding, apprenticeships with bazaar tradesmen, or any of the numerous activities—other than education—that are imposed on the majority of young children in Iran. "The boys become independent and self-reliant at a very early age, and are quite capable of running a shop in the bazaar, working at a trade, or tending a flock of sheep in the mountains."[52] It may well be that this abrupt assignment of adult responsibilities helps explain the finding that a greater proportion of the elite born in less urban areas score insecurely. The evidence presented here is, in fact, insufficient to support this contention. Nonetheless, it is suggestive of the relationships postulated and awaits further examination.

CONCOMITANTS OF PRIMARY INSECURITY

To backtrack, the statement that Iranian elite are relatively secure has meaning only insofar as results derived from Iranian elite responses are comparable with responses from a variety of groups in the United States. However, we have already suggested that any such comparison is highly suspect. A comparison of responses internal to the elite is likely to be more valid, for that analysis avoids the deficiencies inherent in intercultural comparison. Such an analysis does, indeed, prove to be a good deal more interesting. One of the more relevant of these is the relationship between insecurity as measured by Maslow's instrument and responses to the question, "Do you often feel frustrated because you are unable to do as you wish or unable to accomplish what you wish?" as can be seen in table 7.6, the relationship between security and absence of frustration is particularly strong, with the converse relation being less strong. In fact, when age is controlled, the association between these two variables is

---

there is a significant positive relationship between social class and size of city. Those of the elite born outside Tehran tended to have parents of lower social status.

[52] Donald N. Wilber, *Iran Past and Present* (Princeton: Princeton University Press, 1958), p. 178. Actually, the literature on Iran presents a fascinating series of contradictions when it considers child rearing practices. To give but a few examples: "Children are the objects of the most tender parental affection" (*ibid.*, p. 178); and "Discipline is the indispensable instrument of Iranian child training" (Vreeland, *Iran*, p. 262). Other sources are available that suggest that the children are raised by women servants, by men servants, by the women of the household while isolated in the *haram* (women's quarters), with or without physical punishment, etc. None of this literature attempts a serious consideration of these practices by urban-rural residence or social class. On balance, the result is an impressionistic collection of anecdotal materials with little practical applicability.

TABLE 7.6

Feelings of Frustration by Scores
on the S-I Inventory

Level of Security	Level of Reported Frustration		
	Very High	High	Not Very High
Secure	35.0%	37.5%	66.7%
Intermediate	27.5	12.5	12.2
Insecure	37.5	50.0	21.1
Total	100.0%	100.0%	100.0%
N	(40)	(16)	(90)

Note: $x^2 = 15.552$; df = 4; p = .004; gamma = -.415.

strengthened—the higher the insecurity at all age levels, the greater the reported frustrations.

This relationship is to be expected on at least two levels. Accepting Maslow's inventory as tapping the primary or antecedent sources of insecurity and anxiety, then frustration would be expected in terms of dynamic psychiatry. "Freud, in *The Problems of Anxiety*, says that anxiety is felt by a person at the realization of formerly repressed, unacceptable drives and wishes."[53] Frustration would be bound to arise from the stimulus of these impulses and the continued unacceptability or impossibility of acting so as to satisfy these impulses. On the secondary level, i.e., sources of anxiety in adult life, frustration would also be a part of general anxiety or insecurity. Anticipation of negative sanctions—be that defined by an outside observer as fear or anxiety—would in all likelihood produce frustrations. Two commentators see this relationship between frustration and anxiety as so intertwined that they equate the two. "Anxiety," they stress, "is the anticipation of punishment, i.e., of failure to receive positive rewards or expectations of pain or frustration."[54]

The frustration of those of the elite with insecure scores contributes to a general propensity for negativism and pessimism, Many of the elite reported a sense of impending doom or dread of an untoward future. They also looked upon their recent national history in the same fashion. The elite were asked to comment on the most significant changes in Iranian society since World War II. Answers were coded in a number of ways including a count of the number of changes towards which the respondent felt positively oriented and the number to which he felt nega-

[53] Frieda Fromm-Reichmann, "Psychiatric Aspects of Anxiety" in *An Outline of Psychoanalysis*, Clara Thompson, Milton Mayer, and Earl Witenberg (New York: Random House, 1955), p. 115.

[54] John P. Gillin and George Nicholson, "The Security Functions of Cultural Systems," *Social Forces*, 30, no. 1 (Oct. 1951): 183.

tive. The number of positive changes run against insecurity shows that 56 per cent of the more insecure respondents felt that no positive changes whatsoever had occurred in Iran. Only forty-four of the more secure were so inclined. The relationship is soon reversed, however, for more than two-thirds of the secure respondents reported at least one favorable change, whereas only one-third of the less secure held such sanguine views. Clearly, for these respondents insecurity and negativism do go together.

But once said, there is no necessary indication of the direction that such negative attitudes will take. One respondent who scored appreciably more insecure than the mean, felt that the recent changes that had occurred in Iran were meaningless, or worse. He attributed responsibility for this not only to His Imperial Majesty, but also directly to the United States, which he perceived as ultimately the most significant factor in Iranian politics. The United States, he claimed, was losing the immense reservoir of good will created by such men as Morgan Shuster, whose economic mission to Iran in 1911 was subverted by Anglo-Russian pressure on the Iranian government, and Dr. Samuel Jordan, long-time principal of the Presbyterian-run Alborz College.[55] The problem, he suggested, "stems from America's tendency to see money and economic factors as the basis for all human action. The Soviets, however, are masters. When they want to paint a car, they scrape off the old paint and start anew. The United States just tries to throw a new coat of paint over the old standards of thinking." For this respondent, then, the apparent problem was that the United States had failed to intervene enough in domestic Iranian affairs.[56]

[55] It is relevant to note that when discussing their attitudes towards the United States, an overwhelming majority of the political elite expressed positive feelings based on the actions of individual American citizens. Very few regarded the United States in an especially favorable light because of the more than $1 billion that Iran has received in foreign aid. The consensus argued that aid monies were spent for America's own national interest, not for Iran's, and that America had long since been amply rewarded. No sacrifice had been made by the U.S. and no particular gratification need be expressed by Iran—especially because many of the elite felt that the long run result of much U.S. assistance was essentially negative. But, on the other hand, Americans who had made personal sacrifices for Iran were viewed in a totally different perspective and brought the U.S. much of the limited prestige that it still possessed.

[56] This same member of the elite went on to explain that America's stance of non-intervention was nonsense. By massive foreign assistance to the regime, it had intervened as thoroughly as possible. But, he argued, the intervention had served to strengthen the wrong domestic political forces. Or, as another member of the political elite put it, "The United States has spent billions in Iran and saved Iran from the charms of the Soviet Union. But the people hate them. Why? Because the people that they choose to govern us are corrupt, inexperienced, cruel, and arrogant." It might be added that neither of these members of the elite are considered "radical" or in the "opposition."

A host of additional examples relating s-i score to other attitudes might be given. But it is clear that irrespective of any comparison of insecurity levels among the Iranian political elite and a variety of groups in the United States, those members of the political elite who do manifest higher levels of insecurity on the Maslow test display attitudes consonant with Maslow's expectations. This would tend to lend credence to Maslow's assumptions on the cross-cultural applicability of the concept of primary insecurity, as we have labeled it, or "the ontogenetic priority of safety, belongingness, and love," as he has termed it.[57]

What this analysis and that of Maslow suggest is that security-insecurity as measured by the Maslow test is a general character orientation that would affect all areas of a person's striving. Maslow himself suggests that:

In every insecure person with whom the writer has worked, he always found *a continual, never dying longing for security* . . . there were found wide variations in the subjects' individual definitions of the security that they longed for. Some defined it in terms merely of safety, some in terms of dependence upon a stronger person, some in terms of having power and money and a few defined it in what is a more "correct" way, i.e., as a longing to deserve and win back the love and affection of other people.[58]

Much of the evidence from elite responses would support this generalization. Thus, for example, we asked the elite the following question: "How probable is it that you will lose your present position?" Some two-thirds of the elite who felt it fairly probable or very probable that they would lose their present position scored at insecurity levels on the Maslow questionnaire. Conversely, of those who felt it fairly or very improbable that they would lose their positions, 56 per cent had "secure" scores. The spill-over effect so prevalent with the cynicism factor below seems to be operative here, for the elite who manifest high levels of primary insecurity also manifest insecurity in areas far removed from primary psychological concerns—security of job.

But Maslow himself pulls back from complete identification with this primary-secondary spill-over effect. He cautions that: "We do not wish to embark upon any typology and speak of secure and insecure people in a black and white fashion as if they were completely different. . . . Most people in our society can be seen to be both secure and insecure. For example . . . a person secure in the intellectual world may be insecure in the social world."[59] While Maslow quite clearly recognizes, then, that individuals may be secure and insecure in different areas of

---

[57] Maslow et al., *Manual.*
[58] "Dynamics of Psychological Security-Insecurity," p. 336.
[59] *Ibid.*, p. 333, n. 3.

their striving, "his conceptual framework does not lend itself to analysis along these lines."[60]

MANIFEST INSECURITY

What has been proposed, then, is that observations of Iranian society suggest the presence of insecurity as well as an explanation in child rearing practices for its absence among the political elite. Maslow's instrument is replete with difficulties and does not, in fact, indicate high levels of primary insecurity among the respondents. But individual items in the questionnaire relate to the Maslow inventory in ways predictable from his theoretical statements. To untangle these apparent contradictions, a number of additional items were included in the questionnaire. These were meant to tap specific areas of insecurity at the secondary level. When run in a factor analysis with other general characterological variables, these fell out together in an orthogonal rotation. This factor, labeled manifest insecurity (MI), includes the items and headings shown in table 7.7.

From the loadings on the questions related to manifest insecurity and the answers to them that were received, it appears that the conceptual unity of manifest insecurity is similar to that which would be expected on theoretical grounds in the case of secondary insecurity. What coalesces together in this factor are frustration, fear, pessimism, inefficacy, firmness with children, and an authoritarian upbringing. A central issue in the factor appears to be the respondent's expectation that he will lose his present position—that he is not "secure" in that post. Insofar as a formal position within the bureaucracy is so vital for assuring status, communication, access, and, thus, power, loss of position or fear of such loss would be expected to appear as an essential element in manifest or secondary, adult sources of insecurity. Indeed, the elite were almost unanimous in their agreement over the necessity of a formal post. One put it this way:

There is a universal feeling among Iranians that an official administrative position is essential for safety and to be able to protect one's own and family's interests. A "title" is necessary for in running even one's family affairs, one perpetually comes up against the formal structure of the Government. One needs a title to deal with that structure. . . . By law everyone has the same protection, but it remains true that a title or officeholder has the power to use that part of the structure over which he has control and his supporters against other formal officeholders.[61]

[60] Knutson, "Personal Security," p. 224.

[61] Sebastian de Grazia sees the value of formal office holding in different terms. He argues: "The ruler by his presumed regulation of the environment is held

TABLE 7.7

Manifest Insecurity Factor

1.	Do you often feel frustrated because you are unable to do as you wish or unable to accomplish what you wish?	.506
2.	How probable is it that you will lose your present position?	.440
3.	How secure do you think you are in your present position?	.430
4.	To what extent do you feel surrounded and impeded by red tape, petty rules and regulations, and other annoyances?	.392
5.	Respondents favored method for dealing with a disobedient ten-year-old son.	.578
6.	Concerning your personal future, would you say that in general you feel enthusiastic, hopeful, indifferent, anxious, resigned, or embittered?	.377
7.	The best way of life is to walk in the path of our fathers.	.325
8.	What do you consider the likelihood of Iran's overcoming in the next ten years the problems which you have enumerated?	.319
9.	I don't think that really powerful public officials and politicians care much what people like me think.	.301
10.	In terms of what you see around you, would you say there is a great deal of injustice or really not very much?	.294
11.	During your own upbringing, how were most of the major family decisions made?	.291

And as we have shown above, positions have been awarded and withdrawn from individuals without respite for decades. No wonder, then, that such fears would have a solid founding in the realities of Iranian politics.

But, in fact, such fear over the probable loss of official position is surprising. The most recent political history of Iran would argue that the

responsible for the provision of status positions, namely, the approved occupations in a community. Without one of these occupations the person is without status, namely the approval of the community for his activities. The loss of primary status is equated with loss of the affection of attendants and brings on anomic anxiety" (*The Political Community: A Study of Anomie* [Chicago: University of Chicago Press, 1963], pp. 239–40, n. 21). "Anomic anxiety" appears to be identical to meanings of insecurity as we have used that term. Binder, in his study of Iran, combines these two perspectives: "Holding some sort of government position is a mark of honor and means of institutionalizing access and influence, even though the salary involved may be unconsequential" (Iran, p. 69). The lack of honor or status is seen by de Grazia as contributing to "anomic anxiety"—a finding paralleled in our own research.

average tenure of high officeholders is considerably greater than ever before. We have already noted that the average tenure for the prime ministers who have served since the inauguration of the first constitutional government is nineteen months. But more recently, that average has been considerably lengthened. The ministers who were given cabinet-level portfolios with the elevation of Hassan Ali Mansur to the premiership in March of 1964 have continued in their posts, with minor exceptions, to the present.

We have also noted that when high officials have been removed from their posts, they are more likely than not to receive another high commission. To take only some of the more recent examples: when General Hassan Pakravan was relieved of his command of the State Security and Intelligence Organization, he was posted as ambassador to Pakistan; ex-Prime Minister Alam was established as chancellor of the Pahlavi University in Shiraz and more recently, minister of the Imperial Court; ex-Prime Minister Eghbal was made ambassador to UNESCO and then director of the National Iranian Oil Company. This list could be extended indefinitely but the conclusion should already be clear—as long as the official continues to operate within the rules of the political system as established by His Imperial Majesty, some high-level formal position within the governmental bureaucracy is, in the main, a certainty.

Why, then, this concern with loss of formal position? One quite reasonable basis for concern is that while another formal position is statistically a virtual certainty, there are exceptions. A member of the elite recently relieved of his position is not especially interested in aggregate probabilities. Rather, his concern focuses on his own immediate political future. Perhaps more important, however, is the realization by the members of the elite that they exercise virtually no control over their tenure in a given position or over their appointment to any other position. No well-established or generally understood criteria for the maintenance of office appear to exist. In fact, the same is true for achieving office. One respondent, in a story reminiscent of the mythical deputy whose tale was told above, recounted how he happened to become a member of the Senate. "I was in Switzerland," he recalled, "with no intention of being active in Iranian politics. One day in Zurich, I picked up a Swiss newspaper and noticed an article about Iran's new Senate. There was my name. His Imperial Majesty had nominated me as one of the thirty senators he is empowered to select!" Loyalty to His Imperial Majesty, of course, is an absolutely basic criterion for officeholding. But numerous examples indicate that loyalty is a concept difficult to operationalize, to translate into a guide for behavior in office. Moreover, loyalty is only the minimal criterion, insufficient to explain the majority of dismissals that have lately occurred.

The elite are acutely aware of the absence of satisfactory operational meanings for loyalty. The less cynical attribute their success to loyalty in the sense of "efficiency" in executing the monarch's reform plans. The difficulty of measuring such efficiency and the difficulties of assigning responsibility for any governmental action whatsoever suggest that this claim is not taken seriously by either the cynical or the noncynical among the elite. Rather, there appears to be more general importance attached to the concept of loyalty in its more common meaning. On this latter meaning, there is agreement among both the holders of official positions and those of the political elite without such positions. The position of the officeholders was succinctly put this way: "To retain my post, I remain what I must be—*nowkar-e dowlat* [a servant of the government]." A member of the elite without formal position put the matter differently when he told of a private audience he had with the shah:

I told His Imperial Majesty that his sacrifice [i.e., the person being interviewed] was insane. The shah asked why I talked that way. "Because a sane person pursues his own selfish interests and I do not." The shah agreed and asked why I did not do so. "Well," I replied, "the only way to achieve one's interests in this country is to flatter you and to agree with whatever you say. To do so one must be without personal scruples. I am not and so cannot and will not do so." Since then, I have been retired.

Whatever the actual bases for maintaining one's position, it is clear that the general belief among the elite is that those bases are highly elusive and their control is perpetually beyond one's grasp. Being beyond one's grasp, insecurity is generated in the course of the individual's realization that he is not in control of his own, personal fate.[62] Similar conclusions have been reached in countless studies of employment in other countries. As one student of the problem put it: "A good deal of comparative research has found that the workers experiencing the most recurring unemployment and underemployment are the ones most likely to be discontented with the existing order, to conceive of themselves as its 'exploited victims,' to be 'class conscious' and to support the political left in their country."[63] In many ways, the recurring turnover of personnel in high-level government jobs as well as the realization of helplessness in controlling or altering that turnover, is a central source of secondary insecurity among the Iranian political elite.[64]

[62] This observation speaks to one of Harold Lasswell's contentions that "the influential are those who get the most of what there is to get." One of the three principal values for him is "safety." Clearly in Iran this is one value that the political elite do not get. See Harold D. Lasswell, *Politics: Who Gets What, When, and How* (New York: McGraw-Hill, 1936), p. 3.

[63] Maurice Zeitlin, "Economic Insecurity and the Political Attitudes of Cuban Workers," *American Sociological Review*, 31, no. 1 (Feb. 1966): 35. Zeitlin also gives a bibliography of some ten other studies which draw approximately analogous conclusions.

[64] It may be appropriate, in the face of evidence that suggests increased tenure

And expectations of losing formal position, so essential for maintaining political power, contribute to the sense among many of the elite of fear, frustration, and pessimism—which in turn are all central features of manifest insecurity as determined by the factor loadings. In addition, manifest insecurity goes together with relative harshness in dealing with a disobedient son and with childhood upbringings whereby fathers were the dominant individuals and the sole decision makers.

It should be clear to the reader that these items that load highly on the MI factor are the very ones that are significantly associated with scores on the S-I factor. Not surprisingly, then, individuals tend to score similarly on both indexes.

Table 7.8 implies that theorists of security-insecurity are correct in

TABLE 7.8

Comparison of Scores on MI and S-I Factors

S-I Score	MI Score		
	Secure	Medium	Insecure
Secure	38.9%	15.4%	19.4%
Medium	31.5	65.4	35.8
Insecure	29.6	19.2	44.8
Total	100.0%	100.0%	100.0%
N	(54)	(26)	(67)

Note: $x^2 = 15.488$; df = 4; p = .001; gamma = .345.

suggesting a key relationship between primary and secondary sources of insecurity. Thus, "the effect of an emotionally disturbing event may be multiplied as a consequence of the important effects of various antecedent vicissitudes of early life, which come to serve actually or symbolically as analogous prototypes."[65] One immediate difficulty, however, is the problem of the direction of causality. Certainly, in a psychoanalytic sense, primary sources of anxiety or insecurity would affect secondary sources. But does the Maslow instrument measure primary insecurity alone? In fact, does it measure that insecurity at all? It is certainly conceivable that responses to the Maslow items, which ostensibly are unrelated to secondary sources of insecurity, are significantly affected by the level of secondary or manifest insecurity then being experienced by the respondent. Not surprising, then, would be high scores on the Maslow instrument by inmates of penitentiaries. Maslow avoids this dilemma by

for high-ranking elite as well as a near guarantee of subsequent high-level appointments, to reiterate that what is at issue here is not "the facts" but the perception of "the facts" by the individuals in the elite.

[65] Laughlin, *Neuroses*, p. 29.

claiming to measure both types simultaneously—but in the process, also avoiding the issue of whether there are, in fact, two such sources of insecurity, their relationship, and the functional specificity of insecurity.

Among the Iranian political elite, there is a clear propensity for persons who score insecurely on Maslow's instrument to score highly in terms of manifest insecurity. Because this is a study of the political process, moreover, we feel justified in concentrating primarily on this latter type of insecurity—feelings of threat and danger occasioned by adult life experiences primarily encountered in the course of participation in the political process. Undoubtedly, those members of the elite with early childhood experiences most conducive to producing primary insecurity would react most strongly to such later events. And indeed what limited data we have to bring to bear on this point support that contention. But we would also argue that even in the absence of primary insecurity, the reality of participation at high levels of the Iranian political process are conducive to producing the latter, but no less psychically real, secondary insecurity.

Turning then to this manifest or secondary insecurity, we wish to know who among the elite demonstrate these qualities. Who are the insecure? An immediate answer, from interview data, is, "those who participate most actively in the system." Those who are most imbedded in the Iranian political process—as measured by age, reputed political power, degree of participation, number of activities, and social status— these are the most insecure.

Age-Political experience factor. One of the social background factors produced in a rotation of those variables was labeled the age-political experience factor. The variables and factor loadings it contained are shown in table 7.9. Age, parliamentary service, lower education for the respondent and his father, many children, and fewer films were all related in this factor. The results produced when the age-political experience factor was run again the MI factor are shown in table 7.10. The older elite with lower educations and greater parliamentary experience demonstrate by far the highest levels of manifest insecurity.

An intensive review of recent Iranian political history will attest to the validity of these results. The inauguration of Hassan Ali Mansur as prime minister in early 1964 brought to formal positions of power the members of his *dowreh* and a larger group known as the Progressive Center. Coupled with an intensity of royally led reform—rare in the reign of Mohammad Reza Shah—the older elites saw their hold over the key points of power vanishing. The earlier dissolution of both houses of Parliament had eliminated one such vantage point. When the results of the elections to the new houses of Parliament were announced in the fall

TABLE 7.9

Age-Political Experience Factor

1.	Respondent's age at time of interview	.787
2.	Number of Senate sessions in which the respondent was a member	.642
3.	Highest education level achieved by the respondent	.495
4.	Highest education level achieved by the respondent's father	.464
5.	Number of Majles sessions in which the respondent was a member	.430
6.	Number of films which the respondent has seen in the past three months	.429
7.	Number of living children	.342

TABLE 7.10

Scores on the Manifest Insecurity Factor by
Scores on the Age-Political Experience Factor

MI	Age-Political Experience Factor	
	Young	Old
Low	57.6%	40.2%
High	42.4	59.8
Total	100.0%	100.0%
N	(85)	(82)

Note: Yates x^2 = 4.386; continuity corrected; p = .036; gamma = .338.

of 1963, it was obvious that a fundamental change had occurred. The older members of the traditional elite had lost their majority in the lower house, the Majles.[66] Only in the Senate were these traditional wielders of political power still in control.

[66] "Up to, and including, the Twentieth Majles, representatives were almost exclusively drawn from the hereditary elite groups. . . . When the Twenty-First Majles was convened, representation had undergone 'drastic changes' due to shift in control over elections from the traditional elite into the hands of the shah. Former civil servants were in the majority (69%) in a Majles in which 81% of the 200 seats were filled by individuals serving for the first time" (Howard J. Rotblat, "The Patterns of Recruitment into the Iranian Political Elite" [M.A. diss., University of Chicago, 1968], p. 4). Also see Zahra Shaji'i, *Namayandegan-e Shoray-e Melli dar Bist-o-Yek Dowreh-ye Qanungozari* [Representatives of the national assembly in twenty-one legislative assemblies] (Tehran: Institute for Social Research and Studies, University of Tehran, 1966), chap. 6, for data on members of the twenty-first session.

234

But the final blow came with the resignation of Prime Minister Assad-ollah Alam in early 1964. For he and his cabinet were replaced by Mansur and the technocrats. While these individuals were primarily the sons of members of the traditional elite, they brought two new factors to bear in the performance of their executive responsibilities: relative youth and technical educations. Together, these resulted in a degree of vitality and enthusiasm unusual for Iranian politics. In the process, however, it became clear that the Senate, the remaining occupational base of the previous *rejal* (elite), would be insufficient to allow for their exerting influence in Iranian politics as was their custom. As they felt themselves being displaced from positions in the administration—the very center of political power in Iran—their discontent and their manifest insecurity rose markedly. For not only were the older members of the elite being displaced from positions of political power, but the prime virtue that they claimed was now in disrepute. Mansur and his colleagues justified their rapid rise to power on the basis of their technical educations. Mansur claimed that such education more than compensated for any lack of experience. In fact, their lack of experience and lack of slavish adherence to outmoded customs were hailed as beneficial. But perhaps more than any other single criterion, experience had long been prized in Iran. A frequently related proverb makes the point:

> A wise man needs two lives in this world,
> So as to gain experience in the one and apply
> it in the other.

Mansur, then, was not only taking administrative office but in the process denigrating that experience that so many of the elite had used to justify their wielding political power in the past. Bitterness arose between those of the elite who had served in the Majles and Senate and the ministers. The result was growing and often intense insecurity on the part of those who could not lay claim to technical educations or to membership in Mansur's circle.

This combination of variables—age, relatively poor education, and relatively great experience in the Parliament—all contributed in the early 1960s to fostering manifest insecurity. But age is related to insecurity in another fashion. Insofar as age is congruent with length of participation in the political system, increased participation would be expected to lead to heightened levels of manifest insecurity. Operating in the milieu of Iranian politics with its eccentricities and vagaries—over which the individual has no control—can only contribute to heightened levels of manifest insecurity irrespective of the additionally threatening factor of the denigration of one's most valued skills.

235

Activity factor. The connection between involvement and heightened manifest insecurity can be seen more strikingly when we consider yet another of the factors produced in the orthogonal rotation of social background variables. Labeled the activity factor, it grouped together eleven variables, all of which measure, in some fashion, the extent of the respondent's participation in the political system. The variables and loadings are shown in table 7.11. What groups together in this factor are

TABLE 7.11

Activity Factor

1.	Total number of groups, organizations, clubs, etc., to which the respondent belongs	.823
2.	Total number of positions or occupations held for which no remuneration is received	.694
3.	Number of professional and occupational groups or social classes with which the respondent converses a few times per month or more frequently	.582
4.	Frequency of respondent's conversations with various professional and occupational groups or social classes	.573
5.	Membership in a dowreh (circle) of friends or family which meets regularly	.465
6.	Total number of occupations or positions held by the respondent for which he receives remuneration	.458
7.	Number of magazines, in any language, read each month	.382
8.	Recency of respondent's last trip outside Iran	.381
9.	Highest education level achieved by respondent	.360
10.	Reputed power score	.327
11.	Number of trips of any duration made outside Iran by the respondent	.323

variables pertaining to the number of the respondent's remunerated and nonremunerated positions, organizational memberships, *dowrehs*, frequency of his communication with a variety of occupational and social groups, and finally, his reputed power score. All of these relate in the predicted direction—higher levels of reputed power being associated with greater number of occupational positions and organizational memberships and communication. A significant relationship is found when the activity factor is run against MI (see table 7.12).

The greater the immersion of the respondent in the political system, the greater is his level of manifest insecurity. And perhaps more importantly, the greater the reputed power of the respondent, the higher the

TABLE 7.12

Manifest Insecurity Scores by
Scores on the Activity Factor

MI	Activity Level	
	Low	High
Low	56.8%	40.5%
High	43.2	59.5
Total	100.0%	100.0%
N	(88)	(79)

Note: Yates x^2 = 3.803; continuity
corrected; p = .05;
gamma = .318.

level of manifest insecurity. This manifest insecurity appears to be an accompaniment of mobility up the ladder of elite success. Rather than serving to provide the individual member of the elite with a greater sense of safety and protection, increasing power appears to extract its toll in greater insecurity. As the level of power increases so do the rewards— but perhaps to a greater extent so does the insecurity increase. That which is meant to represent higher levels of well-being thus turns on acquisition to be of less substance than one had imagined.[67]

In this sense, this relationship may very well have reciprocal effects. A variety of studies of voluntary associations in the United States have led one observer to conclude: "It is likely that another psychological satisfaction [besides 'the two needs for self-expression and satisfaction of interests through collective action'] provided in other societies mainly by the immediate family and secondarily by the extended family, church, and community, is also being inadequately provided by them in our society. This is the provision of a sense of security."[68] Failing to find that sense of security in the family, church, or community, Americans are seen turning to voluntary organizations—trade unions, clubs, fraternal

[67] Certainly a similar argument is frequently made in terms of national military security where more strategic capability or military power appears directly associated with less national security. See, for example, Richard H. Rovere, "Letter from Washington," New Yorker, Feb. 3, 1968, pp. 85–90.

[68] Arnold M. Rose, The Power Structure: Political Process in American Society (New York: Oxford University Press, 1967), p. 230. See also Charles R. Wright and Herbert H. Hyman, "Voluntary Association Memberships," American Sociological Review, 23, no. 3 (June 1958); Murray Hansknecht, The Joiners (New York: Bedminster Press, 1962); David Sills, The Volunteers (Glencoe: Free Press, 1957); and John Carver Scott Jr., "Membership and Participation in Voluntary Organizations" (Ph.D. diss., University of Chicago, 1948). For an interesting study which examines primary group relationships as a type of security in a setting not traditionally considered in an interpersonal fashion, see Gregory P. Stone, "Sociological Aspects of Consumer Purchasing in a Northwest Side Chicago Community" (M.A. thesis, University of Chicago, 1952).

societies, political groups, etc.—in order to locate that sense of security. The Kluckhohns have suggested this in a slightly different fashion: "Why are Americans a nation of joiners? In part this is a defense mechanism against the excessive fluidity of our social structure. Because of the tension of continual struggle for social place, people have tried to gain a degree of routinized and recognized fixity by allying themselves with others in voluntary associations."[69] We would argue that these factors operate in the Iranian context. Members of the political elite turn to voluntary associations to obtain a sense of security in the face of a changing social system and, more importantly, as a base to attain or maintain political power.

Dowreh. The *dowreh* system in Iran is a telling example of such voluntary organizations, and we have already noted that membership in a *dowreh* is highly associated with manifest insecurity ($p = .001$). The *dowreh* is a small group of people, usually numbering no more than fifteen, who organize about some common purpose and meet on a regular basis.[70] *Dowreh*s exist for card playing, poetry, music, and, of course, politics. Earlier in the twentieth century, the role of these last types of *dowreh* was explained in this manner: "In practice the country is run, one can't say ruled, by small rings of politicians cooperating with a powerful and corrupt bureaucracy, whose aim is to enrich themselves so far as possible before a turn of the political wheel brings their term of office to an end."[71]

As an example of a *dowreh* that typifies many of the qualities of the "ideal type," we may consider the following group of gentlemen:

1. Mehdi Namazi
2. Mohammad Khosrow Shahi
3. Gholem Hossein Khoshbin
4. Abdol Hossein Behnia
5. Nasrollah Entezam
6. Abdollah Entezam
7. Mohammad Najmabadi
8. Ali Ardalan
9. Ebrahim Mahdavi
10. Ali Vakili
11. Ali Amini

[69] Clyde Kluckhohn and Florence Kluckhohn, "American Culture: Generalized Orientations and Class Patterns" in *Conflicts of Power in Modern Culture*, ed. L. Bryson, L. Finkelstein, and R. M. MacIver (New York: Harper, 1947), pp. 249–50, as quoted in Rose, *Power Structure*, p. 231.

[70] For insights into the striking relevance of the *dowreh* for Iranian politics, see Ann K. S. Lambton, "Secret Societies and the Persian Revolution of 1905–1906," *St. Anthony's Papers*, no. 4, 1958, pp. 43–60; and William G. Miller, "The Dowreh and Iranian Politics," *Middle East Journal*, 23, no. 2 (Spring 1969): 159–67. For information on the relevance of the *dowreh* for the formation of political parties, see L. P. Elwell-Sutton, "Political Parties in Iran, 1941–1948," *Middle East Journal*, 3, no. 1 (Jan. 1949), esp. the formation of the Iradeh-ye Melli (National Will) party by Seyyed Zia ed-Din Tabatabaie during World War II.

[71] J. M. Balfour, *Recent Happenings in Persia* (Edinburgh: W. Blackwood and Sons, 1922), p. 90.

These eleven constitute the core of one of the oldest continuously operating *dowreh*s in Iran. It is reported that along with four or five others who have joined or left the group over time, they have been meeting weekly for lunch for over twenty-five years.

The common interests and the satisfactions that their members receive from their association are at the root of the phenomenal prevalence of these *dowreh*s throughout Iran. In order to assess these factors, let us turn to some salient characteristics, shown in table 7.13, of the members of the "ideal type" *dowreh* being considered.

TABLE 7.13

Birth Date, Education, and Occupations of
the Members of an "Ideal-Type" Dowreh

Member Number	Birth Date	Education	Principal Occupation	Secondary Occupation
1	1901	Traditional	Senator	Business
2	1920	European commercial	President, Tehran Chamber of Commerce	Business
3	1898	D.Law, Geneva	Minister of Justice	Banking
4	1907	D.Economics, Paris	Minister of Finance	Business
5	1889	D.Law, Paris	Ambassador to France	Landownership
6	1907	Tehran School of Diplomacy	Director, National Iranian Oil Co.	Landownership
7	1894	D.Law, Paris	Ambassador to Lebanon	
8	1910	D.Law, Paris	Ambassador to Moscow	
9	1901	Agricultural College, Germany	Minister of Agriculture	Farming
10	1908	License, Paris	Senator	Business
11	1905	D.Law, Paris	Prime Minister	Landownership

With few exceptions, these *dowreh* members are all in the same generation and have had similar educational experiences. (Although not true of each participant, the *dowreh* has the reputation of being the "French Doctorate" group.) Within the period of three years in the early 1960s, the members of the *dowreh* held the positions listed in table 7.13. It is not surprising, therefore, that all eleven were included with the 307 most politically powerful Iranians.

The occupations of the members provide one clue towards an explanation of the prevalence of these groups. One member of the elite referred to them as " 'joint stock companies' for the exploitation of the political situation and, less frequently, of the economic situation." With the impossibility of overt political activity, groups are formed—ostensibly on nonpolitical grounds—whose purpose is the mutual furtherance of the members' careers. These groups may even bind their members to secrecy and mutual aid by oaths or various rituals.

The "French Doctorate" circle is an apt example of this type. It "placed," or if that term is too purposive, "has" its members in different positions throughout the political structure. With the assistance of these representatives, the power of almost all significant sections of that structure can be utilized for purposes of mutual welfare. If some members of the group are in while others are out of power, no one need suffer unduly. In addition, these *dowreh*s provide Iranian politics with a significant degree of continuity and stability which a superficial examination would not otherwise reveal. When one of the members of the clique is elevated to a position of political importance, there exists a long-established coterie of fellow elites who can be called upon to fill other offices. The premiership is the most vital of these. Without straying beyond the confines of his own *dowreh*, a new prime minister may locate individuals to hold ministerial portfolios, men who have known each other, communicated with each other on a relatively intimate basis, and developed a more or less common outlook together for a number of years. While the premiership is the most vital example, similar opportunities and problems arise when one member of the *dowreh* accedes to any position of administrative responsibility.

A final key role of the *dowreh*s in the political process is the communication function that they provide. Many Iranians are frequently members of more than one *dowreh*. An individual may belong to a political group, such as the one detailed here. In addition he may also be active in any variety of other *dowreh*s organized for social, cultural, recreational, or intellectual purposes. With the overlapping and interlocking quality of membership which does exist, a message inserted into one *dowreh* will quickly fan out through the entire network. Moreover, *dowreh*s, especially those organized for the last three purposes above, frequently cut across social class lines. As a result, the message will fan out not only within a given social class, but also between social classes. No wonder that a message generated at the Imperial Court will reach the most humble *bazaari* within a day or two. No wonder that this network is so frequently the source of information for members of the Iranian political elite. The elite were asked to mention the three sources from which they most frequently got news about Iranian political and economic affairs; the responses are shown in table 7.14. Of the variety of sources of information about Iranian politics—the mass media, government reports, personal observations, etc.—the most frequently cited single source is "other persons." When an elite mentioned this source of news, he was also asked to mention the kind of person or persons who

TABLE 7.14

Sources of News about Iran

	1st Mentioned	2nd Mentioned	3rd Mentioned
Other persons	35.3%	18.6%	15.0%
All other sources	62.3	62.9	52.1
None, don't know	2.4	18.5	32.9
Total	100.0%	100.0%	100.0%
N	(167)	(167)	(167)

usually served as such a source. "Friends" was the most common answer. It is likely that these friends are those with whom the respondents share membership in a *dowreh*.

Membership in a *dowreh*, then, and in other voluntary organizations, as well as multiple job-holding, tend to serve the same functions for members of the elite. They are used to provide fallback positions, to offer the elite a variety of access points through which to approach the formal structures of political power, to multiply the elite's communication patterns, to provide contact with a diversity of individuals within and without the elite, and to establish reciprocal obligations with as many individuals representing as diverse sectors of Iranian life as possible. All such motives, in short, center around the acquisition of a sense of security.[72]

But the very security that members of the elite seek in multiple association memberships and occupational positions contributes to their felt *insecurity*. For with such participation, they are subjected to the pressures generated by social change and the tenuousness of the political process itself. And the more they are subjected to these processes, the greater is their insecurity. Increased participation in the political system may, in fact, contribute to the objective political or social security of the elite by contributing to the stability of their elite positions. But simultaneously, their psychic security is diminished.

In at least one sense, this conclusion seems contradictory to the literature on group participation and insecurity levels. For such participation is assumed to enhance control over one's environment and such control is assumed to contribute to psychological security. This conclusion, a common one in the literature, is predicated on the assumption that the individual who participates in a variety of organizations will be able to influence the policies of those organizations in directions congruent with the individual's self-interest. By this sense of efficacy derived from molding his environment and by the objective benefits that will flow

[72] The use of these techniques for the acquisition of a sense of security approaches a number of points made by Robert K. Merton, *Social Theory and Social Structure* (Glencoe: Free Press, 1957), pp. 195–206.

241

to the individual from controlling his environment, it is generally assumed that the individual will enhance his sense of security.[73]

But in Iran, it is highly doubtful that these results accrue to individuals who participate so thoroughly in their society. For the chief source of insecurity for the Iranian elite remains perpetually beyond their control. We refer, of course, to His Imperial Majesty, the Shahanshah. Members of the elite can use multiple job-holding and overlapping organizational memberships to acquire wealth and enhance their political power by acquiring control over administrative hierarchies, but they can, with these techniques, never assure themselves of sufficient bases of power to influence the shah. And when he reaches the conclusion that a given member of the elite is dysfunctional, in any sense, no amount of wealth or memberships can save the individual from dismissal, disgrace, or demotion. The fall from grace can be cushioned. It cannot be prevented.

Suzanne Keller has made this same point on a general level, but it applies most directly to the Iranian political elite. She argues that:

Although individuals are increasingly achieving elite status, this status, once won, has grown less rather than more secure. Retirement, dismissal, defeat, or rejection inevitably face members of a strategic elite. In a world that demands flexible accommodation to rapidly changing problems of national and international scope, tenure at the top is apt to be brief and uncertain. For the hereditary elites of old, entrances were signalled by birth, exits mainly by death. There was no fixed route to the top because most of the members were already at the top. If the rules of the game were observed, one's status was secure. This pattern of the past survives only in the Social Register of the present day.[74]

To put the matter slightly differently, the active member of the political elite in Iran can enhance his subjective feelings of success. By providing new areas of striving in which to demonstrate competence and mastery, these subjective feelings of self-esteem may very well lead to an enhanced sense of personal security.[75] But by his awareness of his failure to truly control his destiny, this sense of security will be eroded and, indeed, precluded. In the final analysis, awareness of inefficacy at the most basic level will be paramount and destructive.

Evidence of this is available in the positive and significant association between level of reputed power on the one hand and degree of participation in the system and levels of manifest insecurity on the other. The higher the number of paid or unpaid positions held and the greater the

[73] See, for example, Rose, *Power Structure*, p. 230; and Knutson, "Personal Security," pp. 219–36, passim.

[74] *Beyond the Ruling Class* (New York: Random House, 1963), pp. 213–14.

[75] This point is made most clearly by Knutson, "Personal Security," p. 227, in summarizing general areas of agreement in studies of psychological security-insecurity.

number of organizational memberships claimed, the higher the individual's level of power. Simultaneously, however, the higher is the individual's level of manifest insecurity. As the individual enhances his power, he increases his participation in the system which, in turn, contributes to a further enhancement of his political power. But as his power increases, so does his insecurity. The members of the elite run faster and faster to stay ahead politically. But they continually fall behind psychically. Their dilemma is bitter.

The present prime minister, for example, Amir Abbas Hoveyda, is generally regarded to be the most successful holder of that office during the entire reign of the present shah. No other prime minister has enjoyed a longer tenure in the twentieth century, and his modesty and self-effacing nature have contributed to his enjoying widespread good will.[76] Nonetheless, Hoveyda was recently asked how long he thought he would hold his post. "Hoveyda made no bones about the fact that his job was a question of being here today, gone tomorrow. 'How long I stay in office is not in my hands,' the Premier explained, 'but I work in such a way as to make myself believe that I will be in office for another 1,000 years. At the same time, I am prepared to resign at a second's notice.' "[77]

One final result of these multiple memberships and occupational positions might be mentioned. In a study outlining the relationship between insecurity and radicalism, it was found that "radicalism seems related to insecurity only when it is the radicalism of the 'lone wolf.' "[78] That is, insecurity is likely to be associated with radical political orientations for those who are "individuated" or "degrouped" or socially isolated. As members of the Iranian political elite are so thoroughly not socially isolated, the likelihood of the emergence of radical political ideologies from among them is considerably diminished. The absence of such radical ideologies is a striking feature of Iranian public life.

Social status. In addition to level of reputed political power, the level of an individual's social status is also positively associated with manifest insecurity. As the more powerful display higher levels of insecurity, so do members of the social elite. We compared elite scores on the MI factor with whether or not they claimed to have influential relations. The results, which are shown in table 7.15, while not of unusually high statistical significance, indicate that the more elite—as measured in social

[76] Ahmad Matin Daftari served under Reza Shah from October 25, 1935, to June 25, 1940, a total of 56 months. Dr. Manouchehr Eghbal served for 42 months, from April 4, 1957, to September 30, 1960. Hoveyda, serving as minister of finance, took office as prime minister with the assassination of Mansur on January 25, 1965. As of the end of June 1971, therefore, he had already served for 77 months.

[77] "'Here Today, Gone Tomorrow' is PM's Philosophy," *Kayhan International* (Tehran), Jan. 29, 1967.

[78] Gwynn E. Nettler and James R. Huffman, "Political Opinion and Personal Security," *Sociometry*, 20, no. 1 (1957): 57.

TABLE 7.15

Influential Relations Claimed
by Responding Elite

Level of Manifest Insecurity	Yes	No
Low	24.0%	40.0%
Medium	37.6	40.0
High	38.4	20.0
Total	100.0%	100.0%
N	(125)	(40)

Note: x^2 = 5.85; df = 2; p = .054; gamma = -.352.

terms rather than solely on political grounds—do demonstrate higher levels of manifest insecurity. The more intimately the elite are involved in the present system, on a class basis as well as on a political basis, the more insecurity that is manifested. As King Hussein titled a recent autobiography, *Uneasy Lies the Head*; so with members of the elite.[79]

Foreign travel factor. Another social background factor that is a frequent companion of manifest insecurity and more strongly of its principal component—frustration—is the respondent's personal familiarity with the world beyond the borders of Iran. The greater the number of trips that a member of the elite has made outside Iran, the more likely he is to agree strongly with the question, "Do you often feel frustrated because you are unable to do as you wish or unable to accomplish what you wish?" (See table 7.16.) What appears to be at work is the debilitating effect of firsthand personal experience in other political and social sys-

TABLE 7.16

Number of Foreign Trips Made
by the Respondent

Reported Frustration Level	Number of Trips		
	0-5	6-20	21 or More
Very high	10.8%	21.9%	43.1%
High	10.8	14.1	12.1
Not very high	78.4	64.0	44.8
Total	100.0%	100.0%	100.0%
N	(37)	(64)	(58)

Note: x^2 = 14.437; df = 4; p = .006; gamma = -.435.

[79] H.M. King Hussein, *Uneasy Lies the Head* (London: Heinemann, 1962).

tems. Daniel Lerner has discussed the ways in which a society characterized by physical mobility and social mobility gradually evolved into a society with participant life styles, inhabited by persons with mobile personalities. "The mobile person," he suggests, "is distinguished by a high capacity for identification with new aspects of his environment, he comes equipped with new mechanisms needed to incorporate new demands upon himself that arise outside of his habitual experience."[80]

In support of this point, our data suggest that members of the Iranian political elite who enjoy foreign travel—and the statistics reveal that the vast majority frequently make lengthy stays abroad—do make demands from the political environment that are not conventionally made; neither are they conventionally fulfilled. As the elite with immediate experience in other systems are rebuffed in their attempts to translate that experience into the Iranian context, the results are frustration and higher levels of manifest insecurity.

This relationship portends no lessening of frustration in the future. For foreign travel is one of the benefits of elite membership disproportionately enjoyed by the more powerful ($r = .301; p < .001$). Again the more powerful have yet another basis for their discontent.[81] The powerful demonstrate higher levels of manifest insecurity not only because they are more subject to influences from His Imperial Majesty over which they have no control but also because they enjoy firsthand experience—physical mobility—which exposes them to new life styles inappropriate to Iranian conditions as defined by others of the elite.

All the above variables which are significantly associated with manifest insecurity can be thought of as representing the socialization experiences of elite respondents. Analytically, such experiences need to be separated according to the life stages of the individuals on which they impinge.[82] Experiences peculiar to early childhood, adolescence, and

---

[80] Daniel Lerner, *The Passing of Traditional Society: Modernizing the Middle East* (New York: Free Press of Glencoe, 1958), chap. 2. Lerner also calls attention to the literature on human migration to amplify these points, esp. W. I. Thomas and F. Znaniecki, *The Polish Peasant in Europe and America*, 5 vols. (New York: Alfred A. Knopf, 1927), 5: 5.

[81] Cross tabulations of power, travel, and frustration reveal that relations between power and frustration and travel and frustration continue to be valid. It is assumed that high power and travel contribute independently to the level of perceived frustration and neither is an intervening variable.

[82] See, for example, Lucian W. Pye, *Politics, Personality, and Nation Building: Burma's Search for Identity* (New Haven: Yale University Press, 1962), pp. 195–200; Frederick W. Frey, *The Turkish Political Elite* (Cambridge: M.I.T. Press, 1965), pp. 22–25; Erik H. Erikson, *Childhood and Society* (New York: W. W. Norton, 1963), p. 16; and Fred I. Greenstein, *Children and Politics* (New Haven: Yale University Press, 1965), pp. 1–9. These authors all conceptualize the problem of "socialization" in a different fashion, veering now closer, now further from a narrow, Freudian approach to adult personality and attitudes. The failure of many political scientists even to confront these issues is alarming.

adulthood need to be treated as distinct tiers in the processes of socialization. In addition, one must consider those attributes of the individual
that are relevant to such tiers. In this latter category, one could conceive
of wealth, height, religion, etc., which, while not of direct importance as
a socialization experience are nonetheless vital because they directly
affect the experiences that the individual will undergo in these various
tiers or stages.

Sources of information. We have considered above a number of socialization experiences appropriate to relatively early stages of the individual's development. Child rearing data and education fall into that
category. In addition, we have considered later socialization experiences
—occupations, foreign travel, and the like. Finally, we have discussed
certain personal attributes such as social status and reputed power. Let
us turn, now, to another set of adult socialization experiences.

Another factor from the general body of social background data was
labeled mass media exposure. Items and loadings it contained are shown
in table 7.17. What is associated in this factor is consumption of all
aspects of the mass media in Iran including foreign magazines, news-

TABLE 7.17

Mass Media Exposure Factor

1.	Number of newspapers read per day by the respondent	.628
2.	Frequency with which the respondent listens to the radio	.518
3.	Frequency with which the respondent views television	.497
4.	Number of Persian or foreign-language magazines which the respondent reads per month	.427
5.	Membership in a dowreh (circle) of friends or family which meets regularly[a]	.376
6.	Respondent's service in the Imperial Iranian Armed Forces	.319
7.	Sex of the respondent	.313

[a] It is unlikely that the relatively high loading of
the variable pertaining to dowreh membership on
this factor and on the activity factor would be
sufficient to account for the statistically significant relation of both factors to manifest insecurity. The large number of other variables which
are unique to each of the former factors and the
higher loadings of those variables would suggest
the virtual impossibility of explaining these
relations by only one common variable.

papers, and television films.[83] Membership in a *dowreh*, as in the activity factor, loads with mass media exposure as do sex (male) and service in the Imperial Iranian Armed Forces, but these are appreciably less associated with this factor than the mass media variables.

As might be expected, media exposure and manifest insecurity are positively and significantly associated (see table 7.18). This relationship

TABLE 7.18

Manifest Insecurity by Exposure
to the Mass Media

Manifest Insecurity		Exposure to Mass Media		
		Low	Medium	High
Low		49.0%	16.4%	20.4%
Medium		25.5	46.3	40.8
High		25.5	37.3	38.8
	Total	100.0%	100.0%	100.0%
	N	(51)	(67)	(49)

Note: x^2 = 17.455; df = 4; p = .002; gamma = .272.

was predictable on several grounds. Consumption of the mass media is a prime expression of a "participant style."[84] That is, the greater the individual's consumption of the mass media, the more he is immersed in Iranian society. As we have seen with other measures of such immersion in Iranian life, e.g., number of jobs, number of organizational memberships, etc., the greater is the attendant level of insecurity. The more an individual is a part of contemporary Iranian society, the more he is subjected to the strains and stresses that result in the generation of insecurity.

These strains emanate from the individual's heightened realization of his personal inability to manipulate the environment in ways that will

[83] At the time of the interviews, Tehranis enjoyed two television stations, one run by the Armed Forces Radio and Television Network of the United States. Program content, which was carefully supervised by its own personnel to exclude material that might prove offensive to its Iranian audience or the government of Iran, consisted primarily of American cowboy and detective movies. The second station—National Television of Iran—was owned by a prominent Baha'i, who reportedly had received permission from the shah to establish an indigenously owned TV station when he set up a closed-circuit television transmission of the shah's marriage to the then Farah Diba for the benefit of the shah's elderly mother, too indisposed to attend the wedding ceremonies in person. The content of this channel is remarkably similar to that of AFRTS with the exception of a few programs devoted to Iranian culture and education. Since that time, the government itself has opened a TV channel which broadcasts programs of a more "Iranian" nature. But the vast proportion of television content at the time of the interviews was entirely of foreign, and primarily American, origin.

[84] Lerner, *Traditional Society*, pp. 50–51.

foster autonomy and safety. They also are a product of the individual's being subjected to conflicting value systems. For as with foreign travel, so with exposure to the mass media. Thus, the individual, especially in Iran, is bombarded with stimuli of foreign lifeways and styles. He is made frustratingly aware of the shortcomings of his own society, its backwardness, and the generally low esteem in which it is held in the world at large.[85] No less an authority than His Imperial Majesty comments on the role of the media in this fashion:

We have found it best to control such [subversive] organizations . . . commonly masquerading as devoted indigenous nationalists . . . while at the same time allowing maximum freedom for individual expression. . . . To allow people to speak their minds not only provides a valuable cathartic; it also may serve to uncover abuses. . . . In Iranian bookshops and in the daily Press you can find material that is sharply critical of some of the Government's policies.[86]

But in order to be subversive of the established order, the mass media need not be directly critical; the precedent of foreign example is sufficient. The individuals who consume the mass media are subjected to these stimuli but the effect, as shown by their responses to other items, is not "cathartic" in the least. On the contrary, frustrations are heightened, tensions are made apparent, and insecurity is the result. While the messages in the media may allow political pressures to dissipate, at least

[85] A recent poll of a national sample of Americans asked how much the respondents liked some twenty-eight nations. Only six countries received fewer favorable responses than Iran. The percentages of Americans holding a positive view of the least-liked countries are indicated in table 7.a.

TABLE 7.a

American Attitudes toward
Foreign Countries

Country	Percentage of Favorable Responses
Republic of South Vietnam	62
Iran	54
France	49
Egypt	39
USSR	19
People's Democracy of North Vietnam	7
Cuba	6
Communist China	5

Source: "Gallup Poll Finds U.S. Amity for French Eroded," New York Times, Feb. 7, 1968, p. 5.

[86] Mohammad Reza Shah Pahlavi, Mission for My Country (New York: McGraw-Hill, 1961), p. 128.

partially, they leave the individuals who absorb those messages all the more insecure.

Education. A final word might be offered on the relationship of education to insecurity. Insofar as education, especially technical education, familiarizes its recipient with a culture contradictory to that of traditional Iran, it should be expected to be associated with insecurity. In fact this does not prove to be the case; the data reveal an inverse relation between education and insecurity. We suggest that this apparent contradiction can be resolved by considering education to provide its holder with a power base which, being in high demand by the shah, serves to lessen insecurity. That Mansur was able to invest the higher levels of the bureaucracy with technically educated colleagues and that they have remained in office after their immediate benefactor's death have tended to augment this. In short, the heightened insecurity to be expected from competing ideologies and belief systems is absent because the very education that serves as the source of manifest insecurity also provides the individual with greater control over a central base of power, control that serves to minimize insecurity. Nonetheless, one would be optimistic to expect this satisfactory resolution to continue into the future. Not only will these technically educated elite be subjected to the challenge of an ever-increasing number of even more highly educated and younger men, but they will enjoy greater exposure to other cultures. As foreign travel is positively correlated with power ($r = .301$; $p < .002$), we can expect the technocrats to travel more frequently as they become more powerful. Hence, as Iran's elite are challenged by more firsthand acquaintance with competing ideologies on the one hand and by younger and better trained technocrats on the other, their manifest insecurity with its attendant consequences can be expected to become more pronounced.

In sum, then, we find members of the Iranian political elite beset with manifest insecurity characterized as insecurity of the secondary, adult level. Data exist relating primary insecurity, exemplified by answers to Maslow's Security-Insecurity Inventory, to this manifest insecurity although doubts engendered by the validity and reliability of the former inventory leave the issue in the form of a hypothesis for future testing.

But manifest insecurity is prominently associated with a number of variables that can be reduced to two distinct concepts. First, heightened insecurity is associated with more intensive participation in Iranian society, defined in its fullest sense. Power, status, consumption of the mass media, immersion in the bureaucracy and voluntary associations, and multiple job-holding all symbolize this immersion and all contribute to, and in turn are fed by, higher levels of a sense of insecurity.

Second, exposure to value systems that differ from conventional Iranian culture is an accompaniment to manifest insecurity independent of participation in the society. Harold D. Lasswell has discussed the generation of insecurity through the world-wide dissemination of new symbols. "Propaganda, as the name for the self-conscious spread of symbols to mobilize collective action," he has argued, "tends to maximize insecurities, and hence, crises."[87] Foreign travel, the most prevalent source of immediate experience with foreign symbols and cultures, is widely enjoyed by the political elite and is intimately related to levels of manifest insecurity. Attention to radio, television, newspapers, and magazines in Iran is the most prevalent source of mediate experience with other value systems. And mass media consumption is also intimately related to manifest insecurity.

[87] *World Politics and Personal Insecurity* (New York: Free Press, 1965), p. 87. Sebastian de Grazia makes the identical point about the generation of "simple anomie" with the added caveat that simple anomie is not the "evil outcome of too many ideologies. . . . Simple anomie is, instead, the result of a clash between belief systems or, more precisely, a conflict between the *directives* of belief systems" (*Political Community*, p. 72).

:8:

THE ORIENTATIONS OF THE POLITICAL ELITE, II

CYNICISM

The proper province of doubt
extends to infinity.
Montesquieu, *The Persian Letters*

*T*he attitudinal characteristic of cynicism that has been judged so harmful to the processes of social change is not unknown to students of developing societies.[1] In particular, it has frequently been ascribed to the peoples of the Middle East. Albert Hourani, for example, notes: "This crisis of the Arab mind today is clear. All around is a sea of nihilism: the cynicism of men cut off from their own past, deprived too long of responsibility for their own fate, tied too long to a decaying Empire, exposed too soon to the corruption of wealth and power."[2]

The issues implied by Hourani are those that we wish to clarify and confront here. The *Oxford English Dictionary* defines a cynic as one "disposed to deny human sincerity and goodness." *Webster's* suggests that a cynic is "one who believes that human conduct is motivated wholly by self-interest." But in terms of the philosophy of the Greek cynics, the concept can be considered far more comprehensive. Those

---

[1] Lucian W. Pye, for example, has warned that: "Without a sense of basic trust and faith, political promises and even the most glowing plans for future development are likely to arouse suspicions on the part of the public. When basic trust is replaced by cynicism, a people will suspect that behind the screen of political promises their leaders are really 'out to get everything for themselves' " (*Politics, Personality, and Nation Building: Burma's Search for Identity* [New Haven: Yale University Press, 1962], p. 55).

[2] "Arabic Culture," in *Perspective of the Arab World* (New York: Intercultural Publications, 1956), p. 11, as quoted in "The Arab Middle East: Some Background Interpretations," by George H. Gardner, *Journal of Social Issues*, 15, no. 3 (1959): 20–27.

cynics were "irreverent toward culture, disloyal to the State, resentful to authority, anti-intellectual, and scornful of conventional morality."[3]

In an impressionistic sense, Iranian politics and society appear to be leavened by an unmitigated cynicism of this last, more broadly defined type. The verses of Khayyam, who wrote so effectively of Iranian culture, for example, might have been written instead by Diogenes:

> O Time, who dost thyself confess
> The wrongs by mortal men endured,
> The convent where thou art immured
> Is dedicate to ruthlessness.
> Thy blessings on the base alone
> Are showered; men of nobler part
> Thou punishest; which proves thou art
> A donkey, or a doting crone.[4]

Elite respondents were no less biting in their own perceptions of Iranian society. One told the story of how a foreigner in Tehran had complained about something. An Iranian friend responded: "You're right, you've hit on one of the only two things wrong with Iranian society. The first is what's been bothering you; the second is everything else in the country." A second put his cynicism differently: "To become outstanding in any field of endeavor in Iran," he warned, "requires an appetite for corruption and a taste for personal decay."

The cynicism of the elite was reflected in the cynicism factor. The items related to the cynicism factor and the loadings assigned them, in the varimax rotation, are shown in table 8.1. These items represent a number of indexes that had been formed on a priori grounds before running the factor analysis. The indexes and items that make them up are:

INDEXES	VARIABLE NUMBERS
Personal Cynicism	12, 21, 25
Political and Social Cynicism	5, 7, 8, 10
Personal Efficacy	2, 4, 6, 15, 19, 22
Mobility	14, 17
Authoritarianism	11, 13, 24
General System Orientation	1, 3, 9, 16, 18, 20, 23

The relation of these indexes to the factor illuminates the dynamics of cynicism in Iran. The loadings indicate that personal, social, and political

---

[3] David Clark Hodges, "Cynicism in the Labor Movement," *American Journal of Economics and Sociology*, 21 (1962): 33. Hodges, in line with the subject matter of his study, notes that historians call cynicism "a philosophy of the proletariat." In fact, Donald R. Dudley, author of *A History of Cynicism* (London: Methuen & Co., 1937), calls this notion misleading, for unlike modern proletariats, the cynics had no interest in establishing any new social order (p. xi).

[4] From the "Rubaiyat" of Omar Khayyam, trans. Edward Fitzgerald.

TABLE 8.1

Cynicism Factor

1. On the whole, do you think that the Iranian political system is working very well, not too well, or badly? .723

2. Today, political power in Iran is really controlled by certain foreign governments. .711

3. In terms of what you see around you, would you say there is a great deal of injustice or not so much injustice? .658

4. Politics in Iran is the business of such a small group of people that I usually can't find out what is really going on until the important decisions have already been made. .619

5. In Iran, a person can have himself chosen for almost any government office if he is enough of a bootlicker and flatterer. .605

6. I don't think that really powerful public officials and politicians care much what people like me think. .603

7. The best man is almost always picked for promotion to important positions in Iran's government. .600

8. Lawbreakers are almost always caught and punished in Iran. .589

9. Degree of trust accorded to the mass media in Iran by the respondent. .548

10. In Iran, dishonesty seems to be more prevalent in the government service than in most other careers. .543

11. What we need more than anything else is a strong leader to tell us what to do. .495

12. Most people will use somewhat unfair means to gain a profit or advantage rather than risk losing it. .487

13. People with wild and strange opinions in Iran should not be allowed a public platform from which to preach. .478

14. Mobility Scale (The total number of "yes" answers to: In Iran do you think that any person with the capability and talent, regardless of wealth or family status, is able to become: owner of a small enterprise; owner of a large enterprise; an employee of the government in a high post; a high officer in the army; a prominent politician; an office worker?) .468

15. It's no use getting upset and concerned about broad political issues and public affairs; people like me really can't do anything about them anyway. .458

16. Number of negative or unfavorable changes in the Iranian way of life mentioned by the respondent. .447

17. How easy do you think it is for a high government official to lose his position, status, and wealth? .432

18. Number of positive or favorable changes in the Iranian way of life mentioned by the respondent. .429

19. What do you consider the likelihood of Iran's overcoming in the next ten years the first problem which you have enumerated? .417

20. To what extent do you feel surrounded and impeded by red tape, petty rules and regulations, and other annoyances? .396

21. The average Iranian is overwhelmingly motivated by self-interest, that is, the pursuit of his own, personal interests. .389

22. How much is there that you as an individual can do to solve the first of the personal problems which you mentioned that you are facing? .353

23. Do you feel that in Iran there exists much, enough, little, or no national unity? .326

24. How would decisions usually be made in your own family at the present time? .325

25. Most people in Iran make friends because friends are likely to be helpful and useful to them. .311

---

cynicism are all positively related—higher levels of one is associated with higher levels of the other. Or as reported in a study done in two American cities, "those who are contemptuous of people in general, the personally cynical, tend to be politically cynical as well."[5] The converse is also true. Those who view neither their society nor their fellow countrymen with derision have more sanguinary and positive attitudes toward the political system. What is here implied is that cynicism is a general character orientation that spills over into all aspects of elite perceptions.

Other studies have indicated that personal and political cynicism may, in fact, be related in a different fashion. One hypothesis suggests that an individual might be positively related to those persons or organizations with which he is in most frequent contact. Feelings of hostility or negativism that might prove disruptive of those proximate relations could be displaced on to more distant, and safer, objects. It is frequently alleged that such displacement operates most easily onto symbols that are outside the national political system. It is also possible that these feelings may be displaced to symbols of national politics. The result could be the preservation of immediate interpersonal harmony at the cost of disrupting internal politics or foreign relations. Our data indicate that this

[5] Robert E. Agger, Marshall N. Goldstein, and Stanley A. Pearl, "Political Cynicism: Measurement and Meaning," *Journal of Politics*, 23, no. 476 (1961): 490. Also see Morris Rosenberg, "Misanthropy and Political Ideology," *American Sociological Review*, 21 (Dec. 1956): 690–95.

mechanism is not common among the political elite. Rather, cynicism is equally prevalent in the most immediate interpersonal relations of the respondents as well as in their attitudes towards national politics and international relations.

A second commonly advanced notion about cynicism is that a cynical orientation, or at least a healthy skepticism towards the political system, may be a quite rational and ultimately beneficial response to the political process.[6] It is doubtful that objective, foreign observers with no personal stake in Iranian politics would need delve too deeply before uncovering incidents inducing cynicism. But this rather appropriate cynicism also appears absent from the Iranian system. A constructive and sophisticated skepticism about the possibilities for reform and the social benefits to be derived from political change is absent. Rather, a more diffuse and pessimistic negativism relating to fellow Iranians, to all Iranian society, and to Iranian politics undercuts the social value of all human endeavor. Thus, for example, the elite were asked to specify the most important changes that have occurred in Iranian society since the end of World War II (factor items 16 and 18 in table 8.1). The more cynical invariably recounted an overwhelmingly greater number of negative changes, while the less cynical related a more balanced appraisal.[7]

In addition to the indexes pertaining directly to cynicism, other questions in this factor relate to perceptions of power. Four questions (2, 4, 6, and 15) were designed to tap the respondents' sense of personal, political efficacy. As originally formulated, the questions were used in the United States to assess the subjective political effectiveness of the American citizen.[8] They were adapted to reflect the workings of the Iranian political system, and the role of the elite in it. A fifth question (22)

---

[6] Thus Pye suggests that an "uncritical and childlike trust in the rulers and in all forms of higher authority" is an "obstacle to development" (Lucian W. Pye, "Political Culture and Political Development" in *Political Culture and Political Development*, ed. Lucian W. Pye and Sidney Verba [Princeton: Princeton University Press, 1965], p. 22).

[7] The differences in the responses by the elite may be exemplified with the following quotations on the changes in Iran since World War II. A less cynical response: "Iran has begun to travel the path of the United States: to use the knowledge of the twentieth century to the exclusion of the archaic ideas which have kept us poor, backward, and miserable . . ." A more cynical response: "The Americanization of Iranians: using Kleenex, drinking Coca-Cola, having parties, hanging multicolored drapes in the living room, wearing cowboy pants, dancing the hullygully on the Varamin Plain . . ."

[8] The original items were: (1) Voting is the only way that people like me can have a say about how the government runs things; (2) Sometimes politics and government seem so complicated that a person like me can't really understand what is going on; (3) People like me don't have any say about what the government does; and (4) I don't think public officials care much about what people like me think. See Angus Campbell, Gerald Gurin, and Warren Miller, *The Voter Decides* (Evanston, Ill.: Row, Peterson and Co., 1954).

applied to the sense of efficacy of individual members of the elite in confronting strictly personal problems. And a final item (19) asked for their estimates of the likelihood that Iran could overcome its national problems, i.e., their perceptions of the efficacy of the entire political system.

As with the diffuse sense of cynicism, so with the sense of efficacy. Individuals who report a sense of potency in political matters also report a sense of mastery when confronting their own personal problems and when evaluating the possibilities of their nation's successfully mastering its problems.[9] Once again this spill-over effect seems to be operating. One might expect the elite to displace their feelings of personal inadequacy or incapacity onto the system at large or to identify with the generally recognized impotency of the system while claiming high efficacy for themselves. Conversely, those of the elite who feel helpless before the social change that they are powerless to affect and a political system in which one actor is dominant, might be expected to denigrate their own capacities while attributing nearly magical strengths to the political system with which they are so intimately connected.

But such is not the case. Rather, the similar patterns that the elite manifest in all six questions lends credence to our assumption that the sense of efficacy is "object free," that it approximates a general character orientation. Whether the member of the elite considers his power vis-à-vis his government, the elite, the shah, foreign governments, his personal problems, or the power of the system, he responds in a similar fashion. It appears that in terms of efficacy, as with cynicism, a member of the elite either does have a basic sense of his own mastery and competence (or cynicism) or he does not. If the former is true he is, at least figuratively, ready to take on the world. If the latter holds, he feels weak and ineffective in nearly all areas of life.

But how does this rather unfocused perspective on power relate to the overriding general orientation of cynicism? As the factor loadings demonstrate, they are inversely related. Higher levels of efficacy are associated with lower levels of cynicism, while low efficacy and high cynicism are positively related. Those of the elite who possess this sense of personal potency are less sarcastic and cynical of the political system and other individuals.

This inverse relationship between cynicism and felt efficacy has been well established in studies by Agger et al., Edgar Litt, and others.[10] Mel-

---

[9] For a discussion of the personal efficacy of nonelite and elite, which stresses social factors, see Gabriel A. Almond and Sidney Verba, *The Civic Culture* (Princeton: Princeton University Press, 1963), pp. 180–257. For a discussion which puts more emphasis on the psychoanalytic, see Robert E. Lane, *Political Life: Why People Get Involved in Politics* (Glencoe: Free Press, 1959), pp. 149–55.

[10] Agger et al., "Political Cynicism"; and Edgar Litt, "Political Cynicism and Political Futility," *Journal of Politics*, 25 (May 1963): 312–23.

vin Seeman, for example, in a study of alienation in the work process, suggests that work with little decision-making potentiality leaves the worker with a sense of the world as unmanageable and himself as relatively powerless on "a wide range of social and personal outcomes." Such powerlessness, Seeman suggests, is a key component of alienation in occupations, which leads to the worker's viewing the social order as "less supportive and trustworthy."[11]

Seeman, then, and most of these authors, have considered political cynicism the dependent variable in this relationship, i.e., the failure to develop a sense of efficacy resulting in derision of the political system or of politicians. But there appears no valid conceptual reason why both these concepts should be immediate or superficial accommodations to political reality any more than that they both represent facets of the same underlying characterological dimension. In fact, this is what our factor analysis suggests. These two variables are so intimately related, according to the responses of the political elite, that they fall out on one factor: they cannot be considered statistically independent.

Another set of variables that appears in the cynicism factor pertains to aspects of mobility. Item 14 is an index of responses to six questions in which the elite assay the possibilities for the upward occupational mobility of nonelite. Question 17 represents the converse situation. Here the elite are asked to consider the possibility that high government officials can be downwardly mobile. (For this question, downward mobility was defined as the loss, not only of political power, but of wealth and social status—a rare circumstance in the context of Iranian politics.) The two aspects of mobility are significantly related. The elite who were most optimistic over the life chances of the nonelite were those who felt most strongly that a high government official would not surrender his place or possessions. And similarly, with those who felt it most unlikely that the less wealthy or prestigious would advance in the society. The latter of the elite suggested that downward mobility was not especially unusual for high officials.

In other words, the elite tended to divide into two groups. One group saw a benevolent social system in which sufficient resources could be marshaled to satisfy the desires of both the present and the would-be elite. A second group perceived social mobility and thus, we assume, politics, as a zero-sum game, where the limited resources could satisfy the elite or mass, but not both. While upward mobility was unlikely for the nonelite, those who did rise were counterelite or at least could have their claims to elite status satisfied by denying the rewards of that status to those of the existing elite.

[11] "On the Personal Consequences of Alienation in Work," *American Sociological Review*, 32, no. 2 (April 1967): 274.

But how are these two views of Iranian reality related to the variables of cynicism and efficacy? Respondents who claim a sense of efficacy and lower levels of cynicism have the most benign view of social mobility. Those who are more trusting of persons and politics and who feel more politically potent are optimistic about possibilities for upward mobility for the nonelite and for the continued eliteness of the present elite. On the other hand, the cynical and impotent of the elite see upward mobility as less likely and the fall of high officials as more likely. Where cynicism and powerlessness are rife, pessimism is not absent.

Another set of variables that fell out in this first factor relates to authoritarianism (11, 13, and 24). Those of the elite who are more cynical[12] are the least well disposed to authoritarian leadership. They disagree most strongly with the notion that "a strong leader" who would tell "Iranians what to do" is "what we need more than anything else." This is a remarkable position for members of the political elite. For, after all, Iran already does have such a leader. Disagreement with the statement then implies dissatisfaction with the nature and course of Iranian politics and the very personification of the system itself—His Imperial Majesty. In short, while the question in the abstract has been frequently used to tap authoritarian attitudes, it means that and more in Iran. A predilection for authoritarian leadership constitutes a vote for the political system as it is currently established.

A second item subsumed by this index relates to the willingness of the Iranian political elite to tolerate divergent political opinions. It was originally hypothesized that the less cynical-more efficacious in the elite would be willing to countenance such polemics. Being satisfied with Iranian politics and the righteousness of the system and trusting of others' motives, these individuals might have felt less challenged by contrary opinions. In fact, the opposite is the case. As the less cynical of the elite support decision making by a strong leader, so would they restrict public debate to ideas that are politically and morally acceptable to them. Again, this is a two-pronged question for it refers both to a general character orientation as well as a more narrowly and specifically political concern. Time and again, the shah has made it clear that he will tolerate "opposition" parties and leaders insofar as they clearly operate within the policy directive of his Six- or Eight-Point Reform laws. Thus, nearly the only legitimate issue for intraelite or elite versus nonelite political infighting would be a claim by the "outs" that the "ins" are not sufficiently intent or efficient in implementing the shah's programs.

A willingness to tolerate the expression of opinions that diverge from this code of public conduct is, in effect, a rebuff to the current political

---

[12] Note that henceforth when referring to cynicism we have in mind the entire cynicism factor and also imply low efficacy, pessimism in regard to mobility, etc.

order. The cynical and inefficacious elite are the ones ready to offer such a rebuff. The noncynical are ready to maintain the existing guidelines, exclude threatening opinions, and support the manner in which politics is presently contested.

It was feared that the responses to these items intended to tap general authoritarianism might produce spurious results because of their inevitable connection with contemporary Iranian politics. An additional item was added, therefore, which bears no relevance to those politics but which seeks information on the nature of decision making within the respondents' families. It was hypothesized that the less authoritarian respondents would report more democratic family decision making. Indeed, this was the case. Those who rejected the value of a strong leader and favored the expression of more divergent opinions also claimed that their wives and children more often participated in the running of their families. They personally made fewer of the decisions unadvised and tended to share that authority more readily.

In a society other than Iran, one might be able to argue that, in fact, such respondents are living in households dominated by their women and children. No wonder that cynicism and a sense of powerlessness are not far behind. While our data do not refute this hypothesis, it appears highly untenable impressionistically, in the contexts of both Iranian culture and our data. The latter indicated that only five of the elite (3 per cent) reported that their spouses made family decisions unencumbered by their husbands, and one of the elite claimed that his children made the decisions alone.

The authoritarian item devoid of specifically political content, then, was answered in the same fashion by the same respondents as the more manifestly political items. We feel more confident in suggesting that among the Iranian political elite, cynicism, powerlessness, and non-authoritarianism are all part of one conceptual package.

Finally, a number of individual items measuring elite orientations to the political system are included in the cynicism factor. Two of these—evaluations of the changes in Iranian society since World War II—have been mentioned. But there were a number of other items, and the elite pattern of responses to them is consistent. The higher the level of cynicism and its attitudinal accouterments, the deeper the antagonisms to the system. Not only are negative changes reported more frequently but these elites perceive the political system as bogged down in administrative inefficiencies and their country as totally lacking national unity while they view themselves as trapped in a mire of red tape.

The elite with this set of orientations also tend to perceive their environments as beset by injustice (item 3). In fact, the over-all perception of injustice in Iran was surprisingly high. Responses to the question, "In terms of what you see around you, would you say there is a great deal of injustice or not so much injustice?" are shown in table 8.2. The responses

TABLE 8.2

Perceived Injustice in Iran

A very great deal of injustice	46.7%
A great deal of injustice	25.2
Not very much injustice	18.6
Very little injustice	1.2
Don't know, or refuse to answer	8.3
Total	100.0%
N	(167)

of the Iranian elite may be compared to the attitudes of French and Italian industrial workers as reported by Hadley Cantril (see table 8.3). We note, not surprisingly, one major difference in these statistics—the Iranian elite are more likely to hold an opinion or, at least, to reveal that opinion. The fewer "don't knows" among the Iranian respondents are accounted for by a slight increase in the number reporting "not much injustice" but also by a large increase in the reports of the presence of

TABLE 8.3

Prevalence of Injustice in France and Italy as Reported by Industrial Workers, by Percentage

	France	Italy
Much injustice	63	66
Not so much injustice	17	17
No opinion	20	17
Total	100	100

Source: Hadley Cantril, The Politics of Despair (New York: Collier Press, 1962), p. 50.

injustice. Indeed, the over-all level of perceived injustice is higher among the Iranian elite than among the French and Italian industrial proletariat.[13]

[13] The high level of reported injustice among both cynical and noncynical groups of the Iranian elite lends credence to the notion that perhaps the expectations of an industrial proletariat can be more easily satisfied by improvements in their material conditions than can the expectations or aspirations of an elite group which may be based, to a greater extent, on nonmaterial values. See, for example, Robert Greenway, "Eupsychia—The Good Society," *Journal of Humanistic Psychology*, 1, no. 1 (1962): 1–11. It is also important to note that the Iranian elite chose from two levels of negative answers whereas the industrial workers had only

While the level of perceived injustice is high among the Iranian elite in general, it is at a peak among the more cynical. Thus we removed the injustice item from the factor and ran it against an index of other items in the cynicism factor. The results are shown in table 8.4. The percep-

TABLE 8.4
Perceived Injustice by Cynicism

Cynicism		Perceived Injustice		
		High	Medium	Low
High		43.6%	9.5%	0.0%
Medium		52.6	57.2	24.2
Low		3.8	33.3	75.8
	Total	100.0%	100.0%	100.0%
	N	(78)	(42)	(33)

Note: x^2 = 72.597; df = 4; p = 0.000; gamma = .851.

tion of injustice goes hand in hand with a sense of powerlessness, pessimism over mobility, and general negativism.

Another single item in the factor reveals a similar relationship. The elite were asked to assess the extent to which they believed in the content of Iran's mass media (9). Similar to many of the other items in the questionnaire, this is a multifaceted tool. On the simplest level we can learn elite attitudes to their own mass media. But on another level, attitudes towards the trustworthiness of the mass media, as with the willingness to tolerate the public expression of opinions divergent from current maxims, reflect attitudes towards the political system. For the media are rigidly supervised by the government to exclude any array of information deemed harmful. The mass media, then, tend to reflect the political orientations of the system, and a failure of confidence in the media is a criticism not so much of the fourth estate as of the system as a whole. And on yet another level, the question of confidence in the newspapers, radio, and television of Iran reflects an underlying propensity to trust the environment—to accept, on a manifest level, the content and direction of one's milieu. To what extent do the elite display this willingness? As might be expected, to no great extent (see table 8.5). Whereas only slightly less than one-third of the elite were favorably inclined towards the mass media, nearly one-half of the respondents report that the media are usually not or almost never trustworthy or correct. Only 6 per cent of those scoring high on cynicism reported the converse—that the media were usually or almost always trustworthy. On the other hand, 54 per

one seriously negative choice which perhaps reduced the propensity of those workers to choose the negative answer.

TABLE 8.5

Degree of Trust Accorded the Mass Media
by the Political Elite

The mass media in Iran are:	
almost always trustworthy and correct	8.4%
usually trustworthy and correct	22.8
about equal	9.0
not very trustworthy and correct	26.3
almost never trustworthy and correct	17.4
(not asked or refused to answer)	16.1
Total	100.0%
N	(167)

cent of those who scored low on the cynicism factor expressed trust in the mass media while only 6 per cent of the noncynical felt that the media were usually not or almost never trustworthy or correct $(p = 0.000)$.

This general disbelief in the mass media on the part of the more cynical of the elite serves to fuel Tehran's amazingly well-developed rumor network. That channel is widely assumed to convey more reliable and valid information than do the formal channels of communication. But rumor serves a variety of functions other than the transmission of news and information. One of these is the politically safe expression of hostility or dissatisfaction towards the government. By tolerating such expression, the regime provides a relatively harmless outlet for sentiments that would prove more disruptive were they to be disseminated in the mass media. These informal networks also provide an opportunity for the displacement into gossip of what otherwise might assume the form of derisive and substantive political issues.[14]

A final overview of the orientation of the elite towards their political system is provided by their responses to the item that loaded most highly on this factor (1). The elite were asked to present their over-all appraisal of how well the Iranian political system is working. Their responses are shown in table 8.6. More of the elite were positively oriented towards the workings of the political system than were disposed to be critical. But of greater interest is the relationship between this item, taken alone, and other variables in the cynicism factor. As with the variables above, there is a statistically significant relationship that could be expected to occur virtually never by chance. The greater the score on

[14] See, for example, Rebecca Birch Stirling, "Some Psychological Mechanisms Operative in Gossip," *Social Forces*, 34, no. 2 (Dec. 1955), esp. pp. 264–65. See also Max Gluckman, "Gossip and Scandal," *Current Anthropology*, 4, no. 3 (June 1963): 307–16; and Gordon W. Allport and Leo Postman, "The Analysis of Rumor" in *Personality and Social Encounter*, by Gordon W. Allport (Boston: Beacon Press, 1964), pp. 311–26.

TABLE 8.6
Evaluation of the Performance
of the Political System

Performance Level	Percentage
Very well	15.6
Fairly well	31.7
Not too well	26.3
Badly	15.0
Don't know, refused to answer, or not asked	11.4
Total	100.0
N	(167)

the cynicism factor, the less well that respondent felt the political system to be operating. Conversely, the noncynical of the elite, along with their perceptions of less red tape and injustice, fewer negative changes since World War II, and a more reliable mass media, also see their political system as functioning reasonably well.

An interest in this cluster of attitudinal items that "go together" in the minds of the Iranian political elite should not be restricted to an identification of those items alone. For the identification and interrelationship of items that commonly load highly on a given factor are only the initial phases of our task. We want to demonstrate, in the context of the Iranian political system, that these items intervene between the social background variables that describe the existential experiences encountered by these elite and their policy orientations that give shape and life to the political process of their nation. Let us turn here to the former concern—the social background experiences that contribute to the development of that cynicism—and then examine in the next chapter the policy considerations associated with this orientation.

Two social background factors relate significantly to the cynicism factor: the factors that we have labeled status and foreign exposure. The status factor loaded most highly on two variables generally recognized as an essential component of social status in Iran, landownership (see table 8.7).

What the factor reveals is the tendency for intergenerational landownership in the families of the elite to associate with having influential relatives and frequent conversations with a variety of groups in the society. This latter variable would be expected to occur among those with higher status in the elite. If they restricted their communication to family members alone, they would still manifest high discussion scores as they would be conversing with family members filling important posts. High status in Iran, as in so many other societies, is predicated on land-

TABLE 8.7

Status Factor

1. Do you or your spouse own land? If so, more than one village? More than five?	.691
2. Do or did your mother or father own land? If so, did your mother or father own more than one village? More than five villages?	.665
3. Number of groups or classes mentioned with which the respondent has held discussions or conversations a few times per month or more frequently	.381
4. Conversation score (The frequency of the respondent's conversations with the enumerated classes or groups in Iranian society)	.381
5. Are there influential persons within your or your spouse's family who now hold or have held important positions in the service of the government of Iran or in private enterprise?	.301

ownership, influential relations, and recurrent communications with many social groups.

But how is this factor related to cynicism? The greater the status, the less is the cynicism ($r = .176$, $p = .05$). The higher status respondents bring the least cynicism to bear on their perspectives of other men and their motives.

A number of items were included in the questionnaire whose purpose was to measure the respondents' exposure to and familiarity with non-Iranian culture and stimuli. The results of the questionnaire are shown in table 8.8. This foreign exposure factor groups together all the questions in the interview schedule pertaining to foreign travel. Lengthy residence abroad, many foreign trips, and recent foreign travel are all statistically related. A number of occupational positions also load highly, positions that are associated with foreign travel. Cabinet ministers, military officers, and senators all enjoy foreign travel to a far greater degree than their fellows. Such travel is frequently in the line of duty. Occupants of these posts are sent abroad to conferences or negotiations, for specialized technical training, or to observe the operations of foreign industries, administrative bureaucracies, or parliaments with a view to transferring all or part of those institutions to Iran.

Finally, foreign travel is positively associated with higher levels of reputed power. To some extent, foreigners and foreign experience still convey a mystique among Iranians, who automatically assume that "foreign" and "superior" are synonymous. The elite who are able to demonstrate firsthand familiarity with foreign languages, foreigners, and foreign life styles are not only more "modern" but reputedly more able to cope

264

TABLE 8.8
Foreign Exposure Factor

1.	Length of time which the respondent has spent in foreign countries	.761
2.	Number of languages other than Persian for which the respondent claims knowledge	.587
3.	Number of trips of any duration made outside Iran by the respondent	.583
4.	Respondent's reputed power score	.402
5.	Number of times respondent has served as a cabinet-level minister	.392
6.	Number of living children	.368
7.	Number of magazines, in any language, read by the respondent	.332
8.	Have you ever served in the Imperial Iranian Armed Forces?	.321
9.	Number of Senate sessions in which the respondent was a member	.300
10.	Recency of respondent's last trip outside Iran	.287

with Iran's own development, administrative, and political problems. (The more cynical would argue that this positive association between power and foreign exposure is a reflection of the role that foreigners play in the domestic political process. That is, Iranians with more foreign connections gain power because of the intervention of those foreigners into domestic Iranian politics. While we have no direct evidence that would either support or refute this contention, it appears to us an overly simplistic interpretation of the sophisticated process that is Iranian politics.)

But foreign travel and power are also clearly related in a converse fashion. Those members of the political elite who are already powerful benefit from the political system by being rewarded with opportunities for more officially sponsored foreign travel. This explanation appears far more plausible, for abundant supportive evidence already exists. The connection between certain official positions and travel has already been mentioned, and those positions in Iran, as was suggested above, are the preserve of the more powerful.

Unfortunately, the foreign travel that is so widely enjoyed by the elite appears inimical for the course of political development in Iran. For such travel is one of the principal contributory factors towards the development and maintenance of cynicism (see table 8.9). As the elite are exposed to more stimuli from foreign cultures and countries, their mani-

TABLE 8.9

Cynicism by Scores on the Foreign
Exposure Factor

Cynicism	Foreign Exposure	
	Low	High
Low	57.2%	42.2%
High	42.8	57.8
Total	100.0%	100.0%
N	(77)	(90)

Note: Yates x^2 = 3.697; continuity
corrected; p = .05; gamma = .292.

fest insecurity is enhanced. So is their cynicism. This is demonstrated by a multiple regression analysis where scores on the cynicism factor were considered an independent variable and were run against the social background factors. Status and foreign exposure were the only significantly correlated factors (multiple r = .272; p = .01; f = .257; p = .05).[15]

A final relationship between social background factors and cynicism needs to be mentioned. The regression analysis inversely relates scores on the activity factor and cynicism. That is, the higher the activity level, the less the cynicism, a relationship that violates our hypothesis that greater immersion in the system is more productive of manifest insecurity, cynicism, and mistrust. However, neither the partial correlation produced in the regression equation (r = .123), nor the chi squares or gammas generated in cross tabulations reach levels of statistical significance.

There is an impelling explanation for this weak but inverse relation, nevertheless. Those of the Iranian political elite characterized by the social background variables most frequently associated with cynicism, i.e., relatively low status, low activity level, and high direct exposure to foreign influences, tend to be the younger, better educated, up-and-coming members of the elite.[16] And the younger the respondent, the lower

[15] The actual multiple regression is as follows:

Dependent Variable	Multiple r	F	df
Cynicism	.272	2.57	161

Independent Variable	Partial r	F	Simple r
Status	.179	5.33	.175
Foreign Exposure	−.150	3.70	−.146
Activity	.123	2.46	.119

[16] Interestingly, the lower social status of these more cynical of the elite is reflected in the educational attainments of their fathers. Low status members of the elite are the sons of traditionally educated fathers. In other words, their fathers were far less likely to have had a modern secular education than a traditional

the level of activity. Holding age constant, higher levels of education go with greater activity. But the vast majority of the more active are the older of the elite, while the vast majority of the better educated are the younger respondents. The relation between activity and cynicism is to be explained by the great cynicism of the less active. It is the so-called new men of Iran who manifest the highest levels of cynicism.[17] As a researcher analyzing political elite in Southeast Asia has put it, these men represent the "intelligentsia elites." They are "ruling classes proper: they rule because they are intelligentsia and not because they are educated members of other ruling groups in the society."[18]

These ruling intelligentsia or new men are members of the Iranian political elite not because they can lay claim to the privileges of social status—their families are relatively uninfluential; nor because of their intense activities in political parties or social groups—they are the less active of the elite; but rather because they are the bearers of the "culture of modernization" emanating in the West. From their better educations and more frequent personal contact with *farangistan*, these elites are thought of as the technocrats who will put Iran's government on an administrative basis that is "scientific," "modern," and "Western." Thus, lacking the traditional bases of power that entitle an individual to a claim on elite status, these cynical members of the elite are brought into the system for the skills and special services they offer. They have achieved political power by being co-opted into the elite. In return for their services, their personal rewards have been great, but the political system has had to pay a heavy price for the resulting cynicism.

And there is no reason to assume that with increasing age these new men will lose that cynicism, now so pervasive among them. With the advent of Mansur to the premiership in 1965, their rise from rather unknown young aspirants to cabinet posts and other high places has been brilliant. But in the process, many of the ideals that motivated them as students and as aspirants have been left behind. Those earlier ideals and the contemporary realities are too disparate for easy accommodation.

---

maktab one ($p = .05$). This finding affirms the frequently noted observation that modern education in nineteenth-century Iran was reserved for the children of the elite. Cf. Issa Sadiq, *History of Education in Iran: From Earliest Times to the Present Day*, 3rd ed. (Tehran: Teachers College Press, 1963 [in Persian]), esp. pp. 332–34.

[17] For a description and analysis of these "new men," see Manfred Halpern, *The Politics of Social Change in the Middle East and North Africa* (Princeton: Princeton University Press, 1963), esp. pp. 51–78; Morroe Berger, *The Arab World Today* (Garden City, N.Y.: Doubleday and Co., 1964), esp. pp. 249–58 on the middle class; and William R. Polk, "The Middle East: Analyzing Social Change," *Bulletin of the Atomic Scientists*, 23, no. 1 (1967): 12–19.

[18] Harry J. Benda, "Political Elites in Colonial Southeast Asia: An Historical Analysis," *Comparative Studies in Society and History*, 7, no. 3 (April 1965): 234.

The cynicism that has made that accommodation possible will not be soon forsaken.

MISTRUST
If he is given the egg, he wants the hen.
Iranian proverb

Adam Smith framed much of the subsequent debate about the nature and value of trust when he wrote:

When an animal wants to obtain something either of man or another animal, it has no other means of persuasion but to gain the favor of those whose service it requires. A puppy fawns upon its dam, and a spaniel endeavors by a thousand attractions to engage the attention of its master who is at dinner, when it wants to be fed by him. Man sometimes uses the same arts with his brethren and when he has no other means of engaging them to act to his inclinations, endeavors by every servile and fawning attention to obtain their good will. He has no time, however, to do this upon every occasion. In civilized society, he stands at all times in the need of cooperation and assistance of a great multitude, while his whole life is scarce sufficient to gain the friendship of a few persons.[19]

This early venture into ethology aside, Smith attacked the Hobbesian dilemma by outlining countless means whereby cooperation between individuals in common social units could be achieved in the absence of the dreaded Leviathan. All these means centered about the notion of trust—trust as a sense of assured anticipation with regard to the behavior of others. Smith did not argue that Hobbes was an especially poor judge of human character, i.e., he too believed that individuals could, in fact, be counted upon to pursue their own selfish interests. Smith was able to demonstrate, however, a basic fallacy in Hobbes's reasoning. For under certain conditions, the pursuit of individual interest could contribute to the common good. The conditions under which the common good would accrue to a society of individuals pursuing their own interests centered about the limits of behavior considered legitimate by those actors.

Translated into notions of "enlightened self-interest," these limits have been accepted as the basis for achieving a social optimum from individuals attempting to maximize their own interests. Thus Alexis de Tocqueville identified a crucial difference between the citizens of the United States whom he so artfully observed and those of his own France: "I do not think, on the whole, that there is more selfishness among us than in America; the only difference is that there it is enlightened, here it is not.

[19] *The Wealth of Nations* (New York: Random House, Modern Library, 1937), book 1, chap. 2, pp. 13–14.

Each American knows when to sacrifice some of his private interests to save the rest; we want to save everything, and often we lose it all."[20]

In the process, Tocqueville introduced a second meaning of the concept of trust, that of an assured reliance on another's integrity, virtue, justice. These two meanings of the term—assured reliance on another's behavior and assured reliance of certain types of behavior in another—remain intertwined in the concept of trust as it is commonly used and serve to introduce ambiguities in the concept's application.[21]

For Erik H. Erikson, the notion of trust is relatively restricted to the first of these two meanings. Erikson argues that an infant will develop trust when he has "learned to rely on the sameness and continuity of the outer providers."[22] Lucian Pye, who extends Erikson's analysis in its relevance to the processes of political development, also stresses those aspects of trust that center on fixity and stability of interpersonal relations in the absence of concern for the quality of those relations. He recognizes that: "First, there is the problem of certainty or predictability: people in transitional societies can take almost nothing for granted, they are plagued on all sides by uncertainty and every kind of unpredictable behavior. In their erratically changing world, every relationship rests upon uncertain foundations."[23]

It is in this sense of the concept of trust that Iranian society demonstrates the difficulties of interpersonal relations. The inability of Iranians to count on, to be assured of the meaning of the behavior of others is taught early. So are Iranians taught early in life to mask their own thoughts. *Taqiyah* (dissimulation) is a prevalent notion in Iranian

[20] *Democracy in America*, 2 vols. (New York: Vintage Books, 1945), 2: 131. Tocqueville adds: "The principle of self-interest rightly understood produces no great acts of self-sacrifice, but it suggests daily small acts of self-denial. By itself it cannot suffice to make a man virtuous, but it disciplines a number of persons in habits of regularity, temperance, moderation, foresight, self-command; and if it does not lead men straight to virtue by the will, it gradually draws them in that direction by their habits."

[21] These concepts of virtue, justice, etc. are decidedly not absolutes but are recognized as fluctuating in intensity depending on the context in which they are applied. Lasswell observes, for example, that "The bargaining Yankee is still admired because he knows how to use his head to outsmart the other fellow and this easy toleration of mutual fraud is a major trait of capitalist society" (Harold D. Lasswell, *Politics: Who Gets What, When, and How* [New York: McGraw-Hill, 1936], p. 92).

[22] *Childhood and Society* (New York: W. W. Norton, 1963), p. 248. We emphasize the notion of "relatively restricted" for Erikson seems to argue that trust also contains elements of the second definition, e.g., "Mothers create a sense of trust in their children by that kind of administration which in its quality combines sensitive care of the baby's individual needs and a firm sense of personal trustworthiness" (*ibid.*, p. 249). Here he seems to introduce notions entailing the nature of the relationship and not merely that it has dependability.

[23] *Politics, Personality, and Nation Building*, pp. 54–55.

society dating back to the early centuries of Islam. Iranian Shi'ites took refuge from the threats of their Sunni Arab or Turkish overlords by misstating their own religious beliefs. For these purposes, dissimulation was an accepted, and even honored, technique. Essentially "the weapon of the weak against the strong," the practice was so widely accepted and so useful for self-protection in matters sacred, that its use in areas of secular interpersonal relations became widespread.[24]

The aphorism, "Conceal thy gold, thy destination, and thy creed," is one of a large number of similar caveats that are the stock in trade of acculturated Persians. Indeed, this lesson for living is explicitly taught young Persians and forms the basis of one of the most popular games that youngsters play throughout the society. The game, called *Goosh va Damagh* (Ear and Nose), is played by a group sitting in a circle. The "chief" of the game begins by lightly pulling the ear of the player on his left, or twitching his nose, tickling his sides, etc. That player then passes on to the person on his left a similar set of actions designed to unnerve the recipient. Whoever is unable to control his emotions and laughs, giggles, or makes a noise is a "loser" and must leave the circle. The game continues on until only one player is left—the winner being the child most successful at controlling his emotions and masking his reactions.[25]

This early training in dissimulation is carried on throughout the general socialization process in Iran and contributes to the marked instability in interpersonal relations that is at the root of the distrust so prevalent throughout the society. In a rather unembellished formulation, Andrew F. Westwood, the author of "Politics of Distrust in Iran," notes that Iranians have found it exceptionally difficult to trust one another or to work together over time in any significant numbers.[26]

But the notion of interpersonal relations characterized by mistrust is important not merely because it appears to be widespread in Iran.

[24] Sir Arnold Wilson, *Persia* (London: E. Benn, 1932), p. 5. This readiness for dissimulation apparently flies in the face of the culture of ancient Iran. Herodotus, for example, claimed: "The period of a boy's education is between the ages of five and twenty, and they are taught three things only: to ride, to use the bow, and to speak the truth" (Herodotus, *The Histories*, trans. Aubrey de Selincourt [London: Penguin Books, 1961], p. 70). More striking evidence of the value of truthtelling is provided by the Achaemenid inscriptions at Behistun, in west-central Iran. There Darius the Great had carved the record of his conquest of the pretender, Smerdis. Darius adds: "Thus saith Darius the king: Those who mayest be king hereafter, beware of lies; the man who is a liar, destroy him utterly; thou thinkest (thereby) shall my land remain whole" (*The Scriptures and Inscriptions of Darius the Great on the Rock of Behistun in Persia* [London: British Museum, 1907], p. 66).

[25] The playing of this game was witnessed several times in Iran by the author and is also described in, U.S. Commission for UNICEF, *Hi Neighbor*, Hastings House Publications, no. 4 (New York: Hastings House, 1961), p. 52.

[26] *Annals of the American Academy of Political and Social Sciences*, 358 (March 1965): 124.

Rather, the nature of interpersonal relations, especially with regard to mistrust, is central to the efforts of all developing societies to build meaningful social cooperation and integration as a concomitant of modernization. Pye alluded to this point above, but he has stated it even more explicitly: "The art of modern government and politics requires that people work together in ways that will maximize the forcefulness of the collective effort, while preserving the necessary flexibility to give scope for change and innovation."[27]

But observations in a variety of nations reveal that the success of the collective effort—the social optimum—is not being effectively advanced. Specifically, ambiguities in interpersonal relations stemming from notions of trust appear as one central explanatory factor. From peasant societies to advanced national political systems, trust in interpersonal relations is crucial and all too often lacking. Summarizing much of the literature on national political systems, Verba notes that "unless lessons of political trust have been learned before demands for participation arise, such demands are likely to produce tension and fragmentation."[28] Leonard Binder has commented on just this behavioral ambiguity in his study of Iran:

We have tried to show the lack of integration in the political system [of Iran], a lack of integration resulting in conflicting expectations and uncertainties about strategies, on the part of political actors. Having chosen a strategy based on either traditional or conventional value expectations, the actor may be faced with a response based on the opposite value system. . . .

. . . The resultant uncertainties breed alienation along with a strong sense that no one can be trusted.[29]

To an even greater extent than is the case at the national level, problems of mistrust seem to plague interpersonal relations in developing societies at the village and community level. After reviewing that body of literature, George Foster concludes that "an objective appraisal of a peasant village, however fond the ethnologist may be of his people, will in all likelihood reveal basic strains and tensions in interpersonal relations that make it difficult to understand how the community continues

---

[27] Lucian W. Pye, *Aspects of Political Development* (Boston: Little, Brown and Co., 1966), p. 100. The need for concerting the behavior of large numbers of people is a central theme for Banfield. See Edward C. Banfield, *The Moral Basis of a Backward Society* (Glencoe: Free Press, 1958), esp. pp. 7–12.

[28] "Comparative Political Culture," in *Political Culture and Political Development*, ed. Pye and Verba, p. 560. From the same volume see also the following authors who deal with problems of trust in national political systems: Richard Rose, "England: The Traditionally Modern Political Culture," pp. 83–129; Donald N. Levine, "Ethiopia: Identity, Authority, and Realism," pp. 245–81, and Joseph La Palombara, "Italy: Fragmentation, Isolation, and Alienation," pp. 282–329.

[29] *Iran: Political Development in a Changing Society* (Berkeley: University of California Press, 1962), pp. 306–307.

to function."[30] From Foster's survey it appears that at the root of these tensions lies mistrust—the absence of an assured certainty in the behavioral responses of others.

Despite the ambiguities inherent in the concept as we commonly use it, mistrust in interpersonal relations is a key factor in limiting cooperation essential for organization and development.[31] And that mistrust is a characteristic mode of interpersonal relations in Iran is a subject about which virtual certainty exists among students of Iranian politics. It is not surprising, then, that a number of variables in the elite questionnaire designed to tap this mistrust were grouped together by the factor analysis of general character orientations (see table 8.10). What falls out on this single factor are a number of items pertaining to the respondents' views of interpersonal relations in the family, with people in general, with friends, with occupational associates, and with minority groups.

People in general (items 1, 4, 8, and 9). The four items in this category were included in the questionnaire as an indication of the respondents' approach to interpersonal relations in the absence of any specific referents. The four items differ, however, in pertaining to situations of varying abstractness. Items 1 and 4 concern trust at its most abstract—the world and all men. When confronted with questions tapping highly abstract situations and no specific referents, the elite responded in a manner indicating high levels of trust:

"The world is a hazardous place in which men are basically evil and dangerous."

Agree: 10.2%   Disagree: 82.6%   No Answer: 7.2%
                                           Total: 100.0% (N = 167)[32]

"A person is better off if he does not trust anyone."

Agree: 9.6%   Disagree: 85.0%   No Answer: 5.4%
                                           Total: 100.0% (N = 167)

---

[30] George M. Foster, "Interpersonal Relations in Peasant Society," *Human Organization*, 19, no. 4 (Winter 1960–1961): 176. For other studies that treat of peasant mistrust, see Banfield, *Backward Society*; G. Morris Carstairs, *The Twice Born: A Study of a Community of High-Caste Hindus* (Bloomington: Indiana University Press, 1958); S. C. Dube, *Indian Village* (Ithaca: Cornell University Press, 1955); F. G. Friedman, "The World of 'La Miseria'," *Community Development Review*, 10 (1958): 16–22; Oscar Lewis, *Life in a Mexican Village: Tepoztlan Re-Studied* (Urbana: University of Illinois Press, 1951); Octavio Romano, "Values, Status, and Donship in a Mexican-American Village," 1959, University of Chicago Library, Chicago, Ill.; Ozzie G. Simmons, "Drinking Patterns and Interpersonal Performance in a Peruvian Mestizo Community," *Quarterly Journal of Studies on Alcohol*, 20 (1959): 103–11.

[31] For a study of the success of Communism in overcoming this mistrust and contributing to the effective concerting of people's behavior, see Philip Selznick, *The Organizational Weapon* (Glencoe: Free Press, 1959).

[32] These answers may be compared to responses to the identical question in a cross-national survey of college students, as shown in table 8.a.

TABLE 8.10

Mistrust Factor

1.	The world is a hazardous place in which men are basically evil and dangerous.	.486
2.	Of the following two alternatives, which do you consider worse for a child: that his teachers be too strict or that they be too permissive?	.473
3.	I believe that most of my associates would stab me in the back if it meant that they could get ahead faster that way.	.468
4.	A person is better off if he does not trust anyone.	.462
5.	Could you tell me if you have _ever_ belonged to any group in which all members of the group were truly good friends and from which you received full satisfaction?	.444
6.	Apart from your immediate family, is there anyone to whom you confide your most personal and important problems?	.394
7.	We must do all we can to safeguard our children from the threats and dangers of life.	.393
8.	Most people will use somewhat unfair means to gain a profit or advantage rather than risk losing it.	.369
9.	I mistrust people who are more friendly than I would naturally expect them to be.	.358
10.	Maybe some minority groups in Iran do get treated in a prejudiced fashion, but that is no business of mine.	.328
11.	While some women have made valuable contributions to Iran, women should remain in their proper place--the home.	.300

TABLE 8.a

Various Views on Proposition
that the World is a Hazardous Place
in which Men are Basically Evil and Dangerous

Country	N		Agree		Disagree	
	Men	Women	Men	Women	Men	Women
United States	590	187	17%	10%	83%	90%
Egypt	31	32	55	69	45	31
France	106	25	32	16	68	84
Italy	40	37	17	27	83	73
Germany	20	11	10	9	90	91
Japan	72	117	22	31	78	69
Israel	29	11	34	27	66	73

Source: James M. Gillespie and Gordon W. Allport, Youth's Outlook on the Future (Garden City, N.Y.: Doubleday Papers in Psychology, 1055), p. 58 (table 10).

Items 8 and 9, while still devoid of referents, pertain to interpersonal relations considerably less abstract, and in that sense, considerably more relevant to the common experiences of the elite in coping with others. Answers to these items were markedly different:

"Most people will use somewhat unfair means to gain a profit or advantage rather than risk losing it."

Agree: 59.9%   Disagree: 31.1%   No Answer: 9.0%

Total: 100.0% (N = 167)

"I mistrust people who are more friendly than I would naturally expect them to be."

Agree: 57.6%   Disagree: 36.0%   No Answer: 6.4%

Total: 100.0% (N = 167)

These answers reveal that while in the abstract the elite consider trust to be a laudable stance, in practice it seems to be achieved only with great difficulty. As trust becomes a matter removed from the ideal and a matter for concrete decisions in interpersonal relations, its incidence is diminished.

Minority groups (items 10 and 11). As the objects of interpersonal relations begin to be specified more distinctly, the level of trust accorded those objects diminishes. Minority groups in Iranian society are a case in point. The status of minorities in Iran has long been a source of pride to the regime. While minorities in one developing nation after another have been singled out for harsh treatment—frequently as scapegoats for internal dissatisfaction after the role of colonial power and foreigners has been markedly lessened—Iran has presented a contradictory picture. With only slight exceptions, minorities have continued to enjoy the official protection of the regime.

Studies on the distribution of authoritarianism have demonstrated that for these purposes, minorities can be defined as any readily identifiable group outside the immediate cultural environment of the subjects under study.[33] Thus for members of the Iranian elite, minorities in the broadest sense may be identified as peasants, women, and more narrowly defined, Armenians, Jews, Christians, and Baha'is. As with other referents, as the objects of trust are more narrowly defined, are defined in an increasingly exclusive fashion, so does the level of mistrust accorded them increase.

One respondent seemed to speak for the majority of the political elite when he noted: "Minorities should always be treated with justice, as long as they agree with the goals of the majority. After all, one cannot have a servant or boarder in one's house who disagrees with all you do or wish to do." As long, then, as the minority groups are willing to abide by the rules established by the dominant group, they are accepted. When the

[33] Theodore W. Adorno et al., *The Authoritarian Personality: Studies in Prejudice* (New York: Harper and Row, 1950).

minorities advance claims that differ from those of the dominant group, the minorities overstep their legitimate role.

The parallels between the stance of the political elite toward minority groups, however broadly conceived, and the stance of His Imperial Majesty toward the politically active or mobilized segments of the population are obvious. In both cases, those outside the community live by the grace of the community's leaders. The status of the individual with regard to the Moslem community, the *Dar al-Islam* (Abode of Islam) in the early Moslem centuries, defined the rights of the person in the state. In altered form, the notion continues to function in present-day Iran. The principal alteration in the concept centers around the definition of membership. Now the chief criterion is not acceptance of the Moslem faith or submission to Allah, but submission to the dominant political forces.

By this test, virtually all segments of the population can continue to enjoy the rights of "boarders" in the present political community. Only one major group of the population need be excluded on a priori grounds —the Baha'is.[34] As a widespread and expanding religion, viewed by Islamic traditionalists as a heretical schism of Islam, the Baha'is are automatically disenfranchised on religious grounds. But the present regime does not at all define membership in the dominant community on religious grounds, but solely by the test of political loyalty. Here the Baha'is fare well. Cognizant of the hostilities to them on the part of the Shi'ite ulema, the Baha'is seek the protection of the regime by demonstrating complete political fidelity. Were the protection of the regime to be removed, the Baha'is might once again be subjected to the violence of the majority religion.[35] Indeed the support that the regime derives on these grounds from the Baha'is, and from other religious and ethnic minorities, is one of its principal bases of support. While its support is enhanced from those minorities, however, it lays itself open to the not inconsiderable charge that it is not truly a Moslem government or, even worse, that it thereby serves the interests of foreign governments. Dissidents among the elite frequently relate the status of minorities, and espe-

---

[34] In many respects, the Baha'is of Iran are subject to the criticisms frequently leveled against the Jews of the West. Thus one respondent said: "In two thousand years of our history, the Jews have been the most trusted group. Armenians, however, are of dubious loyalty for in two world wars they have served foreigners. The Baha'is are undoubtedly the worst. They do not recognize our central government, they cluster together, and they work against all people who are not Baha'is." See Bruno Bettelheim and Morris Janowitz, *Social Change and Prejudice* (Glencoe: Free Press, 1964), esp. pp. 111–51.

[35] The most recent occasion on which Moslem hostilities toward the Baha'is was manifest occurred during the June 1963 riots. Then a variety of symbolic and not so symbolic displays of anti-Baha'i sentiment was reported. Previous to these events, Baha'is were subjected to a series of primarily minor indignities, including the near destruction of their religious center in Tehran and its confiscation by the government shortly after the overthrow of Mossadegh.

cially the Baha'is, to foreign influence and use this combination of sins as a means of lambasting the regime. One member of the elite went so far as to explain the recent expansion of the Iranian cabinet in these terms: "The Jews are an economic people, who share the same holy book with us. They live and work side by side with other Iranians. The Baha'is, however, are not part of our traditions. They are spies for the English and want us to forsake our own nationalism to serve Haifa [the headquarters of the Baha'i faith]. Mansur included nine Baha'is in his cabinet but to do so, he had to increase the size of the cabinet to nine-teen."[36] While the regime never responds explicitly to these charges, it is quite conscious of them and misses few opportunities to declare its fidelity to Islam. Nonetheless, it continues to be mistrusted by many of the elite on these grounds.

Occupational associates (item 3). As the referents of the items de-signed to tap trust-mistrust are narrowed, the level of mistrust expressed remains on the positive side:

"I believe that most of my associates would stab me in the back if it meant that they could get ahead faster that way."[37]

Agree: 53.5% Disagree: 40.1% No Answer: 6.6%

Total: 100.0% (N=167)

Elite respondents do tend to perceive their work environment as basically hostile, one in which constant vigilance should be exerted. In the work environment, a high correlation is perceived between mistrust of one's colleagues and the use of language as a tool in interpersonal relations. Those of the elite who mistrusted their counterparts were also likely to feel that the latter would resort to dissimulation when it suited their own ends. Frequent references were made to this belief. One respondent said: "Ideas and words in Iranian society are primary weap-ons in a person's efforts to reach power. Not one person in a thousand believes what he says, but says what he says as a means for achieving success. Centuries of assimilating conquerors have left us with an in-capacity for true belief. We say '*baleh, baleh*' [yes, yes] when we mean '*nah, nah*' [no, no]." One result of this attitude is a condition common

[36] The presence of Baha'is in "high places" in the government is frequently alleged but virtually impossible to demonstrate inasmuch as Baha'is apparently resort to *taqiyah* (dissimulation) about their religion as often as did the Shi'ites of old. Only one of my elite respondents admitted to the faith and he held no official government position. In fact, Mansur's first cabinet had twenty-one mem-bers, five more than did that of his predecessor, Assadollah Alam. A number of the additional members were not full ministers, however, but deputy prime ministers elevated to cabinet rank.

[37] The wording of this question proved to be troublesome, for the concept of a "stab in the back" in Persian bears none of the connotations conveyed by the English phrase. Nonetheless, the meaning of the phrase is unambigious in Persian and it was retained in the final instrument.

in developing societies. The truth value of statements is not inherent in the words used or in the relationship of the words employed to the reality described. Rather, the "truth" of any statement is based on the status of the speaker; in order to validate statements, some relevant in-group authority must be located.[38] The Iranian elite seem perpetually engaged in such a search. But with attitudes suggesting mistrust of other Iranians who might be defined as members of their in-group, such an authority is virtually impossible to locate. As a result, the "truth value" of a statement can never be conclusively established.

Friends (items 5 and 6). As the referents under consideration move appreciably closer to what would be conventionally considered a rather narrowly defined in-group, the levels of mistrust remain relatively high. Only 43 per cent (N = 72) of the respondents admitted to having a close personal confidant other than a member of their immediate families. Similarly, only 39 per cent (N = 65) reported that they ever belonged to a group whose members were truly good friends. Even in the closest personal relations outside the family, then, members of the elite rarely establish ties based on mutual trust. Hafez offered a couplet counseling against mistrust at this level: "With friends—manliness. With enemies—expediency." But although the "manliness" that he supported contains a large dose of interpersonal trust, his counsels, apparently, fall unheeded.

Family (items 2 and 7). Two items that refer more to socialization beliefs than to interpersonal relations within the family appear in the mistrust factor. The question on the value of permissiveness in child raising has the second highest loading on the factor. It is related to the other questions such that mistrust is associated with the reputed desirability of permissiveness. Those respondents who manifest the highest levels of mistrust report that it is worse for a child to have teachers who are too strict. In an apparently contradictory fashion, however, these same individuals manifesting high levels of mistrust also argue that parents should safeguard their children from the dangers of life. Actually, the majority of the elite agree with this latter position:

"We must do all we can to safeguard our children from the threats and dangers of life."

Agree: 80.8%   Disagree: 16.2%   No Answer: 3.0%
Total: 100.0% (N=167)

[38] Ithiel de Sola Pool, "The Mass Media and Politics in the Modernization Process" in *Communications and Political Development*, ed. Lucian W. Pye (Princeton: Princeton University Press, 1963), p. 242. See also, Felix Keesing, Marie Keesing, and Thomas Blair, "Social Structure and Information Exposure in Rural Brazil," *Rural Sociology*, 25 (March 1960): 65–75; and Felix Keesing and Marie Keesing, *Elite Communication in Samoa* (Stanford: Stanford University Press, 1956).

Nonetheless, a far higher proportion of the mistrustful in the elite agree with this notion than the more trustful. How is this contradiction between permissiveness outside the home and strictness within the family to be explained? We would suggest that what is at work here is a disinclination on the part of the mistrusting elite to allow outsiders to play a role in the disciplining and thus in the rearing of their children. Those of the elite who most distrust their fellow Iranians are the most wary of allowing those outsiders a role in dealing with their own children. But, those children must in turn be taught the hazards presented by others and must be protected from them. Thus, the children of the most mistrustful would be most shielded from the dangers of life, and in the process, from the realities of life. As a result, they would be less able to cope with those very dangers, and with those outsiders who perpetrate those dangers. Mistrust would most likely be passed directly from generation to generation; those of the elite who themselves mistrust others would, in turn, contribute to the development of mistrust in their own children by denying them the opportunity to cope successfully with life while they are children. Moreover, the fact that they are the most eager to protect their children would imply that they also fundamentally mistrust their own children. Their offspring need to be protected, for they themselves are incapable of coping with life outside the family.

That this latter point seems to be the case is borne out by the significant association between trust and family disdain (see table 8.11).[39] Clearly, the greater the mistrust of the respondent, as measured by his

TABLE 8.11

Responses to the Family Disdain Factor
by Responses to the Trust Factor

Family Disdain	Trust		
	Low	Medium	High
Low	29.0%	47.8%	54.2%
Medium	29.0	21.7	25.4
High	41.9	30.4	20.3
Total	100.0%	100.0%	100.0%
N	(62)	(46)	(59)

Note: x^2 = 10.100; df = 4; p < .05; gamma = -.240.

[39] The family disdain factor is described above in the chapter on insecurity. Note that that factor and the trust factor share one variable which loads significantly high on both: "Apart from your immediate family, is there anyone to whom you confide your most personal and important problems." While this overlap would clearly affect the significance of association, it is suggested that it would be insufficient to bring about the magnitude of the association found.

responses to a series of questions pertaining to general interpersonal relations, the greater is his disdain and mistrust of his immediate family.

It is widely assumed that the family unit in Iran serves as the principal haven from threatening interpersonal relations. It has been observed that the family often functions in a manner parallel to that of the *dowreh*. Operating under conditions of widespread nepotism, family members are expected to advance the interests of their kinsmen before or even at the expense of others. Families, as is true for *dowreh*s, frequently attempt to place their members in a variety of posts throughout the official and private bureaucracies. From these multiple vantage points, it is assumed that the joint interests of the family can thus be more easily secured.

These observations have led many students of Iranian society to conclude that, therefore, the family in Iran somehow represents a pattern of personal relations that defy conventional morality. Here, then, is that in-group based on trust.[40] In fact, our data refute these allegations. While the family unit may manifest more trust in the relations of its members than do other social units, it is not able to avoid the underlying ethos. For as with cynicism, so with mistrust; individuals who manifest these general character orientations tend to bring them to bear on all of their interpersonal relations. Whatever the nature of these relations, whether they be object free, relate to Iranians in general, minority groups, occupational associates, friends, or family members, Iranians carry over their orientations. And in a majority of cases, the general orientation is one of mistrust.

Mistrust is such a pervasive character orientation of the political elite that the conditions which contribute to such a perspective are more difficult to identify than is the case with other general orientations. Certainly one concomitant of mistrust, as with insecurity (and in an inverse fashion with cynicism), is the level of participation in the political system. The more the elite members participate in the day-to-day operations of the system, the more they manifest mistrusting attitudes. One measure of this is the association between scores on the activity factor and levels of mistrust (see table 8.12). The more active the member of the elite as measured by his participation in voluntary organizations, *dowreh*s, charities, multiple job-holding, and the like, the more apt he is to manifest mistrust.

In his historical view of mistrust in Iran, Westwood described how the almost frenzied activities of the members of the Iranian elite are both a symptom of mistrust and, in turn, a cause: "Expecting betrayal, men

[40] Binder (*Iran*, p. 159) was astute enough to deny the conventional wisdom on Iranian family relations by noting: "Generally speaking, these obligations [of nepotism] stand, *despite a good deal of family friction*, usually the result of sibling rivalry" (italics added).

TABLE 8.12

Level of Mistrust by Scores on
the Activity Factor

Mistrust	Activity	
	Low	High
High	43.2%	58.2%
Low	56.8	41.8
Total	100.0%	100.0%
N	(88)	(79)

Note: x^2 = 3.771; df = 1;
.10 > p < .05; gamma = -.294.

seek to balance political alliance with contradictory alliance, thus each fulfilling the other's prophecy of betrayal. To have lines of alliance in so many directions that no betrayal, no development will leave one isolated and exposed is the ideal and the quest after this ideal, of course, leaves all isolated and exposed."[41]

A further clue to this relationship between political activity and mistrust is revealed by an examination of the number of years that the respondents have filled their present principal positions compared with the level of mistrust that they manifest (see table 8.13). Members of the elite who have served in their present posts for up to ten years demonstrate higher levels of mistrust than do those more permanently placed. But among those of the elite who have served for less than ten years, the longer the tenure, the higher the mistrust. What appears to be at work here is that the elite with the longest tenure in their present posts have been isolated, by dint of that tenure, from the buffetings of the political system. Among this group will be found private businessmen with no formal ties to government bureaucracies, bureaucrats and politicians retired from government service, and the relatively few government employees who have, nonetheless, been successful in holding onto their posts.

But for those who have served for less than ten years, the overwhelming majority of whom are in government service, the relation is altered. Here, longer tenure is accompanied by higher mistrust. As these Iranians settle into a given bureaucratic structure and are socialized into its style of interpersonal relations, they manifest higher levels of mistrust, mistrust that is an appropriate response to the milieu in which they operate. In short, "participation in the system" translated as age or number of years of active political life is too crude a measure. What appears more

[41] "Politics of Distrust," p. 124.

TABLE 8.13

Number of Years in Present Principal
Position by Level of Mistrust

Mistrust		Number of Years in Post		
		Less than 1 - 2	3 - 10	16 or More
High		38.6%	51.4%	26.8%
Medium		27.1	22.9	21.4
Low		34.3	25.7	51.8
	Total	100.0%	100.0%	100.0%
	N	(70)	(35)	(56)

Notes: x^2 = 8.394; df = 4; .10 < p > .05.

This table should be interpreted with the
maximum of caution. It proved exceedingly
difficult to translate "present principal
position" unambiguously into Persian. While
its most obvious meaning was identical with
the concept in English, it could also be taken
to imply not "position" but "occupation."
Thus a member of the Iranian Supreme Court,
for example, who had served on the bench for
over twenty years in a series of lower courts
before being elevated to the highest court of
Iran only months before the interview,
responded, "over eleven years." When the
primary meaning of the question was emphasized, however, he changed his answer to "less
than one year." While the interviewer
attempted to remain sensitive to this ambiguity,
there exists no assurance that all such difficulties were eliminated.

relevant is a composite of the number of years of political participation
plus frequent alterations in position; this combination constitutes a more
nearly modal pattern of experience for the Iranian elite. Lengthy participation with fixed tenure is neither typical nor positively related to the
incidence of the character orientations.

That greater familiarity with and immersion in the government bureaucracy (as defined to include frequent changes in position) contributes to feelings of mistrust is also attested to by the relationship between military service and scores on the mistrust factor. A positive
(gamma = .367) and significant association (p < .02) exists between
the two variables. Respondents who have fulfilled their military service
are more likely to manifest higher levels of mistrust than nonveterans.
Controlling this relationship by a number of other variables—age, social
status, power, etc.—reveals no basic change in the relationship between
military service and mistrust. We suggest that military service represents
but another channel of experience in the political system, experience that
contributes to the orientation of mistrust.

One relationship that seems contradictory needs to be mentioned. It appears that as the elite make more trips outside Iran, their level of mistrust decreases. We have already demonstrated the positive relationship that exists between foreign travel and insecurity. It was suggested that such a connection might be explained by the subjection of the elite travelers to immediate experiences with foreign value systems. The conflict that often arises between the culture of Iran and the foreign culture as experienced by a member of the elite contributes to manifest insecurity. Should it not also contribute to mistrust? In fact, as table 8.14 indi-

TABLE 8.14

Number of Foreign Trips
by Level of Mistrust

Mistrust	Number of Foreign Trips		
	0 - 5	6 - 20	21 or More
High	50.0%	40.6%	25.5%
Medium	21.1	21.9	28.8
Low	28.9	37.5	45.7
Total	100.0%	100.0%	100.0%
N	(38)	(64)	(59)

Note: x^2 = 6.662; df = 4; p < .20; gamma = .259.

cates, the greater the number of foreign trips, the less the mistrust.[42] Indeed, this relationship would be expected on grounds other than the clash of value systems. For as an individual experiences others in a widening network of relationships, as the individual achieves a "decentering from the unit of self to a progressively larger social unit," he would be expected to manifest greater trust toward other individuals.[43] And we have noted that Iranians who demonstrate trust do so throughout the entire social system.

Nonetheless, this notion of foreign travel's expanding the size of the community that is accorded trust in interpersonal relationships does not resolve this dilemma. For participation in the political system, through military service or intensive activity or lengthy service in a bureaucratic position, would also serve to widen the social units in which the individual interacts. Clearly what seems relevant is not so much altering the ratio between inclusivity-exclusivity in terms of the definition of in-

[42] The other variables and factors that are significantly associated with insecurity are all related in a similar direction with mistrust although the relationship does not achieve the same level of significance.

[43] Gordon W. Allport, *Personality and Social Encounter* (Boston: Beacon Press, 1964), p. 175. A similar point is made by J. C. Flugel, "Some Neglected Aspects of World Integration" in *Psychological Factors of Peace and War*, ed. T. H. Pear (London: Hutchinson and Co., 1950); and Foster, *"Interpersonal Relations."*

group versus out-group, but the quality of personal relationships experienced within such networks. Because it would be condescending in the absence of data to imply that the positive association between trust and foreign travel among the elite must be due to a different (and presumably superior) type of interpersonal relations, the resolution of this issue remains unclear.

An alternative explanation, which is supported by the data, is that the greatest foreign travel is experienced by businessmen and government officials who have served over eleven years in their present posts. In this case, their isolation from the values characteristic of the Iranian bureaucracy, rather than their exposure to new value systems, would explain the association.

As a group, then, the Iranian elite are beset by mistrust. They mistrust the motives of other Iranians, their families, their children, and, most likely, themselves, at least partially because they are unable to control their environment and their places within it. Regis Debray, in his primer for revolutionaries, offers three "golden rules" for guerilla fighters—rules that the Iranian political elite seem to have long ago taken for granted. Debray insists on the need for "constant vigilance, constant mistrust, constant mobility."[44]

EXPLOITATION

Chicanery, artifice, and mendacity are our heritage . . .
Member of the Iranian elite

In popular usage, the name of Niccolo Machiavelli is associated with the ruthless pursuit of political power through principles characterized by "cunning, duplicity, and bad faith."[45] In his classic, *The Prince*, Machiavelli sought to inform Lorenzo Medici of the proper governance of an absolute state or monarchy, proper defined here as that which contributes to the maintenance of the rule of the monarch.[46] For that purpose, politics was conceived of as an end in itself and the ruler was counseled to pursue that end in a totally amoral or nomoral fashion. To aid the ruler, Machiavelli elaborated what might be considered a sociopsychological model of interpersonal relations, especially those between the ruler and the ruled. He provided the monarch with a set of predictive

[44] As quoted in Eghbal Ahmad, "A Primer for Revolutionary Guerillas: Revolution in the Revolution?" from *Revolution in the Revolution?*, by Regis Debray (New York: Grove Press, 1967), in *The Nation*, Jan. 29, 1968.
[45] Richard Christie and Robert K. Merton, "Procedures for the Sociological Study of the Values Climate of Medical School," *Journal of Medical Education*, 33, no. 10, part 2 (Oct. 1958): 125–53. Also in H. H. Gee and R. J. Glaser, *The Ecology of the Medical Student*, Report of the Fifth Teaching Institute, Association of American Medical Colleges (Atlantic City, N.J., Oct. 15–19, 1957), p. 134.
[46] *The Prince*, trans. Luigi Ricci (London: Oxford University Press), 1903, p. 2.

statements about those relationships and about means of influencing those relations in ways consonant with the ruler's purposes. Thus, he wrote: "It may be said of men in general that they are ungrateful, voluble, dissemblers, anxious to avoid danger and covetous of gain; as long as you benefit them they are entirely yours; they offer you their blood, their goods, their life and their children."[47]

Much of what Machiavelli suggested as relevant for the maintenance of power in sixteenth-century Florence appears familiar in the context of contemporary Iran.[48] Members of the Iranian political elite, without referring to the ill-reputed Machiavelli, talked as if they were familiar with his thoughts. A well-known member of the elite complained: "There is a great deal of upward mobility in Iran, but very few have made progress by talent alone. Rather, flattery, lying, and *hoghe bazi* [fraud] must be one's tools." Another suggested that: "Iranians are like chameleons: they switch their colors every day and along with their colors, their policies. We never feel we know another person's position or what he thinks, or how we can count on him. If a politician announces a policy, we do one of three things. Either we don't believe it, we wait for him to change it, or we ignore it." What is being charged here and in much of the literature on Iran is the notion that Iranian politics frequently approximate what was a normative model for Machiavelli. In order to test this notion, a variety of items were included in the questionnaire, items about the proper conduct of interpersonal relations.[49] With surprising frequency, these items all grouped together in an orthogonally rotated exploitation factor (see table 8.15). The items grouped in the factor suggest a view of human nature as opportunistic, manipulative, aggressive, immoral, deficient, and other-directed. Men act in Machiavellian ways to achieve their selfish ends, even at the expense of the welfare of others. There are no natural limits on the lengths to which individuals will go to achieve those ends, the possibilities for human behavior being virtually limitless.

[47] *Ibid.*, p. 46. The author goes on to warn the Prince, however, that "the friendship which is gained by purchase and not through grandeur and nobility of spirit is merited but not secured" (*ibid.*).

[48] Indeed the social and political state of sixteenth-century Europe bears striking similarities to contemporary Iran. See, for example, George H. Sabine, *A History of Political Theory* (New York: Henry Holt and Co., 1937), pp. 331–36; and esp. Lawrence Stone, *The Crisis of the Aristocracy, 1558–1641* (London: Oxford University Press, 1965).

[49] Unfortunately, at the time of formulating the testing instrument, the author was unaware of Christie's work in this area. See Christie and Merton, "Procedures," as well as Richard Christie, "A Quantification of Machiavelli," unpublished MS. Milbrath has used Christie's scale in his study of Washington lobbyists and reports on the results in Lester W. Milbrath, "Measuring the Personalities of Lobbyists," Northwestern University, Department of Political Science, 1961, mimeo.

TABLE 8.15
Exploitation Factor

1. Most people in Iran make friends because friends are likely to be helpful and useful to them.	.648
2. The average Iranian is overwhelmingly motivated by self-interest, that is, the pursuit of his own, personal interests.	.542
3. Religious and political minority groups, when they are given too much money and freedom, just misuse the privileges and create disturbances.	.515
4. I mistrust people who are more friendly than I would naturally expect them to be.	.506
5. It is usually better in Iran to "get" one's rival before he gets you.	.506
6. Most people will use somewhat unfair means to gain a profit or advantage rather than risk losing it.	.382
7. One reason why we can't have complete democracy in Iran is that such a large percentage of the population is innately incapable and deficient.	.354
8. A person should adapt his behavior and thoughts to the group that happens to be with him at that time.	.343
9. The present is an immeasurably small fragment of time which has taken its place in the past almost before we are aware of its existence.	.327
10. The present exists only as a product of creation of our senses. The future is still a matter for conjecture. Thus only the past has tangible reality.	.297

Note: Richard Christie and Robert K. Merton ("Procedures for the Sociological Study of the Values Climate of Medical School," Journal of Medical Education, 33 [Oct. 1958], p. 134) describe their wariness in referring to their scale as a Machiavellianism scale. We share many of the same reservations but in addition have applied the title "exploitation" in order to avoid confusion with their work even though similar processes are being measured.

The two items loading most highly on the exploitation factor are the subject of widespread certainty on the part of the elite. Some 70 per cent of the elite agree that the concept of friendship in Iran is translatable into mutual benefit. (Only 25 per cent disagree, while 5 per cent gave no answer.) One of the elite suggested that, in fact, friends were really of two kinds. Some were friends because of the contributions that they could make to one's career. Others were friends because they were genuinely admired. But all men had both types of friends and the secret of success in life was to be adept at parceling out one's acquaintances in these categories so that the former group could be manipulated in ways beneficial to the self.

The second item was the subject of even more certainty. Seventy-nine per cent of the elite believed that their fellow countrymen were overwhelmingly motivated by self-interest. (Only 17 per cent disagreed, while less than 5 per cent offered no answer.[50]) While some of the respondents were wary of probes in this area, many felt free to discuss their responses. In a surprising number of instances, they had a common policy for coping with opportunistic others. In order to prevent being duped or used, especially by one's coworkers, some respondents in positions of administrative responsibility claimed always to hire colleagues or workers who appeared less talented than themselves. "That way," one explained, "I need never fear that my coworkers could impede my progress."

The other items in the factor that tap similar orientations—items 3, 4, and 6—all load in a similar direction. Were no specifically behavioral evidence available, we would be willing to argue, on the basis of these attitudes alone, that the political elite do, in fact, behave in a manner consonant with these attitudes. For it is likely that a self-fulfilling prophecy would tend to operate.[51] If members of the elite truly believed that others do act as they report they believe others act, then they would undoubtedly alter their own behavior to respond to the perceived acts of these other individuals. Their anticipatory responses would lead to real responses in others.

Additional items that load highly imply that this is, in fact, what has occurred. Item 5 refers to the estimate of appropriate behavior as a response to the other attitudinal items. Over 70 per cent of the elite agree that it is better to "get" one's rival before he gets you. (Only 14 per cent of the most powerful Iranians disagreed with the idea.) We have assumed throughout that the behavior of elite members is at least consonant with their attitudes. If this is the case, then these members of the elite would strive to "get" their rivals rather than wait to respond to the attack that they are certain will occur. If this is the case, then their own

---

[50] Foreigners have been noting this phenomenon for centuries. One struck a particularly contemporary ring at the beginning of the twentieth century: "The Persian newspapers have been telling their readers for years that what they lack is public spirit—the spirit of cooperation. Well-meaning foreigners have asked them why they do not organize trade guilds and merchant guilds as Europeans did in their Middle Ages. They reply that they are too fond of intrigue, that they suspect each other too much, that their standard of business morality is too uncertain, that their ideas are too volatile. The Persian likes advice, but has always a fairly sound reason for not accepting it" (Anthony Hale, *From Persian Uplands* [New York: E. P. Dutton and Co., n.d., ca. 1915], p. 31).

[51] See Robert K. Merton, *Social Theory and Social Structure* (Glencoe: Free Press, 1957), pp. 421–36.

aggressive behavior, whether or not it be perceived as anticipatory to a certain set of aggressive behavior from another or only to a potential set of aggressive behavior, would undoubtedly occasion that behavior in another. (The situation is highly analogous to strategic thinking vis-à-vis the Soviet Union. If we believe that the Soviets will eventually launch a nuclear attack against us, then we should launch at first strike to pre-empt the advantage of initial attack. But if they believed that we believed that they would launch an attack and that we would respond with a first strike, then they . . . , etc., etc.[52])

Another item that poses these same dilemmas is that which suggests that an individual should adapt to the group of which he is then a member. This question raises the specter of the David Riesman-Daniel Lerner-Abraham Maslow debate on the nature and value of disparate personal reference figures and "other-direction."[53] The relevance of those issues in terms of the striking similarity between the question of adapting to the group and the factor as a whole and the previous quotation on the chameleonlike qualities of Iranians is obvious. The point also bears striking parallels with Machiavelli, who counseled: "It is necessary to be able to disguise this character [of faithlessness] well and to be a great feigner and dissembler; and men are so simple and so ready to obey present necessities, that one who deceives will always find those who allow themselves to be deceived."[54] We seem to be coming full circle, back to the maxim on *taqiyah* (dissimulation) cited in the section above. But there is more at work among the Iranian elite than Machiavelli's notion of feigning and dissembling. For the distinctive characteristic of chameleons is that they do actually change color. They do not merely take on a neutral shade or effectively look like the color of their environment; they become the color of their environment.

What the factor item was proposing is precisely this: that an individual not dissimulate by mouthing the beliefs of the group he happened to

[52] Such arguments led explicitly to the recognition of insuring a massive second strike capability which could survive intact an initial attack. In the process, the value of launching a first strike may be reduced. See Herman Kahn, "The Arms Race and Some of Its Hazards" in *Arms Control, Disarmament, and National Security*, ed. Donald G. Brennan (New York: George Braziller, 1961), pp. 89–121; and Herman Kahn, *On Thermonuclear War* (Princeton: Princeton University Press, 1961), esp. pp. 190–218. This situation of anticipatory behavior is one that has been dealt with at length in the literature on stable solutions in game theory. See, for example, R. Duncan Luce and Howard Raiffa, *Games and Decisions* (New York: John Wiley and Sons, 1964), esp. pp. 199–236.

[53] The principles of this debate, never framed as such, may be found in David Riesman, *The Lonely Crowd—A Study of the Changing American Character* (Garden City, N.Y.: Doubleday and Co., 1956); Daniel Lerner, "Comfort and Fun: Morality in a Nice Society," *American Scholar*, 27, no. 2 (Spring 1958): 153–65; and Abraham H. Maslow, *Toward a Psychology of Being* (Princeton: D. Van Nostrand Co., 1962).

[54] *The Prince*, p. 70.

be with, but that he actually adapt his behavior and thoughts to the group. He should not merely appear as if he belonged to the group. He should become a full-fledged member. The common, high factor loading suggests that this is what goes together in the minds of the elite. In a sense, the consummate fraud is perpetrated: one becomes what one pretends to be. Indeed, it appears that certain members of the elite perceive their situation as analogous to role playing. In their interactions with others of the elite, a set of roles generally considered appropriate for each of the politically powerful actors seems to exist. In order to function in the political process, the elite would have to assume the norms of the roles. Otherwise, harsh sanctions could be expected and an actor might be disenfranchised from further participation.[55]

Of importance to us is the large body of research that concludes that role playing can be effective in altering the most fundamental and deeply held attitudes and values.[56] Merely participating in a game—even though the game be as important as Iranian elite politics—will tend to foster attitude change in a direction concordant with the activities of the game and its rules. This process appears to be occurring among some of the political elite. The variables that are principally associated with the factors already discussed and with the exploitation factor (which we shall note below) are those relating to the specific type of involvement with Iranian politics experienced by the elite. The greater the involvement of members of the elite in Iranian politics, as defined above, the more likely are they to score highly on the first three factors. The greater the tenure of the members in one position, the more likely are they to score highly on the exploitation factor. Gerth and Mills come upon a similar conclusion from different premises. Beginning with Mead's concept of the "generalized other," they argue:

[55] For an analysis of the relationship between whites and blacks in the United States in terms of role theory, see Thomas F. Pettigrew, *A Profile of the Negro American* (Princeton: D. Van Nostrand Co., 1964), esp. pp. 3–26; and idem, "Complexity and Change in American Racial Patterns: A Social Psychological View" in *The Negro American*, ed. Talcott Parsons and Kenneth Clark (Boston: Beacon Press, 1965), pp. 325–59.

[56] For some of this research, see: F. J. Culbertson, "Modification of an Emotionally Held Attitude Through Role Playing," *Journal of Abnormal and Social Psychology*, 54 (1957): 230–33; I. L. Janis and B. T. King, "The Influence of Role Playing on Opinion Change," *Journal of Abnormal and Social Psychology*, 49 (1954): 211–18; Herbert C. Kelman, "Attitude Change as a Function of Response Restriction," *Human Relations*, 6 (1953): 185–214; B. T. King and I. L. Janis, "Comparison of the Effectiveness of Improvised Versus Non-Improvised Role Playing in Producing Opinion Changes," *Human Relations*, 9 (1956): 177–86; Milton J. Rosenberg et al., *Attitude Organization and Change: An Analysis of Consistency among Attitude Components* (New Haven: Yale University Press, 1960); W. A. Scott, "Attitude Change Through Reward of Verbal Behavior," *Journal of Abnormal and Social Psychology*, 55 (1957): 72–75; and idem, "Attitude Change by Response Reinforcement: Replication and Extension," *Sociometry*, 22 (1959): 328–35.

The content of a person's generalized other generally depends upon the normative attitudes of "the society" only as these attitudes have been selected and refracted by those who have been and who are authoritatively significant to the person. Accordingly, persons who have moved along different career lines will accordingly feel quite different "pangs of conscience" in regard to given actions. And, on the other hand, persons who have occupied similar institutional positions will have similar generalized others.[57]

One qualification based on the research on attitude change needs to be added to this conclusion. It is generally the case that the greater the coercion attached to the role playing, the less the subsequent attitude change. Persons who feel coerced into fulfilling the norms of a given role will be less likely to change their attitudes in a direction prescribed by those norms. It is interesting that in these cases, the definition of coercion extends even to accepting a payment for playing the role. The larger the payment, the greater is the perceived coercion and the less the attitude change.[58] In many respects, the co-optative style of His Imperial Majesty establishes conditions approximating the coercion of the inducement payments of laboratory experiments. The ability of the elite to convince themselves that their outward conformity to their roles was the sole result of the coercion of the shah would contribute to the maintenance of their attitudinal integrity.

While a number of the respondents alluded to this type of reaction, it seems unlikely that it could be completely effective in preventing any attitude change. What seems to result, instead, is an amalgam of opinions, attitudes, and beliefs reflecting various degrees of commitment and hostility to the political system and the actors therein. In the process, the elite do not develop a commonly held body of beliefs that could serve as the foundation for political development. The contradictions and ambiguities in the value structures of the elite mean that while the process called identification takes place, it is an identification that feeds on insecurity, mistrust, and cynicism on the one hand, and exploitation on the other.[59]

---

[57] Hans Gerth and C. Wright Mills, *Character and Social Structure: The Psychology of Social Institutions* (New York: Harcourt, Brace and World, 1953), p. 96.

[58] See, for example, Scott, "Attitude Change by Response Reinforcement"; idem, "Attitude Change Through Reward of Verbal Behavior"; and Rosenberg, et al., *Attitude Organization and Change*.

[59] Parsons refers to "identification" as "the process by which a person comes to be inducted into membership in a collectivity through learning to play a role complementary to those of other members in accord with the pattern of values governing the collectivity. The new members come to be *like* the others with respect to their common membership status and to the psychological implications of this—above all, the common values thereby internalized" (Talcott Parsons, *Social Structure and Personality* [New York: Free Press, 1964], p. 91).

A final set of items that load highly on this exploitation factor refer to the sense of time perspective. One of the more widely commented upon characteristics of Persian society has been this very issue—that Iranians have little regard for time. As one of the respondents put it, "In Iran, time is not money." A well-known aphorism expresses this same time sense:

> Baleh, Baleh, Insha'allah;
> Chashm, Chashm, Pasfardah.
>
> Yes, Yes, God be willing;
> O.k., o.k., The day after tomorrow.[60]

The two items loading on the factor are similar. The present is either incalculably brief or has no real existence at all. What they are assumed to imply is a certain sense of *taqdir* or *kismet* (fatalism). For if the present is brief (at worst) or does not exist (at best), then whatever goes on in the present can be more easily tolerated. A certain callousness would result, a capacity for enduring suffering. An individual with such time perspectives would not be expected to rail against the indignities or unpleasantnesses of the present, however defined.

But some means of reacting to those indignities must be found. Rather than attempting to confront them directly, those of the elite with attitudes deprecating the present respond, we would argue, by coping, not by challenging. And one copes by wheedling and adapting, in short, by manipulating others. Indeed, there is a significantly positive relationship between the two items tapping time perspective and those comprising the principal body of the exploitation factor. Those who hold attitudes supporting interpersonal exploitation place slight stock in the importance of the present, remembering a better past—a past that was, perhaps, less beset by the upsetting interpersonal relations that do characterize the present.

We wish to relate this exploitation factor to its antecedents, the variety of social background data, personal experiences, and the like, with which it is significantly associated. Many of the same social background factors that we have identified and related to the orientations of insecurity, cynicism, and mistrust also relate significantly to the exploitation factor. But they relate significantly in an inverse fashion. To illustrate this point, it

---

[60] Originally related to the author by Professor Richard W. Frye, whose storehouse is practically limitless. For other references to time in Iranian society, see Joseph M. Upton, *The History of Modern Iran: An Interpretation*, Harvard Middle Eastern Monographs (Cambridge: Harvard University Press, 1960), p. 34; Wilson, *Persia*, p. 10; Wilfred Sparroy, *Persian Children of the Royal Family: The Narrative of an English Tutor at the Court of H.I.H. Zillu's-Sultan, G.C.S.I.* (London: J. Lane, 1902), p. 19; and Arthur C. Millspaugh, *Americans in Persia* (Washington, D.C.: Brookings Institution, 1946), p. 79.

will suffice to present but one of the possible relations, that between exploitation and the number of years in which the elite respondents have served in their present, principal positions. Table 8.16 illustrates that

TABLE 8.16

Scores on the Exploitation Factor
by Number of Years in Post

Exploitation		Number of Years in Present Position			
		1 or less	1 - 2	3 - 10	11 or more
Low		25.9%	37.0%	29.7%	28.6%
Medium		48.1	43.5	54.1	21.4
High		25.9	19.6	16.2	50.0
	Total	100.0%	100.0%	100.0%	100.0%
	N	(27)	(46)	(37)	(56)

Note: x^2 = 19.831; df = 6; p = .003; gamma = .179.

those of the elite who have been locked into a given position for more than ten years are most prone to score high on the exploitation factor. For respondents who have served in their posts ten years or less, the percentage at the medium level of interpersonal exploitation increases, although in none of the categories is there ever a majority found at the lowest levels. This is not surprising, inasmuch as a relatively high level of positive orientation toward manipulation is a sine qua non for elite membership. But of relevance for us is the fact that the elite who have achieved relative stability of tenure in their positions manifest higher percentages of manipulative responses. Rather than gaining a sense of permanence from their tenure and deprecating the role of the manipulative politician, the game of politics in Iran with all its interpersonal exploitation is supported to an increasing degree.

What is being suggested is that the members of the elite who have been least beset by the turmoil of the political system, as indicated by infrequent job changes, are most likely to manifest attitudes conducive to interpersonal manipulation. That is, they seem most likely to act the role of politician. But, in fact, they do not appear to do so. An overview of all four factors demonstrates this point.

THE GENERAL CHARACTER
ORIENTATION FACTORS: AN OVERVIEW

The four factors that we have already considered at length have been analyzed in terms of their component variables and their relationship to the social background factors. In the next chapter, their relationship to factors made up of political and social attitudes will be examined. Here, we turn to the relationship of the four character factors to data on elite communications patterns as well as to each other.

Elite respondents were asked the frequency of their conversations or discussions with eleven groups in Iranian society:

1. Officers of the Imperial Iranian Armed Forces
2. Big businessmen
3. Peasants or agricultural workers
4. Workers or laborers
5. Syndicate or labor leaders
6. University students
7. Members of the national police[61]
8. Foreigners
9. Members of the royal family
10. Religious leaders
11. Members of the present cabinet

The elite were presented with eight answer choices offering frequencies from "never" to "a few times per day." Correlation coefficients based on the extent of elite communications with each of the groups were then computed for each of the eleven groups for all 167 respondents. We wished to find out whether the eleven groups could be viewed as a single communication network from the viewpoint of the elite or whether subnetworks comprising particular groups existed.

Indeed, on the basis of common correlation coefficients, which represent the communication patterns of all of the elite with specific subgroups in the society, three identifiable subnetworks of the eleven groups emerged and one group appeared as the nexus of the three subnetworks. Figure 8.1 illustrates these identifiable groups. The networks are identified by lines based on the magnitude of the correlations among the groups. Taking the uppermost group as an example, the figure illustrates that those members of the elite who communicate frequently with union leaders are also very likely to communicate frequently with workers and are also likely to communicate with members of the business elite and with peasants. They are also very likely to communicate with members of the national police and somewhat less likely to communicate with officers of the armed forces.

The second major grouping indicates that those in the elite who communicate frequently with members of the royal family are very likely to

---

[61] The national police in Iran are responsible for a number of law enforcement duties which are dispersed among several agencies in the United States. Their duties include border patrol, passports, and customs; traffic and automobile supervision; the enforcement of the criminal law code; narcotics, food, and drug law administration; counterfeiting control; and certain aspects of state security and intelligence.

communicate frequently with members of the cabinet and officers of the armed forces. They are also apt to converse frequently with foreigners and somewhat less likely to communicate frequently with the national police. The third grouping indicates that the elite who converse with religious leaders are also very likely to converse with the national police and somewhat less likely, with students. Note that all the communications links among these groups that represent a correlation coefficient of .295 ($p < .001$) or greater are indicated.

Several interesting conclusions about Iranian politics are revealed by these subnetworks alone. It is clear that the national police bind together the major groups of Iranian society. Only one other group communicates directly with a group in a different subnetwork—the military. These agencies of repression are the sectors of the official bureaucracy which unify the major parts of the social structure. In that sense, these groups are responsible for transmitting downward the policies of the regime.

In the process, however, the police and the military are particularly unsuited for mobilizing the population behind those regime policies. In many other societies, these functions tend to be performed by political parties, their inherent advantage being that they are ideally suited to serve as two-way channels of communication, not only transmitting the policies of the regime to the masses but also aggregating the interests of the masses and articulating those interests to the government. Even the most unlikely political parties have demonstrated a capacity for these latter functions. The Republic People's party of Ataturk began to demonstrate this capacity early. The Communist party of the Soviet Union seems to be developing that capacity at present. But in no case have the police or armed forces been able to function as two-way channels.

The links that the national police possess also reveal the present security concern of the regime. Syndicate and union leaders are an especially important concern, for they are the officers of the officially sanctioned unions created as a challenge to Communist domination of organized labor or even a non-Communist but independent body of organized labor.[62] The ulema has proven to be especially troublesome to the regime and it remains one of the few, if not the only, organized or, at least, semiorganized, group that the regime has been unable to co-opt or thor-

[62] See the following on labor in Iran: George B. Baldwin, "Labor Problems in a Developing Economy," *Current History*, 37, no. 216 (1959): 91–95; and idem, *Planning and Development in Iran* (Baltimore: Johns Hopkins Press, 1967). For a review of this latter work see the author's review in the *American Political Science Review*, 62, no. 2 (June 1968): 645–47. See also International Labor Organization, "Evolution of Labor Legislation and Administration in Iran," *International Labor Review*, 69 (March 1959): 273–95; and U.S. Department of Labor, Bureau of Labor Statistics, Office of Labor Affairs, *Summary of the Labor Situation in Iran* (Washington, D.C.: U.S. Government Printing Office, 1955).

FIGURE 8.1

Communications Networks for the Elite

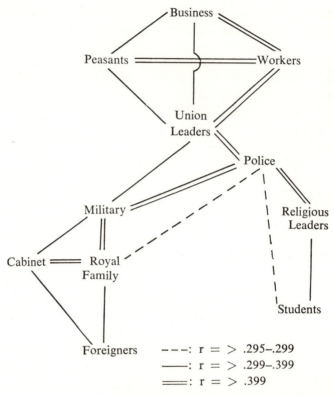

--- : r = > .295–.299
—— : r = > .299–.399
=== : r = > .399

oughly permeate. Because of this independence and their resulting reputation for rectitude, ulema members assume the role of the only independent group outside the official bureaucracies. And the ulema have
used that position to challenge the regime on a number of occasions:
land reform and the reputed rigging of the 1963 parliamentary elections
representing only two of their more serious challenges. If the regime's
charges of religious connections to the June 1963 riots are valid, then the
ulema are indeed a serious threat. No wonder, then, that they remain a
focus for police activities. That the police have direct communication
links with university students is also understandable in the context of
recent Iranian politics. Students at the University of Tehran have demonstrated on numerous occasions their fidelity to the ideals of Mohammad
Mossadegh and his National Front and a proportionately great resentment toward the regime. Many of the active leaders of the Front have
faculty and research appointments at the university and with the stu-

dents have participated in a number of serious and often violent demonstrations.

Finally, the ties between the royal family and the national police are of interest on two grounds. First, they lend credence to the notion that the Pahlavi princes and princesses are not the unified and closely knit family group that they claim to be. Their loyalty to their reigning sib is perpetually suspect and subject to scrutiny. Second, however, only the Pahlavis and the military of all the elite or governmental groups who would be expected to have frequent communications links with the police, do so. The ties of the military to the police are accountable on the basis of their common undertaking in security affairs. But the monarch prevents other elite groups from establishing communication links to the police for fear of the threat that would then result to his rule.

The communication links also reveal the fragmentation that exists in the society. A key elite subnetwork is made up of the Imperial Iranian Armed Forces, the cabinet, and foreigners, all linked together by the royal family (network M, C, R, F). A second subnetwork is composed of the economically productive group in the society—peasants, business leaders, workers, and union chiefs (network P, B, W, U). Finally, the ulema and students exist on the periphery of the political and economic sectors with links to each other and through the police to the remainder of the society (network R, S).[63]

When we turn from an examination of the relations internal to these sectors to an examination of their relation with the four factors, additional insights are produced. We ran the factors in zero order cross tabulations against the extent to which the elite communicated with each of

[63] Besides the internal composition of each sector, the frequency with which the elite reported conversing with each of the four groups is revealing. We calculated the mean number of responses for each of the sectors by combining responses for the appropriate groups (see table 8.b). Not surprisingly, but fortunately for the credibility of our data, the members of the political elite converse most frequently with members of the four groups which compose the more elite communication subnetwork. The ulema and students are communicated with the least.

TABLE 8.b

Mean Frequency of Reported Communication
Level with Each of the Three Subnetworks

Frequency	MCRF	PBWU	RS
Never	12.3	14.3	23.5
Once or twice	2.8	4.0	6.0
A few times/life	9.8	18.8	18.5
A few times/year	34.3	35.0	42.0
A few times/month	38.3	31.8	27.5
A few times/week	41.0	32.5	23.0
Every day	17.5	17.5	12.5
A few times/day	5.0	7.2	8.0

the three major communication subnetworks (see table 8.17). Irrespective of the significance level obtained in the cross tabulation, in every case the association was positive for the first three factors. That is, the higher the scores on these factors—the more insecurity, the more cyni-

TABLE 8.17

Direction of Relationship (+ or -) and Probability
of Obtaining the Chi Square Produced in a Cross
Tabulation of the Four Character Factors and
the Extent of Elite Communication with
each of the Communication Subnetworks

Subnetwork	Character Factor			
	Insecurity	Cynicism	Mistrust	Exploitation
M, C, R, F	+	+	+	-
	.05	.04	.04	.02
P, B, W, U	+	+	+	-
	n.s.	.12	.08	.25
R, S	+	+	+	-
	.005	.15	.04	n.s.

cism, the more mistrust—the more frequent the communication with all the subnetworks. Of these subnetworks, however, the most positive association was consistently found between the factors and the military, cabinet, foreigners, and the royal family.[64] This is consonant with our findings above: the more intimate the participation of the elite in the political system—here measured by frequency of communication with the most powerful groups in the communications subnetworks—the more likely are the members of the elite to manifest those general character orientations by which we have depicted them.

But what of interpersonal exploitation? Of the four factors, only this one bears a negative association—greater orientation toward manipulation is associated with lower communication. This is consonant with our original hypothesis of the incidence of these general orientations. For only those of the elite who are most firmly ensconced in their positions are isolated from the *sholugh-polugh* (moil and toil) of the political system. And their greater isolation is signified by their more infrequent communication with key groups in the society. That is, those members of the political elite who express orientations conducive to the exploitation or manipulation of others appear to hold positions that limit their ability to exercise such exploitation. They are structurally isolated from other key groups in the society. Not communicating with their countrymen, those with lengthy job tenure are not in a position to manipulate them to any great extent.

[64] As measured by the size of the statistic "gamma" derived from the cross-tabulation.

But what of the elite who do communicate with their countrymen? What of their ability to manipulate or exploit others? We have found that the greater the extent of elite participation in the Iranian political system, the more likely are those elite to be characterized by cynicism, insecurity, mistrust, and lower levels of exploitation.

Those of the elite who communicate frequently with key groups in the society do not indicate the character orientations of exploitation. We would hypothesize that the ability to manipulate others and the attitudes conducive to such manipulation imply and, indeed, necessitate relatively low levels of insecurity, cynicism, and mistrust. Individuals distinguished by high levels of these characteristics would be uninterested or incapable of interpersonal manipulation. The cynical person would not consider it worthwhile to manipulate others; he would be too contemptuous of other persons and too disparaging of the value of such behavior to engage in the manipulative relation. The insecure person would be too unsure of himself and his capabilities as well as too immersed in his own dissatisfactions and frustrations to step outside his own framework long enough to form a relationship in which manipulation might occur. The mistrustful would be incapable of calculating the responses of others as well as his own attitudes or responses. Unable to depend on his own or the responses of others, he cannot exploit them in ways that will achieve his ends. Those of the elite who are incapable of trust, security, and sincerity and commitment, are equally incapable of working with others in mutually beneficial relations or even in relationships that promise to be beneficial to at least one of the pair.[65]

Thus we would expect to find little exploitation among the Iranian elite as a whole. Those who demonstrate the character orientations conducive to such exploitation, i.e., low levels of cynicism, insecurity, and mistrust, and an orientation of manipulation, appear to be poorly located in the structure of the system for such behaviors. They are the isolates. But those of the elite who do communicate with their countrymen manifest those orientations that would limit their ability to exploit or manipulate others. In short, insofar as exploitation or manipulation are integral parts of "politics" as it has been defined in the West, the nature of "politics" in Iran would be expected to differ considerably.

In order to measure these relationships more adequately, the factor loadings produced in the principal components factor matrix were subjected to an oblique rotation, as well as to the varimax rotation. The resultant nonorthogonal loadings were then correlated; the results are

[65] Lucian W. Pye, in a discussion with the author, made a remark more perceptive than appeared at first sight. We were attempting to understand the failure of the long-heralded revolution to occur. After listening to the author's explanations, he exclaimed, "Why, they're just too incompetent to fall apart!"

shown in table 8.18. While all of these correlations do not reach levels of statistical significance, they are all in the expected direction. They demonstrate that higher levels of cynicism, mistrust, and insecurity are all positively associated with each other while negatively associated with

TABLE 8.18

Correlation of Factors Produced
in an Oblique Rotation

	Cynicism	Manifest Insecurity	Mistrust	Exploitation
Cynicism	x	.291	.078	-.108
Manifest Insecurity	.291	x	.103	-.080
Mistrust	.078	.103	x	-.277
Exploitation	-.108	-.080	-.277	x

exploitation. That is, the members of the elite who score highly on the cynicism factor are likely to have high scores on the manifest insecurity and mistrust factors as well. Similarly, they are likely to have low scores on the exploitation factor. The insecure, the cynical, the mistrustful fail to develop the psychic equipment necessary to play the game of politics as it is conventionally defined.

:9:

THE CONSEQUENCES OF ELITE ORIENTATIONS

Work requires knowledge and will,
the one without the other produces no honor.
Persian proverb

$\mathcal{T}$he internal composition of the general character orientations has been examined and their antecedents have been analyzed. But of more immediate import is their relevance. That is, do these orientations of manifest insecurity, cynicism, mistrust, and exploitation affect the more narrowly defined political attitudes of the elite? If these orientations that we have described do not affect elite policy perspectives, then we can assume that they are interesting, but largely irrelevant to the nature of Iranian politics, insofar as those politics are directed or influenced by the elite. In fact, these general orientations are highly relevant.

In order to examine their applicability, let us turn to the factors produced in yet another factor analysis, factors that have been labeled xenophobia, orientation to the shah, social disdain, family disdain, populist-nonelite orientation, and government disdain.[1] These factors are

[1] The factors were drawn from a standard principal components factor analysis on a selected array of 141 variables and then subjected to an orthogonal rotation approximating a simple structure varimax rotation. Sixteen factors were produced, which explained approximately 46 per cent of the total variance. The six factors that we have specified as reflecting more narrowly political concerns explained 14.9 per cent of the total variance, as follows:

		Percentage Variance Explained	Percentage Total Variance Explained
1.	Social disdain	3.3	7.2
2.	Xenophobia	3.0	6.4
3.	Populist	2.3	5.0
4.	Family disdain	2.3	5.0
5.	Government disdain	2.2	4.8
6.	Orientation to shah	1.8	3.8
		14.9	32.2

assumed to represent, by the nature of their component variables, less an indication of the general character orientation of the elite than indications of more manifest political attitudes, opinions, and beliefs. As the former set of factors may be considered to delineate elite orientations toward human nature and interpersonal relations at a rather abstract level, these latter factors tap the more mundane, but for our purposes, more relevant, political issues. Let us turn to these factors and their relation to the general character orientations.

XENOPHOBIA

The issue of the role of foreign governments in the domestic political process of Iran is central to the attitudes of the elite and nonelite to the present regime. In the late nineteenth century, Lord Curzon observed:

Perhaps a special sympathy is due a sovereign [Naser ed-Din Shah, who ruled from 1848 to 1896], the exigencies of whose rank and position render it almost impossible for him to receive the assistance which tried and independent counsellors can afford even to the wearer of a crown. . . . The foreign Ministers are probably almost the only source from which he learns facts as they are, or receives unvarnished, even if interested, advice.[2]

That the only source of reliable counseling on which the monarch could depend was the foreign ambassadors appears analogous to the situation as it exists to this day. The American and British diplomatic representatives still seem to constitute the most trusted advisers of the shah. But the ability of these foreigners to gain the ear of the monarch does not result in the greater regard of the population for either. On the contrary, the king is sometimes viewed as a tool of foreign governments, while the latter are viewed as continuously meddling in the internal affairs of an independent nation.

But this is by no means a recent development, having begun not with Naser ed-Din Shah, but centuries earlier. The first of what was to prove an interminable series of foreign interventions apparently began with the Sassanians. Chosroes II is reported to have gained his throne in A.D. 590 or 591 with the aid of "Byzantine troops sent by the Emperor Maurice against the usurper Bahram Chubin."[3] Once begun, the call for assist-

[2] Lord George N. Curzon, *Persia and the Persian Question*, 2 vols. (London: Longmans, Green and Co., 1892), 1: 401–402. He continues: "With the best intentions in the world for the undertaking of great plans and for the amelioration of his country, he has little or no control over the execution of an enterprise which has once passed out of his hands and has become the sport of corrupt and self-seeking officials. Half the money voted with his consent never reaches its destination, but sticks to every intervening pocket with which a professional ingenuity can bring it into a transient contact" (*ibid.*).

[3] Richard N. Frye, *The Heritage of Persia* (London: Wiedenfeld and Nicolson, 1962), p. 239.

ance to foreign powers—especially at the time of kingly succession—became common.

But their help was by no means restricted to the problems of succession. Shah Abbas called on the British for aid in driving the Portuguese from the trading center of Hormoz.[4] Later, Shah Tahmasp, who proclaimed himself king after the Afghan invasion of 1722, signed a treaty with Russia whereby he agreed to cede to Russia the Caspian provinces of Gilan, Mazandaran, and Gorgan as well as the towns of Baku and Darband in return for the expulsion of the Afghans and the restoration of his authority.[5]

In more recent times, the pace of foreign intervention has accelerated. When Fath Ali Shah died in 1834, for example, a three-way struggle for the throne developed. According to Lord Curzon, only because of "the inexhaustible energy and influence of Sir John Campbell, then British Minister and to the assistance of British officers [especially Sir Henry Lindsay Bethune] in command of the Persian troops," was Mohammad Shah, "the rightful heir," able to accede to the throne.[6] On the latter's death, in 1848, a series of rebellions broke out in major cities throughout the country, but the swift action of the British and Russian ministers helped Naser ed-Din achieve supreme power.[7]

All the subsequent monarchs of the Qajar dynasty benefitted to at least a similar extent by the willingness of the British to tip the scales of power in their favor at the time of a troubled accession. Even Reza Khan is not immune from charges of British favoritism in effecting the 1921 coup and subsequently mounting the throne in 1925. Harold Nicolson has put the case most elegantly: "After the collapse of Lord Curzon's Anglo-Persian treaty of 1919, it was evident that Persia was heading for complete disintegration; the only hope was that she could be renovated under strong leadership from within; Sir Percy [Sykes, then British minister at Tehran] rightly foresaw that Reza Khan was capable of such regeneration. And thus it came about that the Kajar Dynasty was deposed by the Majles."[8] And the present monarch, of course, came to power

---

[4] Curzon, *Persia*, 2: 390.

[5] Edward G. Browne, *A Literary History of Persia*, 4 vols. (Cambridge: Cambridge University Press, 1953), 4: 130.

[6] *Persia*, 1: 406. The other two claimants were Zillu's-Sultan and Farman-Farma, both of whose descendants have been active in Iranian politics to the present time.

[7] *Ibid.*

[8] *Friday Mornings, 1941–1944* (London: Constable, 1944), p. 7. Another observer notes: "The British cooperated with Reza Khan and Zia ed-Din, rendering every assistance to the former, and enabling him to collect some sort of an army from the ragtag and bobtail forces in Kasvin. Everything that they lacked in the way of arms and ammunition was found for them by the British" (F.A.C. Forbes-Leith, *Checkmate: Fighting Tradition in Central Persia* [London: George G. Harrop and Co., n.d.], p. 79). British State Papers reveal, moreover, that the British government was overwhelmingly favorable to Reza Khan and welcomed the

only with the grace of Britain and the Soviet Union then occupying Iran and responsible for Reza Shah's deposition.

But much of the intervention of foreign powers was occasioned not by the requests of Persian sovereigns for assistance in their internal political struggles, but rather by the international political concerns of those powers themselves. As early as the seventeenth century, numerous diplomatic missions were dispatched by various European countries to enlist Persian assistance against the Ottomans. It was hoped that Persian aggression in the East combined with European pressure from the West would so weaken the Ottomans as to eliminate their threat to Christendom.[9] Later, a much more compelling set of reasons arose for British interest in Iran: the defense of India. Both the India and Foreign offices viewed Iran as a bulwark against a land invasion of the empire. The English believed that it was "in the power of the sovereigns of that country to repress or assist the host of barbarians ready at all times to precipitate themselves on India as on a certain prey."[10] Having determined early that Persia guarded the only major overland invasion route to India, the next one hundred fifty years witnessed perpetual efforts on the part of the British to control Iran so as to eliminate it as such a route.

The intervention of the foreign powers took on all the elements of an intense wooing campaign, complete with all those gifts that are conventionally loaded on monarchs. One of the earliest of the English ministers, Sir John Brydges, told how he curried the favor of Fath Ali Shah in the early eighteenth century:

L'exhibition d'un beau diamant 'gage d'amitié du Roi d'Angleterre ainsi que d'une bonne quantité d'objets précieux et de monnaie sonnante destinés au Soverain et à son entourage influent appuyaient favorablement les allégations de l'astucieux Ambassadeur.[11]

---

coup. See Rohan Butler and J.P.T. Bury, *The Near and Middle East, January 1920–March 1921,* Documents on British Foreign Policy 1919–1939, 1st series, vol. 13 (London: Her Majesty's Stationery Office, 1963), pp. 735–37. It might also be noted that not until April 1921, three months after Seyyed Zia ed-Din and Reza Khan's coup, did the British remove their troops from Iran. More conclusive information awaits the publication of a manuscript on the coup by Seyyed Zia, who has given instructions that it not be published until his death. (Personal communication to the author, May 12, 1965.)

[9] Busbecq, Ferdinand's ambassador at the Court of Sulayman, is quoted as saying: " 'Tis only the Persian stands between us and ruin. The Turk would fain be upon us, but he keeps him back . . ." (Foster and Daniell, *Life and Letters of . . . Busbecq* [London: 1881], 221–22, quoted in Browne, *Literary History,* p. 11).

[10] From a dispatch by General Stuart in 1880 quoted in R. L. Greaves, *Persia and the Defence of India, 1884–1892* (London: University of London, Athlone Press, 1959), p. 24. See also a dispatch from the government of India to the secretary of state for India, in Council, dated September 21, 1899, as reproduced in W. Morgan Shuster, *The Strangling of Persia: A Record of European Diplomacy and Oriental Intrigue* (London: T. Fisher Unwin, 1912), p. 231.

[11] Ali Akbar Siassi, *La Perse au Contact de l'Occident* (Paris: E. Leroux, 1931), p. 638.

By this period, the campaign for influence in Iran was limited to Britain and Russia. From their compulsion and largesse, Iran was buffeted throughout the century, in the process sacrificing its most valuable assets to the foreign powers in the form of concessions. The rights to operate, control, and own telegraphs, banks, the issue of internal currency, railroads, mines, petroleum, customs, armed forces, tobacco, and fisheries were parceled out to the Russians or British or their subjects.[12]

The Constitutional Revolution can be viewed as the principal internal reaction to the ceding away of Iran's sovereignty. But that revolution against the Qajars, who had so abysmally managed the fortunes of their realm, was carried out with all the ambiguities common to Persian politics. For it was conducted with the material assistance of the British government and its representatives in Tehran. This first of the Middle Eastern nationalist revolutions was made possible by the intervention of the British in allowing dissident merchants to encamp on the grounds of the summer embassy and by otherwise pressuring the Qajars. Thus was demonstrated a peculiar condition of Iranian nationalism, strains of which are still evident. Persia's ills are laid squarely at the feet of interventionist foreign governments. But simultaneously, foreign governments are somehow perceived as the principal and most efficacious means of altering that condition and preserving Iran's independence.[13]

But with the intrusion of foreign governments in its nationalist revolution, not surprisingly, foreign intervention did not cease.[14] The British, thereafter, advanced a monthly subsidy to the Qajars of 15,000 tomans per month.[15] The new Soviet government renounced all Tsarist concessions in Iran but proceeded to invade Iran and support secessionist movements.[16] While such overt intervention declined during the rule of

[12] For information on concessions in nineteenth-century Iran, see Eugene Aubin, *La Perse d'aujourd'hui* (Paris: A. Colin, 1908), p. 221; Nikki R. Keddie, *Religion and Rebellion in Iran: The Tobacco Protest of 1891–1892* (London: Frank Cass and Co., 1966); Siassi, *La Perse*; L. E. Frechtling, "The Reuter Concession in Persia," *Asiatic Review*, 34 (July 1938): 518–33; and Firuz Kazemzadeh, *Britain and Russia in Iran, 1864–1914* (New Haven: Yale University Press, 1968), pp. 148–385.

[13] For a similar position, see Richard W. Cottam, *Nationalism in Iran* (Pittsburgh: University of Pittsburgh Press, 1964), p. 212.

[14] The classic study of foreign intervention in the immediate postrevolutionary years is still Shuster, *Strangling of Persia*.

[15] Butler and Bury, *Near and Middle East*, pp. 538–39. After discussing the continuation of the subsidy, the report continues on that Ahmad Shah "is now thoroughly well disposed towards us and determined to work with us in his own rather odd way. Best method of keeping him in this frame of mind is to give him or obtain for him as much money as we can for that is what he loves most in the world."

[16] See Sepehr Zabih, *The Communist Movement in Iran* (Berkeley: University of California Press, 1966), esp. pp. 1–35; and George Lenczowski, *Russia and the West in Iran, 1918–1948: A Study in Big Power Rivalry* (Ithaca: Cornell University Press, 1949).

Reza Shah, the lightning destruction of the Iranian armed forces in 1941 was testament to the relative strength of Iran vis-à-vis her more powerful neighbors. Wartime occupation, the Kurdish and Azarbaijan separatist movements, the overthrow of Mossadegh, American, and, more recently, Soviet foreign aid are all well-known instances of contemporary foreign intervention and require no retelling here.

The legacy of such intervention, however, deserves careful analysis. Perhaps the single most salient political issue in contemporary Iran is the evaluation of these instances of foreign encroachment on Iranian sovereignty and their relevance for domestic politics. For while Iran, unlike her immediate neighbors, was able throughout recent history to maintain its independence, that independence has been but nominal. And while its neighbors have experienced unifying struggles for national identity and independence, Iran has not. The Mossadegh experiment is generally regarded as the Iranian analogue to other nations' independence struggles. But that was an unambiguous failure as the monarch was able to regain control and enhance his power. Thus Iran can boast of lengthy independence, but an independence in which foreign manipulation subverted the integrity of many domestic institutions while depriving the nation of a unifying struggle for national independence.

Unfortunately, the interviews on which this work is based were all conducted before the conclusion of the most important agreements with the Communist nations: the steel mill-gas pipeline and arms accords with the USSR and the barter trade agreements with the European bloc nations. Nonetheless, we doubt that these recent manifestations of Iranian independence from the United States have altered the basic attitudinal ambiguities of the elite toward foreign powers. And these ambiguities are profound. One member of the elite summed up the last several centuries of Iranian history as follows:

Whenever two external powers competed for influence in Iran, we were comfortable. When there were three or more foreign powers, or only one, we invariably have lost our comfort and peace. Those two powers, whether democratic or dictatorial, allowed us to deal with one and then the other. But the day when the third power arrived, most recently the United States, the government felt that the third power could save it from the other two, and the independence and integrity of Iran were destroyed. The leader of our country forgot us in his job of becoming a partisan of this third power.

It is not surprising, then, that with the lessening of Great Britain's role in the Middle East following World War II, and the subsequent predominance of the United States, the shah would make a move to restore Iran's position as a classic example of the buffer state by establishing closer ties to the Soviet Union. It is not surprising, too, that the United

States should be viewed with such mixed feelings. Another respondent expressed these ambiguities:

The United States spent billions of dollars in Iran and saved Iran from the chains of the USSR, but the people hate them. My opinion is the same as almost the entire nation. The United States imposed prime ministers on the king and the people; prime ministers with programs prepared in Washington with little knowledge of Iranian conditions. When the program proved unfeasible, the solution was to put aside the prime minister. Thus much of the cursing of the United States stems from prime ministers who are independent, arrogant, and inexperienced, and who derive their power from the support of the United States.[17]

These ambiguities extend most profoundly to policies as well as to personnel. Those of the monarch's policies that constitute social reforms are viewed as American inspired and directed, even by the elite who support them. Three such policies in particular are viewed as hothouse American transplants. The first and most castigated in periodic references in the press is the government's moves toward equalizing the distribution of wealth in Iran. In the questionnaire, members of the elite were given a list of ten issues and asked to rank them in order of importance. In terms of mean scores, "more nearly equalize the distribution of wealth" was the eighth issue. The only two issues considered less important were the suggestions that the government build houses for the poor (considered irrelevant in a land where building materials—sun dried or glazed bricks —are inexpensive) and that Iran reduce its foreign trade to strive for economic self-sufficiency (considered economically suicidal). There was little doubt that this was a U.S.-imposed issue. "Why," one member of the elite asked, "does America force this equalization of wealth upon us when it has great inequalities in its own country? This is communism."

A second major policy area that has enhanced the disaffection of the elite toward the United States is the effort to reduce corruption. From the shah's first trip to the United States in 1949 and his subsequent efforts to lessen corruption upon his return, the United States has been viewed as the prime mover behind his campaign. Only 4.8 per cent of the elite

[17] The prime ministers most consistently named as U.S. imposed were Ali Amini and Hassan Ali Mansur. Interestingly, a sizable number of the elite put Dr. Mossadegh in this category—a position which is similar to that taken by the USSR. One of the elite assured me that eight months before Mansur became prime minister, the director of AID informed the respondent that "Mansur was groomed for the premiership, was now ready for it, and should have the post." The respondent added, "I immediately wrote the then Prime Minister Alam to tell him that Mansur would be his successor." While the conclusion that the statement of the AID director meant that Mansur was imposed by the U.S. has dubious logical validity at best, such is the evidence on which most political conclusions in Iran are drawn.

agreed with the idea that "corruption in the government apparatus really isn't such a bad thing—it helps 'oil the wheels' of government and gets things done" (90 per cent disagreed, 78.4 per cent strongly disagreed). Yet despite this nearly unanimous view that corruption is not beneficial, most of the elite reacted violently to the suggestion that its elimination was essential. I was perpetually reminded that "an honest fool is not as good as a slightly corrupt man who can be controlled." But when challenged on the evils that corruption represents, many charged that: "Most of the corruption in government stems from foreigners. Our corruption does not come from people passing a tip to some third-rate government servant in order to get a license. No, the corruption stems from the foreign carpetbaggers who are here." The pressures to eliminate corruption, then, are judged to be American hypocrisy. For what the Americans propose to eliminate, according to many of the elite, is everyone else's corruption. Then the field will be open for American efforts.

The third of these policies attributed to American intervention is the land reform. While this issue is relatively popular, its inception is generally regarded as the handiwork of the United States AID mission and the American embassy. One of the critics of the program charged that:

Land reform is an example of the way everything is done in this country: with no prior investigation, no knowledge, no money, and no plans. One result is a drop in production. Another is the creation of conditions whereby the government must now deal with millions of landlords, the peasants, while before it dealt with a few thousand. Now when the crops are poor those millions of peasants will turn to the owner of them all, the shahanshah, rather than to their former landlords. But this was forced on us by the United States.

For all three of these policies, the relevant issue is not whether the elite are in favor or opposed. Nor is it the actual role of the United States in influencing Iran or the shah toward implementing such policies. Of greater significance is the tendency of the elite to lay responsibility for the major policies of their own government on the United States. The resultant psychic conflicts over national integrity and independence in the face of alleged foreign responsibility are perpetually troublesome. This is the case even when the charge of "foreign pressure" is leveled solely as a means of rationalizing a policy for which the individual policy maker wishes to avoid responsibility. That such a charge can be made and be accepted as at least minimally credible bespeaks the immense ambivalence of the elite toward their own country. Insofar as the feelings of these elite include as a significant component the efficacy, integrity, and independence of the nation, then such attitudes must be ambiguous, as well as ambivalent.

For the elite, His Imperial Majesty is the direct symbol of that ambivalence. His filling this role is based not solely on his responsibility for the policies of the government. It comes, instead, from his own complicated relation to foreigners and foreign governments. We have mentioned his consultations with foreign, and especially the British and American, ambassadors. But in addition, the monarch's connection to foreign, and particularly the American, governments is enhanced by the presence of large numbers of U.S. diplomats, military personnel, technical advisers, and the like; the massive U.S. financial and military assistance with all the concomitant tales of its being siphoned in corruption; the sometimes, almost slavish accession to U.S. foreign policy; the alleged role of the U.S. in overthrowing Mossadegh to return the shah his throne, etc. No wonder, then, that xenophobia in Iran has far-ranging connotations for domestic politics, connotations that imply dissatisfaction with the contemporary balance of political power within Iran.

In order to measure these attitudes in an indirect, but reliable, fashion, a ten-item index of xenophobia was designed. The index elicits elite attitudes to a variety of foreign influences that presently impinge on Iranian society and politics. In the factor analysis, all ten items loaded highly with one factor. Along with one other question, they constitute the xenophobia factor.

TABLE 9.1

Xenophobia Factor

Which of the following external influences on Iranian culture do you consider on the whole "very beneficial" or "somewhat beneficial" and which influences do you consider on the whole "very harmful" or "somewhat harmful" for Iran?

1.	Radio stations from other countries broadcasting to Iran	.546
2.	Books and magazines from abroad	.530
3.	Foreigners being allowed to live in Iran	.526
4.	Foreign films and television programs	.515
5.	Advertising from foreign countries trying to sell their products in Iran	.495
6.	The growing popularity of travel abroad	.476
7.	Iranian youth studying in foreign countries	.469
8.	Foreign economic assistance	.454
9.	Foreign military assistance	.452
10.	Maybe some minority groups do get treated in a prejudiced fashion, but that's no business of mine.	.343
11.	Foreign investments in Iran	.273

The ten items on the original xenophobia index, called foreign usefulness, were scored from one to nine, with lower scores indicating more
approving attitudes. Combining scores for the ten individual items
reveals that the respondents grouped at the lower, nonxenophobic end
of the scale.

TABLE 9.2
Elite Scores on Foreign
Usefulness Index

Scores	Percentage	Scores	Percentage
10-19	9.0	60-69	0.6
20-29	13.2	70-79	0.0
30-39	34.7	80-89	0.0
40-49	28.1	Don't know	
50-59	9.0	or no answer	5.4
		Total	100.0
		N	(167)

Among the ten items, there were appreciable differences in the extent
of elite approval, as is shown in table 9.3. Books and magazines from
abroad are highly valued by the elite. Only twenty-three of the elite
(13.8 per cent) did not regularly read such a publication. Half of the
elite reported that their primary source of news about international affairs was foreign media. The consumption of foreign news sources is so
prevalent that twenty-two of the elite (13.2 per cent) reported that the
foreign media serve as their principal source of news about Iranian
events. Another thirty-six individuals (21.6 per cent) reported foreign
publications as the second most important source for such news.

TABLE 9.3
Elite Responses to Items in the Foreign Usefulness Index,
by Percentage

Item	Very Beneficial	Somewhat Beneficial	Neither	Somewhat Harmful	Very Harmful	Not Applicable or Don't Know	Total
Books and magazines	55.7	31.7	4.8	1.2	0.0	6.6	100.0
Investments	43.7	35.9	2.4	9.0	1.2	7.8	100.0
Study abroad	41.3	34.1	3.6	12.6	3.0	7.8	100.0
Economic aid	37.7	35.9	8.4	8.4	2.4	7.2	100.0
Travel	36.5	35.3	7.2	12.6	2.4	6.0	100.0
Foreign residents	34.1	41.9	12.0	2.4	1.8	7.8	100.0
Military aid	28.1	36.5	4.2	7.2	6.6	17.4	100.0
Films and TV	16.8	28.7	12.6	26.9	4.2	10.8	100.0
Broadcasts	15.0	30.5	21.6	21.0	3.0	9.0	100.0
Advertising	9.0	29.9	22.8	25.1	6.6	6.6	100.0
							(N=167)

Study and travel outside Iran are also considered beneficial but have come under significant attack in recent years. Both represent immense drains on foreign currency reserves and both are considered the principal means whereby Iranians lose the best of their own culture. While travel has consciously been used for just this purpose—socialization into new life styles—many of the elite have come to feel that the only aspects of the exotic culture adopted are the most superficial and trivial. As one of the elite expressed it: "We go to Europe or America and send our youth to study there. Our people are mimics, but too often of the frivolities of your culture. They return having learned the latest Western fashions but not self-discipline, hard work, savings." As a result, there is mounting sentiment in Iran opposed both to sending students abroad, except in special circumstances, and to general tourism. Partly in reflection of this, the government imposed in 1965 a 10,000 rial tax ($133) on all Iranians leaving their country.

The most widely ill-considered foreign influences are films and television programs which have come under severe attack for allegedly teaching American-style sex and violence to the youth of Iran. A rather vast campaign was undertaken in Iran, including hostile speeches in the Majles, calling for banning of these Western products. Advertising, the second of these little valued influences, has never been subject to any public criticism. Elite comments indicate, however, that advertising by foreign companies is considered an attempt by foreigners to raid the Iranian economy and damage the growth of internal industry. The third of these, foreign broadcasting, has been the subject of much public concern and even of several official exchanges between the government of Iran and Communist governments. At least two clandestine radio stations are supported and operated in the USSR and bloc countries, stations whose sole content is antiregime and anti-American propaganda, broadcast primarily in Persian but also in other Iranian languages.

Finally there are a number of items reflecting intergovernmental relations. As a whole they tend to be viewed as less beneficial than most other items. The least beneficial of these is military aid. Here is an item of such intense importance to the regime that the number of "refused answer" responses was relatively very high.[18] Foreign residents are seen primarily as employees of foreign governments and are also relatively devalued. Only economic aid of all intergovernmental relations is found in the first five of these foreign influences.

[18] The attitude of many of the elite toward military aid is reminiscent of a quotation attributed to Naser ed-Din Shah. When he was counseled to modernize and reequip his armed forces, his reply was, "What does Persia want with rifles? Let England and Russia fight it out" (Donald Stuart, *The Struggle for Persia* [London: Methuen and Co., 1902], pp. 209–10). Indeed, it is arguable that the very military weakness of Persia was a major factor in her retaining independence.

On balance, then, it is clear that the elite cannot be considered generally xenophobic, although their aversion to foreign influences on the government is conspicuous. When we turn to subsectors of the elite, however, more interesting patterns emerge. Of the social background factors, only one bears any significant association with these attitudes. The age factor is inversely associated with xenophobia. The older the member of the elite, as measured by factor scores, the less the xenophobia ($x^2 = 14.810$; df $= 4$; p $= .005$; gamma $= .131$). Recall what variables made up the age factor. Primarily, the factor combined increasing age with more service in the Senate and the Majles and lower levels of education for both the respondent and his father. The relation of the two factors indicates that the younger and better educated of the elite are the most xenophobic. This relation holds even when we take into account another variable that is significantly associated with age—the amount of foreign travel experienced. There is no relationship between the amount of foreign travel and xenophobia, irrespective of age. The better educated, younger members of the elite most strongly bridle at the association of the shah with foreign governments and at the nearly pervasive intervention of foreigners in Iranian affairs.

When we turn to the association between the general character orientations and xenophobia, more telling results are produced. All four of these orientations are significantly related. The most startling is that association with manifest insecurity (see table 9.4). The entire agglomera-

TABLE 9.4

Xenophobia by Manifest Insecurity

Xenophobia	Manifest Insecurity		
	Low	Medium	High
Low	56.1%	27.3%	26.8%
Medium	36.6	40.0	26.8
High	7.3	32.7	46.4
Total	100.0%	100.0%	100.0%

Note: $x^2 = 20.568$; df $= 4$; p $< .001$; gamma $= .418$.

tion of variables that make up the manifest insecurity factor would suggest that the elite do displace their own insecurities within Iranian society onto distant, and safer, objects.[19] But this displacement in Iranian society

[19] See Herbert C. Kelman, ed., *International Behavior: A Social Psychological Analysis* (New York: Holt, Rinehart and Winston, 1965), for views on the operation of displacement in international politics. For a more theoretical treatment of displacement as it applies to conflict situations in general, see Lewis Coser, *The Functions of Social Conflict* (New York: Free Press, 1956), esp. pp. 40–48. Coser also gives a number of references to particular studies of displacement.

operates in a different fashion than would be expected. For by expressing dissatisfaction with the extent and nature of foreign involvements in Iran, the elite are also able to express their dissatisfactions with His Imperial Majesty. Here is a relatively safe means for criticizing domestic politics. For in the minds of most of the elite, the shah and foreign governments, especially the United States, but increasingly the Soviet Union, are intimately associated. Thus an attack on the policies of those governments in terms of their activities in Iran can be accepted as an expression of dissatisfaction with the king and his policies. Thus, rather than the phenomenon of displacement, as it is conventionally understood, the high xenophobia of the insecure represents a manifestation of a general hostility to all those forces viewed as responsible for the condition of politics in contemporary Iran.

ORIENTATION TO THE SHAH

That there is a general hostility to all such forces becomes clear when we compare scores on the manifest insecurity factor with scores on another factor encompassing political attitudes, a factor entitled orientation to the shah.

TABLE 9.5

Orientation to the Shah

1.	Number of references to His Imperial Majesty made in answering the question of changes in the Iranian way of life	.503
2.	Assuming you were to lose your present occupational position, in that case do you think that you would also lose your present position in Iranian society?	.445
3.	Concerning your personal future: would you say that in general you feel enthusiastic, hopeful, anxious, or embittered?	.383
4.	Do you ordinarily like to be with people rather than alone?	.316

We have already mentioned the question that asked the elite to state what they thought to be the most striking changes in the Iranian way of life since the end of World War II. In addition to coding the substantive responses to that question, we recorded the number of times in which each respondent mentioned the shah in any context regarding the changes. The number of references loaded most highly on the factor. What groups together are numerous references to the shah, the fear that one's social position is tied to one's occupational position, an optimistic

311

appraisal of one's future, and a desire to be with people rather than alone. On a post facto basis, what this factor appears to express is the realization that one's fate is tied to the shah. That is, the elite who are positively oriented to the shah retain thereby their optimism, especially because they are aware and undoubtedly fearful of losing their social status along with their occupational position (and failure to support the shah would probably result in such a loss).

Table 9.6 shows the results when orientation to the shah is run against the manifest insecurity factor. As expected on the basis of the alleged

TABLE 9.6

Orientation to the Shah
by Manifest Insecurity

Manifest Insecurity		Orientation to the Shah	
		Low	High
Low		39.6%	60.5%
High		60.4	39.5
	Total	100.0%	100.0%
	N	(91)	(76)

Note: Yates x^2 = 6.469; continuity corrected;
p = .01; gamma = -.402.

connection between foreign influences in Iran and the position of the shah, as insecurity is related to xenophobia, so it is related to orientation to the shah. The greater the antecedent insecurity, the greater the xenophobia and the less the positive orientation to the shah.[20] The more insecure the elite, the less is their attachment to the shah and the greater is their hostility to foreign influences, especially to the United States.

A social background characteristic of members of the elite that also plays a telling role in their attitudes toward the shah is foreign travel (see table 9.7). As the elite's foreign travel increases and as, concomitantly, their dissatisfactions with the Iranian political system mount, so do their disaffections with their monarch. This relationship disappears, however, when foreign travel is held constant and the attitudes conducive to negative orientations to the shah are varied. That is, foreign travel per se is not productive of this neglect or worse of the king; what

[20] Once again it will be noted that there is no necessity for these statements to have causal significance. It seems plausible that insecurity would result in greater dissatisfaction with domestic and foreign policy. It also seems plausible, however, that in a relatively authoritarian political system, policy dissatisfactions would conduce to fostering a sense of insecurity. We believe, however, that the causal flow is likely from the opposite direction. On this point see Gwynn E. Nettler and James R. Huffman, "Political Opinion and Personal Security," *Sociometry*, 20, no. 1 (1957): 57.

TABLE 9.7

Number of Years the Elite have Resided Outside
Irán by Orientation to the Shah, by Percentage

Orientation to Shah	Number of Years Abroad		
	0 - 4	>4 - 10	>10
High	45.3	27.3	24.2
Medium	34.0	25.0	30.6
Low	20.7	47.7	45.2
Total	100.0	100.0	100.0
N	(53)	(44)	(62)

Note: x^2 = 11.166; df = 4; p = .025; gamma = .294.

is so productive are the generalized orientations of insecurity, cynicism, and mistrust. Table 9.7 is included here because foreign travel is itself so conducive to the development of those attitudes. And despite regime attempts to limit general tourism, foreign travel is widespread and increasing for the political elite. The result can only be the nurturance of more orientations antithetical both to political development and to the security of His Imperial Majesty.

The relationships outlined here are unusual in that they cover the spectrum of all the elite. We have noted previously that the older the individual, the greater was the accompanying manifest insecurity; here we have shown the connection between insecurity and xenophobia. On the other hand, we have also argued here for the propensity of the younger, better educated of the elite to be xenophobic. What appears to be at work are multiple roots of xenophobia, roots that affect virtually the entire body of the elite.[21]

Cynicism and mistrust also relate significantly and positively to xenophobia.[22] The higher the level of cynicism, the greater the antiforeign feelings (x^2 = 17.633; df = 4; p = .002; gamma = − .320). A similar association exists for mistrust (x^2 = 30.889; df = 16; p = .01; gamma = − .251). Again, these are relationships explicable in terms of general dissatisfaction with the political system. But those of the elite who manifest high levels of exploitation also manifest low levels of xeno-

[21] In a multiple regression analysis, xenophobia, treated as an independent variable, was run against the four general character orientations and the social background variables (separately and in groups). The four orientations were most significantly correlated with xenophobia (manipulation was negatively correlated) when the social background variables of age and foreign exposure were held constant. In other words, at a given age level, the more the foreign exposure, the greater the insecurity, for example, and the greater the insecurity, the greater the xenophobia and the less the orientation to the shah.

[22] The association and correlation between cynicism and orientation to the shah is in the expected direction; the relation is inverse but does not reach significance levels.

phobia, as would be predicted from our understanding of those who can and do manipulate their fellows in the elite ($x^2 = 27.684$; df $= 16$; p $= .035$; gamma $= - .185$). Those of the elite who have enjoyed the longest tenure in their posts and have developed a propensity for manipulating others, manifest the least dissatisfaction with foreign influences and ipse dixit with the shah himself.

SOCIAL DISDAIN

A charge frequently leveled at politically active Iranians is their propensity for belittling the contributions of their fellows. The natural political counterpart to general orientations of cynicism and individualism would be a belief in the disutility of others and their service to society. It was felt that a reliable test of this phenomenon would have to go beyond an evaluation of other individuals, however, for in any highly competitive political system feelings of personal animosity would likely be present. Thus a more broad-gauge evaluatory scale would be required. To tap these attitudes, then, the elite were asked a series of questions about entire social, political, and occupational groups. These fell out in the orthogonal rotation in a factor labeled social disdain (see table 9.8).

In the original questionnaire, an evaluation of the contribution of ten groups was sought. Attitudes towards one group—the ulema—did not load highly on the factor. This group was the only one of the ten subject

TABLE 9.8

Social Disdain Factor

Please consider each of the following groups in Iranian society and indicate whether you think each group is performing a positive, negative, or neutral service for the country.

1.	University professors	.642
2.	The peasants	.629
3.	Judges	.626
4.	The police	.611
5.	The armed forces	.531
6.	Businessmen	.477
7.	Members of the Majles and Senate	.419
8.	Government officials	.388
9.	Those who inform the country through the press, radio, and television	.380
10.	Number of negative or unfavorable changes in the Iranian way of life since the end of World War II mentioned by the respondent	.438
11.	Estimate of the value to Iran of foreign economic assistance	.419
12.	Estimate of the value to Iran of foreign military assistance	.344
13.	Frequency of discussion of career and work affairs with spouse	.341

to general disapprobation. Some two-thirds of the elite felt that the ulema were performing a negative service for Iran—a rather conclusive demonstration of the fundamental bifurcation between the religious and political elite and a rationalization for the political campaign being waged against them. Inasmuch as the regime has been unsuccessful in mobilizing the religious elite for regime policies, the regime's response has been overwhelmingly negative, both against the ulema themselves and against religion per se (although this latter point is not one that would be conceded by the regime).

But how do the remaining groups fare? As a whole, remarkably well. The over-all attitudes of the elite are positive, while only two groups— the Majles and Senate and government officials—fail to win majority support for the positive nature of their contribution. But this is directly supportive of our original hypothesis. For while the elite are willing to concede to groups outside the political process, the same is not true for those within that process. And of all ten groups, only the two here are legitimately part of the political process. While university professors, the military, the employees of the mass media, judges, and police are entirely or in large measure employees of the government, the shah strives to exclude them totally from politics. In the Iranian context, of course, exclusion from politics means isolating those groups from the influence of anyone but the shah, not isolating them from political influence in toto. Their insulation leaves the administrative bureaucracy and the Parliament as the legitimate arena for politics. And these two groups are the least positively received of any of the groups within the factor.

The remaining items in the social disdain factor are loaded in such a fashion as to demonstrate positive attitudes not only to other groups in the society but also to more general aspects of the system. Those of the elite who feel positively toward other groups also report few negative changes since World War II, welcome foreign economic and military aid, and tend to discuss their careers with their spouses.

When we turn to the relationship of antecedent variables to social disdain we note that cynicism is most strongly associated with that set of attitudes (see table 9.9). The greater the cynicism, the greater is the social disdain.

FAMILY DISDAIN

In addition to the social disdain factor, another factor was generated that defined disdain for another significant set of referents for the respondents, their families (see table 9.10). While this factor has been partially dealt with above, we repeat it here for its immediate relevance to

TABLE 9.9

Cynicism by Social Disdain among
the Political Elite

Social Disdain	Cynicism		
	Low	Medium	High
Low	46.3%	32.0%	18.9%
Medium	44.4	32.0	34.0
High	34.4	36.0	47.2
Total	100.0%	100.0%	100.0%
N	(54)	(50)	(53)

Note: x^2 = 20.761; df = 4; p = .000; gamma = .436.

TABLE 9.10
Family Disdain

Frequency with which the respondent has discussed the
following topics with his spouse:

1.	The upbringing of his children	.657
2.	The education of his children	.646
3.	The family budget	.453
4.	Birth control	.386
5.	His career and occupational matters	.344
6.	Apart from your immediate family, is there anyone to whom you confide your most personal and important problems?	.367
7.	How old would you think a child had to be before he could be trusted with information on family finances?	.356

the issues we are now raising. The family disdain factor includes all the items originally conceptualized as a measure of family integration on the basis of intrafamilial communication. The factor also loads highly on variables that pertain to intra-familial trust and interpersonal trust. Little communication within the family, a disinclination to trust children with matters of family importance, at least until they are well into their twenties, and an absence of personal confidants outside the family are suggested as a common behavioral pattern among the elite.

As with xenophobia and social disdain, so with family disdain. This latter factor also is positively and significantly related to cynicism (x^2 = 14.004; df = 4; p = .007). The elite manifest a rather universal contempt extending from their most intimate personal relations to others in the political process to foreigners. This recalls the charges brought against first-century, A.D., Greek cynics. "They despise everyone," a contemporary critic decried, "and call the man of good family effeminate, the low-born, poor spirited, the handsome man a debauchee, the ugly person simple minded, the rich covetous, and the poor greedy."[23] But while these attitudes of the Iranian political elite are reminiscent of the Greek cynics, they are in sharp contrast to the findings of much other research. It has frequently been argued, for example, that individuals displace their hostilities and aggression from proximate relationships on to distant, and presumably safer, objects. From his analysis of nonindustrialized societies, Robert A. LeVine has concluded that "there appears to be a correlation of internal solidarity, trust, and sociability with external hostility."[24] Our findings, on the contrary, suggest a correlation between internal solidarity, trust, and sociability with external solidarity, trust, and sociability.[25]

In the context of Iranian politics, it is this pervasive contemptuous and derisive view of other men—all other men—and interpersonal relations in general that serves as the attitudinal bulwark for the behavioral independence, or individualism, for which Iran is so justly renowned.[26] However, this individualism falls far short of the self-reliance and autonomy that the concept suggests to be the ideal in the West. Rather, it assumes the form of self-seeking behavior, reinforced by cynicism, mistrust, and insecurity, while restrained only by considerations of relative power.

But this individualism is not restricted to Iran. It appears to be a condition of much of the developing world. President Nasser, for example, recognized these same attitudes after the 1952 coup in Egypt:

If I were asked then what I required most, my instant answer would be, "To hear but one Egyptian uttering one word of justice about another, to see but one Egyptian not devoting his time to criticize willfully the ideas of another."

. . . Personal and persistent selfishness was the rule of the day. The word "I" was on every tongue. It was the magic solution of every difficulty and the effective cure for every malady.[27]

But as Nasser so quickly realized, these propensities are inimical to the very root of political development: the concerting of behaviors through

---

[23] Donald R. Dudley, *A History of Cynicism* (London: Methuen & Co., 1937), pp. 136–37, quoting *Dio Cassius*, 65.13.

[24] "Socialization, Social Structure and Intersocietal Images" in *International Behavior*, ed. Kelman, p. 68.

[25] The abundance of research findings and observations of developing societies which tend to support LeVine's conclusion must give pause to any effort to question them. An intensive re-examination of these relations was conducted with no change in results, however. A survey of the survey instrument was then made to seek to uncover other objects of displacement, but none were found. It appears that cynical, mistrustful, and insecure elite members in Iran do, in fact, display contemptuousness "across the board."

[26] See, for example, Norman Jacobs, *The Sociology of Development: Iran as an Asian Case Study*, Praeger Special Studies in International Economics and Development (New York: Praeger, 1966), pp. 252–53.

[27] Gamal Abdel Nasser, *The Philosophy of the Revolution* (Buffalo: Economica Books, 1959), p. 34.

the strengthening of organizations. Lucian W. Pye comments: "The development of effective organizations depends fundamentally upon the capacity of individuals to associate with each other. This capacity calls into question a wide range of basic human values and the ability of individuals to make commitments—commitments as to the goals and purposes of group action, the means and spirit of associational relationships, the appropriate limits of such associations and the integrity of the self."[28] Yet when we asked the members of the elite what they would do if the government of Iran were contemplating an action that they considered harmful or unjust, only one respondent suggested that any type of organized, group activity—either through a political party or the Parliament—would be appropriate. (And that respondent was one of the half dozen women in the panel of respondents![29])

Even more telling were the responses indicating what the elite would do in response to unjust or harmful government treatment. Their responses were significantly associated with levels of cynicism, mistrust, and insecurity and conversely with exploitation. Table 9.11 examines

TABLE 9.11

Reported Behavior Contemplated by the Elite in
Response to Unjust or Harmful Government
Proposals, by Cynicism

Proposed Behavior	Cynicism			
	High	Medium High	Medium Low	Low
Nothing	65.2%	44.4%	42.1%	3.3%
Some action	34.8	55.6	57.9	96.7
Total	100.0%	100.0%	100.0%	100.0%
N	(23)	(18)	(19)	(30)

Note: x^2 = 23.499; df = 4; p = 0.000; gamma = .659.

elite responses as related to cynicism. Nearly two-thirds of the most cynical would do nothing if the government were contemplating a harmful action. Only 3.3 per cent (1) of the least cynical would so respond.

This policy of behavioral inaction by the political elite in the face of prospective injustice constitutes a clear instance of the operationalization of cynicism, insecurity, and mistrust. In all likelihood, the proposed measure would be enacted; its probable personal consequences would be assessed by each of the elite, and if judged personally harmful, some

[28] *Politics, Personality, and Nation Building: Burma's Search for Identity* (New Haven: Yale University Press, 1962), p. 39.

[29] To respond to this point with the charge that the government considers group action in opposition to its policies as anathema is to beg the question of the paucity of meaningful group action of any kind in Iran.

attempt to evade or divert the measure would be made. But no confrontation would be risked, no group or even individual action considered. For that type of response would require psychic equipment beyond the grasp of these members of the elite. The minimal levels of trust, security, and sincerity which make manipulation possible, the basic tools in trade of politicians in every society, are generally absent in Iran. As a result, the political response would be post facto and personal, with the effect that the outputs of the Iranian political system are rarely predictable and usually remote from prior expectations.

GOVERNMENT DISDAIN

A set of ten policies that were being pursued or discussed by the government at the time of the survey were presented to the elite for their evaluation. Of the ten, one loaded highly, and the thrust of that policy has been used to identify this factor—the government disdain factor.

TABLE 9.12

Government Disdain Factor

1.	Dissolving government-owned monopolies is an important policy worthy of implementation	.479
2.	Government officials are performing a rather harmful service for the country	.454
3.	It's no use getting upset and concerned about broad political issues and public affairs; people like me really can't do anything about them anyway	.437
4.	That person, living or dead, in all the world who is most respected by the respondent	.423
5.	I don't think that really powerful public officials and politicians care much what people like me think	.371
6.	Second most respected person, living or dead	.321

That single policy of the ten issues that loads on this factor urges that the government disband its monopolies in the economy. This has been an important issue in Iran for several years, having its roots in the period of Reza Shah's rule. For the indigenous bourgeoisie were first presented with the conditions for strengthening their role in Iran's economic life by Reza Shah. He centralized the country's administration, established security, built railroads and highways, expanded the secular education system, and established a university.[30] The wartime occupation of Iran by the Allies added impetus to their growth by providing new oppor-

[30] Mohammad Zavosh, "Why Is Iran Industrially Backward?" *Economic Reports*, Echo of Iran Press, no. 11 (December 1961), esp. pp. 1–5.

tunities for profit. These were not lost on Iranian businessmen.[31] With the beginning of United States economic aid after the war and the resumption of oil production after the overthrow of Mossadegh, the private sector experienced phenomenal growth, growth that devasted foreign exchange reserves and led to the economic slowdown of the early 1960s.[32]

But by this period, a new factor became significant in the contribution of the private sector toward economic development. The ownership of agricultural land had lost some of its previous luster. Partly as a result of the opportunities for gain in light industry and importing, but more from the gathering government momentum to effect land reform, capital began to flow from land in the countryside to urban land or to other parts of the economy.[33] The result was not only that the economy received a much needed fillip, but that the ex-landlords, recently recruited to the side of the bourgeoisie, made demands on the government seeking a loosening of government control over the economy. This control not only consisted of the usual customs and tariff rates, foreign exchange regulations, taxes and licenses, but involved outright government ownership of the major industrial units throughout virtually all sectors of the economy. Textiles, sugar refining, etc. are the major productive parts of the economy, and the lion's share of their capacity was claimed by the government.[34]

The demands for foreign exchange, government subsidies, and the like continued. But now demands of a different type were being voiced:

In this economy, all roads lead to the State. The State produces textiles, shoes, canned fruit, chairs, desks, wire, and even poultry. The State is a businessman, dealing in sugar, paper, automobiles, oil, typewriters, and even cosmetics. The State is a farmer and a fisher; the State is a dairyman selling milk and eggs, the Government breeds cattle, it operates bakeries and groceries.

When we talk of the Government, we do not refer to the cabinet, but to the Administration. They oppose the transfer of the State monopolies to the people. It obstructs this as long as it can and then it spoils the whole thing . . .[35]

[31] For insight into the economic opportunities during this period, see Arthur C. Millspaugh, *Americans in Persia* (Washington, D.C.: Brookings Institution, 1946).

[32] This is the gist of George B. Baldwin's analysis in *Planning and Development in Iran* (Baltimore: Johns Hopkins Press, 1967).

[33] This assertion, which is, in fact, being advanced in the form of a hypothesis, has also been made by Peter Avery in a communication with the author, March 6, 1968.

[34] Ministry of Interior, Department of Public Statistics, *Amare Namaye Mossavar Ba'azi az Fa'aliatha va Pishrafthaye Keshvar dar Salhaye Akhir* [Illustrated statistics of internal activities and progress in recent years] (Tehran, 1961).

[35] Dr. B. Shari'at, "State or Free Enterprise," *Tehran Economist*, March 5, 1965. This editorial occasioned a good deal of debate, for it seems actually to have been

And, surprisingly, these demands received the sympathetic attention of the cabinet. In his first major economic address to the Majles, the then Prime Minister Mansur declared that "one of our guiding principles is to transfer the affairs of the people to the people themselves . . . which has amounted to the Government relinquishing its commercial and profit making operations."[36]

In practice, the government grouped together a large number of industrial enterprises in a government-owned factories corporation. Shares in this corporation were then sold to the public or exchanged for land reform vouchers.[37] But this came too late with too little and the debate over government monopolies continued, its intensity revealed by the position of the item in the factor.

The second item grouped on the factor mirrored respondents' attitudes toward government officials. Members of the elite who urged the dissolution of government monopolies considered these same officials to be harmful for the welfare of the country. When the elite were asked to specify persons whom they most respected, these respondents invariably chose persons long since dead. Their reference figures were no contemporary political figures—like Reza Shah Kabir or even the present shah, not Taghizadeh or Mossadegh. Nor did they mention contemporary literary figures or foreigners. Kasravi and Sadegh Hedayat, Kennedy and de Gaulle were infrequently mentioned by them. These elite reverted to the more distant past for their reference figures. Shah Abbas, Darius, or Cyrus; Mohammad the Prophet or Ali, his son-in-law, even Jesus or Moses; non-Iranians such as Lincoln; and, of course, the great Iranian poets, Hafez, Sa'adi, and Ferdowsi—these were the reference figures for those with high scores on the factor. Invariably their dissatisfaction with contemporary politics was reflected in their inability to specify contemporary figures as worthy of respect or admiration.

---

ghostwritten by one of the most powerful of the private industrialists, Eng. Taleghani, one-time minister of agriculture, then director of the B. F. Goodrich Factory in Iran.

[36] Hassan Ali Mansur, "Iran's Program for Economic Prosperity," *Facts About Iran*, Iranian Ministry of Information, no. 191, April 30, 1964, p. 15. Mansur, who had a penchant for offending people, also said in that speech: "The Government, under the law, can take any action it desires against private companies" (*ibid.*, p. 16). There was little understanding of the specific law to which he was referring.

[37] While this move was clearly not satisfactory to the private sector, it was unusual in comparison with most of the developing nations. Several reasons can be advanced to explain the government's action. It is generally conceded that the GOF Corporation was composed overwhelmingly of the least profitable public enterprises. Secondly, distribution of ownership in GOF to landlords would eliminate future demands for payment of their land reform vouchers. Thirdly, it was widely rumored that while the corporation was formed, it had been dragging its feet and offered but few shares to the public, its principal function being a propagandistic one.

Finally, two items that loaded highly on this factor refer to the elite's sense of mastery vis-à-vis the political process. Those who wished to dissolve the monopolies, who thought government officials were, on balance, harmful, and who turned to the past for reference figures—these respondents also felt the least sense of relevance to and control over the political process.

When we turn to the antecedents of this package of variables expressing disenchantment with the present political system, we find the strongest association with scores on the mistrust factor (see table 9.13). The

TABLE 9.13
Scores on the Mistrust Factor by Scores
on the Government Disdain Factor

Government Disdain	Mistrust	
	Low	High
Low	67.5%	36.7%
High	32.5	63.3
Total	100.0%	100.0%
N	(77)	(90)

Note: Yates x^2 = 14.608; continuity corrected; p = 0.000; gamma = .565.

elite who are mistrustful of others are the most eager to reduce the role of the government in Iranian life, apparently "to turn the affairs of the people over to the people." The same association exists with the other variables of insecurity and cynicism. As the elite manifest higher levels of these orientations, they report a progressively increasing tendency to wish the government ill, to lessen its impact on Iranian life, and to disperse political power more broadly from its present allocation.

POPULIST—NONELITE ORIENTATION

How broadly the elite choose to allocate political power is an issue not answered by the government disdain factor. For more insight, we need to turn to yet another of the political factors—the populist-nonelite factor (see table 9.14). Grouped here are a number of additional policies which members of the elite were asked to rank in terms of their importance for Iran. The effect generated by the issue of income equalization has already been mentioned. Many of the elite railed at the notion, associating it with American naiveté larded with Marxism. But its loading on this factor was to the contrary, implying support for the policy.

While those with high scores advocated government measures to reduce income disparities, they did not consider an increase in Iran's share

TABLE 9.14

Populist-Nonelite Factor

1.	The government should undertake policies whose result would be to equalize more nearly the distribution of wealth in Iran among individuals	.598
2.	Increasing the share which Iran derives from oil production is an important policy for the government to implement	.473
3.	That type of loyalty which is most important to teach a child in Iran	.428
4.	Iran's culture is so unique that it has always subverted would-be conquerors and "Iranized" them	.376
5.	Land reform should be accelerated	.324
6.	The civil service of Iran should be reformed	.319
7.	Foreign military assistance is, on balance, a harmful influence on Iranian society	.318

of the oil revenues to represent a salient issue. But why should elite oriented toward all the social and political changes in Iranian society implied by equalization of wealth not support a policy of increasing the wealth flowing to Iran? The explanation is rooted in recent political history. For a basic belief on the part of many of the elite and nonelite is that the oil revenues are the foundation on which the present system of politics maintains its stability. The oil revenues have not proved conducive to the types of social change that are advocated. Rather, they serve oppositely. For the massive oil revenues make possible the system of co-optation which we have described as the basic component of His Majesty's style of rule. And those revenues have been massive and continually increasing. From the resumption of oil production in 1954 to the present, Iran's total annual earnings in foreign exchange from petroleum have mounted nearly 2,200 per cent (see table 9.15). Since 1960, her total earnings from petroleum have been growing at an average rate of 15 per cent per annum. Revenues were flowing into the country at the rate of $755 million per year as of 1966. Since then, revenues have mounted sharply. With the stoppage of production in Arab crude oil following the June 1967 war with Israel and the mounting pressures that Iran has been applying to the consortium for increased production, Iran's oil revenues were by 1970 at an annual rate of slightly more than one billion dollars per year. But still more revenues were needed. In March of 1971, after lengthy negotiations in Tehran (significantly, presided over by the shah), all the Persian Gulf exporting nations signed a new agreement with the oil companies. The new agreement provides for vastly increased revenues. Prime Minister Hoveyda explained that "the his-

TABLE 9.15

Foreign Exchange Receipts from Oil,
1954-1970, $ Millions

Year	Oil Revenues	Purchases from:		Total	Annual Percentage Increase
		Oil Consortium	Other Oil Companies		
1954-55	$ 22	$ 12	$	$ 34	-
1955-56	92	47		139	318.80
1956-57	140	40		180	43.88
1957-58	208	48		256	42.22
1958-59	245	74	25	344	34.37
1959-60	261	77		338	- 1.74
1960-61	285	74		359	6.21
1961-62	291	100		391	8.91
1962-63	342	91	5	438	12.02
1963-64	388	81	2	471	7.53
1964-65	480	77	197	754	60.08
1965-66	514	76	23	613	- 18.70
1966-67	653	81	26	760	23.98
1967-68	752	83	23	858	12.89
1968-69	854	83	22	959	11.77

Source: Central Bank of Iran, Bulletin, 5, no. 30 (March - April 1967): 1088-89; vol. 6, no. 32 (July - August 1967): 276-77; vol. 9, no. 52 (Nov. - Dec. 1970): 470.

toric oil victory and other increases in the public revenues will permit us to expand the ordinary budget by 23% and the development budget by 30%."[38]

These immense revenues underlie the co-optation system, for His Imperial Majesty's chief means of co-optation are financial means. But of significance to the shah is not only the annual level of these revenues. Although they must be high, their absolute level is but part of the equation. In addition, these revenues must continually expand, just as do the expectations of the elite and their "needs." In order to continually satisfy these, His Majesty must see to it that oil revenues perpetually increase. Fortunately for his style of rule, he has been successful.

[38] Premier Amir Abbas Hoveyda's speech to the Majles while presenting the new budget. Pars News Agency, *News and Documents*, Vol. II, no. 49, March 1, 1971, p. 7. Such pressure for increased revenues is not new. "In an attempt to force the international oil consortium in Iran to make a dramatic 17 per cent increase in production, the Government of Iran is threatening to deprive the Western companies making up the group to forsake all or part of their exploration area" (Dana Adams Schmidt, "Iran Is Pressing the West on Oil," *New York Times*, Nov. 7, 1966, p. 43). Subsequently, the consortium agreed to relinquish virtually all its concession areas not then under production and to increase production by 14 per cent annually. But this soon proved inadequate for the shah and he began mounting new pressures on the consortium in 1966, pressures that have continued to the present. Even so, by late 1965, Iran's oil revenues amounted to "about half the government's running expenses and development spending" (Thomas F. Brady, "International Oil Group in Iran Lifts Output Fivefold in Decade," *New York Times*, Dec. 20, 1965, pp. 59-60).

But this very success explains the disinclination of certain of the elite respondents to press for increased oil revenues, as do so many of their peers. For they appreciate the relation between the increase of such revenues and the maintenance of the present distribution of power within Iran. One presented an extreme position when he argued: "What is the curse of Iran? The curse of Iran is its oil. Look at the greatness of the United Kingdom. That greatness originates in the fact that Great Britain has nothing." While most of the respondents would disagree with this view and with the "oil-less Iran" policy attributed (incorrectly) to Mossadegh, neither do they place a high priority on forcing those revenues upward, given their present use.

Another variable whose political meaning is similar to that of oil is the issue of military assistance from foreign nations. Such assistance is frequently perceived as not serving the purpose of helping Iran protect itself from foreign aggression, but rather as maintaining the power of the regime. This most crucial issue of contemporary politics in Iran was not one about which it was simple to allude in interviews. But oblique and telling criticisms of military assistance were frequently leveled. Comments such as, "Our armed forces are performing a positive service for Iran: they defend us against Afghanistan," were not rare. This item, then, loaded in a fashion similar to the issue of oil. Those of the elite with high scores on this factor held unfavorable attitudes toward the value of foreign military assistance.

Another set of variables loading on the populist-nonelite factor was the kinds of loyalty that the elite felt most important to teach a child. The types of loyalty from which they were asked to choose and the responses are listed in table 9.16. The choices were framed so that responses could be placed on a continuum of abstractness from universal, inclusive symbols (all Moslems, all Iranians) to parochial, exclusive symbols (the

TABLE 9.16
Type of Loyalty to Teach a Child for
the Iranian Elite

Type of Loyalty	First Choice	Second Choice
Loyalty to Islam	12.6%	5.4%
Loyalty to the nation	28.1	32.9
Loyalty to His Imperial Majesty	18.0	22.8
Loyalty to the profession or organization where he works	3.0	4.8
Loyalty to the family	6.6	7.8
Loyalty to the self	15.6	2.3
Other, no answer	16.1	24.0
Total	100.0%	100.0%
N	(167)	(167)

child's family, the child himself). Loadings of these answers on the factor indicate that those who are least disposed to accept the existing distribution of power (and of income) most favor the inculcation of universalistic symbols in their children. In other words, the definition of the community to which loyalty is due is broad rather than narrow, is universal rather than parochial, and is inclusive rather than exclusive—a very non-elitist approach to the polity and to interpersonal relations.

Two other policies whose implementation is accorded high priority according to their factor loadings are the acceleration of land reform and the reform of Iran's civil service. The former is clearly a policy with populist implications (even in the sense of Populism as it existed in the United States). The latter policy has similar implications. For civil service reform would undoubtedly produce two results. First, the efficiency of the administration would be enhanced. Consequently, the many policies of the government whose implementation would conduce to far-reaching changes in the social structure would stand a better chance of being implemented in fact. Second, the bureaucracy would serve less as a source of employment and an instrument for co-optation and more as the administrative organ for which it was originally designed.

The Populist-nonelite factor grouped a number of variables whose impact was that the government of Iran should pursue policies that would reduce disparities of wealth, speed land reform, and reform the civil service. Increased oil revenues and foreign military assistance are, on balance, not valuable. Finally, the political community should be as broadly defined as possible and, concomitantly, that definition is facilitated by a disinclination to view Iran's culture as unique. The orientation of these variables in the factor suggests that those of the elite who advocate a reduction in the sway of the government, according to the previous factor, would score highly on the populist-nonelite factor. But such is not the case.

The mistrustful, cynical, and insecure of the respondents deprecated the performance of the government and, accordingly, scored highly on the government disdain factor. But these same respondents had low scores on the populist-nonelite factor. In a regression analysis, the three general character orientations correlated with scores on the populist factor in this fashion (multiple $r = .313$; df $= 162$; $p = .001$). In other words, while these respondents wished to reduce the role of the government, they were not in favor of transferring that power to any other sector of the populace. As there was a general spill-over of disdain for other persons, so is there a general disaffection for government as it does exist and government as it might exist. One result is that these elite approach the essence of the Greek cynics in the modern-day inception of their political belief: anarchism. The principal difference is that these elite continue to operate in political life, their cynicism and mistrust feeding their insecurities and all serving to lessen their effectiveness as political actors while rationalizing their being co-opted.

These elite evince in certain surprising ways attitudes characteristic of major segments of the Iranian political opposition. We have discussed the unwillingness of the opposition to participate in Iranian politics in order to avoid the kind of co-optation that has befallen high-level government officials. Their stance recalls that of Bakunin, who argued that the capitalists hold their capital by the grace of the state (unlike Marx, who made an opposite argument). Bakunin concluded that inasmuch as, "the state is the main evil, nothing must be done which can keep the state . . . alive. Hence complete abstention from all politics. To commit a political act . . . would be a betrayal of principle."[39] But in a very definite sense, this is also the stance of the present elite. They would appear to salve the guilt of their "betrayal of principle" by maintaining the orientations that they do and by maximizing the material rewards that the system is so willing to offer them.

When we turn to those of the elite who do not evince cynicism and mistrust and the accompanying insecurity—those who score highly on the exploitation factor—we find different political attitudes. Those who can manipulate their fellows in the elite show little inclination to lessen the power of the government (see table 9.17). These same respondents

TABLE 9.17
Scores on the Exploitation Factor
by Scores on the
Government Disdain Factor

Government Disdain	Exploitation	
	Low	High
Low	40.5%	60.2%
High	59.5	39.8
Total	100.0%	100.0%
N	(79)	(88)

Note: Yates x^2 = 6.478; continuity corrected; p = .02; gamma = -.380.

see little cause to "return the affairs of the people to the people" and in that sense are the most "elitist" of the political elite. For their disinclination to disperse political power and increase reciprocity in the system is based on their own competence in dealing with the system, their lengthy

[39] Friedrich Engels in a letter to Theodore Cuno, London, January 24, 1872, in Karl Marx and Friedrich Engels, *Basic Writings on Politics and Philosophy*, ed. Lewis S. Feuer (Garden City, N. Y.: Doubleday and Co., 1959), p. 443.

tenure in their positions within and without the political system, and the sense of psychic security that they manifest. Not "a plague on all your houses," which is the message of the insecure and cynical, but rather, "a plague on only your house" seems to be the message of the exploitative.

In short, what appears to be operating among the political elite is a nearly universal disinclination to broaden the base of political participation. In this sense, the behavioral consequences of all four general character orientations are similar. Those of the elite who are relatively removed from day-to-day operations of the political process or those who have successfully mastered the art of manipulating others for their own benefit are disinclined to disperse power. They see no need to do so. On the other hand, those of the elite beset by insecurity, cynicism, and mistrust react by disparaging foreign influences, the shah, their fellow elite, other Iranians, and their families. They are disinclined to share political power with anyone and would seem to be characterized by a disaffection or alienation from the political process in general.[40]

With such intense feelings of hostility to politics by such a large segment of the most politically powerful actors, we may well ask why the political system has been immune from collapse. With these general orientations of insecurity, cynicism, and mistrust and the political attitudes of xenophobia, social disdain, family disdain, and government disdain, why has Iran not emulated so many of its Middle Eastern neighbors? Why has Iran been immune from the *coups d'état* and revolutions that seem to characterize so many developing nations? Why has the shah-

[40] In order to test the validity of these conclusions and to search for intervening variables which might offer alternative explanations for these relationships, a series of some two hundred regression analyses were computed. In each case, one of the six political factors was specified as the independent variable and a combination of general character orientations and social background factors were specified as the dependent variables. Two principal conclusions can be derived from these computations. First, for virtually every combination of variables, the general character orientations are better predictors of the political attitudes than are the social background variables. Second, even when controlling for any or all social background factors, the relationships between those general orientations and political attitudes continue to hold.

Within these general conclusions, several specific findings and qualifications need to be advanced: (1) cynicism and insecurity were the strongest predictors of the social disdain factor; (2) insecurity and mistrust were the most efficient predictors of xenophobia; (3) insecurity was the best predictor of orientation to the shah; (4) insecurity and mistrust were the best predictors of scores on the government disdain factor; (5) mistrust, insecurity, and age were the best predictors of family disdain; (6) activity level was the best predictor of scores on the populist-nonelite factor; (7) holding constant the factors of age, foreign exposure, occupation (private or government), and status in concert with insecurity and mistrust enhanced the predictive capability of the latter two variables for xenophobia; and (8) holding foreign exposure constant enhanced the predictive capability of insecurity for orientation to the shah and government disdain scores.

anshah been able to boast so correctly that Iran is a "sea of tranquillity and stability" in the midst of the world's political chaos?[41]

Fundamentally, the answer lies in the success of the monarch in creating a consensus among the political elite. Contrary to his efforts, however, the consensus revolves neither about his person nor about his policies. The consensus is rooted in a pervasive sense of the immutability of the system in the face of an equally pervasive sense of personal inefficacy on the part of the vast majority of the elite. Beset by personal insecurities, mistrustful of themselves and their fellows, and cynical about the motives of all persons and the outcomes of all programs, the elite respond by coping with the system, not by attempting to alter it in fundamental ways. And the process of coping consists, basically, of learning to operate within its norms while maximizing the benefits that can be derived from it.[42]

Such is the consensus that has been formulated. But while conducive to stability, the consensus is maintained only at great costs to the processes of political development in Iran. It is to these costs—the costs of politics in Iran—that we need, finally, to turn.

[41] These claims permeate the monarch's public utterances and may be found even more profusely in his new book, *Enghelabe Sefid* [The white revolution] (Tehran: Pahlavi Foundation, 1967).

[42] This point is similar to a conclusion of another study which bears striking similarities with my own. After his examination of the U.S. State Department, the author determined that: "The network of interconnected coercive processes [within the Department of State] creates a tight system with the ability to make individuals behave according to the system's demands. All participants now will experience the system as all-powerful and unchangeable. Although they may dislike the system, they will tend to feel a sense of helplessness and resignation about changing it" (Chris Argyris, *Some Causes of Organizational Ineffectiveness Within the Department of State*, Washington, D.C.: Department of State, Center for International Systems Research, Occasional Papers, no. 2, 1967, p. 33).

:10:

THE COSTS OF POLITICS IN IRAN

All problems of man stem from men;
all solutions, from understanding men.
Member of the Iranian elite

*T*homas Mann has argued that in
our century, destiny works itself out in political terms. In order to assess
the "working out" of "destiny" in Iran, we have turned to the political
process of that country. For politics in Iran does present opportunities
for the acquisition of those rewards that are available in Iran, rewards
in the Weberian sense of class, status, and political power. Whereas
these rewards are conventionally available from alternate areas of human
endeavor in other societies, in Iran they emanate almost exclusively from
the political process which thus becomes so much more central than
other areas.

And persuaded of the caveat of the elite respondent quoted above, it
seemed appropriate to examine Iran's political process through a study
of its political actors. But why, you may ask, study the political *elite*?
Tocqueville has provided us with one answer:

When the world was full of men of great importance and extreme insignifi-
cance, of great wealth and extreme poverty, of great learning and extreme
ignorance, I turned aside from the latter to fix my observations on the
former alone, who gratified my sympathies. But I admit that this gratification
arose from my own weakness: it is because I am unable to see at once all
that is around me that I am allowed thus to select and separate the objects
of my predilection from among so many others.[1]

[1] Alexis de Tocqueville, *Democracy in America*, 2 vols. (New York: Vintage
Books, 1945), 2: 350.

Iran, beset by the social change now characteristic of most nations, presents contrasts of this nature. Unable to grasp all aspects of this change in all parts of Iranian society, an analysis of only one area of society, the most politically powerful, was undertaken.

Once defined, it became necessary to locate these politically powerful individuals. Using a two-stage attributional method, 307 individuals were identified and labeled the political elite. Of this universe, 167 were interviewed with a detailed and lengthy questionnaire.

We found that the contemporary elite claim the highest degrees of formal Western education, counting many Ph.D.'s, Doctorates, and M.D.'s in their number. They are inordinately well traveled, having spent many years in residence outside their own country. Attuned to the West, they are well informed of developments in Europe and the United States, and are frequent and avid readers of Western publications.

In recent years, especially with the assumption to the premiership of the late Hassan Ali Mansur, the shah has broadened the base from which his elite are drawn. He has raised men to cabinet-level posts with few or no social connections to the traditional elite. As a result, he has successfully begun to alter the base of power from its traditional sources of wealth and social status to expertise and technical competence.[2] In the process, this democratizing of recruitment to positions of political power has served the shah well. For with a growing pool of technically educated Iranians from which to select his elite, he has enhanced his control over the political process. No longer need he feel constrained to select officials from the families of the traditional social elite. And no longer do the social elite have any claims for official position on the king.

But this process of democratization involved a key challenge to the traditional style of rule that the king had constructed. While the technically educated Iranians would be personally more dependent on the monarch for their power, and thus contribute to his control over politics in Iran, they have been the most vociferously critical of his rule in the past. That the shah has been successful in overcoming their criticism has been one of his finest achievements and a great contribution to the continuity and stability of his rule.

In essence, he has co-opted his former critics by making available to them rewards over whose distribution he maintains control.[3] The bases

---

[2] These are essentially the findings of the study by Howard J. Rotblat, "The Patterns of Recruitment into the Iranian Political Elite" (M.A. diss., University of Chicago, 1968). For a case with interesting parallels, cf. Lloyd A. Fallers, ed., *The King's Men: Leadership and Status in Buganda on the Eve of Independence* (London: Oxford University Press, 1964).

[3] An interesting and relevant anecdote exemplifies the co-optative style of the king. During an audience with a foreign visitor, the shah was asked whether he appreciated that the young men of the army's Literacy Corps were "subverting"

of class, status, and power are all within his province. He has dispatched those bases in a most effective fashion, with the result that he has silenced the opposition, withdrawn power from those over whom he had less control, and brought to power younger men who owe their present elevated positions entirely to the shah while placing their technical competence at the service of his rule.

But the very manner in which he has accomplished all this has had dysfunctional consequences for political development in Iran. It is generally acknowledged that kings "measure their friends and foes by the sole standard of expediency."[4] But the co-optative style of His Majesty carries this ancient practice to new levels. Two principal results accrue. First, the members of the elite have little independence of action vis-à-vis the shah. "In general, the fewer the rewards a society offers members of a particular group in the society, the more autonomous will the group prove to be with reference to the norms of that society."[5] The elite appear incapable of stepping outside their political roles to view the entire system with perspective.

Second, many of the elite who are being co-opted into the system were, at least in their student days, ardent critics of the regime. By acceding to the regime's efforts to recruit them to positions of power, the elite contribute to the markedly high levels of political cynicism that already exist in Iranian society. The opposition who formerly counted the newly co-opted elite as one of them, now must question the sincerity and motives of all their members. These defections from "outs" to "ins," so common in Iran, have debilitating effects on the efforts of members of the opposition to alter the style of His Majesty's rule.

But more importantly, acceding to co-optation contributes to the cynicism of the elite themselves. And it is cynicism, one of the principal general character orientations of the political elite, which takes such a heavy toll in Iranian politics. This propensity to discredit the sincerity and integrity of all human motivations and actions virtually forestalls the pos-

---

their pupils. "Don't worry," replied the shah. "We know just who those young men are and will be offering them high-level jobs as appropriate." (Related to the author by Dr. Israel T. Naamani, who was the foreign visitor.)

[4] Donald R. Dudley, *A History of Cynicism* (London: Methuen & Co., 1937), p. 76, quoting *Polybius*, ii, p. 48.

[5] Lee Rainwater, "Crucible of Identity" in *The Negro American*, ed. Talcott Parsons and Kenneth Clark (Boston: Beacon Press, 1966), p. 200, n. 5. In terms of an analogous form of co-optation, Walter Lippmann explained his decision to move from Washington, after decades of living there, to New York: "Cronyism is the curse of journalism. It is impossible for an objective newspaperman to be a friend of a President. Cronyism is a sure sign that something is wrong and that the public is not getting the whole journalistic truth. He [President Johnson] shouldn't be calling us up and asking us for advice. That sort of relationship is very corrupting" (*Washington Post*, Dec. 30, 1966).

sibility of concerting the behavior of the political elite in socially beneficial ways.

Once within the political elite and participating in the political process, the values of the system and the experiences undergone do nothing
to lessen the cynicism bred by the co-optative means of recruitment.
Rather, this cynical orientation is reinforced and others are introduced.
Insecurity and mistrust are the common plight of the elite. Meeting frustrations in their efforts to exercise their technical competence, subject to
frequent and unpredictable changes of position over which they have virtually no control, beset by a huge and amorphous bureaucracy which
even they cannot make respond, they react in a predictable fashion.

Those of the elite who are cynical, mistrusting, and insecure withdraw
from aggressiveness and in-fighting.[6] They get along by going along with
their superiors and with others who might conceivably one day be their
superiors. But since this latter group includes virtually the entire political
elite, active cooperation with everyone becomes impossible. Many in the
elite come to see themselves playing a role in which interpersonal relations within the elite are never ruffled, harmony being the main goal.

But the very artificiality of this resolution contributes to their frustration, their insecurity, and their cynicism. Indeed, a decidedly circular
process is at work here, so that the values and attitudes of these elite alter
their expectations from the political process and from others, which in
turn causes them to adjust their behavior in appropriate ways. In response, others behave toward them in ways that reinforce their original
values and expectations, confirming the wisdom of their initial behavior.

The elite themselves enjoy taking refuge in this type of analysis. An
avoidance of confrontation can be rationalized by reference to the profound complexity of cause and effect. Another of *mullah* Naser ed-Din's
exploits is advanced by them as supporting evidence:

"What is Fate?" Naser ed-Din was asked by a scholar.

"An endless succession of intertwined events each influencing the other."

"That is hardly a satisfactory answer. I believe in cause and effect," replied the scholar.

"Very well," said the Mullah. He pointed to a procession passing in the
street. "That man is being taken to be hanged. Is that because someone gave
him a silver piece and enabled him to buy the knife with which he committed the murder; or because someone saw him do it; or because someone
stopped him?"[7]

---

[6] A similar point is made by Chris Argyris, *Some Causes of Organizational Ineffectiveness Within the Department of State*, Washington, D. C.: Department of
State, Center for International Systems Research, Occasional Papers, no. 2, 1967,
pp. 8–9.

[7] Idries Shah, *The Exploits of the Incomparable Mulla Nasrudin* (London:
Jonathan Cape, 1966), p. 112.

Concomitant with their withdrawal from personal confrontation and their refuge in a sense of the complexity of the world, there is a flight from responsibility. Ann K. S. Lambton has argued that in the past Iranians had a sense of group responsibility stemming from the corporate nature of Iranian life.[8] Guilds, religious orders, *anjuman*s or *dowreh*s, sectors of the city, etc. all served as focuses for that responsibility. But with the destruction of those institutions as viable forces in Iranian society, the sense of group responsibility and loyalty was also destroyed.

Within the political elite, this lack of responsibility takes on an additional form. The system is highly conducive to the avoidance of assuming responsibility for any bureaucratic act. Conflicts are pushed ever higher in the bureaucracy for resolution. Still more committees and groups are created for decision making, but even they tend to assume ritualistic functions whose ceremonial contributions are far greater than their purposive contributions.

One result is a continued reinforcement of the tendencies of the elite to avoid challenging others and the system. Virtually no member of the elite can ever firmly attribute responsibility for any policy to any other member. To respond, then, would be virtually impossible. Far better to play it safe by coping with the system and agreeing with everyone about everything. If need be, the execution of the policy can be secretly subverted, but any attempt at a personal showdown would be disruptive, probably based on a miscalculation of the other relevant members of the elite, and, ultimately, likely to arouse the attention of His Imperial Majesty.[9]

This fear of coming to the attention of the monarch, especially in the guise of a disrupter of the political quietude, introduces the second major consequence of the flight from responsibility—the congruity between the interests of the elite and of His Imperial Majesty. The elite wish to minimize their role in decision making for fear of the consequences; the shah wishes to make the maximal number of decisions so as to maximize his control over the political process.

In an unusual sense, this process has reciprocal effects. Occasionally the secrecy inherent in the political system and the desire of the shah to husband control by personal decision making allows a member of the elite to act while attributing responsibility for that act to the king. This can be done directly or by claiming that the act is in accord with the shah's wishes. Like the charisma of Weber, which rests on belief in a gift of grace, these elite seek to cloak themselves in the mantle of kingly power. But this is at best a risky policy. For kingly retribution would be swift

[8] "Islamic Society in Persia" (Lecture delivered at School of Oriental and African Studies, University of London, March 9, 1954), p. 31.
[9] Cf. Argyris, *Department of State*, p. 33.

in coming were it brought to his attention. The shah seeks to strip his elite of responsibility for major acts while enhancing his own. A member of the elite individually making important decisions or especially decisions under the guise of the king's wishes approaches a *hubris* rarely tolerated.

Note also the extent to which it is in the interests of the shahanshah to maintain this flight from responsibility. Fred Riggs has noted that:

The more differentiated a system becomes, the more difficult and delicate becomes the task of coordinating the highly specialized roles. One of the major functions of the government for a differentiated system becomes precisely the task of assuring the reciprocal adjustment of highly interdependent structures. This task can be accomplished only in part by the voluntary co-operation of the interacting units, because it seems unavoidable that at certain points, their interests would diverge. Hence, there must be someone —some institutions or roles—standing outside the interdependent units to define "rules of the game" and assure their observance.[10]

The role that performs these functions in Iran, of course, is that filled by the monarch. As the political system in Iran becomes more differentiated and as the insecurity, cynicism, and mistrust of the elite enhance their tendencies to withdraw and avoid responsibility, so do the decision making and coordinating functions of the shah become greater. There is almost an inverse relation between the operations of the political process and the quality of the bureaucracy with the utility of the monarch.[11]

One result of this relation is the introduction of profound ambiguities into the processes of political development. For political modernization "involves the differentiation of new political functions . . . and autonomous, specialized, but subordinate organs arise to discharge those 'tasks.' "[12] The growth of these specialized functional subunits is very much in the interests of a monarch committed to social change as well as to political longevity. The proliferation of such units is perceived as contributing to the efficiency of the administration and to enhancing

[10] Fred W. Riggs, *Thailand: The Modernization of a Bureaucratic Polity* (Honolulu: East-West Center Press, 1966), p. 376.

[11] Cf. Tocqueville: "Despotism, which by its very nature is suspicious, sees in the separation among men the surest guarantee of its continuance, and it usually makes every effort to keep them separate. No vice of the human heart is so acceptable to it as selfishness: a despot easily forgives his subjects for not loving him, provided they do not love one another. He does not ask them to assist him in governing the state; it is enough that they do not aspire to govern it themselves. He stigmatizes as turbulent and unruly spirits those who would combine their exertions to promote the prosperity of the community; and, perverting the natural meaning of words, he applauds as good citizens those who have no sympathy for any but themselves" (*Democracy in America*, 2: 109).

[12] Samuel P. Huntington, "Political Modernization: America vs. Europe," *World Politics*, 18 (Oct. 1965–July 1966): 378.

opportunities for kingly control.[13] They also provide opportunities for greater numbers of personnel and, thus, more options for the exercise of royal co-optation. But the autonomy of these subunits, so vital to the very development process that he also seeks, is perceived as incompatible with the political control that the monarch cherishes.

The growth of functionally specific subunits within the bureaucracy is also very much to the interest of the political elite. They are very much aware of the commensurate increase in the number of prestigious new appointments that are opened. Moreover, these new sectors provide even greater opportunities to delay the making of decisions, to avoid responsibility and personal confrontation, and to force all of these—decision, confrontation, and responsibility—to the highest levels of the bureaucracy.[14]

In short, these members of the elite, beset by insecurity, cynicism, and mistrust, seem to react to their plight in ways similar to those of subordinates in other societies. Active resistance appears foolhardy and useless. But passive resistance can safely be used to restore one's self-esteem.[15] And in the Iranian context, that passive resistance takes several forms. Ceaseless vigilance is maintained in interpersonal relationships along with timidity and apprehension. Caution and conservatism mark their approach to innovation and political policy. Cooperation with others is unwise, for joint behavior represents both a direct threat and a loss of personal control. Independence in thinking is as unwise as independence in behavior. Any marked display of intelligence may single one out as too threatening. Gossip and rumor allow the legitimate expression of hostilities and aggression, by providing inside information they enhance the sense of efficacy, and participation in these informal networks of communication provides a sense of communality, otherwise so lacking. Finally, maximal efforts are devoted to the acquisition of material wealth, as a mainstay for the day when the elite member will fall from power and as a symbol of his own worth and independence from others of the elite and the vagaries of the political process.

We have also identified a subset of the contemporary elite who cannot be characterized by these general orientations. Manifesting relatively low

[13] Mannheim, for example, supports this notion. "The more elites there are in a society," he argues, "the more each individual elite tends to lose its function and influence as a leader, for they cancel each other out (Karl Mannheim, *Man and Society in an Age of Reconstruction* [London: Kegan Paul, 1946], p. 86).

[14] Cf. Argyris, *Department of State*, pp. 32-33.

[15] See John Dollard's *Caste and Class in a Southern Town* (New Haven: Yale University Press, 1937), for ways in which Negroes in the southern United States engaged in such passive resistance. Feigned ignorance and childishness, laziness, impulsivity, irresponsibility are all seen as such techniques.

levels of insecurity, mistrust, and cynicism, they bring a certain psychic strength to their interpersonal relations. Consequently, they are able to act in ways conventionally defined as political. Expecting their fellows in the elite to be manipulative, they respond in kind. Rather than avoidance and passive resistance, they too can manipulate and exercise their political skills in interpersonal confrontation. But these "politicians" exist rather at the periphery of the formal structures of the political process. If they have appointments within the governmental bureaucracy, they tend to be locked in, frequently having served for over ten years in their present positions. More likely, they are retired from government service and can survey Iranian politics from a safe and distant perspective. Or, they are not employed by the bureaucracy at all, being part of the private sector, but, nonetheless, exercise considerable political power. As a result, these more secure of the elite are atypical of the elite as a whole, who would be characterized by active formal involvement in the government bureaucracy with all the alterations of power and position which that implies. While those who manipulate would, undoubtedly, be more successful as the modernizing cadre required to effect the ambitious reform programs of the shah, they are not so strategically placed in the administration to make that role a feasible one for them.

The problems of governance in Iran are profound. Inefficiency is their hallmark; the general character orientations of the centrally placed political elite, their bulwark. An inability to predict, with surety, the behavior of others; a disbelief in the sincerity and integrity of others (and, in a real sense, of oneself); absence of cooperation and mutual interdependence; a flight from responsibility and decision making; and the pursuit of personalized, systematically nonsubstantive goals characterize the elite and their political system. The bureaucracy, principally charged with the task of implementing measures designed to move Iran closer to modernity and the more developed West, does not and cannot function in ways that will contribute in an appreciable degree to these goals.

Also, the human resources that must be part of the development process are not being mobilized. Just as there exists a fear of losing control and a mistrust of others, so there are fears of a broad-based involvement of the population at large in the processes of modernization. There is a disinclination to foster any widespread participation. So is there a disinclination to strengthen the organs of government most suitable for mass mobilization. The goals of political parties and their operations are highly suspect. Not only might they involve large sectors of the population that are now quiescent and thus capable of being ignored in the allocation of the large but nevertheless limited resources over which the regime has control, but those very parties perpetually threaten to channel demands upward, demands that would result in reciprocal influence and a loss of control by the pinnacle of elite power.

As a result, only superficial acknowledgement is accorded to the importance of political parties in the developmental processes. And stringent efforts are made to limit their bases of support and efficacy. Rather more attention is lavished on those reliable organs of the government that can be used for mobilization. The national police, the Imperial Iranian Armed Forces, and the State Security and Intelligence Organization have become the principal vehicles for elite communication with and conscription of the nonelite. But while these arms of the bureaucracy have demonstrated a capacity for the control of the populace, they have been considerably less successful in organizing that populace behind the modernization programs of the regime.

But the Iranian political elite is unable to serve as an effective modernizing cadre for yet another reason. For the elite are incapable of demonstrating the self-discipline required to carry out the ambitious proposals of the monarch. Organized largely to satisfy their own material aspirations, the elite cannot and do not desire to enforce the type of austerity required of them. As Fred Riggs has so perceptively noted in Thailand:

A bureaucratic polity . . . cannot impose a tight system of centralized control, as can a single party dictatorship. Such a control system requires that the state officials themselves be subjected to iron discipline so that they can be relied upon to carry out the unpleasant and arduous tasks imposed upon them by the ruling party. A bureaucratic polity, run in the interests of the state officials, is so self-indulgent that such discipline is impossible.[16]

While these elite appear too devoid of discipline to serve as effective leaders of modernization and while the very basis of a "political community" in Iran is buffeted by the insecurity, mistrust, and cynicism of its members, the regime has demonstrated an astounding capacity for survival and stability.[17] While monarchs and presidents throughout the Middle East and the developing world have been deposed or dismissed and political chaos has been rife, Iran does appear as an island of stability. From Egypt to Iraq, Algeria to Indonesia, neither royal blood nor political charisma have proved sufficient for the preservation of the ruler and his political stability.

The shah has pursued those goals and for the present and foreseeable

---

[16] *Thailand*, p. 379.

[17] For comments on the disintegration of the political community from the skepticism of its members, see Sebastian de Grazia, *The Political Community: A Study of Anomie* (Chicago: University of Chicago Press, 1963), p. 189; and Gaetano Mosca, *The Ruling Class* (New York: McGraw-Hill, 1939), chap. 2.

future has accomplished them. Four pillars of his style of rule have been major contributories to his success. First, the shah has been able to broaden the bases of political recruitment from the traditional elite alone to nonaristocratic aspirants to power. More widespread access to secondary, and especially higher, education has resulted in the acquisition, by nonaristocratic elements of the population, of technical educations which the shah has pressed into the service of his regime. Gaetano Mosca also saw the value of this recruitment process: "The best regimes, that is, those lasting a long time and able to avoid the violent convulsions which have plunged mankind into barbarism, are the mixed regimes. We call them mixed because in them neither the autocratic nor the liberal principle rules supreme, and the aristocratic tendency is tempered by a gradual, but continuous renewal of the ruling class, enabling it thus to absorb the better elements into its ranks."[18]

Second, the shah has been successful at recruiting the new aspirants to political power without in the process alienating any significant sector of the traditional, aristocratic elite. He has managed this by husbanding the immense oil revenues over which he has control while using them to markedly expand the bureaucracy. This has created sufficient new positions so that satisfying the aspirations of would-be elite members was not and, indeed, did not have to be done at the expense of the existing elite. In addition, immense resources have been expended in satisfying other elite aspirations. Luxury imports, automobiles, modern water and electricity systems for Tehran and major cities are all part of this latter concern.

Third, the shah has contributed to a breakdown of the sense of community of his elite. Along with the clash of traditional Iranian value systems and those from the West, the structure and operating procedures of the bureaucracy foster this breakdown, or anomie, as that term is used by de Grazia. That any decisive set of the politically relevant population could combine to effect his overthrow has been a negligible possibility since the fall of Mossadegh.

Finally, where all other means of political control have failed, the shah has not hesitated to reply with strength. Exile, house arrest, imprisonment, and other means for isolating dissident members of the elite from politics have all been part of His Majesty's political tools. All have been used, but only in a highly selective fashion and as a last resort.[19]

---

[18] "Storia della dotrine politiche," trans. by James Meisel and included as the supplement to the latter's *The Myth of the Ruling Class: Gaetano Mosca and the "Elite"* (Ann Arbor: University of Michigan Press, 1962), p. 390.

[19] Merle Kling has made the point that, "*Continuismo,* prolonged office holding by a strong *caudillo,* in its essence represents the reverse side of the shield of political instability. *Continuismo* signifies not the absence of political instability, but the effective suppression of potential and incipient rebellions by competing

But while the monarch has achieved the stability he so eagerly sought and in the process insured the preservation of his own throne, he and Iran have been forced to pay the costs. Tocqueville long issued the admonition:

I readily admit that public tranquility is a great good, but at the same time, I cannot forget that all nations have been enslaved by being kept in good order. Certainly it is not to be inferred that nations ought to despise public tranquility, but that state ought not to content them. A nation that asks nothing of its government but the maintenance of order is a slave at heart, the slave of its own well-being, awaiting only the hand that will bind it.[20]

We can see the fruition in Iran: a low priority assigned to the essential components of political and economic development; grossly inequitable distribution of resources; the development of attitudes and orientations conducive to stability but not to stable change, to order but not to orderly growth, to mobility but not to democracy, to tranquillity but not to legality.

And yet herein is not the ultimate irony. That term must be reserved for the present and future course of Iran's political life. For all the above were meant to be but the prelude to a different work. With the establishment of the preconditions by Reza Shah, Iran could be dragged into the twentieth century. Then under Mohammad Reza Shah those preconditions could be elaborated and refined for the transition to a national, developed, powerful, unified, democratic state.

But it is on this transition that Iran has foundered. The very policies and elite orientations that brought Iran to its present condition—a relatively admirable one in the context of much of the developing world—hinder its moving on to a new stage in its development. Political reform from the bottom up has become virtually impossible. But such reform from the top down, now referred to as the White Revolution, has become increasingly unattainable. For the political relations of the elite, the shah, the already mobilized segments of the population, the tribes and the peasantry have become more intractable as they have become more enduring. Like a commercial enterprise beset by threatening competition,

---

caudillos. Continuismo in fact may be regarded as perpetuation in office by means of a series of successful anticipatory revolts" (Merle Kling, "Towards a Theory of Power and Political Instability in Latin America" in *Political Change in Underdeveloped Countries: Nationalism and Communism*, ed. John H. Kautsky [New York: John Wiley and Sons, 1962]). While this interpretation alone is insufficient to explain the *continuismo* in Iran, it needs to be counted as one of the major explanatory variables.

[20] *Democracy in America*, 2: 150.

the government of Iran has responded by creating a cartel to insure its survival and profitability.[21]

But unlike monopolies, hedged by the tariff walls of beneficent governments, political systems cannot insure themselves against competition from abroad. Most especially is Iran incapable of doing so. The press of foreign values and life styles, of alien ideologies and conflicting norms, cannot be excluded from Iran as might the wares of foreign manufactories. And as long as that competition whose market is the mind bears on the ideologies, myths, and values of the present regime, its stability remains tenuous, and its power, problematic.

[21] Christopher Jencks, "Is the Public School Obsolete?" *The Public Interest*, no. 2, Winter 1966, pp. 18-27, makes this point and a number of others about urban, public school systems which are strikingly parallel to our analysis.

APPENDICES

BIBLIOGRAPHY

INDEX

APPENDIX I

IDENTIFYING THE POLITICAL ELITE

*O*ne problem that has long interested political scientists is the variance between the distribution of power according to the formal institutions and structures of government and its actual distribution in the political system. The majority of empirical studies of foreign elites have failed to confront this problem but have been content, with some efforts at rationalization, to assume that the holders of formal positions—be they legislators, cabinet members, political party members, or what have you—were in some way coterminous with the political elite.[1] The present study attempts to avoid this pitfall while hazarding the often problematic method of elite selection through a two-stage reputational analysis.

Preliminary investigations suggested that Iran is illustrative of those societies with a vast differential between the actual and formal distributions of power. To assume that this was not true for purposes of identify-

---

[1] See, for example, the following: George E. Schueller, "The Politburo" in *World Revolutionary Elites: Studies in Coercive Ideological Movements*, by Harold D. Lasswell and Daniel Lerner (Cambridge: M.I.T. Press, 1966), pp. 97–178 (a study of the members of the Politburo); Frederick W. Frey, *The Turkish Political Elite* (Cambridge: M.I.T. Press, 1965), (a study of members of the Turkish Parliament); Lester G. Seligman, *Leadership in a New Nation: Political Development in Israel* (New York: Atherton Press, 1964), (a study of members of the Israeli Knesset); and P. C. Lloyd, ed., *The New Elites of Tropical Africa* (London: Oxford University Press, 1966). In his introduction, Lloyd discloses that participants at the International African Institute's seminar "determined" that "the overwhelming majority of the elite of independent African states are in Government bureaucratic employment" (p. 7).

ing the political elite might result in a gross falsification of Iranian politics. Unfortunately, the nature of politics in Iran makes it impossible to pursue an issue analysis. Reliable information on the processes and participants in the making of key decisions is especially difficult to obtain: decisions attributed to politicians, civil servants, or other officials would denigrate the role and thus the aura of His Imperial Majesty, the Shahanshah. (But to accord sole importance to His Majesty would sully the purported democratic cast of the Iranian polity.)

Thus an investigation that attempts an empirical examination of the actual distribution of political power must do so through some other method. This study is based on one such method, a two-stage reputational analysis. A general elite was identified and the names of the members of this general elite offered to a panel of ten rankers, who attributed varying degrees of political power to each. Specifically, the following steps were undertaken.

On the assumption that the government is the central political institution in Iranian society, present and past holders of official positions were included in the general elite. Members and officeholders of organizations such as political parties, interest groups, etc., which have both formal and informal relationships with the government, were also included. Finally, the names of holders of various social, economic, or occupational positions in Iran, irrespective of any manifest link with the national political system, were added.[2] The categories whose members were arbitrarily considered members of the general elite are as follows:

1. All members of the Pahlavi dynasty, including spouses and ex-spouses, children, and in-laws
2. All ex-prime ministers
3. All ministers in all cabinets since the accession to the throne of His Imperial Majesty Mohammad Reza Shah in 1941
4. All deputy ministers, assistant ministers, director-generals, and department chiefs in all ministries during the tenure of the last three prime ministers (1961–1965)
5. All military officers holding positions of administrative or command responsibilities in the Imperial Iranian Armed Forces, gendarmerie, or national police during the tenure of the last three prime ministers
6. All directors, administrative officers, board members, and department directors in all government agencies and departments (i.e., nonministerial agencies at the national level: The Plan Organization, the Central Bank, the National Iranian Oil Company, the Department-General of Civil Aviation, the office of the prime minister, etc.) for the period 1961 to 1965

[2] These categories tend to conform and overlap with the eight base values specified by Lasswell in his elite studies. See Harold D. Lasswell, *Power and Personality* (New York: W. W. Norton, 1948), pp. 16–19; or idem, "Introduction: The Study of Political Elites" in *World Revolutionary Elites*, by Lasswell and Lerner, p. 8.

7. All provincial governors-general, governors, mayors of large cities, and department directors of major provincial administrative offices (1961–1965)
8. All officials of the Imperial Court, including secretaries, aides, civil and military adjutants to the various members of the royal family
9. All members of the twentieth and twenty-first sessions of the Majles (the lower house of Parliament) and the third and fourth sessions of the Senate
10. All committee chairmen and officers of the eighteenth and nineteenth sessions of the Majles and second session of the Senate
11. Politically influential or important members of all twenty-one sessions of the Majles and four sessions of the Senate
12. All present and past members of the Supreme Court of Iran
13. All heads of diplomatic missions (ambassadors, consuls general, cultural attachés) during the tenure of the last three prime ministers
14. Officers and members of the central committees or boards of all political parties (e.g., the Iran Novin party, the National Front, the *Mardom* party, the *Melliyun* party, the Pan-Iran party, the Socialist Front of Iran, the Tudeh [Communist] party of Iran, the Freedom Movement of Iran, the Iran party, etc.)
15. Political influentials not holding official governmental or political party affiliations
16. Chiefs and heads (khans, il-khans, il-beigis, etc.) of principal tribes
17. Leading merchants and businessmen as well as officers and board members of commercial organizations (e.g., the Chamber of Industry and Mines, the Chamber of Commerce of Iran, the Syndicate of Iranian Industries, etc.)
18. Directors of all labor guilds, syndicates, and unions
19. Directors, managers, and members of the boards of all private banks and major fiduciary institutions
20. Principal religious leaders (*Ayatollahs, mullahs, mojtahedin*)
21. Journalists who receive frequent by-lines in all Iranian publications, and publishers, editors, and managing directors of the press
22. Leading intellectuals and members of the Iranian Academy of Letters, the Cultural Council of Iran, etc.
23. Chancellors, deans, noted professors, members of university senates and the Central Council of Iranian Universities
24. Lawyers
25. Physicians
26. Engineers
27. Officers and directors of women's organizations, members of the High Council of Iranian Women's Organizations, etc.
28. Officers and members of boards of directors of Iranian-foreign cultural and friendship societies (e.g., Iran-American Society, Irano-Soviet Friendship Society, Goethe Institute, Iran-Pakistan Cultural Society, etc.)
29. Officers, directors, members of the board, of leading fraternal and social organizations (e.g., the Rotary Club, Lions Club, Iran Javan, Tehran Club, the Key Club, Gorgan Club, the Freemasons, etc.)

30. Leaders of *Zurkhaneh* [athletic organizations] and the fruit and vegetable bazaars, and important *choqu-keshan* (knifewielders)—leaders of semicriminal or criminal factions or gangs usually based in particular neighborhoods of major cities

Obtaining the names of members of the thirty categories often proved a difficult task. For certain of the categories (specifically categories 1 through 10, 12–13, 17–19, 22–23, 27–29), lists of appropriate individuals were available from Iranian encyclopedias, almanacs, yearbooks, or more frequently catalogs or records kept by the agency concerned. Thus, for example, the director of the Senate graciously made available to me his official lists giving committee assignments, officers, etc. for members of the Senate.

For the remainder of the categories, lists of names were either unavailable or inclusion of all the names relevant to that category was assumed to be inappropriate. As an example of the former—to my knowledge there is no one list stating the names of all religious leaders or even the principal ones. On the other hand, as an example of the latter, lists of names of all lawyers in Iran were available. But it appeared unlikely that all members of that profession could be considered members of a general elite.

For each of categories 11, 14–16, 20–21, 24–26, and 30, two methods were used to locate members of this general elite from within the given categories. On the one hand, names of officers of professional organizations were obtained when possible (lawyers, doctors, engineers, etc.). On the other hand, interviews were held with at least three individuals who would be considered not only members of that category but representative of diverse tendencies within that group, e.g., French- and American-educated lawyers were interviewed, as were pro- and antigovernment religious leaders. Each person interviewed was asked two questions: (1) "What are the names of those Iranian lawyers (or religious leaders or doctors or engineers, etc.) who are generally considered to be outstanding in the performance of their professional tasks?" and (2) "What are the names of those Iranian lawyers (or others) who are generally considered to be outstanding because of their alleged political power?"

The names acquired through these various methods were then added to lists acquired for other categories and checked for overlap. While no statistical analysis will be presented of individuals appearing in more than one of the thirty categories above, one example of such agglutination might be given. Dr. Manouchehr Eghbal appeared in the following categories:

1. One of Dr. Eghbal's daughters was at the time of the study married to His Highness Mahmud Reza Pahlavi, stepbrother of His Imperial Majesty,

2. Ex-prime minister, 1957 to 1960,
3. Held the posts of minister of Health, Education, Roads, Communications, Interior, P.T.T., and the Imperial Court, 1943 to 1950 and 1956,
6. Chairman of the board and general managing director of the National Iranian Oil Company, 1963 to present,
7. Governor-general of Azarbaijan,
8. Civil adjutant to His Imperial Majesty,
9. Elected to the Twentieth Majles,
10. Chairman, Health Committee, second session of the Senate,
11. Considered a politically influential member of the Majles and the Senate,
13. Ambassador to UNESCO, 1961,
14. Member, Central Committee, *Melliyun* party,
17. Member, board of directors, Chamber of Industry and Mines of Iran,
19. Member of the board, Iranian Development Bank,
23. Ex-chancellor of the University of Tehran, 1955 to 1957,
25. Considered a politically influential physician, M.D. degree, Paris, 1933, and
29. Officer, Rotary Club of Iran.

While Dr. Eghbal is an exceptionally active and successful member of the Iranian political elite, there were a vast number of other duplications and overlap. When these cases were eliminated, some 3,100 different individuals remained who were considered the general elite of present-day Iran.

The names of the 3,100 individuals who appeared in one or more of the thirty categories, and thus are considered members of the general elite, were then typed on file cards in preparation for power attribution by the panel of readers. The selection of individuals for this panel was based on the criteria that the members of the panel be as knowledgeable about the intricacies of Iranian politics as possible; be widely reputed to be men of integrity and truthfulness; be willing to cooperate and especially, able to devote sufficient time to the ranking process (which required up to forty hours); and represent diverse interests and political orientations (whatever their pretentions at objectivity, two panels of rankers, one group all partisans of the monarch and the other left-leaning intellectuals, would probably produce less than perfect consensus on the composition of the political elite). With these criteria as a guide, the following panel of ten was selected:

1. A newspaper publisher with a diverse and lengthy career in and out of Iranian politics. Known for his objectivity, he is nevertheless of strong personal opinions, but intimately acquainted with all aspects of Iranian politics.
2. A magazine editor and scholar. He is the author of numerous published and unpublished works on Iranian political and social institutions.

349

3. A member of the central committee of the National Front. He possesses a number of higher degrees from Iran and abroad. His refusal to accept proffered cabinet-level positions has reinforced his widely acclaimed reputation for integrity.

4. A professor in the Faculty of Law at the University of Tehran. An older man with lengthy service in a variety of capacities within and without the government, he is especially well versed in Iranian politics because of his wide-ranging family and social ties.

5. An ex-prime minister. He has over thirty-five years of experience in a majority of the most important posts in the Iranian government. His personal integrity and independence are widely acclaimed.

6. A professor of political science at the National University of Iran. While not personally involved in Iranian politics, he has had extensive professional training in the United States and has conducted perceptive research in Iran.

7. A journalist and long-time student of Iranian politics. His earlier fiery political career and equally cogent political analyses have earned him the enmity of the government censors, who now forbid the publication of his works.

8. An undersecretary of a government ministry. From an important family whose predecessors were key figures in the Constitutional Movement, this political activist is widely known and knowing.

9. A banker. Educated as a lawyer and now a practicing banker, he has a deep understanding of Iran's economy and the role of the private sector. His family is known for its professionals, poets, and politicians.

10. A foreign diplomat. The only non-Iranian ranker, this individual has years of diplomatic service throughout Iran and is recognized by Iranians as particularly sensitive, aware, and candid about their politics.

The panel members were individually visited and the nature of the project was explained, including the concepts of political power and political elite. They were then presented with the file cards bearing the names of the general elite and asked to assign a rating of political power to each individual. This they did by assigning the cards to one of four groups: "This man is politically very powerful in Iran today" (2); "This man is politically powerful in Iran today" (1); "This man is not politically very powerful in Iran today" (−1); "I don't know whether this man is or is not politically powerful in Iran today," or "I don't know who this man is" (0).

Weights were assigned to the four power groupings (as indicated in the parentheses above) and the thirty-one thousand rankings (ten members of the panel attributed power or the lack of power to 3,100 individuals) were arranged in a power scale, with scores of from 20 (all ten rankers considered the individual politically very powerful) to −10 (all ten rankers considered the individual not politically very powerful). The distribution of individuals receiving scores of 0 to 20 is shown in table i.1

TABLE I.1

Number of Members of the General Elite who
Received Political Power Attribution
Scores of Zero to Twenty

Power Rating Score	Number of Individuals		Cumulative Total
	Receiving Score	In Each Internal Score Category	
20	4	4	4
19	3	3	7
18	7	2/5	14
17	2	2	16
16	5	2/3	21
15	5	5	26
14	10	1/2/1/6	36
13	18	3/5/10	54
12	14	1/2/5/6	68
11	18	2/1/1/3/11	86
10	32	1/6/8/13/9	118
9	18	1/3/5/3/6	136
8	35	3/5/5/5/12/5	171
7	52	1/5/15/4/17/7	223
6	57	1/1/14/11/7/20/3	280
5	76	1/1/1/1/13/9/1/25/16/8	356
4	72		428
3	82		510
2	108		618
1	107		725
0	159		884

It was then decided to establish a cutoff point for delineating the political elite from the general elite on the basis of reputed political power. This was arbitrarily established at 10 per cent of the general elite. Thus, the first 310 individuals in the power hierarchy were considered to be the most politically powerful individuals in Iranian society at the time of the power attributions. The cutoff point accomplished one of our objectives in identifying the elite—differentiating the elite from the non-elite on the basis of the distribution of the value of political power.[3]

A second objective was to establish an internal differentiation among those identified as the most politically powerful individuals in Iranian society. This was accomplished in two ways. First, the elite were internally differentiated by the actual score received from assigned weightings (as indicated in column two of table I.1). Second, they were more distinctly differentiated by means of rank orderings within similar scoring categories. (Column three of table I.1 lists the distribution of the elite within identical score categories.) This differentiation within score categories was accomplished by listing elite with identical scores on the basis of the numbers of "politically very powerful" and "politically powerful" attributions received. For example, seven individuals received scores of 18. But the score of 18 could be achieved on the basis of

[3] The extent of my intellectual debt to Harold D. Lasswell can hardly be over-emphasized here.

351

nine "politically very powerful" ratings and one "don't know" $(9 \times 2 + 1 \times 0 = 18)$ or eight "politically very powerful" and two "politically powerful" ratings $(8 \times 2 + 2 \times 1 = 18)$. In actuality, two individuals received scores of 18 in the former method and five in the latter. The two individuals have been ranked first, for they received the highest number of "politically very powerful" ratings.

As the scores decrease, the number of permutations of ratings which will result in that score increases, as the table illustrates. Nonetheless, elite within each score category were ranked in a similar fashion, by listing individuals on the basis of the number of "very powerful" attributions received, then the number of "powerful" attributions received.

These 307 individuals[4] distinguished from their fellow Iranians then ranked internally—and distinguished from each other—were considered the elite universe and subject to intensive study.

[4] It was through this means for ranking within score categories that individuals were selected for the elite near the cutoff point. It will be noted that the cutoff point of 10 per cent of the general elite falls within the group of general elite with scores of 5 ($N = 76$). But a total of 280 individuals had already been selected for inclusion (individually with scores of 20 to 4). The problem was to select 30 of the elite from the group of 76 to constitute a total elite of 310 without doing violence to the ranking on the basis of attributed power. This was made possible by the methods outlined for ranking of elite within similar score categories. The chart indicates that identification of the 27 most powerful individuals with scores of 5 was accomplished through such internal rankings $(1 + 1 + 1 + 1 + 13 + 9 + 1$ individuals). These 27 individuals produced an elite total of 307 (280 + 27). Rather than select an additional three names at random from the next group of 25, the cutoff point was established for convenience after the seventh subcategory of the score category of five.

THE PHENOMENON OF NONRESPONSE

AMONG THE POLITICAL ELITE

$\mathcal{T}$he following is an analysis of the phenomenon of nonresponse in this study of the Iranian political elite, of whom 167 were actually interviewed in the period December 1964 to May 1965. One hundred and forty members of the universe, therefore, were nonrespondents and are the subject of this inquiry. Specifically, we wish to determine the biases, if any, introduced into the results of the elite interviews by the exclusion of the 140 nonrespondents.

NONRESPONSES BY POWER RANKING

The universe of 307 from which the respondents were drawn were given power rank orderings (PRO) of 1 to 307 with power and rank in an inverse relationship, i.e., the lower the PRO, the higher the reputed political power. Comparing the mean PRO of the 167 respondents and the 140 nonparticipants with the mean PRO of the universe, we find a spread of some 20 PRO between the respondents and the nonparticipants (see table II.1). Considering all respondents and all nonparticipants, we find that the latter group are reputedly politically more powerful.

We may consider the 307 members of the elite to be stratified into thirteen power clusters. A comparison of the PRO by such clusters gives the results in table II.2. We note that in only six of the thirteen clusters is the PRO lower for respondents than for nonparticipants. (It should be noted again that the lower the PRO, the higher the reputed political power.)

TABLE II.1

Mean PRO of Respondents and Nonrespondents

Respondents	Universe	Nonrespondents
163.6	152.3	143.7

TABLE II.2

Comparison of PRO of Respondents and
Nonparticipants by Cluster

PRO by Cluster	Number of Respondents	Average PRO/ Respondents	Number of Nonparticipants	Average PRO/ Nonparticipants
1-25	7	16.8	18	11.5
26-50	12	36.2	13	39.7
51-75	10	60.3	15	64.8
76-100	16	88.2	9	87.7
101-125	15	113.2	10	112.7
126-150	15	138.1	10	137.8
151-175	14	164.4	11	161.3
176-200	15	188.2	10	187.7
201-225	17	212.3	8	214.5
226-250	11	237.9	14	238.1
251-275	16	261.8	9	265.1
276-300	12	285.3	13	290.5
301-307	7	304.0	0	0
Universe total and average	167	163.6	140	143.7

Treating the response data among the 307 members of the universe in this gross fashion belies the availability of respondents. In fact, not all members of the universe were potential respondents. Because of problems of access, some seventy-five members of the elite had to be excluded from the universe.

EXCLUDED MEMBERS OF THE ELITE

Military. From the inception of this study, the probability of being able to interview, on a formal basis, highly placed officers in the Imperial Iranian Armed Forces was considered very low. Indeed, when the Shahanshah of Iran gave his official permission for the conduct of this study, the military was conspicuously absent from the list of groups sanctioned for interviewing. Despite repeated attempts to gain access to this group through other channels, no member of the elite whose primary occupations were in the military was ever available for formal questioning and, thus, must be considered members of the excluded elite. The average PRO of the twenty-nine military officers in the universe is 145.4, slightly more powerful than the average member of that universe.

Out of Iran. Some thirty-one members of the universe were discounted as potential respondents because of their residence outside Iran during the period of the interviews. Of these, twenty-four were serving the government of Iran in foreign posts, three were in exile, and four were undergoing medical treatment. The PRO averages of these three categories are 180.7, 141.3, and 281.0, respectively.

Jail or arrest. Six members of the political elite were either in jail or under house arrest during the period of interviewing. They all were serving sentences, usually of unspecified duration, for "political crimes against the state." Their average PRO is 153.1. Another six members of the elite had been released from incarceration within a period of twelve months preceding the interview period. Still politically inactive during the time of the survey, in their search for security through anonymity, they were also excluded from consideration (average PRO: 189.0). Some seven members of the "political opposition" who had not as recently served jail sentences did participate in the survey (PRO: 156.1). (Since my departure from Iran, two of the seven have been arrested for treason and are now being held incommunicado—for reasons unrelated to participation in this project.)

Illness or death. Two members of the political elite with an average PRO of 137.5 were ill and undergoing medical treatment during the entire interview period. One member of the elite, the late Prime Minister Hassan Ali Mansur (PRO: 6), was assassinated on the day before my scheduled interview appointment.

Thus, from the universe of 307 persons, seventy-five members of the Iranian political elite, with an average PRO of 158.5, were excluded from consideration as potential respondents because of their political or physical unavailability.

Who, then, were the remaining sixty-five of the elite who were neither interviewed nor excluded—the actual nonrespondents?

NONRESPONDENTS

Cabinet ministers. The following cabinet ministers were nonrespondents:

	PRO
Prime minister	32
Minister of foreign affairs	47
Minister of labor	49
Minister of state	66
Minister of state	90
Minister of state	91
Minister of state	149
Minister of education	177
Average PRO of nonrespondents in cabinet	87.6
Number of non-respondents in cabinet	8

The present prime minister of Iran, with a PRO of 32, was not the prime minister at the time the attributional power ratings were made. The then prime minister, PRO: 6, was subsequently assassinated in early 1965, and was replaced by the then minister of finance (PRO: 32) and present prime minister. All PRO given in this book represent attributions of power made in the year 1964. The position attributed to the given member of the elite, however, is the position held by that individual at the present time.

The following cabinet ministers were interviewed:

	PRO
Minister of economy	23
Minister of finance	31
Minister of culture	35
Minister of agriculture	36
Minister of interior	87
Minister of justice	88
Minister of development	92
Minister of state	125
Minister of water and power	258
Average PRO of responding ministers	86.1
Number of responding ministers	9

There is only a slight difference in the PRO averages of the two cabinet groups. The reasons interviews were not obtained with the excluded ministers suggest that no special biases were introduced.

The present prime minister, upon his accession to the prime ministership made vacant by the assassination of his closest personal friend, was too emotionally disturbed to grant interviews to anyone. Subsequently, he did grant some interviews to foreigners, but only to official persons.

The ministers of state who did not respond all worked directly for the office of the prime minister in the latter's suite of offices. The conditions applicable to the prime minister apply here also, with the additional factor that these ministers were the most burdened with the day-to-day business of the government during the transition period following the assassination.

The minister of foreign affairs granted me time for an interview on four different occasions, none of which were carried out. The four scheduled meetings and the reasons for their cancellation are as follows: (1) the day after the shooting of the late prime minister; (2) the day of the funeral of the late prime minister; (3) the day on which President Bourguiba of Tunisia, then visiting Iran, announced the cancellation of his scheduled visit to Iraq and extended his remaining stay in Iran by a week; and (4) the day after the attempt on the life of the shahanshah.

The minister of labor acceded while minister to the post of secretary-general of the ruling Iran Novin party upon the death of the prime minister. The demands on his time as a result of this new post in combination with the fact that he had no articulate policy for running the party made him loathe to grant interviews, especially to foreigners.

Senators. Ten of the bureaucrats or government personnel who were neither excluded elite nor respondents were members of the Senate. Their PRO average is 115.5. Aside from these nonrespondents in the Senate, thirty-nine senators with a PRO average of 137.5 were interviewed. The nonrespondent senators, therefore, tended to be politically more powerful than the respondents. My impression is that the ten nonrespondents were older, more conservative persons who felt more hostile to the group in ministerial positions, more hostile to the United States, who, they have assumed, forced the shah to accept these men as ministers, and basically more dissatisfied and frustrated than other senators. Fundamentally, their dissatisfaction stemmed from the fact that they, the more mature, experienced voices of wisdom, had been excluded from positions of administrative power by the younger technocrats and the latter's protectors, the United States. I was seen as a representative of this type of person and thus incurred their hostility.

Miscellaneous posts. The eight nonrespondent bureaucrats holding various jobs in the government civil service had a PRO average of 100.9. As their reputational PRO indicates, they tended to be more powerful than the average member of the universe. This is borne out by an examination of the positions represented:

1. Director, National Iranian Oil Company (NIOC)
2. Director, Central Bank of Iran
3. Director, Plan Organization
4. Director, National Bank of Iran
5. Deputy minister of finance
6. Governor-general, Gorgan Province
7. Member, board of directors, NIOC
8. Member, board of directors, NIOC

I would suggest that the four individuals filling directorships did not grant me an interview because I had already interviewed their deputy directors. I am quite certain from conversations with their appointments secretaries that the directors believed I obtained all the information possible on that organization's policies from the deputy directors and that an interview with the director himself would have been redundant. It was impossible to convince the nonrespondents that I was not interested in organizational policy, but rather personal attitudes.

Private and retired. A second major group of nonrespondents were persons in private business and those who had recently retired from government service and had begun to engage in private business or had remained idle. These fourteen individuals had a PRO average of 186.6. Of the fourteen, seven could be described as pure businessmen with no previous governmental connections (PRO: 229). Eight other pure businessmen (PRO: 179.2) were among the respondents. I would suggest that the willingness of the latter to be interviewed and the unwillingness of the former can be explained by the wide disparity in average reputed power. It is likely that the nonparticipation of the less powerful businessmen is a reflection of the same processes as are found among American businessmen who do not participate in politics, i.e., an unwillingness to jeopardize their profit-making potentials.

The other seven nonrespondents in this category (PRO: 151.3) were elderly men who were once active in politics but are no longer. Their collective approach might be summarized by the comments that one of them, who was about seventy years old, made when I walked into his living room to explain the project: "Do you know what the trouble with the world is today? The trouble with the world today is that it is being run by the young. They are running this country and the world to ruin. And I don't want to hear about or take part in your study because it is stupid. It has to be stupid—you're young."

Royal family. Eleven of the nonrespondents were members of the royal family (PRO: 104.4). As a whole, members of this group were reluctant to involve themselves in a situation whereby they might be asked for information, the giving of which would be demeaning or embarrassing or potentially embarrassing. The three members of the royal family (PRO: 63.7) who consented to a formal interview and completed the questionnaire have reputations as being among the more outspoken members of the Pahlavi family.

Religious leaders. Seven religious leaders (PRO: 93.0) indirectly declined to involve themselves in the interview. Six of these leaders are residing outside Tehran in other religious centers. To meet with them, one contacts their representative in the capital. These representatives are without exception extremely cautious and conservative. While receiving the usual infinite number of promises from these representatives, I also received ultimately no results. The religious leaders would not, except under unusual circumstances, meet with an American in any case. One of the three religious leaders who did consent to be interviewed is not only considerably less reputedly powerful (PRO: 198) but was a serious student of psychology and the social sciences!

Ministry of Court. The six officials of the Ministry of Court (PRO: 126) who refused to be interviewed may be considered in a situation analogous to members of the royal family. The highly sensitive nature of their positions, e.g., minister of court, private secretary to His Imperial Majesty, private secretary to the empress of Iran, etc., preclude participation in even potentially awkward, embarrassing, or even unusual projects. (In fact, no employee of the court was interviewed.)

Ministry of Justice. Four employees of the Ministry of Justice were included in the universe of 307 elite members. The minister of justice (PRO: 88) was interviewed, primarily, he confided, because his son is a university student in the United States. The other three members of the Ministry (PRO: 94.7) declined to participate on the grounds that such participation would be incompatible with their judicial positions: chief justice of the Iranian supreme court, public prosecutor general of Iran, and director of the Iran Bar Association.

Let us turn to an overview of the problem of nonresponse in this survey. Table II.3 presents PRO figures broken down to represent the excluded elite and the nonrespondents.

TABLE II.3
Comparison of PRO of Respondents, Excluded Elite, and Nonrespondents
by Cluster

PRO by Cluster	Respondents		Excluded Elite		Nonrespondents	
	Number	Average PRO	Number	Average PRO	Number	Average PRO
1-25	7	16.7	10	12.4	8	10.5
26-50	12	36.2	2	39.0	11	38.3
51-75	10	60.3	8	65.5	7	64.0
76-100	16	88.2	4	91.5	5	86.5
101-125	15	113.2	7	114.7	3	108.0
126-150	15	138.1	6	133.7	4	144.4
151-175	14	164.4	3	160.0	8	161.8
176-200	15	188.2	7	187.7	3	187.7
201-225	17	212.3	5	215.4	3	213.0
226-250	11	237.9	5	246.8	9	233.2
251-275	16	261.8	5	264.2	4	266.3
276-300	12	285.3	13	290.5	0	0
301-307	7	304.3	0	0	0	0
Total and average	167	163.6	75	151.8	65	137.6

Table II.3 demonstrates that the PRO average of the nonrespondents is considerably less than the PRO average of the respondents (163.6). Despite the disparity, however, I would argue that there is no significant bias introduced into the interview data because of the unbalanced coverage of the potential respondents. Nonetheless, there were some biases so introduced.

Members of the Iranian armed forces, a vital element in Iranian politics, have been totally excluded from the survey. While this group would have been an extremely interesting one to investigate, this analysis of the Iranian political elite must limit itself to a study of the civilian elite.

Most members of the active political opposition excluded themselves from participation in the interviews. Nonetheless, I would hypothesize that their attitudes are adequately reflected in responses by others of the elite. Some seven active opposition leaders were interviewed. Moreover, personal observation in Iran convinces me that opposition opinion has been sufficiently reflected in the responses of nonopposition elite.

The respondents who were outside Iran during the interview period do not, on an examination of their social backgrounds, appear significantly different from other members of the political elite who were in Iran and who did participate.

I have tried to demonstrate that nonresponse among members of the cabinet is not particularly likely to have introduced biases in respondent data.

There is little doubt in my mind that the ten senators who refused to participate did so because they were dissatisfied and frustrated with the distribution of political power in Iran. A sense of actual or alleged deprivation in the exercise of that political power resulted in their noncooperation. These feelings seem to be widespread throughout the Senate. It may be hoped that the thirty senators who were interviewed would constitute a sufficiently large group to reflect the dissatisfactions prevalent among the ten nonrespondents. If this does not prove to be the case, one can assume that the data have been biased in the direction of greater satisfaction and less frustration.

Of the eight nonrespondents holding relatively influential positions in the governmental hierarchy, only four need concern us here. The less important of the four positions are not particularly distinctive, as many other holders of the same positions have been interviewed. The first four on the list, while more powerful than the average respondent, do not appear at all unusual in their reputed attitudes, public positions, or social backgrounds. I do not assume that their present high positions are a reflection of a particularly distinctive or unusual set of beliefs or attitudes. In fact, quite the opposite argument might be legitimately advanced, i.e., that they are what they are specifically because they are not distinctive.

The absence of the generally less powerful businessmen from the respondents probably does not introduce any particular distortion into the data. Other businessmen were respondents. The self-exclusion of the elderly, the more frustrated, dissatisfied, and generally hostile, would bias the data, if at all, in a direction similar to the nonrespondent senators.

It is very likely that interviews with all members of the royal family would have resulted in fairly similar responses, determined not only by common family backgrounds and life experiences but also by the dictates of membership in the ruling family. The three interviewed members of the family, however, were not standardized. One respondent presented the answers to be expected from a brother of His Imperial Majesty. The other two respondents are known as the family misfits—they are better educated, more democratic, less venal. They were strongly outspoken critics of present policy in Iran. It is likely that these two types of interview introduced all shades of Pahlavi opinion.

The religious leaders are one civilian group for which problems of access are as difficult as for the military. In the Iran of today, these leaders tend to be the most outspokenly critical of the government, hostile to the United States, and opposed to the rule of the shah. Unfortunately, their views could not be included explicitly in the response data.

The ten members of the Ministries of Court and Justice who excluded themselves from participation did so because of the sensitive nature of their positions. Aside from their obvious discretion, there is no reason to assume that they are particularly different from the respondents.

In conclusion, then, the following seem to be the principal factors contributing to the phenomenon of nonresponse:

Exclusion of a total occupational group from failure to obtain approval for their being interviewed

Impossible conditions of physical access, e.g., residence outside Iran, hospitalization, incarceration

Fear of political reprisals

Hostility to the interview technique

Unwillingness to spend the time required for the interview

A feeling of nonparticipation in Iranian politics per se and thus the belief that participation in a study of Iranian "politics" or about "political" elite attitudes would be inappropriate

On balance it seems that any biases introduced by the exclusion of the nonrespondents would tend to alter the data toward a less positive orientation to the regime. Such being the case, the character orientations and political attitudes that were uncovered are all the more striking.

SELECTED BIBLIOGRAPHY

IRAN

Adams, Robert M. "Agriculture and Urban Life in Early Southwestern Iran." *Science*, 136, no. 3511 (April 1962): 109–22.

Amini, Ali. *L'institution du monopole du commerce extérieur en Perse*. Paris: Rousseau and Co., 1932.

Amuzegar, Jahangir. "Administrative Barriers to Economic Development in Iran." *Middle East Economic Papers*, 1958, pp. 1–21.

———. *Technical Assistance in Theory and Practice*. New York: Praeger, 1966.

Arasteh, Reza. *Education and Social Awakening in Iran*. Leiden: E. J. Brill, 1962.

———. *Man and Society in Iran*. Leiden: E. J. Brill, 1964.

Arberry, A. J. *Aspects of Islamic Civilization as Depicted in the Original Texts*. New York: A. S. Barnes & Co., 1964.

Arfa, General Hassan. *Under Five Shahs*. London: John Murray, 1964.

Aubin, Eugene. *La Perse d'aujourd'hui*. Paris: A. Colin, 1908.

Avery, Peter. *Modern Iran*. London: Ernest Benn, 1965.

Bahar, Malek ol-Shu'ara. *Tarikh-e Azab-e Siasi* [A history of political parties]. 2 vols. Tehran: Amir Kabir Publishers, 1944.

Baldwin, George B. "The Foreign-Educated Iranian: A Profile." *Middle East Journal*, 17, no. 3 (Summer 1963): 264–78.

———. "Labor Problems in a Developing Economy." *Current History*, 37, no. 216 (1959): 91–95.

———. *Planning and Development in Iran*. Baltimore: Johns Hopkins Press, 1967.

Balfour, J. M. *Recent Happenings in Persia*. Edinburgh: W. Blackwood and Sons, 1922.

Banani, Amin. *The Modernization of Iran, 1921–1941*. Stanford: Stanford University Press, 1961.

Bayne, Edward A. *Persian Kingship in Transition, Conversations with a Monarch Whose Office Is Traditional and Whose Goal Is Modernization*. New York: American Universities Field Staff, Inc., 1968.

Benjamin, Samuel Greene Wheeler. *Persia and The Persians*. Boston: Ticknor and Co., 1887.

Berger, Morroe. *The Arab World Today*. Garden City, N. Y.: Doubleday and Co., 1964.

———. *Bureaucracy and Society in Modern Egypt: A Study of the Higher Civil Service*. Princeton: Princeton University Press, 1957.

Bill, James A. "The Social and Economic Foundations of Power in Contemporary Iran." *Middle East Journal*, 17, no. 4 (Autumn 1963): 400–418.

Binder, Leonard. "The Cabinet of Iran: A Case Study in Institutional Adaptation." *Middle East Journal*, 16, no. 1 (1962): 29–47.

———. *Iran: Political Development in a Changing Society*. Berkeley: University of California Press, 1962.

———. *The Ideological Revolution in the Middle East*. New York: John Wiley and Sons, Inc., 1964.

Bogdanov, L. "The House and Life in Persia." *Islamic Culture*, 5 (1931): 407–21; and vol. 6 (1932): 290–306, 468–85.

Browne, Edward G. *The History of the Persian Revolution, 1905–1909*. London: Adam and Charles Black, 1910.

———. *A Literary History of Persia*. 4 vols. Cambridge: Cambridge University Press, 1953.

———. *Press and Poetry in Modern Persia*. Cambridge: Cambridge University Press, 1914.

———. *A Year Amongst the Persians*. London: Adam and Charles Black, 1893.

Brydges, Sir Harford Jones, trans. *The Dynasty of the Kajars*. London: J. Bolin, 1833.

Burton, Sir Richard F. *Personal Narrative of a Pilgrimage to Al-Madinah and Meccah*. 2 vols. London: Tylston and Edwards, 1893.

Butler, Rohan and J. P. T. Bury. *The Near and Middle East, January 1920– March 1921*. Documents on British Foreign Policy 1919–1939, 1st series, vol. 13. London: Her Majesty's Stationery Office, 1963, Document Number 477.

Chardin, Sir John. *Voyages du Chevalier en Perse et autre lieux de l'Orient*. Paris: La Normant, 1811.

Christensen, Arthur. *L'Iran sous les Sassanides*. Paris: Gennther, 1936.

Cottam, Richard W. *Nationalism in Iran*. Pittsburgh: University of Pittsburgh Press, 1964.

Courtuis, V. "The Tudeh Party." *Indo Iranica*, 1954, pp. 14–22.

Curzon, Lord George N. *Persia and the Persian Question.* 2 vols. London: Longmans, Green and Co., 1892.

Ebtehaj, Abol Hassan. "A Program for Economic Growth." Paper delivered at the International Industrial Conference, San Francisco, September 1961.

Echo of Iran, *Iran Almanac,* 1964, 1965, 1966, 1967, 1968, 1969, 1970. Tehran: Echo of Iran Press.

Elwell-Sutton, L. P. "Political Parties in Iran, 1941–1948." *Middle East Journal,* 3, no. 1 (January 1949): 45–62.

Empire de l'Iran, Ministère de l'Instruction Publique, Service de la Statistique. *Annuaire, 1935–1936.* Tehran: Imprimeur Madjless, n.d.

Entner, Marvin L. *Russo-Persian Commercial Relations, 1828–1914.* University of Florida Monographs, Social Sciences, no. 28. Gainesville: University of Florida Press, 1965.

Esfandiary, Fereidoun. *The Day of Sacrifice.* London: William Heinemann, 1960.

––––––. *Identity Card.* New York: Grove Press, 1966.

Farmanfarmaian, Khodadad. "Social Change and Economic Behavior in Iran." *Explorations in Entrepreneurial History,* 9, no. 3 (1957): 178–83.

Farman Farmayan, Hafez. "The Forces of Modernization in Nineteenth Century Iran." In *Beginnings of Modernization in the Middle East,* edited by William R. Polk and Richard Chambers. Chicago: University of Chicago Press, 1968, pp. 119–51.

Fateh, Mustafa Khan. *The Economic Position of Persia.* London: P. S. King and Son, 1926.

Fattahipour Fard, Ahmad. "Educational Diffusion and the Modernization of An Ancient Civilization—Iran." Ph.D. dissertation, University of Chicago, 1963.

Fischer, John. "The Land of the Charming Anarchists: A Report from Iran, Part I." *Harper's,* March 1965, pp. 20–30.

––––––. "The Shah and His Exasperating Subjects: A Report from Iran, Part II." *Harper's,* April 1965, pp. 24–32.

Forbes-Leith, F. A. C. *Checkmate: Fighting Tradition in Central Persia.* London: George G. Harrap and Co., n.d.

Frechtling, L. E. "The Reuter Concession in Persia." *Asiatic Review,* 34 (July 1938): 518–33.

Frye, Richard N. *The Heritage of Persia.* London: Weidenfeld and Nicolson, 1962.

Gable, R. W. "Culture and Administration in Iran." *Middle East Journal,* 13, (1959): 407–21.

Gallagher, Charles F. *Contemporary Islam: The Plateau of Particularism— Problems of Religion and Nationalism in Iran.* American Universities Field Staff Reports Service, South West Asia Series, Iran, vol. 15, no. 2, 1966.

Gastil, Raymond Duncan. "Iranian General Belief Modes as Found in Middle Class Shiraz." Ph.D. thesis, Harvard University, 1958.

––––––. "Middle Class Impediments to Iranian Modernization." *Public Opinion Quarterly,* 22, no. 3 (Fall 1958): 325–29.

Gobineau, Comte de. *Les Dépêches Diplomatiques de Perse de Comte de Gobineau.* 10 vols. Geneva: E. Droz, 1961.

Gordon, Sir Thomas Edward. *Persia Revisited, With Remarks on H.I.M. Mozaffar ed-din Shah.* London: E. Arnold, 1896.

Greaves, R. L. *Persia and the Defence of India, 1884–1892.* London: University of London, Athlone Press, 1959.

Hale, Anthony. *From Persian Uplands.* New York: E. P. Dutton and Co., n.d. (ca. 1915).

Halpern, Manfred. *The Politics of Social Change in the Middle East and North Africa.* Princeton: Princeton University Press, 1963.

Hambly, G. R. G. "An Introduction to the Economic Organization of Early Qajar Iran," *Journal of the British Institute of Persian Studies,* 2 (1964): 69–82.

Hanway, Jonas. *An Historical Account of British Trade Over the Caspian.* 4 vols. London: Sold by Mr. Dodsley, 1753.

Herbert, Sir Thomas. *A Description of the Persian Monarchy Now Beinge.* London: W. Stansby and J. Blonne, 1634.

Hudson, Bradford B., ed. *Cross Cultural Studies in the Arab Middle East and United States: Studies of Young Adults. Journal of Social Issues,* 15, no. 3 (1959).

Ibn Iskandar, Kai Ka'us. *Qabus Nama* [A mirror for princes], translated and introduction by Reuben Levy. London: Cresset Press, 1951.

International Labor Organization. "Evolution of Labor Legislation and Administration in Iran." *International Labor Review,* 69 (March 1959): 273–95.

Iranian Ministry of Agriculture, Department of Information. *Avalin Congreye Melliye Sherkathaye Ta' avaniye Rusta'iye Iran* [The first national congress of rural cooperative societies of Iran]. Tehran, March 1961.

Iranian Ministry of Education, Office of Studies and Programs. *Amar-e Farhang-e Iran* [Educational statistics of Iran]. Tehran, 1964.

Iranian Ministry of Interior, Department of Public Statistics. *Amare Namaye Mossavar Ba'azi az Fa'aliatha va Pishrafthaye Keshvar dar Salhaye Akhir* [Illustrated statistics of internal activities and progress in recent years]. Tehran, 1961.

Iranian Ministry of Interior, Department of Public Statistics. *National and Province Statistics of the First Census of Iran: November 1956.* 2 vols. Tehran, 1961. Vol. 1, *Number and Distribution of the Inhabitants for Iran and the Census Provinces.* Vol. 2, *Social and Economic Characteristics of the Inhabitants for Iran and the Census Provinces.*

————. *National Census of Population and Housing—November 1966;* esp. Vol. CLXVIII, "Total Country-Settled Population," March 1968.

Jacobs, Norman. *The Sociology of Development: Iran as an Asian Case Study.* Praeger Special Studies in International Economics and Development. New York: Frederick A. Praeger, 1966.

Kazemzadeh, Firuz. *Britain and Russia in Iran, 1864–1914.* New Haven: Yale University Press, 1968.

————. "Ideological Crisis in Iran." In *The Middle East in Transition*, edited by Walter Z. Laquer. New York: Frederick A. Praeger, 1958, pp. 196–203.

————. "The Origin and Early Development of the Persian Cossack Brigade." *American Slavic and East European Review*, 15 (1956): 342–53.

Keddie, Nikki R. "Religion and Irreligion in Early Iranian Nationalism." *Comparative Studies in Society and History*, April 1962, pp. 265–95.

————. *Religion and Rebellion in Iran: The Tobacco Protest of 1891–1892.* London: Frank Cass and Co., 1966.

Kia, Abbas Chams-ed Din. *Essai sur l'histoire industrielle de l'Iran.* Paris: M. Lavergne, 1939.

Kitab, Kulsum Naneh. *Customs and Manners of the Women of Persia, and Their Domestic Superstitions.* London: J. Atkensons, 1832.

Krusinski, Father. *History of the Revolution of Persia,* translated by Father du Cercea. 2 vols. Dublin, 1729.

Lambton, Ann K. S. "The Impact of the West On Persia." *International Affairs*, 33 (1957): 12–25.

————. "Islamic Society In Persia." Lecture delivered at School of Oriental and African Studies, University of London, March 9, 1954.

————. *Landlord and Peasant in Persia.* London: Oxford University Press, 1953.

————. *The Persian Land Reform, 1962–1966.* London: Clarendon Press, 1969.

————. "Persian Political Societies 1906–1911." *St. Anthony's Papers*, no. 16, 1963.

————. "Persian Society under the Qajars." *Journal of the Royal Central Asian Society*, 48 (April 1961): 123–39.

————. "Quis custodiet custodes? Some Reflections on the Persian Theory of Government." *Studia Islamica*, 5 (1956): 125–48; vol. 6 (1956): 125–46.

————. "Secret Societies and the Persian Revolution of 1905–1906." *St. Anthony's Papers*, no. 4, 1958.

————. "The Tobacco Regie: Prelude to Revolution." *Studia Islamica*, 22: 71–90.

Lenczowski, George. *Russia and the West in Iran, 1918–1948: A Study in Big Power Rivalry.* Ithaca: Cornell University Press, 1949.

Lerner, Daniel. *The Passing of Traditional Society: Modernizing the Middle East.* New York: Free Press of Glencoe, 1958.

Levy, Reuben. *The Social Structure of Islam.* Cambridge: Cambridge University Press, 1962.

Lingeman, E. R. *Report on the Finance and Commerce of Persia, 1925–1927.* London: His Majesty's Stationery Office, 1928.

Mahdavy, Hossein. "The Coming Crises in Iran." *Foreign Affairs*, October 1965, pp. 134–46.

Malcom, Sir John. *The History of Persia.* 2 vols. London: John Murray, 1815.

Mansur, Hassan Ali. "Iran's Program for Economic Prosperity." *Facts About Iran*, Iranian Ministry of Information, no. 191, April 30, 1964.

Massé, Henri. *Persian Beliefs and Customs*. New Haven: Human Relations Area Files, 1954.

Matine-Daftary, Ahmad. *La Suppression de Capitulations en Perse: L'ancien régime et le statut actuel des étrangers dans l'Empire du "Lion et Soleil."* Paris: Les Presses Universitaires de France, 1930.

McDaniel, Robert A. "The Shuster Mission and the Culmination of the Persian Revolution of 1905–1911." Ph.D. dissertation, University of Illinois, 1966.

Mehdevi, Anne Sinclair. *Persian Adventure*. New York: Alfred A. Knopf, 1953.

Miller, William G. "The Dowreh and Iranian Politics." *Middle East Journal*, 23, no. 2 (Spring 1969): 159–67.

Millspaugh, Arthur. *The American Task in Persia*. New York: Century Co., 1925.

————. *Americans in Persia*. Washington, D.C.: Brookings Institution, 1946.

Minorsky, Vladimir. "Iran: Opposition, Martyrdom, and Revolt." In *Unity and Variety in Muslim Civilization*, edited by G. E. von Grunebaum. Chicago: University of Chicago Press, 1955, pp. 183–206.

Morgan, Jacques de. "Feudalism in Persia: Its Origins, Development, and Present Conditions." In *Annual Reports of the Board of Regents, 1913*. Washington, D.C.: Smithsonian Institution, 1914.

Morier, James. *The Adventures of Hajji Baba of Ispahan*. London: Oxford University Press, 1959.

Mostaufi, Abdullah. *Sharhe Zendeganiye Man ya Tarikhe Ejtema'i va Edariye Dowreya Qajariyeh* [The history of my life or a social and administrative history of the Qajar period]. 2nd printing. 2 vols. Tehran: Ketab Forushi Zavvor, n.d.

Naficy, Dr. Habib. "The Brain-Drain: The Case of Iranian Non-Returnees." Paper presented at the annual conference of the Society for International Development, Washington, D.C., March 17, 1966.

National Institute of Psychology, Marketing and Public Opinion Research Division. *A Preliminary Survey of Literate Iranians' Attitudes*. Tehran: National Institute Press, 1962.

Newberry, Daniel. "GENMISH—United States Army Military Mission With the Imperial Iranian Gendarmerie." Tehran, mimeo, n.d.

Nicolson, Harold. *Friday Mornings, 1941–1944*. London: Constable, 1944.

Pahlavi, Mohammad Reza Shah. "Address of His Imperial Majesty, the Shahanshah of Iran." Speech delivered at the National Press Club of the United States, Washington, D.C., April 13, 1962.

————. *Mission for My Country*. New York: McGraw-Hill, 1961.

Pfaff, Richard H. "A Single Party System for Iran," *Echo of Iran—Monthly Review*, 1, no. 2 (February 28, 1963).

Polak, Jakob Edvard. *Persien: das land und seine bewohner*. Leipzig: F. A. Brockhaus, 1865.

Polk, William R. "The Middle East: Analyzing Social Change." *Bulletin of the Atomic Scientists*, 23, no. 1 (1967): 12–19.

————. "Social Modernization in the Middle East: The New Men." Mimeo, 1963.

Powell, E. Alexander. *By Camel and Car to the Peacock Throne*. Garden City, N.Y.: Garden City Publishing Co., 1923.

Qajar, Naser ed-Din Shah. *The Diary of His Majesty, the Shah of Persia, During His Tour Through Europe in AD 1873*, translated by T. W. Redhouse. London: John Murray and Sons, 1874.

————. *A Diary Kept by His Majesty, the Shah of Persia, During his Journey to Europe in 1878*, translated by A. H. Schindler and Baron L. de Norman. London: Richard Bentley and Son, 1879.

Ramazani, R. K. "Modernization and Social Research in Iran." *The American Behavioral Scientist*, 5, no. 6 (1962): 17–20.

————. *The Foreign Policy of Iran, 1500–1941, A Developing Nation in World Affairs*. Charlottesville: University Press of Virginia, 1966.

Rawlinson, George. *The Seventh Great Oriental Monarchy or Geography, History, and Antiquities of the Sassanian or New Persian Empire*. 2 vols. New York: Dodd, Mead, and Co., 1882.

Ringer, B. B. and Sills, D. L. "Political Extremists in Iran: A Secondary Analysis of Communications Data." *Public Opinion Quarterly*, 16 (Winter 1952–1953): 689–701.

Rotblat, Howard J. "The Patterns of Recruitment into the Iranian Political Elite." M.A. dissertation, University of Chicago, 1968.

Sadiq, Issa. *Dowreye Mokhtasere Tarikhe Farhange Iran* [The contemporary era of the history of Iranian education]. Tehran: Sherkate Sahamiye Tabqe Ketab, 1961.

————. *History of Education in Iran: From Earliest Times to the Present Day*. 3rd ed. In Persian. Tehran: Teachers College Press, 1963.

Saghaphi, Mirza Mahmoud Khan. *In the Imperial Shadow*. Garden City, N.Y.: Doubleday, Doran, and Co. 1932.

Sanson. *The Present State of Persia: with a faithful account of the manners, etc., of that people*. London: M. Gilliflower, 1695.

Sayili, Aydin. *Higher Education in Medieval Islam: The Madrasa*. Ankara: Ankara Universitesi Yilligi, 1948.

Shah, Idries. *The Exploits of the Incomparable Mulla Nasrudin*. London: Jonathan Cape, 1966.

Shaji'i, Zahra. *Namayandegan-e Shoray-e Melli dar Bist-o-Yek Dowreh-ye Qanungozari* [Representatives of the national assembly in twenty-one legislative Assemblies]. Tehran: Institute for Social Research and Studies, University of Tehran, 1966.

Sheil, Lady Mary Leonora. *Glimpses of Life and Manners in Persia*. London: J. Murray, 1856.

Shoberl, Frederic. *Persia*. Philadelphia: J. Gigg, 1828.

Shuster, W. Morgan. *The Strangling of Persia: A Record of European Diplomacy and Oriental Intrigue*. London: T. Fisher Unwin, 1912.

369

Siassi, Ali Akbar. *La Perse au Contact de l'Occident*. Paris: E. Leroux, 1931.

Skrine, Sir Clarmont. *World War in Iran*. London: Constable and Co., 1962.

Sparroy, Wilfred. *Persian Children of the Royal Family: The Narrative of an English Tutor at the Court of H.I.H. Zillu's-Sultan, G.C.S.I.* London: J. Lane, 1902.

Stuart, Donald. *The Struggle for Persia*. London: Methuen and Co., 1902.

Sykes, Christopher. *Wassmuss: "The German Lawrence."* London: Longmans, Green and Co., 1936.

Sykes, Ella C. *Persia and Its People*. London: Methuen and Co., 1910.

Sykes, Sir Percy Molesworth, *The Glory of the Shia World, The Tale of a Pilgrimage*. London: Macmillan Co., 1910.

————. *A History of Persia*. 2 vols. London: Macmillan Co., 1921.

Tavernier, Jean Baptiste. *The Six Voyages of Tavernier . . . through Turkey into Persia and the East Indies finished in the year 1670*. London: R. L. and M. P., 1678.

ul-Mulk, Nizam. *Siyasat-Nama* [The book of government or rules for kings], translated by Hubert Drake. London: Routledge & Kegan Paul, 1960.

Upton, Joseph M. *The History of Modern Iran: An Interpretation*. Harvard Middle Eastern Monographs. Cambridge: Harvard University Press, 1960.

U.S. Army. *Area Handbook for Iran*. Washington, D.C.: Special Operations Research Office, American University, 1963.

U.S. Congress, Senate. Committee on Foreign Relations. *Activities of the Development and Resources Corporation in Iran*. Hearing, 87th Cong., 2nd sess. Washington, D.C.: U.S. Government Printing Office, 1962.

U.S. Department of Labor, Bureau of Labor Statistics, Office of Labor Affairs. *Summary of the Labor Situation in Iran*. Washington, D.C.: U.S. Government Printing Office, 1955.

U.S. Office of Statistics and Reports, International Cooperation Administration. *Foreign Assistance and Assistance From International Organizations, July 1, 1945 through June 30, 1966*. Washington, D.C.: U.S. Government Printing Office, 1967.

Vreeland, Herbert H., ed. *Iran*. New Haven: Human Relations Area Files, 1957.

Watson, R. G. *A History of Persia*. London: Smith, Elder and Co., 1886.

Westwood, Andrew F. "Elections and Politics in Iran." *Middle East Journal*, 15 (1960): 397–415.

————. "Politics of Distrust in Iran." *Annals of the American Academy of Political and Social Sciences*, 358 (March 1965): 123–35.

Widengren, George. "The Sacral Kingship of Iran." *Numen*, supplement 4, 1959, pp. 242–57.

Wilber, Donald N. *Iran Past and Present*. Princeton: Princeton University Press, 1958.

Wilson, Lt. Col. Sir Arnold. "National and Racial Characteristics of the Persian Nation." *Asiatic Review*, April 1929, pp. 1–14.

————. *Persia.* London: E. Benn, 1932.

Windle, Charles. "The Accuracy of Census Literacy Statistics in Iran." *Journal of the American Statistical Association,* September 1959, pp. 578–81.

Wishard, John G. *Twenty Years in Persia: A Narrative of Life under the Last 3 Shahs.* New York: F. H. Revell Co., 1908.

Woodward, E. L. and Rohan Butler, eds. *Documents on British Foreign Policy 1919–1939, First Series Vol. IV, 1919.* London: Her Majesty's Stationery Office, 1952.

Young, T. Cuyler. "Iran in Continuing Crisis." *Foreign Affairs,* 40 (January 1962): 275–92.

————. "The Social Support of Current Iranian Policy." *Middle East Journal,* 6 (1952): 125–43.

Zabih, Sepehr. *The Communist Movement in Iran.* Berkeley: University of California Press, 1966.

Zavosh, Mohammad. "Why Is Iran Industrially Backward?" *Economic Reports,* Echo of Iran Press, no. 11 (December 1961).

Zonis, Ella. *The Dastgah Music of Iran.* Cambridge: Harvard University Press, forthcoming.

Zonis, Marvin. *Education and Development: Selecting a Sample of Iran's Secondary Schools.* In Persian. Tehran: Institute for Educational Research and Studies, National Teachers' College Press, 1965.

————. "Higher Education and Social Change in Iran." In *Iran Faces the 1970's,* edited by E. Yar-Shater. New York: Praeger Press, 1971.

————. "Iran." In *Comparative Politics in the Middle East,* edited by Tareq Ismael. Homewood, Ill.: Dorsey Press, 1970, pp. 150–80.

————. "Political Elites and Political Cynicism in Iran." *Comparative Political Studies,* 1, no. 3 (October 1968): 351–71.

————. Review of *The Communist Movement in Iran,* by Sepehr Zabih. In *American Political Science Review,* 62, no. 2 (June 1968): 645–47.

————. Review of *Planning and Development in Iran,* by George B. Baldwin. In *American Political Science Review,* 62, no. 2 (June 1968): 645–47.

————. Review of *Persian Kingship in Transition,* by E. A. Bayne. In *Middle East Journal,* 24, no. 1 (1970): 98–99.

————. Review of *The Shah of Iran,* by Ramesh Sanghvi. In *Middle East Journal,* 24, no. 1 (1970): 98–99.

————. "The Search for A Political Elite: Reputational Analysis and the Occupational Bases of Power." In *Political Power in Islamic Iran,* edited by Amin Banani. Forthcoming.

————. *A Study of the Future "Technocrats" of Iran: The Formation of the Development Cadre.* In Persian. Tehran: National Teachers' College Press, 1965.

————. "Themes in Contemporary Iranian Political History." In *The Contemporary Middle East,* edited by Michael Adams. London: Anthony Blond, forthcoming.

IRANIAN PERIODICALS

Bank Markazi Iran (Central Bank of Iran). *Bulletin.*
Diplomat (Persian).
Donya (Persian).
Echo of Iran. *Daily Bulletin: Economic Edition.*
──────. *Daily Bulletin: Political Edition.*
──────. *For Your Information.*
Ettela'at (Persian).
Farman Magazine.
Iranian Department General of Publications and Broadcasting. *Bulletin* (Persian).
Iranian Ministry of Foreign Affairs, Information and Press Department. *Iran—Basic Facts.*
Iranian Ministry of Information. *Facts About Iran.*
Kayhan (Persian).
Kayhan International.
Khandaniha (Persian).
Khushe (Persian).
Mehre Iran (Persian).
Peighame Emruz (Persian).
Sahar (Persian).
Tehran Journal.

POLITICAL ELITES AND POWER

Abrahamsson, Bengt. "The Ideology of an Elite—Conservatism and National Insecurity." Paper presented at the Working Group on Armed Forces and Society, Sixth World Congress of Sociology, Evian, France, September 1966.

Agger, Robert E. "Power Attributions in the Local Community: Theoretical and Research Considerations." *Social Forces*, 34, no. 2 (May 1956): 322–31.

Aron, Raymond. "Classe sociale, classe politique, classe dirigeante." *European Journal of Sociology*, 1, no. 2 (1960): 260–81.

──────. "Social Structure and the Ruling Class." *British Journal of Sociology*, 1, no. 1 (March 1950): 1–16; vol. 1, no. 2 (June 1950): 126–46.

Bachrach, Peter and Morton S. Baratz. "Two Faces of Power." *American Political Science Review*, 56, no. 4 (December 1962): 947–52.

Balogh, Thomas. "The Apotheosis of the Dilettante." In *The Establishment*, edited by Hugh Thomas. New York: Clarkson N. Potter, 1959, pp. 83–126.

Baltzell, E. Digby. *An American Business Aristocracy.* New York: Collier Books, 1962.

Benda, Harry, J. "Intellectuals and Politics in Western History." *Bucknell Review*, 10 (1961): 1–41.

————. "Non-Western Intelligentsias as Political Elites." In *Political Change in Underdeveloped Countries: Nationalism and Communism*, edited by John H. Kautsky. New York: John Wiley and Sons, 1962, pp. 235–51.

————. "Political Elites in Colonial Southeast Asia: An Historical Analysis." *Comparative Studies in Society and History*, 7, no. 3 (April 1965): 233–51.

Borgatta, E. F. "Some Findings Relevant to the Great Man Theory of Leadership." *American Sociological Review*, 19, no. 6 (December 1954): 755–59.

Bottomore, T. B. *Elites and Society*. New York: Basic Books, 1964.

Burnham, James. *The Machiavellians: Defenders of Freedom*. London: Putnam and Co., 1943.

Carlyle, Thomas. *On Heroes, Hero Worship, and the Heroic in History*. London: Oxford University Press, 1963.

Coleman, James S. "Community Disorganization." In *Contemporary Social Problems*, edited by Robert K. Merton and Robert A. Nisbet. New York: Harcourt, Brace and World, 1961, pp. 553–604.

Dahl, Robert A. "The Concept of Power." *Behavioral Science*, 2, no. 3 (July 1957): 201–15.

————. "A Critique of the Ruling Elite Model." *American Political Science Review*, 52, no. 2 (June 1958): 463–69.

Davies, James C. *Human Nature in Politics*. New York: John Wiley and Sons, 1963, pp. 274–330.

Dick, Harry R. "A Method for Ranking Community Influentials." *American Sociological Review*, 25, no. 3 (June 1960): 395–99.

Edinger, Lewis J. "Continuity and Change in the Background of German Decision-Makers." *Western Political Quarterly*, 14, no. 1 (March 1961): 17–36.

————. "Political Science and Political Biography, I and II." *Journal of Politics*, 26, no. 1 (May 1964): 423–29; no. 2 (August 1964): 648–77.

————. "Post-Totalitarian Leadership: Elites in the German Federal Republic." *American Political Science Review*, 54, no. 1 (March 1960): 58–82.

————, ed. *Political Leadership in Industrial Societies: Studies in Comparative Analysis*. New York: John Wiley and Sons, 1967.

————, and Donald D. Searing. "Social Background in Elite Analysis." *American Political Science Review*, 61, no. 2 (June 1967): 428–45.

Ehrlich, Howard J. "The Reputational Approach to the Study of Community Power." *American Sociological Review*, 26 (December 1961): 926–27.

Frey, Frederick, W. "Power Analysis." Mimeo, n.d.

————. *The Turkish Political Elite*. Cambridge: M.I.T. Press, 1965.

Gee, H. H. and R. J. Glaser. *The Ecology of the Medical Student*. Report of the Fifth Teaching Institute, Association of American Medical Colleges, Atlantic City, N.J., October 15–19, 1957.

Glaser, William A. "Doctors and Politics." *American Journal of Sociology*, 66 (November 1960): 230–45.

Goldhammer, Herbert and Edward Shils. "Types of Power and Status." *American Journal of Sociology*, 45 (1937): 171–82.

Guttsman, W. L. *The British Political Elite*. London: MacGibbon and Kee, 1963.

Hansknecht, Murray. *The Joiners*. New York: Bedminster Press, 1962.

Hook, Sidney. *The Hero in History: A Study in Limitation and Possibility*. New York: John Day, 1943.

Hunter, Floyd. *Community Power Structure: A Study of Decision Makers*. Garden City, N.Y.: Doubleday and Co., 1965.

———. *Top Leadership, U.S.A.* Chapel Hill: University of North Carolina Press, 1959.

Janowitz, Morris. "The Systematic Analysis of Political Biography." *World Politics*, April 1954, pp. 405–12.

Keller, Suzanne. *Beyond the Ruling Class*. New York: Random House, 1963.

Kimball, S. T. and M. Piersall. "Event Analysis as an Approach to Community Study." *Social Forces*, 34 (1955): 58–63.

Lasswell, Harold D. and Abraham Kaplan. *Power and Society: A Framework for Political Inquiry*. New Haven: Yale University Press, 1950.

——— and Daniel Lerner. *World Revolutionary Elites: Studies in Coercive Ideological Movements*. Cambridge: M.I.T. Press, 1966.

March, James G. "Influence Measurement in Experimental and Semi-Experimental Groups." *Sociometry*, 19, no. 4 (1956): 260–70.

———. "An Introduction to the Theory and Measurement of Influence." *American Political Science Review*, 59, no. 2 (June 1955): 431–51.

Marvick, Dwaine, ed. *Political Decision-Makers*. Glencoe: Free Press, 1961.

Matthews, D. R. *The Social Background of Political Decision-Makers*. New York: Doubleday, 1954.

Meisel, James H. *The Myth of the Ruling Class: Gaetano Mosca and the "Elite."* Ann Arbor: University of Michigan Press, 1962.

———, ed. *Pareto and Mosca*. Englewood Cliffs: Prentice-Hall, 1965.

Mills, C. Wright. *The Power Elite*. New York: Oxford University Press, 1959.

Mosca, Gaetano. *The Ruling Class*. New York: McGraw-Hill, 1939.

Nadel, S. F. "The Concept of Social Elites." *International Social Science Bulletin*, 8, no. 3 (1956): 413–24.

Naraghi, E. "Élite ancienne et élite nouvelle dans l'Iran actuel avec une note sur le système d'éducation." *Revue des Études Islamiques*, 25 (1951): 69–80.

Pareto, Vilfredo. *The Mind and Society*. 4 vols. London: Jonathan Cape, 1935.

Parsons, Talcott. "The Distribution of Power in American Society." *World Politics*, 10, no. 1 (October 1957): 123–44.

———. *Structure and Process in Modern Societies*. New York: Free Press of Glencoe, 1960, pp. 170–98.

Polsby, Nelson W. *Community Power and Political Theory*. New Haven: Yale University Press, 1963.

———. "The Sociology of Community Power: A Reassessment." *Social Forces*, 37, no. 3 (March 1959): 232–36.

———. "Three Problems in the Analysis of Community Power." *American Sociological Review*, 24, no. 6 (December 1959): 796–814.

Presthus, Robert. *Men at the Top: A Study in Community Power*. New York: Oxford University Press, 1964.

Quandt, William B. *Revolution and Political Leadership: Algeria, 1954–1968*. Cambridge: M.I.T. Press, 1969.

Rose, Arnold M. *The Power Structure: Political Process in American Society*. New York: Oxford University Press, 1967.

Ross, Ralph Gilbert. "Elites and the Methodology of Politics." *Public Opinion Quarterly*, Spring 1952, pp. 27–32.

Rustow, Dankwart. "The Study of Elites: Who's Who, When, and How." *World Politics*, 18, no. 4 (July 1966): 690–717.

Sanders, Irwin T. "Research With Peasants in Underdeveloped Areas." *Social Forces*, 35, no. 1 (October 1956): 1–10.

Schulze, Robert O. and L. V. Blumberg. "The Determination of Local Power Elites." *American Journal of Sociology*, 63 (1957–1958): 290–96.

Seligman, Lester G. "Elite Recruitment and Political Development." *Journal of Politics*, 26, no. 3 (August 1964): 612–26.

———. "The Study of Political Leadership." *American Political Science Review*, 44, no. 4 (December 1950): 904–15.

Sereno, Renzo. *The Rulers*. New York: Frederick A. Praeger, 1962.

Shils, Edward. "The Intellectuals in the Political Development of the New States." In *Political Change in Underdeveloped Countries: Nationalism and Communism*, edited by John H. Kautsky. New York: John Wiley and Sons, 1962, pp. 195–234.

Simon, Herbert. "Notes on the Observation and Measurement of Political Power." *Journal of Politics*, 15, no. 4 (November 1953): 500–16.

Singer, Marshall R. *The Emerging Elite: A Study of Political Leadership in Ceylon*. Cambridge: M.I.T. Press, 1964.

Stone, Lawrence. *The Crisis of the Aristocracy, 1558–1641*. London: Oxford University Press, 1965.

Tannebaum, Arnold S. "An Event Structure Approach to the Problem of Power Comparability." *Behaviorial Science*, 2, no. 3 (July 1962): 315–31.

Waterbury, John. *The Commander of the Faithful, The Moroccan Political Elite—A Study in Segmented Politics*. New York: Columbia University Press, 1970.

Wolfinger, Raymond E. "Reputation and Reality in the Study of Community Power." *American Sociological Review*, 25, no. 5 (October 1960): 636–44.

PSYCHOLOGY

Adler, Alfred. *Superiority and Social Interest: A Collection of Later Writings*, edited by Henry L. Ansbacher and Rowena R. Ansbacher. Evanston, Ill.: Northwestern University Press, 1964.

Adorno, Theodore W., Else Frenkel-Brunswik, Daniel J. Levinson, and R. Nevitt Sanford. *The Authoritarian Personality: Studies in Prejudice.* New York: Harper and Row, 1950.

Agger, Robert E., Marshall N. Goldstein, and Stanley A. Pearl. "Political Cynicism: Measurement and Meaning." *Journal of Politics,* 23, no. 476 (1961): 477–506.

Ainsworth, Leonard H. "Rigidity, Insecurity, and Stress." *Journal of Abnormal and Social Psychology,* 56 (1958): 67–74.

Ainsworth, Mary D. and L. H. Ainsworth. *Measuring Security in Personal Adjustment.* Toronto: University of Toronto Press, 1958.

Allport, Gordon W. and Leo Postman. "The Analysis of Rumor." In *Personality and Social Encounter,* edited by Gordon W. Allport. Boston: Beacon Press, 1964, pp. 311–26.

Arsenian, J. M. "Young Children in Insecure Situations." *Journal of Abnormal and Social Psychology,* 38 (1943): 225–49.

Ball, D. W. "Covert Political Rebellion as Resentment." *Social Forces,* 42 (1964): 93–101.

Bettelheim, Bruno and Morris Janowitz. *Social Change and Prejudice.* Glencoe: Free Press, 1964.

Bonham-Carter, Violet A. *The Impact of Personality in Politics.* Oxford: Clarendon Press, 1963.

Bonner, Hubert. "Sociological Aspects of Paranoia." *American Journal of Sociology,* 56, no. 31 (November 1950): 255–62.

Brill, A. A. "Poetry as an Oral Outlet." *Psychoanalytic Review,* 18 (October 1931): 357–78.

Brim, Orville G., Jr., David C. Glass, David E. Lavin, and Norman Goodman. *Personality and Decision Processes: Studies in the Social Psychology of Thinking.* Stanford: Stanford University Press, 1962.

Cameron, William Bruce and Thomas C. McCormick. "Concepts of Security and Insecurity." *American Journal of Sociology,* 59, no. 6 (May 1954): 556–64.

Cantril, Hadley. *The Politics of Despair.* New York: Collier Press, 1962.

Cattell, R. B. and I. H. Scheier. "The Nature of Anxiety: A Review of Thirteen Multivariant Analyses Comprising 814 Variables." *Psychological Reproductions,* 4 (1958): 351–88.

Christie, Richard and Robert K. Merton. "Procedures for the Sociological Study of the Values Climate of Medical School." *Journal of Medical Education,* 33, no. 10, part 2 (October 1958): 125–53.

Clark, J. P. "Measuring Alienation in a Social System." *American Sociological Review,* 24 (1959): 849–52.

Clarkson, E. P. "The Problem of Honesty." *International Journal of Opinion and Attitude Research,* 4 (1950): 84–90.

Culbertson, F. J. "Modification of an Emotionally Held Attitude Through Role Playing." *Journal of Abnormal and Social Psychology,* 54 (1957): 230–33.

Dai, Bingham. "Some Problems of Personality Development Among Negro Children." In *Personality*, edited by Clyde Kluckhohn and Henry A. Murray. New York: Alfred A. Knopf, 1953, chap. 35.

De Fleur, Melvin L. and W. R. Catton Jr. "The Limits of Determinacy in Attitude Measurement." *Social Forces*, 35, no. 4 (May 1957): 295–300.

de Grazia, Sebastian. *The Political Community: A Study of Anomie*. Chicago: University of Chicago Press, 1963.

Deutsch, Morton and Robert M. Krauss. "Studies of Interpersonal Bargaining." *Journal of Conflict Resolution*, 6, no. 1 (March 1962): 52–76.

Erikson, Erik H. *Childhood and Society*. New York: W. W. Norton, 1963.

Eysenck, H. J. *The Psychology of Politics*. London: Routledge & Kegan Paul, 1954.

Field, M. J. *Search for Security: An Ethno-Psychiatric Study of Rural Ghana*. Evanston: Northwestern University Press, 1960.

Flugel, J. C. "Some Neglected Aspects of World Integration." In *Psychological Factors of Peace and War*, edited by T. H. Pear. London: Hutchinson and Co., 1950, pp. 111–38.

Frenkel-Brunswik, Else. "Interaction of Psychological and Sociological Factors in Political Behavior." *American Political Science Review*, 46, no. 1 (March 1952): 44–65.

Freud, Sigmund. *The Problem of Anxiety*, translated by H. A. Bunker. New York: Norton and Co., 1936.

Froman, Lewis A. "Learning Political Attitudes." *Western Political Quarterly*, 15 (1962): 304–13.

Fromm-Reichmann, Frieda. "Psychiatric Aspects of Anxiety." In *An Outline of Psychoanalysis*, edited by Clara Thompson, Milton Mayer, and Earl Witenberg. New York: Random House, 1955.

Gerth, Hans and C. Wright Mills. *Character and Social Structure: The Psychology of Social Institutions*. New York: Harcourt, Brace and World, 1953.

Gilbert, G. M. *The Psychology of Dictatorship*. New York: Ronald Press, 1950.

Gillespie, James M. and Gordon W. Allport. *Youth's Outlook on the Future*. Doubleday Papers in Psychology. Garden City, N.Y.: Doubleday, 1955.

Gillin, John P. "Personality Formation from the Comparative Cultural Point of View." In *Personality in Nature, Society, Culture*, edited by C. Kluckhohn and H. A. Murray. New York: Alfred A. Knopf, 1948, pp. 164–75.

——— and George Nicholson. "The Security Functions of Cultural Systems." *Social Forces*, 30, no. 1 (October 1951): 179–84.

Greenstein, Fred I. "The Impact of Personality on Politics: An Attempt to Clear Away the Underbrush." *American Political Science Review*, 61, no. 3 (September 1967): 629–41.

Hallowell, A. I. "The Social Function of Anxiety in a Primitive Society." *American Sociological Review*, 6 (December 1941): 869–81.

Hallowell, A. I. "Socio-Psychological Aspects of Acculturation." In *The Science of Man in the World Crisis*, edited by Ralph Linton. New York: Columbia University Press, 1945, pp. 171–200.

Hirschmann, Edward. *Great Men: Psychoanalytic Studies*. New York: International Universities Press, 1956.

Hodges, David Clark. "Cynicism in the Labor Movement." *American Journal of Economics and Sociology*, 21 (1962): 29–36.

Inkeles, Alex. "Personality and Social Structure." In *Sociology Today*, by R. K. Merton, Leonard Broom, and Leonard S. Cottrell Jr. New York: Basic Books, 1959, pp. 249–76.

Janis, I. L. and B. T. King. "The Influence of Role Playing on Opinion Change." *Journal of Abnormal and Social Psychology*, 49 (1954): 211–18.

Kaplan, Bert, ed. *Studying Personality Cross Culturally*. New York: Harper and Row, 1961.

Kardiner, Abram. *The Psychological Frontiers of Society*. New York: Columbia University Press, 1945.

Kelman, Herbert C. "Attitude Change as a Function of Response Restriction." *Human Relations*, 6 (1953): 185–214.

———. ed. *International Behavior: A Social Psychological Analysis*. New York: Holt, Rinehart and Winston, 1965.

King, B. T. and I. L. Janis. "Comparison of the Effectiveness of Improvised Versus Non-Improvised Role Playing in Producing Opinion Changes." *Human Relations*, 9 (1956): 177–86.

Knutson, Andie L. "The Concept of Personal Security." *Journal of Social Psychology*, 40 (1954): 219–36.

Kutner, B., Carroll Wilkins, and Penny R. Yarrow. "Verbal Attitudes and Overt Behavior Involving Race Prejudice." *Journal of Abnormal and Social Psychology*, 47 (July 1952): 649–52.

Lane, Robert E. *Political Life: Why People Get Involved in Politics*. Glencoe: Free Press, 1959.

La Pierre, R. T. "Attitudes Versus Actions." *Social Forces*, 13 (December 1934): 230–37.

Lasswell, Harold D. *Power and Personality*. New York: W. W. Norton, 1948.

———. *Psychopathology and Politics*. Chicago: University of Chicago Press, 1930.

———. "The Selective Effect of Personality on Political Participation." In *Studies in the Scope and Method of "The Authoritarian Personality,"* edited by Richard Christie and Marie Jahoda. New York: Free Press, 1954, pp. 197–225.

———. *World Politics and Personal Insecurity*. New York: Free Press, 1965.

Leggett, John C. "Economic Insecurity and Working Class Consciousness." *American Sociological Review*, 29 (April 1964): 226–34.

Litt, Edgar. "Political Cynicism and Political Futility." *Journal of Politics*, 25 (May 1963): 312–23.

Mannoni, O. *Prospero and Caliban: The Psychology of Colonization*, translated by Pamela Powesland. New York: Frederick A. Praeger, 1964.

Maslow, Abraham H. "The Dynamics of Psychological Security-Insecurity." *Character and Personality*, 10 (1942): 331–44.

———. "Further Notes on the Psychology of Being." *Journal of Humanistic Psychology*, 4 (1964): 45–58.

———. *Motivation and Personality*. New York: Harper & Row, 1954.

———. "Synergy in the Society and in the Individual." *Journal of Individual Psychology*, 20 (November 1964): 153–64.

———. *Toward a Psychology of Being*. Princeton: D. Van Nostrand Co., 1962.

———, E. Birsh, I. Honigmann, F. McGrath, A. Plason, and M. Stein. *Manual for the Security-Insecurity Inventory*. Palo Alto, Calif.: Consulting Psychologists Press, 1952.

——— and R. Diaz-Guerrero. "Delinquency as a Value Disturbance." In *Festschrift for Gardner Murphy*, edited by John G. Peatman and Eugene L. Hartley. New York: Harper and Co., 1960, pp. 228–40.

Milbrath, Lester W. "Measuring the Personalities of Lobbyists." Northwestern University, Department of Political Science, 1961, mimeo.

Mussen, Paul and Anne Wyszynski. "Personality and Political Participation." *Human Relations*, 5 (1952): 65–82.

Nettler, Gwynn E. and James R. Huffman. "Political Opinion and Personal Security." *Sociometry*, 20, no. 1 (1957): 51–66.

Neumann, Franz. "Anxiety in Politics." *Dissent*, Spring 1955, pp. 135–41.

Parsons, Talcott. *Social Structure and Personality*. New York: Free Press, 1964.

Riesman, David. *The Lonely Crowd—A Study of the Changing American Character*. Garden City, N.Y.: Doubleday and Co., 1956.

Rosenberg, Milton J., Carl I. Hovland, William J. McGuire, Robert P. Abelson, and Jack Brehm. *Attitude Organization and Change: An Analysis of Consistency Among Attitude Components*. New Haven: Yale University Press, 1960.

Rosenberg, Morris "Misanthropy and Political Ideology." *American Sociological Review*, 21 (December 1956): 690–95.

———. "Self Esteem and Concern With Public Affairs." *Public Opinion Quarterly*, 26 (1962): 201–11.

Sarnoff, Irving and Philip G. Zimbardo. "Anxiety, Fear and Social Affiliation." *Journal of Abnormal and Social Psychology*, 62 (1961): 356–63.

Scheler, Max. *Ressentiment*. New York: Free Press of Glencoe, 1961.

Scott, W. A. "Attitude Change by Response Reinforcement: Replication and Extension." *Sociometry*, 22 (1959): 328–35.

———. "Attitude Change Through Reward of Verbal Behavior." *Journal of Abnormal and Social Psychology*, 55 (1957): 72–75.

Seeman, Melvin. "On The Personal Consequences of Alienation in Work." *American Sociological Review*, 32, no. 2 (April 1967): 273–85.

Siegel, Bernard J. "High Anxiety Levels and Cultural Integration: Notes on a Psycho-Cultural Hypothesis." *Social Forces*, 34, no. 1 (October 1955): 42–48.

Smelser, Neil J. and William T. Smelser, eds. *Personality and Social Systems*. New York: John Wiley & Sons, 1963.

Srole, Leo. "Social Dysfunction, Personality, and Social Distance Attitudes." Paper delivered at the annual meeting of the American Sociological Society, Chicago, September 1951.

———. "Social Integration and Certain Corollaries: An Exploratory Study." *American Sociological Review*, 21 (December 1956): pp. 709–16.

Stirling, Rebecca Birch. "Some Psychological Mechanisms Operative in Gossip." *Social Forces*, 34, no. 2 (December 1955): 262–67.

Straus, Murray A. "Childhood Experience and Emotional Security in the Context of Sinhalese Social Organization." *Social Forces*, 33, no. 3 (December 1954): 152–60.

Taylor, J. A. "A Personality Scale of Manifest Anxiety." *Journal of Abnormal and Social Psychology*, 48 (1953): 285–90.

Thomas, W. I. "The Unadjusted Girl." In *Source Book for Social Psychology*, edited by Kimball Young. New York: Crofts, 1931.

Thompson, Clara, Milton Mazer, and Earl Witenberg, eds. *An Outline of Psychoanalysis*. New York: Random House, Modern Library, 1955.

White, Robert W. *Lives in Progress*. New York: Holt, Rinehart and Winston, 1952.

———, ed. *The Study of Lives*. New York: Atherton Press, 1963.

Zeitlin, Maurice. "Economic Insecurity and the Political Attitudes of Cuban Workers." *American Sociological Review*, 31, no. 1 (February 1966): 35–51.

GENERAL

Almond, Gabriel A. and Sidney Verba. *The Civic Culture*. Princeton: Princeton University Press, 1963.

——— and James S. Coleman, eds. *The Politics of the Developing Areas*. Princeton: Princeton University Press, 1960.

Apter, David E. *The Politics of Modernization*. Chicago: University of Chicago Press, 1965.

Argyris, Chris. *Some Causes of Organizational Ineffectiveness within the Department of State*. Occasional Papers, no. 2. Washington, D.C.: Department of State, Center for International Systems Research, 1967.

Bakan, David. *On Method: Toward a Reconstruction of Psychological Investigation*. San Francisco: Joseey-Bass, 1967.

Banfield, Edward C. *The Moral Basis of a Backward Society*. Glencoe: Free Press, 1958.

Berelson, Bernard R., Paul F. Lazarsfeld, and William N. McPhee. *Voting: A Study of Opinion Formation in a Presidential Campaign*. Chicago: University of Chicago Press, 1954.

Bowman, Mary Jean and C. Arnold Anderson. "Concerning the Role of Education in Development." In *Old Societies and New States*, edited by Clifford Geertz. New York: Free Press of Glencoe, 1963, pp. 247–79.

Campbell, Angus, Gerald Gurin, and Warren Miller. *The Voter Decides.* Evanston, Ill.: Row, Peterson and Co., 1954.

Carstairs, G. Morris. *The Twice Born: A Study of a Community of High-Caste Hindus.* Bloomington: Indiana University Press, 1958.

Coleman, James S., ed. *Education and Political Development.* Princeton: Princeton University Press, 1965.

Coser, Lewis. *The Functions of Social Conflict.* New York: Free Press, 1956.

Deutsch, Karl. *Nationalism and Social Communication.* Cambridge: M.I.T. Press, 1953.

Dollard, John. *Caste and Class in a Southern Town.* New Haven: Yale University Press, 1937.

Dube, S. C. *Indian Village.* Ithaca: Cornell University Press, 1955.

Easton, David. *A Framework for Political Analysis.* Englewood Cliffs: Prentice-Hall, 1965.

Eisenstadt, S. N. "Sociological Aspects of Political Development." *Economic Development and Cultural Change*, 5, no. 4 (July 1957): 289–307.

Fallers, Lloyd A. *Bantu Bureaucracy: A Century of Political Evolution among the Basoga of Uganda.* Chicago: University of Chicago Press, 1965.

————, ed. *The King's Men: Leadership and Status in Buganda on the Eve of Independence.* London: Oxford University Press, 1964.

Ford, Clellan S., ed. *Cross-Cultural Approaches: Readings in Comparative Research.* New Haven: Hraf Press, 1967.

Foster, George M. "Interpersonal Relations in Peasant Society." *Human Organization*, 19, no. 4 (Winter 1960–1961): 174–84.

Frey, Frederick W. "Political Development: Power and Communications in Turkey." In *Communications and Political Development*, edited by Lucian W. Pye. Princeton: Princeton University Press, 1963, pp. 298–326.

————. "Political Science, Education, and National Development." Paper delivered at the Conference on Comparative Education, University of California at Berkeley, March 25–27, 1966.

Friedman, F. G. "The World of 'La Miseria.'" *Community Development Review*, 10 (1958): 16–22.

Gluckman, Max. "Gossip and Scandal." *Current Anthropology*, 4, no. 3 (June 1963): 307–16.

Greenstein, Fred I. *Children and Politics.* New Haven: Yale University Press, 1965.

Hagen, Everett E. *On the Theory of Social Change: How Economic Growth Begins.* Homewood, Ill.: Dorsey Press, 1962.

Huntington, Samuel P. "Political Development and Political Decay." *World Politics*, 17 (April 1965): 386–430.

————. "Political Modernization: America vs. Europe." *World Politics*, 18 (October 1965–July 1966): 378–414.

Keesing, Felix and Marie Keesing. *Elite Communication in Samoa*. Stanford: Stanford University Press, 1956.

————, Marie Keesing, and Thomas Blair. "Social Structure and Information Exposure in Rural Brazil." *Rural Sociology*, 25 (March 1960): 65–75.

Kling, Merle. "Towards a Theory of Power and Political Instability in Latin America." In *Political Change in Underdeveloped Countries: Nationalism and Communism*, edited by John H. Kautsky. New York: John Wiley and Sons, 1962, pp. 123–39.

Kluckhohn, Clyde and Florence Kluckhohn. "American Culture: Generalized Orientations and Class Patterns." In *Conflicts of Power in Modern Culture*, edited by L. Bryson, L. Finkelstein, and R. M. MacIver. New York: Harper, 1947, pp. 106–28.

Kornhauser, William. *The Politics of Mass Society*. New York: Free Press, 1959.

Lasswell, Harold D. *Politics: Who Gets What, When, and How*. New York: McGraw-Hill, 1936.

Lazarsfeld, Paul F., Bernard R. Berelson, and Hazel Gaudet. *The People's Choice*. New York: Columbia University Press, 1948.

Leites, Nathan. *The Operational Code of the Politburo*. New York: McGraw-Hill, 1951.

————. *A Study of Bolshevism*. New York: Free Press, 1953.

Lerner, Daniel. "Comfort and Fun: Morality in a Nice Society." *American Scholar*, 27, no. 2 (Spring 1958): 153–65.

Levine, Donald N. *Wax and Gold: Tradition and Innovation in Ethiopian Culture*. Chicago: University of Chicago Press, 1965.

LeVine, Robert A. *Dreams and Deeds: Achievement Motivation in Nigeria*. Chicago: University of Chicago Press, 1966.

Lewis, Oscar. *Life in a Mexican Village: Tepoztlan Re-Studied*. Urbana: University of Illinois Press, 1951.

Lipset, Seymour Martin. *Political Man: The Social Bases of Politics*. Garden City, N.Y.: Doubleday and Co., 1959.

———— and Reinhard Bendix. *Social Mobility in Industrial Society*. Berkeley: University of California Press, 1959.

Mannheim, Karl. *Man and Society in an Age of Reconstruction*. London: Kegan Paul, 1946.

Mansur, Fatma. *Process of Independence*. London: Routledge & Kegan Paul, 1962.

Merton, Robert K. *Social Theory and Social Structure*. Glencoe: Free Press, 1957.

Moore, Barrington, Jr. *Political Power and Social Theory*. Cambridge: Harvard University Press, 1958, pp. 30–88.

Nair, Kusum. *Blossoms in the Dust*. New York: Frederick A. Praeger, 1962.

Nasser, Gamal Abdel. *The Philosophy of the Revolution*. Buffalo: Economica Books, 1959.

Ortega y Gasset, José. *The Revolt of the Masses*. New York: W. W. Norton, 1957.

Pool, Ithiel de Sola. "The Mass Media and Politics in the Modernization Process." In *Communications and Political Development*, edited by Lucian W. Pye. Princeton: Princeton University Press, 1963, pp. 234–53.

Pye, Lucian W. *Aspects of Political Development*. Boston: Little, Brown and Co., 1966.

————. "The Non-Western Political Process." *Journal of Politics*, 20, no. 3 (August 1958): 464–85.

————. *Politics, Personality, and Nation Building: Burma's Search for Identity*. New Haven: Yale University Press, 1962.

———— and Sidney Verba, eds. *Political Culture and Political Development*. Princeton: Princeton University Press, 1965.

Riggs, Fred W. *The Ecology of Public Administration*. New Delhi: Indian Institute of Public Administration, 1961.

————. *Thailand: The Modernization of a Bureaucratic Polity*. Honolulu: East-West Center Press, 1966.

Romano, Octavio. "Values, Status and Donship in a Mexican-American Village." University of Chicago Library, Chicago, Illinois, 1959.

Selznick, Philip. *The Organizational Weapon*. Glencoe: Free Press, 1959.

————. *TVA and Grass Roots: A Study in the Sociology of Formal Organization*. Los Angeles: University of California Press, 1953.

Sills, David. *The Volunteers*. Glencoe: Free Press, 1957.

Simmons, Ozzie G. "Drinking Patterns and Interpersonal Performance in a Peruvian Mestizo Community." *Quarterly Journal of Studies on Alcohol*, 20 (1959): 103–11.

Tansky, Leo. *U.S. and U.S.S.R. Aid to Developing Countries—A Comparative Study of India, Turkey, and the U.A.R.* New York: Frederick A. Praeger, 1967.

Wright, Charles R. and Herbert H. Hyman. "Voluntary Association Memberships." *American Sociological Review*, 23, no. 3 (June 1958): 284–94.

383

INDEX

A'alam, Dr. Jamshid, 99
Abadi, Engineer Malek, 60
Achaemenid Dynasty, 119, 176
activity factor, 236–37
Afshar, Dr. Hassan, 174n
Afshartus, General Mahmud, 128
age-political experience factor, 233–35, 310
Agricultural Bank, 54
Ahmad, Eghbal, 283n
Akram, Sardar, 123n
Ala, Hussein, 63, 128
Alamuti, Nour ed-Din, 67
Alborz College, 168n, 226
Amini, Ali, 43, 47, 49, 50, 54, 57, 58, 61–62, 67, 72, 74, 91–92, 105–6, 305n
Amirani, A. A., 184n
Anis ed-Dowleh, 123
anxiety, feelings of, 211–12
Arabic language, elite's knowledge of, 153–54, 178–80
Aramesh, Ahmad, 67, 115
Armed Forces, Imperial Iranian, 4, 21, 85, 102–16, 180–81, 292–96, 309n, 338, 354
Arsanjani, Hassan, 53–60, 91, 94
Aryamehr Technical University, 42n
Assadollah, Alam, 8, 28n, 65, 71, 73, 83, 84, 88, 99, 160n, 230, 235
assignment to foreign posts, 53–62
Ataturk, Kemal, 293
authoritarianism, 258–59
autocracy, 126
Azadegan (Partisans of Freedom) group, 148–49n

Azadi (Liberty) group, 54

Bagha'ee, Mozaffar, 70
Baha'ism, 147, 148n, 274–76
Bahrein Island, 89
Bakhtare Emruz (*The West Today*) newspaper, 70
Bakhtiar, General Teimur, 47–52, 73, 85, 114
Bakhtiari tribe, 47, 103, 180
Bazargan, Mehdi, 72, 76, 91
Behbehani, Seyyed Abdollah, 50
Behbehani, Seyyed Ja'afar, 50
Behbehanian, Mohammad Ja'afar, 57n
Behdad, S., 72
Bethune, Sir Henry Lindsay, 301
Binder, Leonard, 11, 129, 132, 138, 271
birthplace of elite, 134–44
Borujerdi, Ayatollah, 45, 193
Borumand, Abdul Rahman, 71
bureaucracy, inclusivity, 188–89; overlapping responsibilities, 84–91

cabinet, 83, 95–97, 128–33, 147, 193
Campbell, Sir John, 301
capitulations, 165
Central Bank of Iran, 94, 96, 99
Central Treaty Organization, 53
child rearing, 219–24, 277–79
Chubin, Bahram, 300
Clapp, Gordon R., 67–69
Congress of Farmers, 54
Congress of Free Men and Free Women of Iran, 87
Congress of Rural Cooperatives, 58–59
Conquest, Robert, 5n

385